FIRST NATIONS GAMING IN CANADA

FIRST NATIONS GAMING IN CANADA

EDITED BY YALE D. BELANGER

UNIVERSITY OF MANITOBA PRESS

University of Manitoba Press
Winnipeg, Manitoba
Canada R3T 2M5
uofmpress.ca

Printed in Canada on chlorine-free, 100% post-consumer recycled paper.

Cover and interior design: Jess Koroscil

Library and Archives Canada Cataloguing in Publication

First Nations gaming in Canada / edited by Yale D. Belanger.

Includes bibliographical references and index.
ISBN 978-0-88755-723-1 (pbk.).—ISBN 978-0-88755-402-5 (e-book)

1. Indians of North America—Gambling—Canada. 2. Gambling on Indian reservations—
Economic aspects—Canada. 3. Gambling on Indian reservations—Social aspects—Canada.
4. Compulsive gambling—Canada. I. Belanger, Yale Deron, 1968–

E98.G18F57 2011   338.4'779508997071   C2010-906074-1

The University of Manitoba Press gratefully acknowledges the financial support for its
publication program provided by the Government of Canada through the Canada Book Fund,
the Canada Council for the Arts, the Manitoba Department of Culture, Heritage, and Tourism,
the Manitoba Arts Council, and the Manitoba Book Publishing Tax Credit.

MIX
Paper from
responsible sources
FSC® C013916

CONTENTS

I. LEGAL HISTORICAL ISSUES

II. SOCIO-ECONOMIC AND RESEARCH CONSIDERATIONS

III. HEALTH

IV. CHALLENGES AND FIRST NATIONS GAMING

ACKNOWLEDGEMENTS

This project began innocently enough following my appearance on the Aboriginal Peoples Television Network news program *Contact* in February 2008 discussing—you guessed it—First Nations gaming. Within days University of Manitoba Press director David Carr sent me a congratulatory e-mail that also suggested I contemplate preparing an edited volume on the topic. The idea gained traction and here we are. I must thank David and the University of Manitoba Press for recruiting me and for providing the resources needed to finalize this volume. Glenn Bergen and Cheryl Miki both deserve kudos for both their scheduling flexibility and patience with an academic who often times has trouble saying "no" to new and exciting projects, a skill I have been working on of late!

I must also thank Laura Cardiff for her meticulous copy-editing and fine suggestions, which clarified the text in several places. The assistance of Ashley Haughton and Gabrielle Weasel Head cannot be overstated, in particular Gabrielle's role reformatting citations and resolving several critical copy-editing issues. Thanks to Drs. Rob Innes (Saskatchewan) and Darrel Manitowabi (Sudbury) for reviewing parts of this manuscript, and for their first-rate suggestions, which improved several aspects of this volume; and to the two anonymous reviewers for their helpful comments. Sakej Henderson (Saskatchewan) was gracious in responding to several e-mail requests for clarification of complex legal issues related to First Nations gaming; and federal and provincial jurisdictional issues related more generally to Aboriginal people. Drs. Robert Williams and david Gregory (Lethbridge) responded to various questions and concerns while remaining supportive. I owe a debt of gratitude to the fourteen authors whose contributions appear in this book for their fine work and, above all else, perseverance. I do hope that we will work together in the future. My apologies to any colleagues I may have overlooked.

Finally, a special thanks is extended to Tammie-Jai. What can I say that hasn't already been said (or written for that matter)? Throughout this process she has remained a source of inspiration, and her encouragement and support once again enabled project completion. Love ya!

Yale D. Belanger
August 2010
Lethbridge, Alberta

FIRST NATIONS GAMING IN CANADA

INTRODUCTION

Prior to the 2006 publication of *Gambling with the Future: The Evolution of Aboriginal Gaming in Canada*, no book-length study probed the exigencies of reserve casino operations, or Aboriginal gambling in Canada. Exploring first and foremost the evolution of the First Nations gaming industry, that book was intended to distil complex socio-political and -economic processes into an accessible discussion highlighting why First Nations leaders willingly gravitated to such a controversial industry and what they had to date achieved. At the time every First Nations casino in Canada was profitable, although success was variable, ranging from the marginally profitable casinos in The Pas, Manitoba, and Casino of the Rockies (Cranbrook, British Columbia) to the larger and significantly more lucrative Casino Rama (Rama, Ontario). Barely a decade old at the time, many critics still framed the First Nations gaming industry, or more specifically reserve casinos, as an ad hoc political response to regional economic pressures. Most overlooked the fact that the majority were developing into efficient businesses that augmented both First Nations' social capital and provincial economies. Impressive employment statistics were overlooked, as were First Nations casino operators' increasingly beneficial donations to mainstream charities. It was still an industry in its infancy and apt to unique pressures, the latter of which the print and electronic media found most fascinating.

Now well into its second decade of operations, reserve casinos are considered a permanent fixture of First Nations politics that increasingly come to guide long-range economic and community development strategies. Since 2006, five casinos have opened in Alberta, two in Saskatchewan, with another slated for construction in Manitoba. More people are employed (greater than 7000) than anyone had initially anticipated in the 1990s. The Province of Ontario recently assigned 1.7 percent of provincial gambling revenues to the province's First Nations, which amounts to more than a $3-billion allocation over twenty-five years beginning in 2011. The Federation of Saskatchewan Indian

Nations (FSIN) initiated what has evolved into ongoing negotiations with Justice Department representatives to amend the Criminal Code of Canada that would authorize First Nations to regulate reserve casino operations. In June 2010 the First Nations Summit of British Columbia similarly announced its intention to form a gaming commission to regulate First Nations casinos, and to initiate legal action to secure a percentage of provincial gambling revenues. Soon afterward First Nations leaders in Saskatchewan announced their intent to institute a national Aboriginal gaming commission in an effort to gain greater control of what they described as the huge revenues generated by the nation's First Nations casinos.

Despite this rapid change, and the success engendered by the industry, only a handful of studies have been produced in the last five years probing these and like issues. This is fascinating, considering the issues are simultaneously historical and contemporary in perspective, multidisciplinary in scope, politically charged, and culturally oriented. There are critical questions that extend beyond simple academic fascination, frequently impacting First Nations individuals, their communities, and their host communities. In sum, despite our improving understanding—which could accurately be described as a surface understanding—a grave need exists for community-based research to determine a casino's overarching regional and provincial impact and how revenues are being spent to ensure accountability and transparency. These important questions notwithstanding, these environments are virtually devoid of any significant work enabling a broader understanding of First Nations casinos' overall effects, and would benefit from insights provided by legal scholars, economists, historians, sociologists, political scientists, geographers, anthropologists, women's studies scholars, urban and regional planners, constitutional scholars, marketing and management scholars, and environmental scientists, to name a few.

The idea for this book originated at several conferences, speaking events, and discussions where the editor often struggled to respond to basic questions. The book's premise was thus established: provide additional research to better understand gambling and its impact on First Nations individuals, their communities, and the host communities (i.e., the provinces). Prolonged dialogues with many of the contributors followed, and it was decided to develop a book that would supply current and future researchers the foundation needed to expand their respective research agendas, whilst adding to the literature on First Nations gaming and Aboriginal gambling. Three objectives guided this book's development: (1) to draw some of Canada's leading gambling researchers into the First Nations gaming and gambling research domains; (2) to highlight critical research issues currently challenging the scholars in the field; and (3) to convince future and current graduate students to pursue First Nations gaming and Aboriginal gambling-related studies in order to grow a critical mass of researchers who can help and expand our current understanding of the issues. In addition to acting as a reference text for graduate and undergraduate students and academics interested in working in the field of First Nations and Aboriginal gambling studies, *First Nations Gaming in Canada* should be of interest to industry professionals, federal policy makers, and laypersons interested in the emergence and operations of First Nations casinos across Canada.

This book has four sections: (1) Legal and Historical Issues; (2) Economic Development; (3) Health; and (4) Challenges and First Nations Gaming.

In the first section, Chapter 1 situates indigenous games and wagering practices in historical perspective. Using recent Supreme Court of Canada decisions denying that First Nations have an Aboriginal right to control reserve casinos due to an historic absence of regulatory regimes to control high-stakes gambling, this chapter uses a political economy framework to highlight the diplomatic and economic aspects of games and wagering that to date have largely been overlooked. Thematically similar, Chapter 2 adopts a case study approach to argue on behalf of the Kahnawa:ke First Nation's existing Aboriginal right to regulate gaming through an online website that hosts cyber-casinos and patron wagering. Written by Morden Lazarus, partner with the law firm Lazarus Charbonneau in Montreal, and two associates, Edwin Monzon and Richard Wodnicki, the authors' analysis considers historic Mohawk gaming and wagering practices through the lens of contemporary case law and concludes that the Kahnawa:ke First Nation meets the Supreme Court of Canada's threshold for suggesting it has an Aboriginal right to regulate virtual casinos through an online server located on reserve. The section's final chapter builds on this theme and examines the Kahnawa:ke and Alexander First Nations' assertions that they enjoy a historically protected treaty right normally assigned to sovereign political bodies, which is the internal ability to independently determine community-appropriate economic development strategies. The two communities insist that their sovereign treaty rights permit their operating online casino servers, something the provincial hosts contest. Collection editor Yale Belanger and internationally renowned gambling expert Robert Williams acknowledge the difficulty of applying existing definitions of sovereignty when analyzing First Nations political issues. Accordingly, they pursue a culturally contextual analysis that situates competing First Nations, federal, and provincial sovereignty claims within contemporary case law, provincial and federal policies related to gambling, and First Nations treaty interpretations.

Williams initiates the second section by presenting a set of methodological principles the author deems requisite for conducting socio-economic analyses that can be used as an analytical framework for any type of gambling research, including First Nations gambling. A crucial framework for anyone interested in conducting socio-economic research in First Nations communities, this research model combines cost-benefit analysis (CBA) with a meaningful account of the social impacts of gambling that has been successfully used for conducting socio-economic analyses of gambling across Canada. Nationally recognized gambling authority Harold Wynne follows with an extended discussion about how participatory action research (PAR) can facilitate partnerships between the community and academic researchers examining First Nations gambling-related issues. Providing a comprehensive overview of PAR's benefits, the author presents a process-oriented research model to help merge research agendas and ensure successful partnerships.

Nationally recognized gambling research specialist Garry Smith, along with doctoral student Cheryl Curie and psychologist James Battle, next presents the findings from a comparative, participatory action research project conducted at the Ermineskin and Samson Cree Nations in Alberta. Lamenting the lack of relevant frameworks needed to measure the socio-economic effects of gambling in First Nations communities, the authors highlight that their efforts help to improve individual First Nations' awareness of a casino's likely influence on their community. The authors intended for their research process to assist band members' decisions about implementing casino gambling and to prepare to reduce negative impacts if a casino venture materialized. Using participatory action research to create a culturally relevant framework for measuring the socio-economic impacts of gambling in Aboriginal communities was a central objective, as was testing their framework by collecting survey data in two Alberta First Nations communities. The final chapter evaluates the problematic nature of First Nations-province gaming agreements, which deny urban band members access to gambling revenues technically destined for all provincial First Nations populations. This chapter anticipates an organized urban Aboriginal group, now recognized by Canada's courts as a political community akin to a First Nation, legally contesting these restrictions thus pitting urban Aboriginal interests against First Nations economic demands.

The third section begins with a chapter by Williams, Rhys Stevens, and Gary Nixon that reviews the historical aspects of Aboriginal gambling and then moves into a detailed discussion of the current situation, with specific reference to the meaning of gambling for Aboriginal people, current patterns of gambling behaviour, and the prevalence and causes of problem gambling within this population. We do not understand fully why Aboriginal people gamble at significantly higher rates than non-Aboriginal individuals, however it is important to comprehend the dynamics of Aboriginal gambling behaviours prior to engaging in research. In this vein, Chapter 9, written by University of Lethbridge professors Sharon Yanicki (population health), david Gregory (nursing), and Bonnie Lee (addictions counselling), considers First Nations gambling as a population health matter with inherent opportunities and challenges. The authors develop a critical socio-ecological framework, specifically one that embraces qualitative and quantitative data, which they argue is needed to offer a broader understanding of the determinants of Aboriginal gambling.

The book's final section is a set of three chapters exploring a variety of issues. The first chapter is a case study examining the Saskatchewan Indian Gaming Authority's (SIGA) corporate response to a highly publicized case of internal mismanagement that bordered on misappropriation of funds. The chapter develops a thematic analysis drawn from 367 print media articles (2000–2004) to ascertain the corporate strategy employed to counter criticism and ensure the public's trust. Darrell Manitowabi follows with an examination of neoliberalism's impact in Ontario, specifically how it influenced popular understanding of Casino Rama's role in provincial and First Nations economies. First Nations claim the casino is a symbol of self-determination and nation building. Provincial officials counter that it is a provincial establishment located on reserve lands and nothing more. Despite this polarization, the author argues that First Nations have helped expand the societal dialogue and understanding of what the casino represents to provincial First Nations' interests. The book's final chapter examines the contentious issue of labour unions and First Nations casinos. In recent years, several court actions have been initiated by First Nations seeking to keep unions from their casino operations, and by union organizers seeking access to those workers. Although resolved in Ontario and Saskatchewan, these and like issues are destined to become prominent in Alberta, for instance, as Aboriginal workers nurture a labour consciousness, and non-Native workers seek union protection from First Nations political intrigue and to improve wages and working conditions. The author reflects on First Nations casino operators' resistance to union organizing through historic, social, and political lenses in an effort to help answer why this has become such a contentious issue.

The year 2011 represents Casino Rama's fifteenth anniversary, as it does SIGA's opening four casinos in Saskatchewan. No longer are we able to claim that the First Nations gaming industry is in its infancy. It is academics' analyses of the associated issues that are in their infancy, and that is slowly changing on several fronts. With books such as this and *Gambling with the Future*, the foundation is now firmly established enabling extended analyses. This text has drawn various gambling experts and public health scholars into the First Nations and Aboriginal research domains, with the hope that many will continue the work featured here. Finally, this book continues a tradition initiated by larger longitudinal socio-economic studies' inclusion of First Nations and Aboriginal issues. The Socio and Economic Impacts of Gambling in Alberta (SEIGA) study, of which the editor is a co-author, is an excellent example of this growing trend. Commissioned in 2008 by the Alberta Gaming and Liquor Commission, the final report evaluating the provincial impact of all forms of gambling has a spring 2011 publication date. The final report contains what will be the most comprehensive evaluation of a provincial First Nations gaming industry, and the role it plays in a larger provincial industry, produced to date. This parallels several studies that in previous years had identified First Nations and Aboriginal peoples, albeit on a much larger scale.

As we have seen, economic considerations frame our contemporary understanding of First Nations gaming and Aboriginal gambling. The innovative nature of this textbook's contributions has forced us to reconsider old assumptions, and to ask new questions stimulating additional research.

PART I

LEGAL HISTORICAL ISSUES

CHAPTER 1

TOWARD AN INNOVATIVE UNDERSTANDING OF NORTH AMERICAN INDIGENOUS GAMING IN HISTORICAL PERSPECTIVE

YALE D. BELANGER

INTRODUCTION

Did gaming (wagering on the outcomes of games of chance) play an important role in historic indigenous communities?[1] This simple question continues to challenge most scholars investigating indigenous gaming, and as a result limits their focus to gaming's ceremonial and religious importance. In this chapter I argue that this approach obscures insights into the nature of historic North American indigenous gaming, specifically the centrality of gaming to indigenous political economy. Reliance upon narrow categories hampers our ability to appreciate how gaming informed complex political and economic ideologies and practices. Only by broadening the accepted taxonomies that situate gaming as a largely ceremonial and religious practice can scholars develop more profound insights into the nature of indigenous gaming. This is admittedly a difficult chore, and likely the reason why few economic and political histories have been produced explicating the importance of gaming to trade, inter-nation diplomacy, military ideologies, or education and social development. It has important contemporary implications, because Canadian courts rely upon similar assessments when formulating legal decisions, in particular when responding to debates concerning whether First Nations have authority to regulate gaming on reserves based on the asserted centrality of gaming to their communities.

An expansion of our gaze is needed if we are to interpret gaming among pre-European-contact indigenous peoples as they viewed it. When communities gathered for trade and political meetings, and gaming was common, what rules were utilized to ensure peaceful interface? Why did games like lacrosse become popular intercultural encounters between nations previously at war? Why was the outcome of these matches so important to all involved that occasional deaths occurred in the field, and communities wagered everything they owned with their rivals? Drawn from a review of the extant literature examining indigenous gaming, these and similar questions suggest games were central features of diplomatic, economic, social, and political practices in pre- and post-contact indigenous communities, in addition to being essential ceremonial and religious features. They also suggest that new investigative models are needed to tease out new perspectives and ways of knowing related to gaming. This chapter proceeds in three parts with these ideas in mind. The first section examines how the courts understand historic indigenous gaming within the context of Aboriginal rights litigation. The second section highlights how historic taxonomies that developed to interpret gaming continue to inform how we understand the role gaming did and continues to play in First Nations communities, which in turn informs our historic and legal interpretations. The final section presents five categories, and within them numerous research streams, calculated to broaden our understanding of historic indigenous gaming practices, thus expanding our interpretation of historic indigenous political economy.

THE COURTS AND ABORIGINAL RIGHTS

In 1996, the Supreme Court in *R. v. Pamajewon* determined that the Shawanaga and Eagle Lake First Nations in Ontario did not possess the Aboriginal right to control and regulate casino gaming in their reserve communities. The Court determined that the litigants failed to demonstrate gaming's centrality to Ojibwa culture or its practice as connected to "the self-identity and self-preservation of the aboriginal societies involved here."[2] Concluding that gaming was not an Aboriginal right, the Supreme Court determined that on-reserve gambling facilities were not exempt from provincial legislation regulating gaming. Although the possibility of recognizing Aboriginal rights in another case has not been exhausted, the original claim that gaming was an inherent Aboriginal right was answered for the Shawanaga and Eagle Lake First Nations. The case was related to self-government as an Aboriginal right, and not exclusively to self-government as an exercise of Aboriginal title.[3] The litigants asserted a broad right of self-government, and they claimed that this right included the authority to regulate gaming activities on the reserve, an argument the Court declined to consider. Instead, it deferred to the lower court of appeal, which indicated, "there is no evidence that gambling on the reserve lands generally was ever the subject matter of aboriginal regulation. Moreover, there is no evidence of an historic involvement in anything resembling the high-stakes gambling in issue in these cases."[4]

The *Pamajewon* court was critical of the litigant's claim, citing it as too general, while concluding that for an activity to be recognized an Aboriginal right it must be "related to a particular custom, practice, tradition or activity."[5] The Court's analysis was informed by *Van Der Peet* demanding the activity in question be in place in the period prior to European contact.[6] Aboriginal rights were thus characterized as historical rights, informed by the attendant customs and practices at the time of contact with Europeans, that had a limited ability to evolve. Should the practice have evolved post-contact date it cannot be acknowledged as an Aboriginal right. Finally, should historical exercise in any way become disengaged from contemporary practice, historic continuity and tradition are shattered and the Aboriginal right is considered non-existent. This test has been widely criticized and is being subtly restructured, even if it remains the metric that guides justices when determining Aboriginal rights claims.

The First Nations involved in the *Pamajewon* case offered a unique, historically based interpretation to characterize their Aboriginal right to control reserve gaming. The justice writing for the majority in this case, which rested on significant historical interpretation of fact and action, fashioned two conclusions: first, the historical evidence was not compelling enough to recognize a right to gamble or regulate gambling on reserve, and second, the First Nations' history of both gaming and gambling lacked continuity and as such they could not be acknowledged as an Aboriginal right. In each of these considerations, the historical evidence provided by the plaintiff and defendant was weighed in chambers and a final decision rendered by a court of legal experts. Interestingly enough, the Court did not rule that the First Nations did not have an Aboriginal right to conduct and regulate gaming. Rather, it "found that the evidence presented was insufficient to support the existence of such a right."[7] The Court's reluctance to rule on the historical bases of indigenous gaming is expected, considering historic gaming and wagering practices are commonly portrayed as little more than personal activities engaged in when not hunting and fishing. According to this view, gambling was a simple pastime that lacked the societal foundation to evolve into something more significant than a hobby.

Canadian courts have been hesitant to define the nature of Aboriginal rights, and policy makers continue to rely largely upon the Indian Act to define who Indians are and, by virtue of that definition, to what rights they may be entitled. These rights are often confined to reserve environments and emerge as discussion points after the courts are petitioned to ascertain their existence. The courts have interpreted Aboriginal rights as "activities, customs or traditions integral to the distinctive culture of Aboriginal peoples" that must be interpreted within the context of the Canadian Constitution. Such a reading tends to historically freeze Section 35 Aboriginal rights.[8] Referring to *Van Der Peet* to assist in determining whether a practice is constitutionally protected, the Supreme Court has ruled that a community must show that the disputed practice is an integral feature of the pre-contact indigenous culture and that it can be reconciled with non-Native perspectives, ensuring equal legal weighting.

This ruling and the historical record combined have arguably obscured the historic role of gaming in indigenous communities. As First Nations have argued, the right to control community gaming and gambling should be considered a protected Aboriginal right by virtue of its centrality to historic indigenous societies, as reflected in prevailing governing structures regulating both behaviours. Supporting this interpretation is Sakej Henderson, who persuasively argues for the *sui generis* existence of Aboriginal rights by virtue of indigenous nations' practising of governance within their traditional territories. He asserts that the courts are charged with extending "Constitutional equality before and under the law to these *sui generis* Aboriginal orders and treaty federalism."[9] In his discussion of the nature of Aboriginal rights, Brian Slattery identifies two forms of Aboriginal rights recognized by the courts: generic rights and specific rights. The latter "are rights whose nature and scope are defined by factors pertaining to a particular Aboriginal group," which means they vary from group to group; whereas the former "are rights of a uniform character whose basic contours are established by common law of Aboriginal rights."[10]

Generic Aboriginal rights include, but are not limited to, the right to conclude treaties, the right to customary law, the right to honourable treatment by the Crown, the right to an ancestral territory, the right to cultural integrity, and the right to self-government.[11] A general reading of Henderson's and Slattery's work would suggest that gaming should be an acknowledged aspect of historic indigenous societies and, as such, a protected Aboriginal right. Gaming would fit what the Court described as a "particular custom, practice, tradition or activity." Unfortunately, a paucity of literature hinders our developing a systematic interpretive framework needed to establish this right's existence, thus obstructing academic and juridical attempts to consider and comprehend alternative perspectives. Even when contemporary literature is available, the modern interpretation is equally flawed—as evidenced by the Canadian courts' interpretation of the available evidence.

Henderson advocates we abandon this rigid construal of gaming, thereby expanding upon what were dynamic processes inherent in North American indigenous communities. Lacking insight into what these processes meant, and how ideas about them continue to inform contemporary First Nations, the *Pamajewon* court was arguably predisposed to ruling against the right to control gambling as an Aboriginal right. This highlights two interrelated issues associated with determining Aboriginal rights claims: first, the important role historians continue to play, and second, perhaps more importantly, the role justices play as historians when developing their decisions. The point is not to advocate for mandatory historical education for justices but rather to highlight the need to advance our general understanding of historic indigenous gaming practices in order to enable lawyers and historians pursuing similar cases and research agendas to more effectively situate gambling within the overall context of indigenous societies. It would allow the experts to speak to the evolutionary quality of gaming practices as consisting of customs that continue to inform First Nations economic and societal development, thereby informing the courts in their decision-making process. This hurdle will be discussed in the next section.

HISTORIC INDIGENOUS GAMING

Our contemporary understanding of historic First Nations gaming practices dates to the work of late nineteenth-century scholars Frank Cushing and Stewart Culin. The latter published a massive, 846-page inventory of indigenous gaming practices in 1907 that remains the field standard. In addition to cataloguing thirty-six games among the 229 North American tribes he observed, this work framed games and gambling as a central aspect of indigenous culture. Primarily focussed on how games and gambling informed indigenous ceremony and spirituality, Culin's work, as chief of the United States Bureau of Ethnology W. H. Holmes concluded, improved both our collective "understanding of the technology of games and of their distribution," and our "appreciation of native modes of thought and of the motives and impulses that underlie the conduct of primitive peoples generally."[12]

Holmes's proclamation aside, a brief overview of the more important recent works to emerge examining indigenous gaming practices suggests that ceremony and spirituality remain focal points.[13] Kathryn Gabriel and Margo Little in particular underscore gambling's centrality in securing spiritual guidance, and they discuss its inclusion in various contexts.[14] For example, games and gambling were often used to predict the future or curry favour with creation and its various manifestations. In those instances where human beings beat the odds, they were seen as spiritually sheltered.[15] Ceremonies promoting a good hunt or harvest often involved gaming, as did various curative measures and funerary customs.[16] Other writers have suggested that the intensity and prevalence of indigenous gaming practices resulted from the demand for inter-tribal competition.[17] Few, however, have taken the opportunity to determine the importance of gaming practices to pre- and post-contact indigenous political economies, a process that would necessitate studying how they influenced trade, diplomacy, politics, education, and kinship. Some recent studies have expanded on gaming's contemporary role in First Nations communities,[18] as have several professional and government reports, dissertations and theses examining gaming's legality, potential policy initiatives, and the political nature of First Nations casinos.[19] Yet the fact remains that the historic role of gaming in indigenous societies has been marginally explored.[20]

Consider the influence of historians and anthropologists working with indigenous peoples during this period. Culin and his contemporaries constructed their representations of events from data largely produced by non-Native authors. The British historian Hugh Trevor Roper, writing in the mid-twentieth century, adopted his contemporaries' disdain for writing indigenous histories, claiming that the pre-contact history of Africa was one of darkness, "like the history of pre-European, pre-Columbian America," while adding that "darkness is not the subject of history." He also argued that the historian's role was not to write about the "unrewarding gyrations of barbarous tribes in picturesque but irrelevant corners of the world."[21] Such sentiments echoed European philosopher Georg W.F. Hegel's proclamation a century earlier that suggested the indigenous peoples of Africa and America were people without history.[22] Noted British historian E.H. Carr countered these ideas, insisting that the serious historian recognizes the historically conditioned character of all values and avoids claiming for his own values an objectivity beyond history. He also added that it is impossible to write history prior to the historian achieving "some kind of contact with the mind of those about whom he is writing."[23] Arguably, contemporary historians and jurists engaged in pronouncing on historic indigenous gaming lack similar contextual understanding about their meaning within specific cultural frameworks.[24]

The concern here is that Culin's work is still frequently referenced by influential scholars studying historic indigenous gaming. *Games of the North American Indians,* for instance, is more a combination of field observations and literature reviews of previously published sources related to indigenous games and gambling than it is a comprehensive overview of the centrality of gaming in historic indigenous communities. Take Culin's use of the *Jesuit Relations* as an example.[25] Culin frequently referenced this rich written record, composed of seventy-one volumes published between 1610 and 1791, which at times discusses indigenous gaming practices. As one scholar has shown, however, the *Jesuit Relations* portrays indigenous games and gambling as an idolatrous pastime, centring on lazy individuals seeking improved living conditions through games of chance. The missionary authors claim indigenous gamblers often lost their possessions and take this as confirmation that these were the actions of uncivilized peoples.[26] Similar beliefs were reinforced by the Puritans, who exploited the evils of gaming to justify draconian measures aimed at altering indigenous socio-cultural practices.[27] As the colonies became power bases, the Puritans' ability to employ their ideology to civilize the "savage" evolved into a process later described as using "the Indian as justification and rationale."[28] As Francis Jennings has argued, the "Catholic imperative for converting and including the heathen compelled Catholics to learn something about them in order to do the holy work effectively," even if "the Protestant principle of elitism worked out in practice of exclusionism and indifference."[29] By the late seventeenth century, the social internalization of the above-mentioned beliefs about indigenous games and gambling led to their vilification, so much so that by the time of Culin's work mainstream society considered indigenous gaming, once a hallmark of indigenous society, the purview of the uncivilized.

Nowhere is this more evident than in Culin's cited work, which heavily relied upon the observations of Pacific Fur Company member Alexander Ross, one of "four writers upon whom we depend for much that is known about the early exploration of and fur trade in this vast Columbia river basin."[30] The other three are New York lawyer Lewis Henry Morgan, whose 1851 field work among the Seneca resulted in his publications about the League of the Haudenosaunee;[31] German geographer, ethnologist, and travel writer Johann Georg Kohl and his accounts of his visits among the United States Lake Superior Ojibwa;[32] and Wesleyan pastor John MacLean, who wrote about Canada's "savage folk" in western Canada.[33] Culin utilized these four writers' findings to classify North American indigenous gaming practices as either games of chance or games of dexterity—a system that is still employed today.[34] Ross wrote about gaming, and Morgan identified six games the Iroquois played and highlighted the frenzied wagering associated with the competition. Similarly, Kohl detailed an assortment of Ojibwa games while clarifying the differences between games used to "exercise the skill of their fingers and senses, which is so necessary for them in hunting, fishing, etc." and "social sports."[35] MacLean classified games into two categories and in the process became one of the few early writers to separate games and gambling into separate categories, seemingly signifying the conscious separation of the two practices within indigenous societies. This is troubling for several reasons. However, this literature and the budding scholarly frameworks to emerge enabled Culin to situate indigenous gaming in comparative context while establishing the basic taxonomy most future writers adopted, and which is still regularly cited.

By the early twentieth century scholars examining indigenous gaming appraised these activities according to Culin's model. In 1907, the same year *Games of the North American Indians* was published, Frederick Webb Hodge published *Handbook of American Indians*, which included an indigenous games section that stated, "Indian games may be divided into two general classes: games of chance and games of dexterity."[36] One century later, the *Encyclopedia of the Great Plains Indians* (2007) characterized Indian games precisely the same way.[37] Hodge's almost verbatim description is not surprising, considering he and Culin shared their findings. (Culin thanked "Mr. F.W. Hodge" for contributing information to his 1907 collection.)[38] By this period, indigenous gaming in Canada appeared to be dying off as the result of a federal Indian assimilation policy outlawing historic traditions. Anthropologists seeking to capture the last vestiges of once proud "Indian" nations catalogued their vanishing practices, and gaming was increasingly presented in a historical framework. Anticipating vanishing ways of life, Culin's model was an appropriate evaluative framework, and his contemporaries presented games and gambling as little more than custom and tradition. In certain instances, such as the journals of seventeenth-century French government agent Nicolas Perrot, published by E.H. Blair, indigenous gambling was additionally portrayed as a vice.[39]

Analyses of indigenous games and gambling appeared from time to time in contemporary academic publications, but less attention was devoted to these issues as the century progressed. The anthropologist Diamond Jenness's work is a case in point. In *The Indians of Canada* (published in 1932), the first Native Studies text influencing our contemporary understanding of indigenous cultures in Canada, "Indians" were described as inordinate gamblers and indigenous gaming as "universal across Canada." Jenness portrayed British Col-

umbia Natives, for instance, as aggressive gamblers who wagered all possessions, including their wives and children. On the other hand, Prairie indigenous
people were considered more conscientious gamblers.[40] Never hopeful about
indigenous cultural survival, Jenness (writing as the head anthropologist for the
Department of Mines and Resources in 1932) stated that their "old world has
fallen into ruins, and, helpless in the face of a catastrophe they cannot understand, they vainly seek refuge in its shattered foundation."[41] As a member of the
Department of National Defence, in 1946 he was asked to give evidence before a
special joint parliamentary committee examining the *Indian Act*. Testifying that
the Indian problem could be removed over a twenty-five-year period, Jenness
proposed eliminating, "gradually but rapidly, the separate political and social
status of the Indians (and Eskimos); to enfranchise them and merge them into
the rest of the population on an equal footing."[42] One could infer from his writings and public presentations that indigenous gaming practices were little more
than ill-conceived customs of a people best relegated to the dustbins of history.

After a comparative dearth of literature produced between the 1920s and
1980s, the 1990s witnessed a resurgence of writing about indigenous gaming
practices. Most notable is Kathryn Gabriel's 1996 publication *Gambler Way*,
which elaborated on Culin's fundamental themes.[43] The following year a Canadian master's thesis revealed gambling to be part of the "Native quest for
spiritual guidance," and gaming to be "often a reflection of the tribe's attempt to
connect with the positive or good forces in the universe."[44] Both writers relied
upon Culin's framework to further explore the ceremonial and spiritual importance of indigenous games and gambling. While these writers did little to expand
on our understanding of gaming's expansive role in indigenous societies, their
work highlighted these issues for the first time in decades. This led to the emergence of new interpretive models elaborating upon Culin's work. For example,
regarding the nuances of indigenous gaming, one scholar has recently argued
that four conditions are common in pre-contact indigenous societies: (1) having and using money; (2) demonstrating social inequality; (3) social complexity; and (4) experiencing competitive inter-tribal relations.[45] This may be helpful in explaining gambling's presence in pre-contact North America. The use
of concepts such as money and social inequality within the context of historic
indigenous communities is not without its problems, however. Among much of
the northeastern North American indigenous population, for instance, wampum was a popular form of currency. And while many would argue that social
inequality did not occur in this oft-described "utopian" environment, among
the Blackfoot an owner of dozens of ponies was considerably less wealthy than

one who owned thousands of ponies. The latter was also considered politically influential and in many regards a more commanding leader. Hence, social and political stratification based on possessed wealth did occur.

These are but a few of the concerns associated with interpreting the meaning of gaming in historic and contemporary First Nations communities, and in many cases they are easily dealt with by probing the indigenous perspective. For the most part academics remain bound to tried and true interpretive models. It should therefore not be surprising that Canadian courts are inundated with evidence emphasizing the ceremonial and spiritual aspects of gambling and wagering, while there is little acknowledgement of or expansion on a framework exploring the political economy of gaming. First Nations gaming will arguably remain either a pre-contact phenomenon considered long vanished, or an affectation of modernity that First Nations embrace in an attempt to buttress sagging economies, and that thus demonstrates limited ties to the past.

TOWARD AN IMPROVED UNDERSTANDING OF GAMING/GAMBLING'S ROLE

The Supreme Court of Canada has rejected First Nations' claims to historic control and regulation of gaming, as well as the claim that they had historically engaged in high-stakes gambling. This reflects a colonial process identified by the late Lakota philosopher Vine Deloria Jr., who wrote, "Any group that wishes to be regarded as the authority in a human society must not simply banish or discredit the views of their rivals, they must become the sole source of truth for that society and defend their status and the power to interpret against all comers by providing the best explanation of the data."[46] But, as suggested, the purpose of this chapter is to not critique the Supreme Court's decision. Rather, the goal is to probe the nature of indigenous gaming. As suggested, indigenous games have been categorized simplistically for ease of understanding, creating categories reliant upon basic taxonomies to interpret the relevance of gaming practices to contemporary First Nations communities.

There is a need to challenge the existing labels that inform our understanding of the role that gaming played in indigenous societies. Hence, there is a need to reorient our gaze in an effort to see the Native perspective of gaming from a community-based standpoint. A more expansive examination of gaming is thus required to understand not only the religious and ceremonial perspectives, but also how these perspectives and indigenous perceptions of gaming informed the development of internal and inter-national diplomatic protocols and economic development, and of community-based education leading to culturally germane learning outcomes. Such an examination will also probe games' social and entertainment value. Political economy is an important conceptual framework for an attempt to interrogate historic indigenous gaming behaviours within a societal context. It is used to discover how a particular mix of political and economic activities emerged and who benefits from that mix, thereby revealing how particular societies operate. This approach is practical for studying pre-contact North American indigenous communities, specifically because it can help us discern how the forces of politics and economics influence community development, and also because it informs us how community-based ideologies related to both consumption and leadership are structured to help maintain political and economic balance while ensuring the prosperity of community members.

Political economy from an indigenous perspective, then, is defined as the study of the environment's influence on how indigenous political institutions, the political environment, and economic ideologies developed in response to prevailing ecological forces and the dynamics associated with Creation. Never forgetting the centrality of the inter-relational network, it is imperative to consider how the actions of individuals within a community influenced its overall dynamic, and how that one community in turn could affect its neighbours. The following sections will expand on these ideas as regards interpretations of the centrality of gaming practices to historic North American indigenous communities.

RELIGION/CEREMONY — The religious and ceremonial aspects of indigenous games and gambling have to date garnered the majority of academic interest. Culin, Gabriel, and Little all identified the interwoven nature of gambling imagery with creation stories, myths, legends, and songs, represented in a varied cross-section of different indigenous nations.[47] This oral tradition emerges from a world that is in a state of constant change.[48] From an epistemological perspective, a world of constant flux informs gambling practices; partaking in games of chance "recreates and relives the establishment of cosmos and meaning out of chaos."[49] Gambling played an important role by establishing continuity with the past, which is vital according to Little Bear, for "if creation is to continue, then it must be renewed."[50] Since individuals in North American indigenous societies played an important role in creating reality, each individual and separate society came to play an essential role in maintaining place, Creation's general function, and its harmonious operation. Gaming enabled individuals to ensure Creation unfolded as it had earlier, suggesting that this celebration of chance reflects the acknowledgment of "the basic metaphysics of the cosmos, including the power of the trickster and other spirits."[51] Games represented one method of coming to know and understand. "Played on behalf of the whole society," they aided in renewing "the compacts and alliances made with the spirits of the universe."[52]

Many creation stories in various indigenous societies reveal gambling themes. Among the Blackfoot, as explorer Peter Fidler noted in 1792, the gambling exploits of Napi (the Oldman) led to the naming of the Oldman River, which traverses southern Alberta.[53] The coastal Salish tell a story of how a man's continual gambling losses warned him that his good luck had been carried away by spirits of the dead, and that his soul was being enticed to the underworld. In response he needed a medicine man's counsel to recall these spirits and help him re-establish balance within Creation.[54] The Salish also believed a successful gambler owed his good fortune to the powers of Creation.[55] Gambling among the Nuxalk (Bella Coola) involved singing a variety of songs that helped the performers recall their origins.[56] A story among the Klamath, in which a young man loses all his possessions and his parents' respect by gambling, tells of this man's retreat to the mountains for one year. Upon his return, he was not only more worldly, he also proceeded to win back his losses, and more, by gambling.[57] Similarly, the Chinook speak of an ostracized child who, after being raised by four black bears, returns to his village with supernatural powers and proceeds to win the property of all the people, becoming the head chief and marrying the community's most prominent women.[58] In the east, the Mohawks must play the peach stone game before the corn is planted each year. Further east, the Mi'kmaq tell a story of how corn was brought back from the land of the dead by individuals who had won it gambling with Papkootparout, the master of souls. The plants were set out and cultivated accordingly, but successful harvests eluded the people.[59] The waltes game has similar origins: a grieving man went to the land of the souls to retrieve his late son. A waltes game was agreed to by the Keeper of the Land of the Souls, and the old man won. The Keeper enjoyed the game so much he allowed the spirit of the son to return to Mi'kmaq, and he gave the people the gift of fruit trees and bushes. Waltes was played "on behalf of the whole society and may … act to renew the compacts and alliances made with the spirits of the universe."[60] (During the 1950s it was erroneously reported that the Mi'kmaq no longer gambled on waltes, even if gambling remained a popular Mi'kmaq sport. The popular games of the period were identified as poker among the men and bingo and rummy among the women.[61]) Gaming has also been associated with healing and funerary customs in several First Nations communities, while Culin described how, in some cultures, games were held at the request of a sick person in the hopes of becoming well.[62]

A thick reading of these sources suggests that while the ceremonial and religious aspects of gaming are apparent, a complex of relationships is also evident, suggesting gaming to be dynamic and societally informative from several vantage points.[63] Even through the lens of ceremony and religion, one is able to discern gaming's centrality to education, political procedures that inform ideas of territorial sovereignty, medicinal knowledge, food production, funerary customs, wealth distribution, and enjoyment. Several of these ideas are expanded upon below.

SOCIAL EVENTS — Integrating ceremonies and religious activities with social events was a common practice. Yet separations between the ceremonial and spiritual also occurred, suggesting that gaming played a more complex role in the day-to-day unfolding of events in indigenous communities. A simple wagering on who could erect a tipi or lodge the quickest was a common game among Blackfoot and Cree women on the plains. Among the Cree, games of chance were used for relaxation and diversion. Athletic games were used for competitions. Foot races brought about lively betting; hoop games and hiding games were also popular.[64] At Treaty 6 negotiations at Fort Carlton in 1876, following the arrival of nearly 2000 people, games of skill and chance and competitions of strength and endurance were a useful pastime for young and old.[65] In the wintertime, Blackfoot children would slide "down hills on stiff hides" or "play games on the ice—spinning tops with whips, sliding carved sticks known as snow snakes, or batting a round rock with sticks, like hockey."[66] Common foot races "were often made a part of the entertainment with which civil and mourning councils were concluded. The exigencies of both war and peace rendered it necessary for the Iroquois to have among them practiced and trained runners."[67] Competition could be fierce, and it extended to all facets of the community.

An example of the competitive nature of storytelling, for example, is found in Leslie Silko's *Ceremony,* published in 1977. The author describes a fictional storytelling competition in which the assembled participants attempt to outdo one another by telling the most outlandish and horrifying tale possible. In the spirit of the competition, one individual proceeds to tell a story of newcomers from another land that will pollute the land and water, introduce diseases, and kill indigenous peoples out of fear. The others, fearing repercussions, ask the individual to rescind the story, only to be told, "It's already turned loose.

It's already coming. It can't be turned back."[68] In this instance, the impact of this competitive contest effectively unleashed the European invasion of North America, forever altering the lives of the continental indigenous peoples. The story reminds people of the power of their words and thoughts, and that to put something "out" into a universe that embraces a principle resembling observer-created reality could be dangerous—even if it is in the spirit of one-upmanship.

EDUCATION — As Jon Reyhner has observed, "traditionally, the values and skills which a Native American needed for survival were perpetuated through games and sports. Activities often simulated hunting, food gathering, tipi building, relaying vital messages, or fighting." Games also "tested the strength, stamina, speed, pain tolerance, and courage required for life."[69] This is what Peat described as "tacit knowledge," a knowing that is not passed on through reading or verbal instruction but is learned through personal experience or observation. Tacit knowledge "is not so much stored as data in the brain but is absorbed into the whole person."[70] Nuu-Chah-Nulth (Nootka) children "played at various things that were imitations of their elders' activities. They were often encouraged at some of these 'games,' such as the play feasts and potlatches, and the play-Shamans' Dance, although their elders sought to exercise some control over them, especially in regard to the last named." However, "they were not supposed to use the real Shamans' Dance songs in their game, but had special play songs for it."[71] An educational goal often underscored children's activities. This is seen in how, for instance, Dakota children "learned by observing adults and were incorporated into adult activities as soon as their coordination and strength permitted. Games like cup and pin and hoop and pole also taught coordination."[72] However, not all was geared to formal education. Children were expected to have fun and enjoy themselves. In the wintertime, as discussed above, Blackfoot children would slide down hills, place games on ice, in all enjoying themselves from time to time.[73]

DIPLOMACY — Self-government is best described as a set of relationships involving law, politics, financial management, administration, community and economic growth, natural resource development and maintenance, and both individual and community-based entrepreneurship. This suggests a need for neighbouring communities to establish diplomatic relations. As Deloria pointed out, the world was not "a global village so much as a series of non-homogeneous pockets of identity" that "came into conflict because they represent different historical arrangements of emotional energy."[74] Reflecting on the fact that conflict was a common element of pre-contact indigenous cultures, Betty Meggars has suggested that gaming was a well-known outlet for "aggressions provoked by close living but not permitted direct expression."[75] This implies that gaming was likely used to defuse potentially volatile situations, enabling adversaries to interact while gambling instead of engaging in open warfare. Again, additional research is required to clarify these ideas. As stated by Ted Binnema, "Westerners recorded evidence of ... interethnic gambling almost as soon as they encountered indigenous groups on the north-western plains, however, which implies that practices like [this] were well established by the late pedestrian era [early eighteenth century]."[76] Large multi-ethnic gatherings were the norm in the plateau region during the warmer months. These festive events involved socializing, playing the bone game, and horse racing.[77]

Historian Kenneth Cohen concluded that lacrosse was more than a game; it was a diplomatic tool employed to facilitate cross-cultural interaction, both between First Nations and with European and British newcomers.[78] Large multi-ethnic gatherings in British Columbia's plateau region were not unusual occurrences, especially during the warmer months, when the bone game and horse races were regular occurrences.[79] Gaming of this type was a social activity that enabled various bands and larger tribes to interact in a non-hostile environment, permitting the renewal of social, political, and economic relationships.[80] Among the Haudenosaunee Confederacy, lacrosse was not only an important sport, also an important diplomatic mechanism. As Morgan identified in 1851, strife between villages could be resolved through gaming. This was considered an alternative to warfare that helped to avoid diminishing the number of human beings, who were considered a limited resource.[81]

Morgan also observed the resolution through gaming of animosities between "nation and nation, village and village, or tribes and tribes; in a word parties against parties, and not champion against champion. The prize contended for was that of victor; and it belonged, not to the triumphant players but to the party which sent them forth to the contest."[82] Gaming also had a galvanizing effect, assisting communities to promote stability by instilling balance. One academic has written that group cohesiveness "reached beyond those directly involved with the game, to encompass the entire tribe," adding that "the feeling of unity was further reinforced by the numerous intratribal games ... and the stakes placed on intertribal games," stakes that "if lost, could precariously tilt the delicate economic balance of tribes."[83] In such instances, gaming was used to promote peaceful interface, to improve political relations, leading to stable trade relationships, and as a substitute for warfare. Several examples speak of warfare being temporarily halted to allow for horse racing and games of chance to occur. For example, Phillip Stepney and David Goa stated that the Blackfoot would establish "a temporary peace with other tribes just to hold horse races."[84] As the Assiniboine creation story *Gambling Contests* attests, however, there is a strong correlation between gambling and warfare.[85] Similar ideas are evident among the Blackfoot.[86] This further complicates our understanding of the role gaming played in North American indigenous societies, moving us from the realm of simple conclusions to a more dynamic sphere of thought.

ECONOMICS — Games were important trade items, suggesting that the similarity of games among various tribes indicates they were designed for more than gambling; they also promoted cultural interaction through trade. Culin and Hodge identified this trend in 1907, with the latter writing, "A well-marked affinity exists between the manifestation of the same game even among the most widely separated tribes; the variations are more in the materials employed, than the object or method of plays." He added, "Precisely the same games are played by tribes belonging to unrelated linguistic stocks, and in general the variations do not follow the differences in language."[87] The Cree, for example, learned the bone game from the Flathead during the former people's stay in Montana after fleeing Canada during the 1870s.[88] The Kwakiutl of British Columbia learned their stick game from their northern neighbours.[89] The Cree, Mississauga, Nipissing, and Ottawa tribes, whose territories stretch from western Quebec to the prairies, all played the moccasin game. In two separate articles written by anthropologists Alanson Skinner, and Albert Reagan and F.W. Waugh, the Cree of Saskatchewan and the Ojibwa of Fort Bois, Minnesota, were shown to play a variety of similar bowl games, and, in one instance, played "snow snake" in the same manner.[90] Adding to our understanding of the economic value of gaming to indigenous diplomacies, Daniel Sommerfelt's work reveals the exchange of games as a form of trade between the Blackfoot and the Hopi.[91]

Gaming served a diplomatic function, specifically by aiding foreign nations to overcome cultural differences. Gaming was also an important aspect of wealth distribution. As Joseph Oxendine pointed out, inter-tribal gaming was a model of wealth distribution in that the winnings "stayed within the community," something he described as "a type of 'circular economics.'"[92] During card games among the Tlinglit in northwestern British Columbia, an individual's gambling losses were re-circulated throughout the community. In Blackfoot culture, economic stability was often attributable to community members demonstrating what is today described as problem or pathological gambling. Ewers writes about how "some young men were both luckless and inveterate gamblers, who lost all their horses and were forced to return again and again to enemy camps to recoup their losses. Their love of gambling kept them poor and at the same time kept them active as horse raiders."[93] It also kept wealth circulating throughout the community. Among the South Dakota Wahpeton and Sisseton, relatives of southern Manitoba's Dakota communities, gaming was utilized to distribute a dead individual's belongings throughout the community, to the benefit of many.[94] Alexander Ross estimated that most commodities "change hands through gambling" and that the long narrows was "the great emporium or mart of the Columbia, and the general theatre of gambling and roguery."[95]

One of the few to discuss gaming within the context of economic exchange is Robert Boyd.[96] As he concludes, "it appears that gambling was so common a means of redistributing goods that it challenged the expected mechanism of barter."[97] Within this milieu it is likely that gaming played an important role in the fur trade, something the extant literature is silent about. As Carolyn Podruchny has discussed, Native people taught voyageurs various "games or amusements, such as 'pagessan' or 'le jeu au plat' and body tattooing."[98] Internal mechanisms were also used to ensure circulation of wealth. For example, Kwakuitl games were played at the potlatch.[99] A central institution in the social and political life of most plateau and west coast nations, the potlatch was used both to transfer and confirm property rights while enabling the redistribution of community wealth.[100]

CONCLUSION

A great deal of debate surrounds the issue of whether First Nations possess an Aboriginal right to regulate and operate reserve casinos. This has led to extended and oftentimes contentious discussions between various provinces and First Nations communities while the efficacy of situating casinos on reserves is regularly questioned. Bickering tends to obscure important questions concerning the cultural aspect of gaming. In reality, very little is known about gaming among historic North American indigenous populations, save for what we have learned from work examining their spiritual and ceremonial importance. The political economy of gaming is so subtly integrated into historic indigenous society that it at times seems to disappear from the historical record. This thin reading of the historic literature and available contemporary analysis suggests gaming was used for various purposes, ranging from promoting diplomacy and economic development to creating social events and helping in education.[101] By moving away from the religious and ceremonial aspects of gaming, additional work may focus on drawing out the political and economic importance of indigenous gaming.

This work is vital for various reasons. First, it will provide us with an understanding of the role gaming played in indigenous societies, which has largely been obscured by our continued reliance upon Eurocentric taxonomies. Second, with this understanding we may come to better appreciate the commonalities and differences of gaming in various communities demonstrating these behaviours. Third, reasons why each community chose to utilize gaming for diplomatic purposes and economic development will materialize. Finally, we will gain an understanding of how indigenous communities regulated gaming, an understanding that could have contemporary significance. For example, the courts have suggested that no evidence exists to demonstrate how historic indigenous communities regulated gaming. But, would wagering several hundred horses during a stick game not constitute high-stakes gambling? At gatherings involving several different indigenous communities, it was common to adopt the host nation's protocols related to gaming, processes that were strictly monitored to ensure peaceable interface. This appears to be regulatory in scope. Chapter 2 will expand upon this argument in more detail. For now, adopting a multi-disciplinary approach will permit the flexibility required to better determine the importance of gaming to historic indigenous societies. This demands additional research be undertaken to explore the historic notions of gambling for the purpose of contextualizing what gaming represented in these communities.

NOTES

1 The term *indigenous* is utilized to describe the people and communities of Canada prior to Canadian Confederation in 1867. *Indigenous* does not represent a legal category, however. It is used in this textbook to describe: (1) the descendants of groups of people living in the territory at the time when other groups of different cultures or ethnic origin arrived there; (2) groups that have preserved almost intact the customs and traditions of their ancestors, which are similar to those characterized as indigenous; and (3) those who have been placed under a state structure that incorporates national, social, and cultural characteristics distinct from their own. *Aboriginal people* is a constitutionally entrenched term describing Canada's Indian, Inuit, and Métis peoples. Because of the historic time period framing this analysis, the term *Indian* is used in legislation or policy; it also appears in discussions concerning such legislation or policy, as will proper names of communities used historically and today.

2 *R. v. Pamajewon*, [1996] 2 S.C.R. 821

3 Yale D. Belanger, *Gambling with the Future: The Evolution of Aboriginal Gaming in Canada* (Saskatoon: Purich Publishing, 2006).

4 *Pamajewon*, 821–22.

5 Ibid., 826.

6 *R. v. Van der Peet*, [1996] 2 S.C.R. 507 (S.C.C.).

7 Morden C. Lazarus, Edwin D. Monzon, and Richard B. Wodnicki, "The Mohawks of Kahnawá:ke and the Case for an Aboriginal Right to Gaming under the Canada Constitution Act, 1982," *Gaming Law Review* 19, 4 (2006): 376. (This essay is reprinted as Chapter 2 of this text.)

8 John Borrows, "Wampum at Niagara: The Royal Proclamation, Canadian Legal History, and Self-government," in *Aboriginal and Treaty Rights in Canada: Essays on Law, Equity, and Respect for Difference*, ed. Michael Asch (Vancouver: University of British Columbia Press, 1997), 155–172; Russel Lawrence Barsh and James Youngblood Henderson, "The Supreme Court's Van der Peet Trilogy: Naïve Imperialism and Ropes of Sand," McGill Law Journal 42 (1997): 994–1008.

9 James [Sakej] Youngblood Henderson, "Sui Generis and Treaty Citizenship," Citizenship Studies 6, 4 (2003): 429.

10 Brian Slattery, "A Taxonomy of Aboriginal Rights," in *Let Right Be Done: Aboriginal Title, the Calder Case and the Future of Indigenous Rights*, ed. Hamar Foster, Heather Raven, and Jeremy Webber (Vancouver: University of British Columbia Press, 2007), 114.

11 Ibid., 115.

12 W. H. Holmes, *Twenty-fourth Annual Report at the Bureau of American Ethnology* (Washington, DC: United States Government Printing Office, 1907), 39–40.

13 David Hewitt and Dale Auger, *Firewatch on First Nations Adolescent Gambling* (Edmonton: Nechi Training, Research and Health Promotions Institute, 1995); David Hewitt, *Spirit of Bingoland: A Study of Problem Gambling Among Alberta Native People* (Edmonton: Nechi Training and Research and Health Promotions Institute/AADAC, 1994); Research and Health Promotions Institute, *Firewatch on Aboriginal Adolescent Gambling* (Edmonton, 1995); Jill Oakes, *Gambling and Problem Gambling in First Nations Communities* (Winnipeg: Native Studies Press, 2005).

14 Kathryn Gabriel, *Gambler Way: Indian Gaming in Mythology, History, and Archaeology in North America* (Boulder: Johnson Books, 1996); Margo Little, "The Moral Dilemma of High Stakes Gambling in Native Communities" (master's thesis, Laurentian University, 1997).

15 Per Binde, "Gambling and Religion: Histories of Concord and Conflict," *Journal of Gambling Issues 20* (2007): 145–166, http://www.camh.net/egambling/issue20/pdfs/03binde.pdf; Stewart Culin, *Games of the North American Indians* (New York: Dover Publications, 1975 [1907]), 34.

16 Gabriel, *Gambler Way*, 18. Culin, *Games of the North*, 34; Michael A. Salter, "An Analysis of the Role of Games in the Fertility Rituals of the Native North American," *Anthropos 69* (1974): 494–504; Michael A. Salter, "Play in Ritual: An Ethnohistorical Overview of Native North America," in *Play and Culture: 1978 Proceedings of the Association for the Anthropological Study of Play*, ed. Helen B. Schwartzman (West Point, NY: Leisure Press, 1980), 70–82.

17 Binde, *Gambling Across Cultures*, 1–27.

18 Belanger, *Gambling with the Future*; Virginia McGowan and Gary Nixon, "Blackfoot Traditional Knowledge in Resolution of Problem Gambling: Getting Gambled and Seeking Wholeness," *Canadian Journal of Native Studies* 24, 1 (2004): 7–35; Virginia McGowan, Lois Frank, Gary Nixon, and Misty Grimshaw, "Sacred and Secular Play Among Blackfoot Peoples of Southwest Alberta," in *Culture and the Gambling Phenomenon*, ed. Alex Blaszczynski (Sydney: National Association for Gambling Studies, 2002), 241–255; Karen Campbell, "Community Life and Governance: Early Experiences of Mnjikaning First Nation with Casino Rama" (master's thesis, University of Manitoba, 1999); Cathy Nilson, "The FSIN-Province of Saskatchewan Gaming Partnership: 1995 to 2002" (master's thesis, University of Saskatchewan, 2004); Warren Skea, "Time to Deal: A Comparison of the Native Casino Gambling Policy in Alberta and Saskatchewan" (PhD diss., University of Calgary, 1997).

19 John Kiedrowski, *Native Gaming and Gambling in Canada: A Report Prepared for the Department of Indian and Northern Affairs* (Ottawa: Minister of Public Works and Government Services, 2001); Grant Thornton, *Review of First Nations Gaming Commissions: Sources and Uses of Funds Analysis* (Nova Scotia: Office of Aboriginal Affairs, Sept. 2000); Dave Desbrisay, "The Gaming Industry in Aboriginal Communities," in *For Seven Generations: An Information Legacy of the Royal Commission on Aboriginal Peoples* (CD-ROM) (Ottawa: Libraxus, 1996); Paul K. Frits, "Aboriginal Gaming—Law and Policy," in *Aboriginal Issues Today: A Legal and Business Guide*, eds. Stephen B. Smart and Michael Coyle (Vancouver: Self-Counsel, 1997), 220-234; Robin Kelley, *First Nations Gambling Policy in Canada. Gambling in Canada Research Report 12* (Calgary: Canada West Foundation, June 2001); Katherine Marshall, "The Gambling Industry: Raising the Stakes," *Perspectives* (Winter 1998), 7–11; Hal Pruden, "An Overview of the

Gambling Provisions in Canadian Criminal Law and First Nations Gambling," *Journal of Aboriginal Economic Development* 2, 2 (2002), 37-40; Michael Seelig and Julie Seelig, "'Place Your Bets!' On Gambling, Government and Society," *Canadian Public Policy* 24, 1 (1998), 91–106.

20 Francis R. Guth, *Western Values Comparison in Gambling: With a Comparison to North American Aboriginal Views* (Sault Ste. Marie, ON: Algoma, 1994); Constance Deiter-Buffalo, *The Handgame Project* (Hobbema, AB: Indian Association of Alberta, 1996); M.K. Heine, "The Symbolic Capital of Honour: Gambling Games and the Social Construction of Gender in Tlingit Indian Culture," *Play and Culture* 4 (1991): 346–358; Phil Lange, "A First Nations Hand Game: Gambling from Supernatural Power," *Journal of Gambling Issues 11* (2004).

21 Hugh Trevor Roper, *The Rise of Christian Europe* (London: Thames and Hudson, 1966), 9, cited in Shephard Krech III, "The State of Ethnohistory," *Annual Review of Anthropology* 20 (1991): 345.

22 G.W.F. Hegel, *Lectures on the Philosophy of World History: Introduction, Reason in History*, translated from the German ed. of Johannes Hoffmeister by H.B. Nisbet (Cambridge: Cambridge University Press, 1975).

23 Edward Hallett Carr, *What Is History?* (New York: Vintage, 1967), 108–109, 27.

24 Yale D. Belanger, "Epistemological Distinctiveness and the Use of Guided History Methodology for Writing Native Histories," *Indigenous Nations Studies Journal* 2, 2 (2001): 20.

25 Ruben Gold Thwaites, *The Jesuit Relations and Allied Documents: Travels and Explorations of the Jesuit Missionaries in New France* (Cleveland: The Burrow Bros., 1896-1901), 71 vols.

26 Belanger, *Gambling with the Future*, specifically chapter 2.

27 See generally Roy Harvey Pearce, *Savagism and Civilization: A Study of the Indian and the American Mind* (Berkeley: University of California Press, 1988).

28 Robert Berkhofer, *The White Man's Indian: Images of the American Indian from Columbus to the Present* (New York: Knopf, 1978), 119.

29 Francis Jennings, *The Invasion of America: Indians, Colonialism, and the Kant of Conquest* (New York: W.W. Norton and Company, 1976), 57.

30 T.C. Elliott, "Journal of Alexander Ross—Snake Country Expedition, 1824." *Quarterly of the Oregon Historical Society* 14 (Dec. 1913), 366. See also Alexander Ross, *Adventures of the First Settlers on the Oregon or Columbia River, 1810–1813* (Corvallis: Oregon State University Press, 2000 [1849]).

31 Lewis Henry Morgan, *League of the Iroquois, Book II: Spirit of the League* (New York: Corinth Books, 1962 [1851]).

32 Johann G. Kohl, Kitchi Gami: *Life Among the Lake Superior Ojibway* (St. Paul: Minnesota Historical Society Reprint, 1985 [1860]).

33 John MacLean, *Canadian Savage Folk: The Native Tribes of Canada* (Toronto: W. Briggs, 1896).

34 Culin, *Games of the North American Indians*, 31.

35 Kohl, *Kitchi Gami*, 83, 94.

36 Frederick Webb Hodge, ed., Handbook of American Indians: North of Mexico, Pt. 1 (New York: Greenwood Press, 1969 [1907]), 483.

37 Jeff Stuyt and David J. Wishart, "Sports and Recreation," in Encyclopedia of the Great Plains Indians, ed. David J. Wishart (Lincoln: University of Nebraska Press, 2007), 194.

38 Culin, Games of the North American Indians, 194.

39 Emma Helen Blair, ed., The Indian Tribes of the Upper Mississippi Valley and Region of the Great Lakes as Described by Nicolas Perrot, French Commandant in the Northwest; Bacqueville de la Potheria, French Royal Commissioner to Canada; Morel Marston, American Army Officer; and Thomas Forsyth, United States Agent at Fort Armstrong, vol. 1 (Cleveland: The Arthur H. Clark Company, 1911).

40 Diamond Jenness, The Indians of Canada (Toronto: University of Toronto Press, 1977), 159. For a discussion of gambling away family, see T.F. McIlwraith, The Bella Coola Indians, vol. 1 (Toronto: University of Toronto Press, 1948), 159.

41 Jenness, The Indians of Canada, 350. For a discussion of the Indian Problem, see Noel Dyck, "What is the Indian Problem": Tutelage and Resistance in Canadian Indian Administration (St. John's: Institute of Social and Economic Research, 1991). For additional insight into Jenness and his role with Canadian Indian policy generally, see Peter Kulchyski, "Anthropology in the Service of the State: Diamond Jenness and Canadian Indian Policy," Journal of Canadian Studies 28, 2 (1993): 21–50.

42 Canada, Parliament, Special Joint Parliamentary Committee of the Senate and the House of Commons appointed to examine and consider the Indian Act, Minutes of Proceedings and Evidence, no. 7 (25 March 1947), 310–311.

43 Belanger, Gambling with the Future, 27.

44 Little, "The Moral Dilemma," 23.

45 Per Binde, "Gambling Across Cultures: Mapping Worldwide Occurrence and Learning from Ethnographic Comparison." International Gambling Studies 5, 1 (2005): 1-27.

46 Vine Deloria Jr., Red Earth White Lies: Native Americans and the Myth of Scientific Fact (Golden, CO: Fulcrum Publishing, 1997), 26.

47 Belanger, Gambling with the Future, 32.

48 John Boatman, My Elders Taught Me: Aspects of Western Great Lakes American Indian Philosophy (Lanham, MD: University Press of America, 1992), 11.

49 Guth, Western Values Comparison in Gambling, 5.

50 Leroy Little Bear, "Relationship of Aboriginal People to the Land and the Aboriginal Perspective on Aboriginal Title," in For Seven Generations: An Information Legacy of the Royal Commission on Aboriginal Peoples, CD-ROM (Ottawa: Canada Communications Group, 1996), cited in Royal Commission on Aboriginal Peoples, Treaty Making in the Spirit of Co-Existence: An Alternative to Extinguishment (Ottawa: Canada Communications Group, 1994), 48.

51 F. David Peat, Lighting the Seventh Fire: The Spiritual Ways, Healing, and Science of the Native American (New York: Birch Lane Press Book, 1994), 156.

52 Ibid.

53 Peter Fidler, *Journal of Journey to the Rocky Mountains*, 31 December 1792. See also Jay Hansford C. Vest, "The Oldman River and the Sacred: A Meditation upon Aputosi Pii'kani Tradition and Environmental Ethics," *Canadian Journal of Native Studies* 25, 2 (2005): 571–607.

54 Edward S. Curtis, T*he North American Indian: The Indians of the United States, The Dominion of Canada, and Alaska*, vol. 9, ed. Frederick Webb Hodge (New York: Johnson Reprint Corporation, 1913), 110.

55 Lynn Maranda, *Coast Salish Gambling Games, Canadian Ethnology Service Paper* No. 93 (Ottawa: National Museums of Canada, 1984).

56 T.F. McIlwraith, *The Bella Coola Indians*, vol. 2 (Toronto: University of Toronto Press, 1948), 336.

57 Curtis, *The North American Indian*, vol. 11, 195.

58 Marian W. Smith, *Indians of the Urban Northwest* (New York: AMS Press, 1948), 284.

59 Wilson D. Wallis and Ruth Sawtell Wallis, *The Micmac Indians of Eastern Canada* (Minneapolis: University of Minnesota Press, 1955), 19–20.

60 Peat, *Lighting the Seventh Fire*, 156, 171–174.

61 Wallis and Wallis, *The Micmac Indians of Eastern Canada*, 293.

62 Culin, *Games of the North American Indians*, 110.

63 For the discussion of "thick" versus "thin" interpretation, see Clifford Geertz, *The Interpretation of Culture* (New York: Basic Books, 1973), 17–20.

64 Joseph Dion, *My Tribe the Crees* (Calgary: Glenbow Mueseum, 1979), 10–11. Mention of foot races is also found in Edward Ahenakew, *Voices of the Plains Cree*, ed. Ruth M. Buck (Regina: Canadian Plains Research Center, 1995), 42.

65 Deanna Christensen, *Ahtahkakoop: The Epic Account of a Plains Cree Head Chief, His People, and Their Struggle for Survival, 1816–1896* (Manitoba: Ahtahkakoop Publishing, 2000), 222.

66 Beverly Hungry Wolf, *The Ways of My Grandmothers* (New York: Quill, 1982), 25.

67 Ibid., 307.

68 Leslie Marmon Silko, *Ceremony* (New York: Viking, 1977).

69 Jon Reyhner, ed., *Teaching the Indian Child: A Bilingual/Multicultural Approach*, 2nd ed. (Billings: Eastern Montana College, 1988), 255.

70 Peat, *Lighting the Seventh Fire*, 66.

71 Phillip Drucker, *The Northern and Central Nootkan Tribes* (Washington, DC: United States Government Printing Office, 1951), 451.

72 James H. Howard, *The Canadian Sioux* (Lincoln: University of Nebraska Press, 1984), 81.

73 Hungry Wolf, *The Ways of My Grandmothers*, 25.

74 Vine Deloria, *God Is Red: A Native View of Religion* (Golden: Fulcrum, 1994), 65.

75 Betty J. Meggars, "North and South American Cultural Connections and Convergences," in *Prehistoric Man in the New World* (Chicago: University of Chicago Press, 1964), 515. For a general discussion about some of the games played in North American prior to Columbus's arrival in 1492, see Paul S. Martin, George I. Quimby, and Donald Collier, *Indians Before Columbus: Twenty Thousand Years of North American History Revealed by Archaeology* (Chicago: University of Chicago Press, 1947).

76 Theodore Binnema, *Common and Contested Ground: A Human and Environmental History of the Northwestern Plains* (Norman: University of Oklahoma Press, 2001), 59.

77 Gerald Desmond, *Gambling Among the Yakima*. Catholic University of America Anthropological Series 14 (Washington, DC: Catholic University of America Press, 1952).

78 Kenneth Cohen, "A Mutually Comprehensible World? Native Americans, Europeans and Play in Eighteenth-Century America," *American Indian Quarterly* 26, 2 (2001), 67–93.

79 Desmond, *Gambling Among the Yakima*.

80 Belanger, *Gambling with the Future*, 29.

81 Morgan, *League of the Iroquois, Book II*, 292.

82 Ibid., 292.

83 Michael A. Salter, "The Effect of Acculturation on the Game of Lacrosse and its Role as an Agent of Indian Survival," *Canadian Journal of History and Sport and Physical Education* 3 (1972): 29.

84 Phillip H.R. Stepney and David J. Goa, *The Scriver Collection* (Edmonton: Provincial Museum of Alberta, 1990), 39.

85 Robert H. Lowie, *The Assiniboine* (New York: AMS Press, 1909), 218-223.

86 Clark Wissler and D.C. Duvall, *Mythology of the Blackfoot Indians*, 2nd ed. (Lincoln: University of Nebraska Press, 2008), 133.

87 Hodge, *Handbook of American Indians*, 483.

88 David G. Mandelbaum, *The Plains Cree: An Ethnographic, Historical, and Comparative Study* (Regina: Canadian Plains Research Center, 2001), 130.

89 Franz Boas, *Kwakiutl Ethnography*, ed. Helen Codere (Chicago: University of Chicago Press, 1966), 392.

90 Alanson Skinner, "Notes on the Plains Cree," *American Anthropologist* 16, 1 (1914), 68–87; Albert B. Reagan and F.W. Waugh, "Some Games of the Bois Fort Ojibwa," *American Anthropologist* 21, 3 (1919), 264–278.

91 Daniel M. Sommerfelt, "Comparison of Blackfoot and Hopi Games and their Contemporary Application: A Review of the Literature" (master's thesis, University of Lethbridge, 2005).

92 Joseph B. Oxendine, *American Indian Sports Heritage* (Champaign, IL: Human Kinetics Books, 1988), 31.

93 John C. Ewers, *The Horse in Blackfoot Indian Culture: With Comparative Material from Other Western Tribes* (Honolulu: University Press of the Pacific, 2001), 239

94 Culin, *Games of the North American Indians*, 110.

95 Alexander Ross, *Adventures of the First Settlers on the Oregon or Columbia River* (London: Smith, Elder, 1849), 117.

96 Robert Boyd, *People of the Dalles: The Indians of Wascopam Mission* (Lincoln: University of Nebraska Press, 1996), 68.

97 Ibid., 71.

98 Carolyn Podruchny, "Sons of the Wilderness: Work, Culture and Identity among Voyageurs in the Montreal Fur Trade, 1780-1821" (PhD diss., University of Toronto, 1999), 330.

99 Boas, *Kwakiutl Ethnography*, 395–396.

100 For a brief overview of the potlatch's cultural significance, see Tina Loo, "Dan Cranmer's Potlatch: Law as Coercion, Symbol, and Rhetoric in British Columbia, 1884–1951," *Canadian Historical Review* 73, 2 (1992): 125–165; Elizabeth Furniss, "The Carrier Indians and the Politics of History," in *Native Peoples: The Canadian Experience*, ed. R. Bruce Morrison and C. Roderick Wilson (Toronto: Oxford University Press, 1995), 508–545; Douglas Hudson, "The Okanagan Indians," in Native Peoples: The Canadian Experience, ed. R. Bruce Morrison and C. Roderick Wilson (Toronto: Oxford University Press, 1995), 484–507.

101 Geertz, *The Interpretation of Culture*, 17–20.

CHAPTER 2

THE MOHAWKS OF KAHNAWÁ:KE AND THE CASE FOR AN ABORIGINAL RIGHT TO GAMING UNDER THE CONSTITUTION ACT, 1982*

*MORDEN C. LAZARUS, EDWIN D. MONZON,
AND RICHARD B. WODNICKI*

While the past two decades have seen the emergence of the Native American gaming industry in the United States, First Nations groups north of the border have been largely frustrated in their efforts to pursue gaming activity over the same period. The reason for this is quite simple: non-profit gaming is officially outlawed in Canada by virtue of the Criminal Code,[1] with the exception that the provincial governments are authorized to operate gaming enterprises and, in very limited circumstances, to issue licences for private gaming events.[2] The result of this monopoly has been a proliferation of extremely successful provincially owned and operated gaming enterprises throughout the country. Although some First Nations groups have attempted to undertake gaming activity despite the legal ban, these efforts have been largely limited to small-scale bingo halls and sporadic one-time events.

The great exception to the rule can be found about ten kilometres southwest of Montreal, at the Mohawk Community of Kahnawá:ke. The Mohawks of Kahnawá:ke are a Canadian First Nations people of approximately 8000 individuals. A community with a history of self-starting entrepreneurship, the Mohawks recognized early on the opportunities brought by the Internet age, and they made a collective choice to pursue an active strategy focused on the hosting of online gaming websites.

Kahnawá:ke's foray into the world of cybergaming was launched in the late 1990s, with the creation of the Kahnawá:ke Gaming Commission (KGC), which, in 1999, granted an Internet gaming licence to Mohawk Internet Technologies (MIT), the main Internet service provider at Kahnawá:ke. Since then, the KGC has granted client-provider authorizations to more than 100 gaming licencees who have negotiated hosting agreements with MIT. Considering the online gaming generated $12 billion in revenue in 2005,[3] with estimates that this figure will reach $24 billion by 2010,[4] it is evident that the Mohawks are operating a profitable enterprise.

Despite their impressive success in the world of Internet gaming, one inescapable fact continues to loom in the background; namely, non-licenced gaming remains illegal in Canada, and this includes Internet gaming as well. Since they are fully subject to the application of Canadian criminal law, the Mohawks of Kahnawá:ke are theoretically in violation of the Criminal Code provisions relating to gaming, and consequently vulnerable to criminal prosecution. However, despite this, no steps have been taken against them, and they have never been challenged by either federal or provincial authorities. It is arguable that the reason for this can be found in the text of the Canadian Constitution and related to jurisprudence.

As interpreted by the Supreme Court of Canada, Section 35(1) of the Canada Constitution Act, 1982, enshrines the protection of Aboriginal rights. The Court has made it clear that, within reason, where it can be shown that a certain practice has played an important part of an Aboriginal community's way of life since prior to contact with Europeans, that practice is protected and is immune from the application of Canadian law to the extent of any incompatibility. With regard to the Mohawks of Kahnawá:ke, it is indisputable that gaming has long formed a central part of the community's way of life, dating back to well before contact with European peoples. Accordingly, the purpose of this paper is to demonstrate, through an in-depth analysis of their culture and history, that the Mohawks of Kahnawá:ke possess an Aboriginal right to gaming by virtue of the Constitution of Canada. The following review will, therefore, highlight the historical importance of gaming practices in Kahnawá:ke culture and will demonstrate that the Mohawks of Kahnawá:ke fulfill the relevant legal tests and jurisprudence, such that they are able to claim an Aboriginal right to gaming.

CULTURAL AND HISTORICAL EVIDENCE

HISTORICAL GAMING PRACTICES — The range of games played historically by First Nations groups throughout North America is wide and encompasses games of dexterity, such as archery contests, and games of chance, such as dice games. In fact, over 100 dice games are recorded as having been historically played by Native groups throughout North America.[5] Among the games that were played by First Nations peoples are beaver tooth, half shell, and shell disk, to name a few.[6]

If gaming has historically played an important role in the life of North American First Nations groups in general, it has formed a particularly central part of Iroquois, and as a result, Mohawk, culture and history.[7] In fact, it is arguable that the concept of gaming lies at the very root of the way of life of the Mohawks of Kahnawá:ke by virtue of the Great Law of Peace. The founding constitution of the Iroquois Confederacy, the Great Law of Peace set out the principles by which the nations of the Confederacy would co-exist in harmony. It emphasized the fundamental primacy of resolving conflicts through peaceful means. It was as a result of this emphasis on the nonviolent resolution of disputes that the playing of games such as lacrosse emerged as a means of resolving differences among individuals and groups within the Iroquois Confederacy. The Great Law of Peace was the genesis by which aggressions and/or conflicts could be settled in a peaceful manner by wagering on the outcome of a game.[8] The Great Law of Peace therefore forms the basis of the Mohawk culture and practice of gaming.

Among the wide range of Iroquois games played in the community, the game of snowsnake has long been enjoyed by the Mohawks of Kahnawá:ke. Snowsnake competitions were regularly staged between Kahnawá:ke and other communities such as the Oneida, with arrowheads, animal pelts, and food wagered on the outcome of the matches.[9] Plumstone, an antecedent of peachstone, was historically played by the Mohawks of Kahnawá:ke. One such plumstone match was observed in the nineteenth century by a Col. James Smith, who noted, "They put a number of plum stones in a small bowl; one side of each stone is black and the other white; then they shake or hustle the bowl, calling hits, hits, honesy, rago, rago, which signifies calling for white or black or what they wish to turn up; they then turn the bowl and count the whites and blacks."[10]

Hoop and javelin is another game historically played at Kahnawá:ke. Participants were divided among those holding hoops and others throwing sticks toward the hoops. An early observer of one such match played at Kahnawá:ke in the 1700s noted, "The boys are very expert at trundling a hoop, particularly the Cahnuaga Indians, whom I have frequently seen excel at this amusement. The game is played by any number of boys who may accidentally assemble together, some driving the hoop, while the others with bows and arrows shoot at it. At this exercise they are surprisingly expert, and will stop the progress of the hoop when going with great velocity, by driving the pointed arrow into its edge; this they will do at a considerable distance, and on horseback as on foot."[11]

Of all the games historically played by the Mohawks of Kahnawá:ke, few are as well known and unique for the community of Kahnawá:ke as lacrosse. The playing of the game by the Mohawks of Kahnawá:ke dates back to before contact with Europeans. It has been argued that lacrosse was invented sometime in the 1400s,[12] indicating that it existed long before contact with Europeans. Moreover, there appears to be no evidence of non-Natives having taken up the game until the nineteenth century, when Anglophone Montrealers adopted lacrosse, having learned it from the Kahanawa:ke and Akwesasne Mohawks.[13]

HISTORICAL WAGERING PRACTICES — Wagering played an essential and fundamental role in Iroquois and, by extension, Mohawk gaming practices. In fact, as pointed out by an authority on Iroquois gaming, "The idea of gain or loss entered into most contests, and many were played solely for the sake of gambling. The products of hunting, fishing, trading and most wealth were expended in betting."[14] So central was wagering to Iroquois gaming practices that it often got out of hand, to the point where the game was played more for the sake of wagering than for the enjoyment of the game itself: "Betting upon the result was common among Iroquois. As this practice was never reprobated by their religious teachers, but, on the contrary, rather encouraged, it frequently led to the most reckless indulgence.... The excitement and eagerness with which he watched the shifting tide of the game, was more uncontrollable than the delirious agitation of the pale-face at the race-course, or even at the gaming table."[15]

As demonstrated by a European settler's eighteenth-century account, Iroquois wagering was taken to its limits, with participants wagering, and losing, significant portions of their belongings: "The sums bet on the play are immense for the Indians. Some have pledged their cabins; others have stripped themselves of their clothes and bet them against those of the opposing party; others who have already lost everything they possess finally propose their liberty against a small bet."[16]

GAMING REGULATION PRIOR TO CONTACT WITH EUROPEANS — The regulation of gaming formed a fundamental component of the historical gaming practices of the Iroquois peoples, and, by extension, of the Mohawks of Kahnawá:ke. In demonstrating this point, one need only make reference to the writings on Iroquois gaming practices by Henry Morgan, the eminent expert on Iroquois culture and history:

> These bets were made in a systematic manner, and the articles then deposited with the managers of the game. A bet offered by a person upon one side, in the nature of some valuable article, was matched by a similar article, or one of equal value, by some one upon the other. Personal ornaments made the usual gaming currency. Other bets were offered and taken in the same manner, until hundreds of articles were sometimes collected. These were laid aside by the managers, until the game was decided, when each article lost by the event was handed over to the winning individual, together with his own, which he had risked against it.[17]

The game of lacrosse further bolsters the argument in favour of a history of gaming by the Mohawks of Kahnawá:ke. These lacrosse matches involved extensive regulation related to codes of conduct, scheduling rules and regulations, and methods of enforcing outcomes.

The Iroquois also regulated lacrosse through a complex set of rules that governed where, when, and how matches would be held for ritual purposes. Iroquois custom dictated that matches were to be played on occasions of crisis, such as sickness and burial, and such ritual lacrosse matches were regulated by a strict set of rules and procedures which ensured the desired outcome— for example, when the game was properly played as a memorial to the dead, the dead would be at peace and not harm the living. Moreover, ritual lacrosse matches were regulated in the sense that they were played in accordance with the rules of the Sky Holder legend, which structured the match and gave it meaning in the context of the ritual ceremony.[18]

The hosting of lacrosse matches between teams from different Aboriginal communities provides another example of gaming regulation practices. In hosting lacrosse competitions, the Mohawks of Kahnawá:ke regulated the matches through the enforcement of a complex array of rules and procedures that governed the contests and the manner of play. So for example, as evidenced in a 1797 game between the Mohawks and the Seneca, one of the rules was that wagered items were guarded for the duration of the match by men appointed as stakeholders, generally trusted tribal elders.[19]

The preceding review of the historical gaming practices of the Mohawks of Kahnawá:ke demonstrates that gaming has been an integral part of their culture and practices since well before contact with Europeans. The following legal analysis will, in turn, show that, by virtue of this deeply embedded history of gaming, the Kahnawá:ke possess an Aboriginal right to gaming under the Canadian Constitution and related jurisprudence.

LEGAL TESTS

In case law spanning several years and a number of judgments, the Supreme Court of Canada has set forth the legal tests by which an Aboriginal right can be claimed under Section 35(1) of the Canada Constitution Act, 1982. Essentially, where a particular group is able to demonstrate that it has engaged in a particular practice or custom since prior to contact with European peoples, it is able to claim an Aboriginal right and an entitlement to continue engaging in that practice or custom, irrespective of potential legal prohibitions or restrictions. The legal tests set forth by the Supreme Court, and presented in this section, are aimed at providing specific and direct guidelines in evaluating a claim to an Aboriginal right under Section 35(1) of the Constitution.

THREE-PART TEST: R. V. SPARROW — In *R. v. Sparrow*,[20] the Supreme Court of Canada was faced with the question of determining whether Section 35(1) of the Canada Constitution Act, 1982, rendered the terms of a food fishing licence held by Musqueam Indians unconstitutional. Ronald Edward Sparrow was charged under the Fisheries Act with the offense of fishing with a drift net of forty-five fathoms in length instead of the permissible twenty-five fathoms. Mr. Sparrow did not contest the facts alleged by the Crown. In his defence, Sparrow maintained that the terms and restrictions of the fishing licence were inconsistent with Section 35(1) of the Canada Constitution Act, 1982, which states: "The existing Aboriginal and treaty rights of the Aboriginal peoples of Canada are hereby recognized and affirmed." Consequently, he maintained that he was fishing in accordance with the exercise of an existing Aboriginal right, recognized and affirmed by Section 35(1) of the Canada Constitution Act, 1982. In its analysis, the Supreme Court of Canada, under the pen of Chief Justice Dickason, set forth a three-part test that all Aboriginal rights must pass in order to afforded the protection of Section 35(1) of the Canada Constitution Act, 1982.

First part of the test: characterization of the right claimed. The first part of the test pertains to the characterization, assessment, and definition of an existing Aboriginal right. Chief Justice Dickason held that only those Aboriginal and treaty rights existing at the time when the Canada Constitution Act, 1982, came into effect were meant to be protected by Section 35 (1). In addition, he ruled that the claimed Aboriginal right must have existed prior to contact with Europeans. Consequently, extinguished rights were not revived as a consequence of the Canada Constitution Act, 1982. Justice Dickason did, however, recognize the illogical nature of a "frozen rights" approach, which would limit the recognition of an Aboriginal right to its primeval form. Instead, he endorsed a flexible approach that permits the rights claimed to evolve into a current and modern form.

The majority opinion in *R. v. Sparrow* further specified that an Aboriginal right could not be extinguished by the simple fact that an activity may be regulated. In fact, any regulation and/or legislation must be explicitly clear to the effect that it extinguishes a specific existing Aboriginal right: "The test of extinguishment to be adopted, in our opinion, is that the Sovereign's intention must be clear and plain if it is to extinguish an Aboriginal Right."[21]

The Supreme Court of Canada did not elaborate further on the characterization of an Aboriginal right, given that the Crown had failed to effectively dispute the fact that the Musqueams had an Aboriginal right to fish for food. This first part of the test was not clarified or elaborated upon until this same court rendered its decision in *R. v. Van der Peet*.[22]

Second part of the test: infringement. The second part of the test relates to the determination of whether the claimed Aboriginal right has been infringed. The individual and/or group claiming the infringement has the onus of proving a prima facie infringement: "To determine whether the fishing rights have been interfered with such as to constitute prima facie infringement of 35(1), certain questions must be asked. First, is the limitation unreasonable? Second, does the regulation impose undue hardship? Third, does the regulation deny the holders of the right their preferred means of exercising that right? The onus of proving a prima facie infringement lies on the individual or group challenging the legislation."[23]

Third part of the test: justification. If a court comes to the conclusion as to the existence of a prima facie infringement, then the analysis moves to the third part of the test, justification: "The justification analysis would proceed as follows. First, is there a valid legislative purpose? ... If a valid legislative objective is found, the analysis proceeds to the second part of the justification issue.

Here we refer back to the interpretive principle derived from Taylor and Williams and Guerin, supra. That is the honour of the Crown is at stake in dealing with the Aboriginal peoples."[24]

Additionally, other considerations were advanced by the Supreme Court of Canada in R. v. Sparrow: "Within the analysis of justification, there are further questions to be addressed, depending on the circumstances of the inquiry. These include the question of whether there has been as little infringement as possible in order to effect the desired result; whether the Aboriginal group in question has been consulted with respect to the conservation measures being implemented."[25]

ELABORATION OF THE FIRST PART OF THE THREE-PART TEST: R. V. VAN DER PEET — In R. v. Van der Peet,[26] the Supreme Court of Canada elaborated on the first part of the test set out in Sparrow and concluded that in order to identify and characterize an Aboriginal right, said claimed right must pass an "integral to distinctive culture" test. Before addressing the test, the Court outlined some guiding principles. Amongst the guiding principles was the recognition, by the Court, that Aboriginal rights are rights that exist because of their Aboriginal nature. In addition, the Court recognized the fiduciary duty of the Crown vis-à-vis Aboriginal peoples. The Court held that this duty requires that where any ambiguity exists as to what is protected by Section 35(1) of the Canada Constitution Act, 1982, said doubt is to be resolved in favour of the Aboriginal community claiming the right.

In its analysis of Section 35(1), the Supreme Court found that the Aboriginal rights recognized and affirmed by said section are best understood as, first, the means by which the Constitution recognizes the fact that prior to the arrival of Europeans in North America, the land was already occupied by distinct Aboriginal societies, and as, second, the means by which that prior occupation is reconciled with the assertion of Crown sovereignty over Canadian territory.[27]

The Supreme Court then clarified and refined the test for characterizing and identifying an Aboriginal right (integral-to-distinctive-culture test), the whole as can be seen from the following excerpt: "In light of the suggestion of Sparrow, supra, and the purpose underlying § 35(1), the following test should be used to identify whether an applicant has established an Aboriginal Right protected by § 35(1): in order to be an Aboriginal Right an activity must be an element to practice, custom or tradition integral to the distinctive culture of the Aboriginal group claiming the right."[28]

In applying this test, the Supreme Court enumerated the following factors and guiding principles that must be considered:

1) Courts must take into account the perspective of Aboriginal peoples themselves.

2) Courts must identify precisely the nature of the claim being made in determining whether an Aboriginal claimant has demonstrated the existence of an Aboriginal right.

3) In order to be integral, a practice, custom or tradition must be of central significance to an Aboriginal society.

4) The practices, customs and traditions constituting Aboriginal rights are those that have continuity with the practices, customs and traditions that existed prior to contact.

5) Courts must approach the rules of evidence in light of the evidentiary difficulties inherent in adjudicating the Aboriginal claims.

6) Claims to Aboriginal rights must be adjudicated on a specific rather than general basis.

7) For a practice, custom or tradition to constitute an Aboriginal right it must be of independent significance to the Aboriginal culture in which it exists.

8) The integral-to-distinctive-culture test requires that a practice, custom or tradition be distinctive; it does not require that practice, custom or tradition be distinct.

9) The influence of European culture will only be relevant to the inquiry if it is demonstrated that the practice, custom or tradition is only integral because of that influence.

10) Courts must take into account both the relationship of Aboriginal peoples to the land and the distinctive societies and cultures of Aboriginal peoples.[29]

Van der Peet failed the integral-to-distinctive-culture test, in part, because the Supreme Court characterized her claim as an Aboriginal right to exchange fish for money or for other goods instead of Van der Peet's claim that the Aboriginal right in question was the right to provide for a moderate livelihood: "As such, the appellant's claim cannot be characterized as based on an assertion that the Sto:lo's use of the fishery, and the customs and tradition surrounding that use, had the significance of providing the Sto:lo with a moderate livelihood. It must instead be based on the actual practices, customs and traditions related to the fishery, here the custom of exchanging fish for money or other goods."[30] Van Der Peet failed to demonstrate that the exchange of fish for money or other goods was an Aboriginal right of her Aboriginal community. Consequently, the Court did not elaborate and examine the claim on the basis of the remainder of the test provided for in the Sparrow case.

AN ABORIGINAL RIGHT TO GAMING: R. V. PAMAJEWO — The decision in *R. v. Pamajewon*[31] was delivered a day after the Supreme Court of Canada had given greater clarity to the first portion of the Sparrow test. Consequently, counsel for Pamajewon did not benefit from foreknowledge of the integral-to-distinctive-culture test, which was used to determine whether the claimed Aboriginal right was protected under Section 35(1) of the Canada Constitution Act, 1982. Pamajewon claimed that Section 35(1) included the right of self-government and that this particular right included the right to regulate gambling activities on the reserve. The Supreme Court disagreed with Pamajewon's characterization of the nature of the claim and instead ruled that the correct characterization was the participation in, and regulation of, high-stakes gambling activities on the reserve.

In light of the foregoing, the Supreme Court of Canada found that the evidence did not support Pamajewon's claimed Aboriginal right to conduct and regulate high-stakes gaming on the reserve:

> I now turn to the second branch of the Van der Peet Test, the consideration of whether the participation in, and regulation of, gambling on the reserve lands was an integral part of the distinctive cultures of the Shawanaga or Eagle First Lake Nations. The evidence presented at both the Pamajewon and Gardner trials does not demonstrate that gambling, or the regulation of gambling, was an integral part of the distinctive cultures of the Shawanaga or Eagle First Lake Nations.

In fact, the only evidence presented at either trial dealing with the question of the importance of gambling was that of James Morrison, who testified at the Pamajewon trial with regards to the importance and prevalence of gaming in Ojibwa culture. While Mr. Morrison's evidence does demonstrate that the Ojibwa gambled, it does not demonstrate that gambling was of central significance to the Ojibwa people. Moreover, his evidence in no way addresses the extent to which gambling was the subject of regulation by the Ojibwa community. His account is of informal gambling activities taking place on a small scale; he does not describe large-scale activities, subject to community regulation, of the sort at issue in this appeal.[32]

The Supreme Court of Canada did not rule that the Ojibwa and Eagle Lake First Nations do not have the Aboriginal right to conduct and regulate gaming, but it found that the evidence presented was insufficient to support the existence of such a right. In fact, Pamajewon's claimed Aboriginal right was supported solely by the evidence of a single witness who failed to demonstrate the centrality of gaming to the cultures of the Ojibwa and Eagle Lake First Nations. Consequently, the Supreme Court of Canada did not proceed with the remainder of the Sparrow test, namely, the determination of whether or not the claimed Aboriginal right had been infringed. Nor did it address the issue of justification. Sparrow outlined a general three-part test in order to determine if a claimed right should be deemed to be an Aboriginal right under Section 35(1) of the Canada Constitution Act, 1982. Van der Peet clarified and refined the first part of the test, and introduced the integral-to-distinctive-culture notion.

These decisions therefore lay out the exact steps that the Mohawks of Kahnawá:ke need to take to prove they indeed possess an Aboriginal right to carry out gaming activities, by virtue of Section 35(1) of the Canada Constitution Act, 1982.

APPLICATION TO THE MOHAWKS OF KAHNAWÁ:KE — **First part of the test: characterization of the right claimed.** The Supreme Court of Canada stated that courts must identify precisely the nature of the claim being made in determining whether an Aboriginal claimant has demonstrated the existence of an Aboriginal right.[33] The Aboriginal right claimed in Pamajewon was the right of self-government; however, the Supreme Court of Canada disagreed: "When these factors are considered in this case it can be seen that the correct characterization of the appellants' claim is that they are claiming the right to participate in, and to regulate, high stakes gambling activities on the reservation."[34]

As a consequence, and given the similarities of the Pamajewon case to the present matter, the Aboriginal right claimed by the Mohawks of Kahnawá:ke should in fact be characterized as the right to carry out and regulate high-stakes[35] gaming activities. Any other characterization would be too general to meet the requirements set out by the Supreme Court of Canada.

Elaboration of the first part of the three-part test. The primary or core test put forth in Van der Peet was labelled the integral-to-distinctive-culture test and is as follows: "The following test should be used to identify whether an applicant has established an Aboriginal Right protected by section 35(1): in order to be an Aboriginal Right an activity must be an element of practice, custom or tradition integral to the distinctive culture of the Aboriginal group claiming the right."[36]

Gaming and the regulation of gaming has been, and presently is, an element of practice, custom, or tradition integral to the distinctive culture of the Mohawks of Kahnawá:ke. The foregoing is strongly supported by historical and anthropological evidence as well as by testimonial evidence of Kahnawá:ke elders, who were interviewed at length by the authors hereof. Secondly, it cannot be said that the Mohawks of Kahnawá:ke's Aboriginal right to carry out and regulate gaming activities has been extinguished, given that said activities form an integral part of Mohawk culture to this very day. Nevertheless, can it be said that the enactment of the provisions of the Criminal Code of Canada prohibiting gaming had the effect of extinguishing the claimed Aboriginal right to participate in and regulate high-stakes gambling activities?

The Supreme Court of Canada is unequivocal when it states that only an express intention on the part of the sovereign to extinguish an Aboriginal right can effectively extinguish said right. In the matter at hand, no such explicit intention appears from all of the relevant legislation and, more particularly, from the provisions of the Criminal Code of Canada. Accordingly, the enactment of the Criminal Code in 1892 and, more particularly, its provisions related to gaming did not have the effect of extinguishing Aboriginal rights of First Nations in regard to gaming.

Second part of the test: infringement. In *R. v. Sparrow*, the Supreme Court of Canada placed the burden of proving a prima facie infringement on the group and/or individual claiming the Aboriginal right. To this end, three questions must be satisfied:

1) Is the limitation unreasonable? In light of the fact that the Mohawks of Kahnawá:ke have carried out gaming, and the regulation thereof, since before the arrival of Europeans, and that said activities constitute an integral part of their culture and identity, it would be unreasonable to limit and ban their Aboriginal right to pursue those activities in the present day, to their detriment and to the benefit of the province of Quebec.

2) Does the regulation impose undue hardship? The provisions of the Criminal Code of Canada regarding gaming impose an undue hardship on the Mohawks of Kahnawá:ke by disallowing them the opportunity to gain an economic advantage from their Aboriginal right, all the while permitting the province of Quebec to benefit from this very same activity.

3) Does the regulation deny the holders of the right their preferred means of exercising that right? The Criminal Code of Canada provisions regarding gaming forbid the Mohawks of Kahnawá:ke from engaging in any and all forms of gaming without the consent of the provinces and, consequently, they deny the Mohawks of Kahnawá:ke their preferred means of exercising this right.

Third part of the test: justification. The third part of the test relates to the question of justification. To this end, the courts must determine if the infringing legislation has a valid purpose, if the honour of the Crown is at stake, if the infringing legislation effects as little infringement as possible in order to meet the legislation's objective and if the Aboriginal group in question has been consulted. Since its enactment in 1892, the Criminal Code of Canada has included provisions related to gaming. Said provisions are grouped in a section entitled "Offences against Religion, Morals and Public Convenience." The original purpose of said provisions was to outright forbid gambling activities within the territory of Canada. At the time of the drafting of the Code, the Canadian public considered such activities to be vices. Since then, the Canadian public's acceptance of gambling has reached an almost universal level. In fact, since the outright criminalization of gambling, several Criminal Code amendments have permitted the existence of various forms of gambling, albeit under provincial control. For example, in 1985 the provinces were given exclusive jurisdiction to regulate, manage, and conduct lotteries and lottery schemes, and in 1998 Criminal Code provisions banning dice games were eliminated. Since then, the provinces have, arguably, used their jurisdiction to brazenly expand all forms of legal gambling for the sole purpose of increasing their revenue and creating a provincial monopoly:

> Given the wide licence that Government has granted itself, is there still any reason for a residual criminalisation of gambling? If there is, it can no longer be based on a claim that gambling is harmful since the harm is quite clearly not great enough for Provincial Governments to refrain from having become the main operators of this service.
>
> In fact, the creation of a state monopoly has led to such overwhelming expansion of gambling that it is possible to speak of expansionist monopoly. Driven by its unrestrained adoption of a private logic of maximum profit, public Government has applied the substantial resources at its disposal to promote gambling.[37]

The foregoing unequivocally brings into question the criminal nature of the gaming provisions found in the Criminal Code of Canada. According to the justification analysis, the first step would be to determine whether there is a valid legislative purpose. Arguably, criminalization of an activity for the purpose of creating a provincial monopoly, which is used solely for economic gain and which monopoly has been exploited to expand gaming without regard to its ill effects, does not constitute a valid legislative purpose.

Consequently, in granting the province of Quebec an exclusive monopoly over gaming, to the detriment of the Mohawks of Kahnawá:ke, the honour and integrity of the federal government has been breached. In fact, it is arguable that the federal government has failed in its fiduciary duty owed to its First Nations by not having created a mechanism allowing for its First Nations to exercise their sovereign claims to conduct gaming.

In any event, the provisions in the Criminal Code of Canada regarding gaming cannot be said to meet the minimal infringement test in view of the fact that said provisions do not limit gaming and the regulation thereof but, rather, outright forbid the Mohawks of Kahnawá:ke to carry out and regulate any gaming whatsoever, irrespective of their claimed Aboriginal rights. Lastly, the Mohawks of Kahnawá:ke have never been fairly compensated, nor were they ever consulted concerning said provisions and their amendments.

CONCLUSION

The preceding analysis has demonstrated that the Mohawks of Kahnawá:ke satisfy the various legal tests set forth by the Supreme Court of Canada, and are therefore able to rightfully claim an Aboriginal right to conduct and regulate gaming. As demonstrated, gaming has historically played a central and integral role in the cultural, religious, and social practices of the Mohawks of Kahnawá:ke. Indeed, gaming served a variety of integral functions in Mohawk life since well before contact with European peoples, and the long tradition of Mohawk gaming continues to the present day. It is by virtue of this culture and history of gaming that the Mohawks of Kahnawá:ke are able to satisfy the legal tests set forth by the Supreme Court of Canada and are, accordingly, able to claim an Aboriginal right, under Section 35(1) of the Canada Constitution Act, 1982, to conduct and regulate gaming, including the online gaming activity that they are presently pursuing.

NOTES

* Reprinted with permission from *Gaming Law Review* 10, 4 (2006): 369–378. © Mary Ann Liebert, Inc. This article is based in a legal opinion prepared by the Law Offices of Lazarus Charbonneau pursuant to a mandate granted by the Mohawk Council of Kahnawa:ke. The information contained herein cannot be construed as legal, or any form of, advice or counsel.

1 Criminal Code of Canada, sections 201 et. seq.

2 See, e.g., Criminal Code of Canada, section 207(1)(b), which provides for the issuance of provincial licences for the carrying out of limited gaming events for charitable causes.

3 R.J. Bell, *How Much Betting is Really Going On?* http://sportsgambling.about.com/od/legalfacts/a/Betting_Facts.htm (last accessed 15 June 2006).

4 David Silverberg, "Online Poker: Going All-in to Expose the Internet's Billion-Dollar Bet," http://www.digitaljournal.com/print.htm?id=4388 (last accessed 5 May 2006, site no longer active)

5 W. DeBoer, "Of Dice and Women: Gambling and Exchange in Native North America," *Journal of Archaeological Method and Theory* 8 (2001): 215, 217.

6 Ibid., 223–226.

7 The Mohawks form part of the Iroquois Confederacy along with the Cayuga, Oneida, Onondaga, and Seneca nations. Testimony of Kahnawá:ke elders, Mr. Andrew Delisle, and Mr. Billy Two Rivers at Kahnawá:ke, in conversation with the authors, 6 Sept. 2005 Kahnawá:ke.

8 Mr. Billy Two Rivers, in conversation with the authors, Kahnawá:ke, 30 Nov. 2005.

9 Ibid.

10 Stewart Culin, *Games of the North American Indians* (New York: Dover Publications, 1975 [1907]), 105.

11 Ibid., 474

12 See LaxHistory.com, "The On-Line Collection of Lacrosse History," http://www.laxhistory.com (last visited 19 June 2006).

13 Thomas Vennum, "Native American History of Lacrosse," http://Lacrosse/org/museum/history.htm, 3.

14 Karen Lynn Smith, "The Role of Games, Sport, and Dance in Iroquois Life" (master's thesis, University of Oregon, 1975).

15 Lewis Henry Morgan, *League of the Iroquois, Book II: Spirit of the League* (New York: Corinth Books, 1962 [1851]), 293.

16 Smith, "The Role of Games," 103.

17 Morgan, *League of the Iroquois*, Book II, 293.

18 Smith, "The Role of Games," 103.

19 Ibid., 22.

20 *R. v. Sparrow*, [1990] 1 S.C.R. 1097.

21 Ibid., 1099.

22 *R. v. Van der Peet*, [1996] 2 S.C.R. 50.

23 *Sparrow*, 1112.

24 Ibid., 1113–14.

25 Ibid., 1119

26 Van der Peet, 507

27 Ibid., para. 43.

28 Ibid., para. 46.

29 Ibid., para. 49–79.

30 Ibid., para. 79.

31 *R. v. Pamajewon*, [1996] 2 S.C.R. 821.

32 Ibid.para. 28.

33 *Van der Peet*, 51.

34 *Pamajewon*, 26.

35 *The Criminal Code of Canada*, section 207(1) defines "high stakes" wagering as referring to a lottery scheme for which the value of each prize awarded exceeds the sum of $500 and for which the valuable consideration paid to secure a chance to win said prize exceeds an amount of $2.

36 *Van der Peet*, 46.

37 Jean-Paul Brodeur and Genevieve Ouellet, "What is a Crime? A Secular Answer," in *What is a Crime? Defining Criminal Conduct in Contemporary Society*, ed. Law Commission of Canada (Vancouver: University of British Columbia Press, 2004), 27.

CHAPTER 3

VIRTUAL SOVEREIGNTY: EXPLORING CANADIAN FIRST NATIONS INTERNET GAMING VENTURES

YALE D. BELANGER AND ROBERT J. WILLIAMS

INTRODUCTION

Canadian federal law has been interpreted by provincial governments as allowing them to legally operate an Internet gambling website as long as the patronage is restricted to residents within that province.[1] Provincially owned gambling operators in the Atlantic Provinces (Atlantic Lottery Corporation, or ALC) and British Columbia (British Columbia Lottery Corporation, or BCLC) provide online sports betting, online "interactive" lotteries, and the online sale of land-based lottery tickets to residents of their respective provinces.[2] Horseracing in Canada is regulated by the Canadian Pari-Mutuel Agency under the federal Department of Agriculture. The federal agriculture minister made a rule change in 2003 permitting horseracing bets to be placed, not just by telephone, but also by "any telecommunication device." As a consequence, Woodbine Entertainment, a Toronto-based horseracing track operator, began accepting online bets from across Canada in January 2004. The legality of Canadians placing non-horseracing bets with online sites outside of their province is unclear. Thus far, no Canadian resident has been prosecuted for such activity.

First Nations have, however, challenged the provinces of Quebec and Alberta for jurisdictional primacy over the right to regulate online gambling: the Kahnawá:ke First Nation in Quebec and the Alexander First Nation in Alberta both contend that they are sovereign nations empowered to enact their own gambling legislation, following an authority grounded in their respective treaty relationship with the Federal Crown and its predecessors. In the wake of the ongoing debate between the Kahnawá:ke First Nation and Quebec, and the brief encounter between Alberta and the Alexander First Nation (in 2006–07), this chapter seeks to elaborate on two key questions: first, to what extent do treaties establish First Nations as sovereign bodies? and second, do the treaties provide the Kahnawá:ke and Alexander First Nations' peoples the right to operate online gambling?

THE INTERNET AND POLITICAL SOVEREIGNTY

In recent years, several global nations have challenged the spread of online gambling through legislation, a move that is not surprising considering that any external challenge to territorial sovereignty and, ultimately, domestic jurisdiction over local economic initiatives compels a response. Remarkably, such intrusion is seldom framed as a sovereignty issue. Instead it is routinely described as an electronic breach of territorial borders easily remedied through policy, or legislative intervention. No matter how harmless the contravention of borders may appear, the Westphalian principles of political sovereignty suggest that the inability to ensure territorial autonomy is characteristic of the deterioration of the state. State sovereignty in this sense is a rigid, static model based upon an international framework that stresses the centrality of the independent, authoritative state that is likewise considered immune from the intrusions of outside powers.

What is often overlooked is the reality that "the social construction of sovereignty is always in process, and is a never completed project whose successful production never can be counted on totally."[3] Several critics who surfaced during the Internet-fuelled communications revolution of the 1990s thought it essential to embrace sovereignty's adaptive nature and to alter our understanding of sovereignty to rely less on traditional physical boundaries, focussing instead on the state's ability to apply customary regulatory models to electronic commerce.[4] Their claims that sovereignty was being damaged by an electronic medium lacking a centralized controlling body were offset by opponents' claims that fears about the Internet's anticipated challenges to sovereignty were unfounded.[5] As Kevin Bruyneel has written, however, "the politics of sovereignty is the means by which a perpetual effort is made to construct a resolution to this paradoxical relationship between certainty and contingency."[6] This is reflected in sovereignty's extension beyond previously subjective territorial boundaries. The jurisdictional bases have, as a result, expanded to consider actions that, while not taking place within a state's territory, have intended or actual impacts.[7] The United Kingdom's creation of the "White List" is a case in point. The list was developed in accordance with the principle that governance demands autonomous states respond to any and all challenges to their sovereignty.[8]

Recent scholarship suggests that new, borderless, Internet-based economies could facilitate the global economy's development through modern political-regional formations, albeit at the expense of the sovereignty of the nation-state.[9] Others assure us that the nation state will survive, thus dispelling fears about outside challenges to self-rule. From this dynamic dialogue few options have emerged concerning how to address non-state actor participation.[10] In the meantime, state leaders struggle to maintain localized control over domestic development while simultaneously participating in a virtual mega-economy that appears to function without international directive or a centralized control mechanism.[11] Public policy makers and legislators are similarly fettered: unable to publicly confront related issues for fear of compromising internal economic and political confidence, they must create a structured response to online gambling's steady incursion. Otherwise, the risk of being portrayed as reactive rather than proactive is amplified.

Recent events in Canada capture the issues confronting various jurisdictions internationally. Prior to 2001, foreign online casino operators seeking to expand their client base considered Canada an open jurisdiction due to its poor legal and policy regime related to virtual gambling. Commenting in 2000, Bear Stearns, at the time one of the largest global investment banks and securities-trading and brokerage firms, criticized Canada's faulty legal scaffold: "Because Canadian law regarding on-line gambling is as unclear as US law, groups are beginning to test authorities by setting up on both sides of the US-Canada border." The company's report examining Internet gaming identified three specific problems. First, any Canadian could potentially access gaming action over the Internet, even those sites operating outside Canada. Second, enforcement of the Criminal Code of Canada to censure out-of-country online gaming operations would be exceptionally difficult. Finally, upon verification of a clear connection between domestic participation in online gambling and the Internet casino operators, how the Criminal Code would specifically apply was far from clear.[12]

Non-state actors exploited these ambiguities, which authorize provinces to conduct "lottery schemes" on or through an electronic device. Though it is far from clear that sports betting is a lottery scheme, several provinces initiated online sports betting in 2004 (in addition to "interactive lotteries" and traditional lotteries). The legality of Canadians placing bets with online sites remains unclear. Currently before Parliament is a bill (C-13) that would change the language of the Criminal Code to make it clearer that "any means of telecommunication" for the purposes of gambling is an offence (currently the Criminal Code prohibits the use of "radio, telegraph, telephone, mail or express"). In the same vein, this new language is intended to make clear that any means of telecommunication is *legally* permissible for placing horseracing bets. The Senate Committee has stated that it was satisfied that this new language would not have "extra-territorial application."

Canadian officials have endeavoured to secure authority over foreign, virtual companies operating domestically. The catalyst driving this attempt was a Delaware-based Internet software development company operating in Canada. Starnet Communications International, Inc. (SCI) and its various subsidiaries were incorporated in Antigua, where online gaming was legal and where SCI had an online gaming licence. One subsidiary located in Vancouver, British Columbia, was responsible for website administration. Employing nearly 100 people, the Vancouver subsidiary developed the server and client software packages, which permitted customer access to gaming. Suspicions that SCI was accepting online wagers led to a sting operation, during which time British Columbia's police gambled nearly $5,000 on the company's site. Charges were laid in 1999, and in 2001 the BC Supreme Court declared that Canadian-based Internet gambling sites could not legally accept bets from Canadian citizens.[13] A deal was ultimately struck. SCI pleaded guilty to one criminal gambling count under Section 202(1)(b) of the Criminal Code of Canada, was fined $100,000, and forfeited roughly (US) $4 million as proceeds of crime pursuant to Section 462.37 of the Code. Speculation to this point suggested that, prior to establishing sufficient connection to a betting operation and Canadian jurisdiction, applying the Criminal Code would have been difficult.[14] The *Starnet* decision provided clarification: an individual or company interested in offering online gaming in Canada must minimize or eliminate all connections to Canada. Should this prove impracticable, banning Canadian access to the site appears a logical next move.

The unequivocal conclusion reads as follows: Canada will not tolerate external challenges to domestic regulatory authority over online casinos. Aside from the above-mentioned *Starnet* decision, it remains unclear if external forms of Internet gambling fit within existing laws. The law is vague regarding specific provincial and federal responsibilities about online gambling. On the one hand, the law intimates that the federal government can outlaw the establishment of an online gambling site. On the other hand, provinces are authorized to conduct lottery schemes on or through an electronic device. Provincial officials interpret this as assigning them legal authority to operate Internet gambling websites so long as patrons are restricted to provincial residents.[15] This overlap of powers, while not unique, is at odds with the division of exclusive authority of Parliament (Section 91) and the provincial legislatures (Section 92) over matters within their jurisdiction. Ideally "a single matter will come within a class of subjects in only one list."[16] What remains is a latent jurisdictional conflict about who precisely is responsible for Internet gambling and where First Nations' interests lie.

THE NATURE OF FIRST NATIONS SOVEREIGNTY CLAIMS

First Nations leaders contend that reserve gaming operations are shielded from provincial laws by virtue of Section 91(24) of the British North America Act of 1867, which recognizes Canada's sole responsibility for "Indians, and Lands reserved for the Indians." According to this interpretation, state-sanctioned gaming on a reserve is acceptable, but to operate outside legislative strictures is to defy provincial jurisdiction and risk Criminal Code of Canada charges. First Nations respond by citing political and territorial sovereignty over each respective community's land base, which includes the right to determine localized economic development activities. First Nations leaders accordingly consider their communities to be imbued with a self-governing capacity to control reserve gambling activities, both physical and virtual. This self-governing ability is considered an inherent right that saves First Nations from having to accept the popular, delegated Aboriginal self-government model intended to operate within the confines of the Canadian Constitution. As one scholar has argued, indigenous sovereignty, in this instance, is a by-product of Crown–First Nations treaties that acknowledge the First Nations' inherent right to govern according to localized systems of law and rights. Furthermore, it ensures the right for communities to autonomously determine political and economic relationships.[17]

Much has been written in recent years of sovereignty's "fit" with First Nations politics. The concept of sovereignty is linked with exclusive territorial jurisdiction that is understood according to three dimensions: the holder of sovereignty, the absoluteness of sovereignty, and the internal and external dimensions of sovereignty. All sovereign states "should possess jurisdiction over all persons and things within its territorial limits and in all causes civil and criminal arising within these limits."[18] Complicating this definition are political scientist Taiaiake Alfred's writings, which argue that First Nations leaders too often privilege the concept of state sovereignty to the detriment of historic indigenous political models. This false choice offers one avenue—continued colonial imposition rather than true self-determination.[19] Implicit in his argument is the assertion that an alternate form of, or culturally specific notion of, indigenous sovereignty exists in opposition to contemporary political responses stressing state sovereignty's centrality and soundness.

Dale Turner expands upon this debate by considering the role non-indigenous forms of sovereignty played in the dispossession and marginalization of indigenous peoples. Turner maintains that the European tradition from which the sovereignty concept emerged has "created discourses on property, ethics, political sovereignty, and justice that have subjugated, distorted, and marginalized Aboriginal ways of thinking."[20] Elaborating on this point, Thomas Biolsi details how the nation state "structures both political realities and subversive political imaginaries," resulting in sovereignty being accordingly zoned "so as to benefit some citizens systematically and, just as systematically, to disempower or otherwise harm other citizens."[21] Turner admits, however, that our contemporary understanding of sovereignty crudely captures "the unique relationship that Aboriginal peoples have to their territories." Along with Russel Barsh and Sakej Henderson, for instance, Turner identifies the need to formally articulate how this relationship to the land can gain Canadian political and legal expression where, previously, sovereignty meant territorial dispossession and the imposition of colonial social modes and beliefs.[22]

Indigenous sovereignty is closely aligned with the recovery of control over "Indigenous identity and the reproduction of Indigenous cultures."[23] Respecting that the word *sovereignty* is perhaps imprecise when discussing pre-contact ideas related to territoriality and political agency, the preservation of cultural autonomy remains a vital pursuit for First Nations. So too is maintaining political and economic sovereignty while safeguarding territorial integrity to ensure cultural reproduction. The latter is made possible through economic stability, which is difficult to ensure, considering the damage wrought by years of socio-economic malfunction. The resulting higher-than-normal rates of social pathologies and income imbalances continue to undermine First Nations' cultural and political strength.[24] Modern economic outcomes promoted by the state through Canadian policy imposition interfere with First Nations' access to resources, which in turn destabilizes political and economic expression.[25]

This outcome was precisely what indigenous leaders hoped to avoid by signing treaties with the various European powers occupying North America. These agreements established military and political alliances and inter-nation rules regulating trade and regional resource-utilization schemes.[26] An emergent treaty order enabled the institution of principles needed to regulate indigenous and non-indigenous political and economic interface.[27] Initially, the treaty order precluded Europeans seeking access to natural resources and overland travel routes from unilaterally or arbitrarily imposing their political vision upon North American indigenous populations.[28] European leaders and their agents signed more than seventy indigenous-European treaties between 1701 and 1923. These treaties represent a tacit acceptance of indigenous sovereign political status, based on international norms that honoured the binding and inviolable nature of treaties.[29] By the 1920s, however, Canada and the European states embraced new political ideologies stressing international cooperation and global economic growth, which, when interpreted specifically, allowed them to set aside indigenous concerns. Treaties were then used to extinguish Aboriginal land titles, thereby permitting federal officials to carve out an economic stronghold based on territorial gains.

Taking root within this milieu was a hegemonic global political system of nations represented by states that were free from external political coercion. This led to the reaffirmation of the Westphalian principle of non-interference in the internal affairs of states as international leaders seized control and crafted new categorizations of nationhood, statehood, and sovereignty that strategically silenced critics concerned about the treatment of indigenous populations. These new hierarchies did not recognize First Nations in Canada as bona fide and legitimate political actors, and it should not be surprising that indigenous leaders' attempts to define First Nations as sovereign actors were considered preposterous. Indigenous land claims were being denied by the same political actors seeking to bolster their own territorial claims to promote economic reform through the extant system of recognized states and sovereignty.[30] Accordingly, the citation of international political membership in the form of historic treaties and political covenants was no longer sufficient to guarantee recognition of First Nations' political sovereignty within Canada. The resultant devaluation of their political status as partners in Confederation is something First Nations leaders refuse to accept. Canadian officials are consistently reminded that treaties are considered binding nation-to-nation agreements not open to unilateral modification.

Treaty interpretation remains a contentious issue, despite the presence of generally accepted principles to guide our interpretation. Treaties are considered "formal agreements between two or more fully sovereign and recognized states operating in an international forum, negotiated by officially designated commissioners and ratified by the governments of the signatory powers."[31] Section 35 of the Constitution Act, 1982 recognizes and affirms treaty rights. The Supreme Court of Canada concluded that treaties are not contracts or pacts bound by international law but rather *sui generis* accords demanding: (1) a fair and liberal interpretation[32] that is (2) not confined strictly to British/Canadian legal frameworks.[33] Canada all the same adheres to the principle that treaties are akin to land cessions that were negotiated in return for upfront payments and perpetual annuities, and additional government assistance in the form of schools to ease First Nations' transition into Canadian society.[34] First Nations, however, cling to the belief that the treaties created working relationships with Crown officials and ultimately their agreement to *share* the land with the settlers.[35]

TREATY-ACKNOWLEDGED SOVEREIGNTY AND ECONOMIC DEVELOPMENT

In 1999 the Kahnawá:ke First Nation publicly asserted its sovereign right to host online reserve gambling. A similar claim followed a few years later from the Alexander First Nation. In each case, the respective First Nations maintained they were a nation trapped within a nation. Community representatives also alleged to have never relinquished their sovereign authority to determine independently and outside of external coercion what economic development projects to pursue. Furthermore, each community's leaders confirmed that their sovereignty claims were derived from historic treaties signed with the British Crown: Kahnawá:ke's leaders cited treaties dating back to the mid-seventeenth century, whereas Alexander First Nation is a member of Treaty 6 (1876). Following the Kahnawá:ke First Nation's lead, Alexander First Nation's leaders decided it would operate an Internet service provider that welcomed online gambling enterprises as clients.

Here lies the root of the contemporary debate regarding treaties: are they, as Canadian officials contend, simple land sales that have enabled the extension of Canadian sovereignty, and as such federal and provincial laws, into First Nations lands? Or, do they more appropriately recognize First Nations' nationhood status, which suggests that localized laws and governance objectives trump outside concerns? This conceptual (and arguably legal) grey area is the basis of the decade-long dispute being waged between the Kahnawá:ke First Nation and the province of Quebec over the right to control online gaming. This debate for a brief time also occupied the province of Alberta and the Alexander First Nation, located west of Edmonton. In each case, the respective First

Nation proclaimed its reserve a sovereign nation and accordingly immune from provincial and federal legislation outlawing non-government regulation of online gambling. The claimed existing treaty right to territorial sovereignty was interpreted to allow each community the authority to host online casinos through a computer server network located on reserve. The following sections will provide a detailed examination of the significant issues.

KAHNAWÁ:KE — Established in 1996, the Kahnawá:ke Gaming Commission (KGC) has been a major host of online gambling sites since 1999. Currently it is the second-largest worldwide provider of Internet gambling sites. This position is a result of the KGC's established presence as an Internet gambling provider, its very low fees (annual fee of $10,000 with no corporate or gambling taxes), its possession of one of the best hosting and bandwidth capacities, and its status as the only provider physically located within the lucrative North American market.

An additional attraction of the Kahnawá:ke operation has been the belief that it is a "safe haven" for online gambling. When the Unlawful Internet Gambling Enforcement Act (UIGEA) was passed in October 2006, many Caribbean- and Central American-based sites moved their operations to the Kahnawá:ke Territory, in the belief that the United States would be less likely to prosecute individuals from this jurisdiction. Kahnawá:ke is deemed an illegal operation by the Quebec government, and both the provincial and federal governments as well as the Sûreté du Québec (provincial police) have separately initiated several investigations. No prosecution resulted until very recently. In September 2007, Cyber World Group, which administers online casinos located on the Kahnawá:ke reserve, pleaded guilty in Quebec to charges of illegal gambling and was ordered to pay a fine of $2 million.[36] As a result of this ruling, several online operators have moved their operations to other jurisdictions in the past year. (Kahnawá:ke was the world's largest host of online gambling sites in July 2007, with 377 sites, compared to 279 currently.)

In January 2008, Kahnawá:ke Grand Chief Michael Delisle Jr. expressed his disappointment that the United Kingdom's Department of Culture, Media, and Sport rejected the application of Mohawk Internet Technologies (MIT) to advertise its online gambling websites. Instead, MIT ended up on the highly publicized "White List." Delisle indicated that his frustration stemmed from what he portrayed to be a deteriorating political and economic relationship between the Kahnawá:ke nation and the UK that dated to the seventeenth century. As he brusquely stated, "We are keenly disappointed in the UK's decision, which ignored the long-standing alliance between our nations." He also referred to the problematic decision by "our old friends" concerning the failure to acknowledge indigenous peoples' economic development rights.[37] The "old friends," in this case, was a reference to the British Crown; the long-standing alliance was a political relationship dating back to 1664, when the King of England accepted responsibility in the Silver Covenant Chain diplomatic network that "joined the Iroquois and English worlds and organized their discourse, but did not merge them, instead leaving each of them discreet."[38] The King of England was thus integrated into the Haudenosaunee kinship network that likewise emphasized each group's autonomy.[39]

One of several key treaties forged with international allies, the Silver Covenant Chain was based on egalitarian principles embodied by the two-row wampum, or *Gus Wen Tah*, which forms the basis of Kahnawá:ke's sovereignty claims. Emphasizing indigenous political sovereignty and economic agency, the *Gus Wen Tah* personified the principles of sharing, mutual recognition, respect, and partnership signifying indigenous peoples and Europeans to be autonomous nations vested with their own political authority and jurisdiction.[40] These principles informed the multiple political and economic councils that the Mohawks participated in during the first century of contact with the Dutch, French, and British. It is apparent that treaties represent to the Kahnawá:ke First Nation an acknowledgement of nation-to-nation relations, as codified in a 1758 pact with Great Britain that captured the Six Nations' sovereignty claims: "the petition conveys the central concepts underlying the confederacy's understanding of its historical relationship with the Crown," including the Covenant Chain, according to which the "theme of alienation through submission to foreign laws—anathema to the confederacy—is developed."[41] Like concepts are evident in the Oswegatchie Treaty of 1760, whereby in return for Kahnawá:ke's support the British Crown promised not to "deprive any of you of your Lands or Property" while further ensuring the right to continued economic development (i.e., hunting territories).[42] Kahnawá:ke historiography (including oral histories) suggests that Mohawk nationhood status is acknowledged in both the Royal Proclamation of 1763's recognition of indigenous land ownership and the inclusion of land cession procedures structured to facilitate treaty relationships with Indians.[43] To summarize, community leaders "did and continued to promote to colonial officials that their treaties with the British Crown were nation-to-nation pacts" while regularly renewing relationships so that they "remain relevant while strengthening the corresponding political bonds."[44]

Kahnawá:ke's leaders remain concerned with ensuring territorial integrity, as is evidenced by a key dimension of their sovereignty treatise, which is aimed at securing the right to pursue select economic development projects in their territory. In this instance, political and economic sovereignty are considered mutually inclusive concepts. Speaking in 2004, then–Kahnawá:ke Grand Chief and MIT company chairman Joseph Norton stated, "We have an aboriginal right to an economy and it doesn't have to be hunting, trapping, and gathering. We can't do that for a living any more where we live. We don't have any more natural resources." He added that "mainstream economic development" is the avenue to self-sufficiency.[45] Here one in a continuity of treaties with the British Crown ensuring the protection of indigenous economies, the Treaty of Nanfan of 1701 (also known as the Albany Deed), demands consideration. At the heart of the current Caledonia dispute involving the province of Ontario, the Six Nations of Grand River, and non-Native residents living near a disputed construction site located within the Nanfan Treaty boundaries, this treaty has been interpreted by First Nations as a British guarantee of protection against settler encroachment into native lands.[46] Kahnawá:ke's leaders subscribe to the belief that the Nanfan Treaty guaranteed the Iroquois "continued and unimpeded access to their vital hunting grounds."[47] A Kahnawá:ke delegate related to the primary author in October 2008 that the Nanfan Treaty is considered a Crown promise to ensure that the Kahnawá:ke people have the continued ability to engage in economic development activities necessary to ensure community success. It is not specifically about asserting a claim to the land, however. The treaty in this instance is considered proof of continued Crown protection of economic security. The Ontario Court of Justice (General Division) in *Ireland* concluded that the Iroquois right to hunt was protected. No mention was made of economic development, nor did the decision allude to an expansive interpretation of the hunting provisions.[48]

As Levi General Deskaheh, deputy spokesperson of the Six Nations of Grand River Territory's Hereditary Council, proclaimed in a 1920 letter to King George V concerning Iroquoian political beliefs, "We do not wish to be destroyed as a separate people. We have surely done nothing to forfeit our natural right, nor our right under the Royal pledge to continued protection at the hands of the Crown against the aggression by outsiders, making no exception of any Canadian officials who may be the aggressors."[49] The nation-to-nation relationship embodied in the treaties acknowledging Kahnawá:ke territorial protection guided Delisle's contention in 2005 that "We have always asserted that we are a sovereign people, this is our jurisdiction, this is our territory."[50] The risk, in this case, is Canada's threat to Kahnawá:ke's territorial sovereignty and governing authority. In the spirit of nationhood, Kahnawá:ke's leaders also respond to outside threats. In 2008, for example, the Kahnawá:ke First Nation petitioned the Commonwealth of Kentucky to protest its attempted seizure of 141 international online gambling sites. As Delisle explained, "It's not the first time that a government has tried to prevent us from conducting business and it won't be the last. But, rest assured, we will always protect our jurisdiction and the integrity of the Kahnawá:ke Gaming Commission."[51]

Crown officials in Canada have responded by concluding that the Kahnawá:ke people were not international political actors but rather allies requiring protection. Kahnawá:ke leaders counter these claims and cite a continuity of treaties dating back to the seventeenth century as surety of their sovereignty. At times they have physically fended off federal attempts at territorial alienation before determining in 1990 that it was time to challenge "the Canadian government's assertion of jurisdiction [which in turn] assumes the proportion of a people struggling for their very existence."[52] This resistance flared into the Oka Standoff, a seventy-nine-day, $500-million clash that occurred after Kahnawá:ke First Nation members asserted territorial sovereignty in an attempt to reject the expansion of a nine-hole golf course from Oka Township into a community burial ground shaded by sacred pine trees.[53] Even in the wake of resistance, Canadian officials claim that no outstanding treaty promises to economic development exist and that the Kahnawá:ke First Nation is at present in contravention of federal statute restricting the operation of casinos or housing online casinos without provincial or federal approval.

ALEXANDER FIRST NATION — Like Kahnawá:ke, the Alexander First Nation closely examined the value of offering network server capacity to online casino operators, and in March 2006 established the Alexander Gaming Commission (AGC) pursuant to the provisions of the Alexander First Nation Band Council resolution. Alexander Internet Technologies (AIT), located twenty minutes from downtown Edmonton, was also established. According to an AGC spokesperson, "We are pleased to be able to offer on-line gaming licences to qualified applicants, and are confident that the regulations will ensure a safe, high quality environment for on-line gamers." The spokesperson added that the AGC's goal was to "provide leadership in evolving and enforcing comprehensive, socially responsible internet gaming regulations."[54] Adopting the mantle of self-government, Alexander First Nation empowered the AGC to regulate and control gaming and gaming-related activities undertaken within the community. Announcing that it was accepting applications at a fee of $20,000 each, the community appeared prepared to compete with the Kahnawá:ke First Nation and MIT for a share of the lucrative online gambling business.[55]

With the exception of small mineral revenues and limited service-sector employment, the Alexander First Nation had few economic prospects. Leaders sought additional economic ventures that would provide long-term and well-paying jobs. During the late 1990s, federal and provincial officials began promoting the Internet as an effective means of improving Aboriginal economic development. Many First Nations accessed available programs and funding opportunities to launch Internet communications' technology-focussed business ventures.[56] At this point, the Alexander data centre was proposed. AIT managers anticipated similar trends to those of Kahnawá:ke, where non-gambling businesses make up a proportion of overall sites hosted. Plans were initiated in 2006 for the construction of a 25,000-square-foot data centre that would permit online gambling sites. Provincial officials immediately informed the provincial media that the Alexander First Nation was operating in contravention of the Criminal Code of Canada. Chief Arcand attempted to assuage provincial officials with his promises that Alexander would establish a strict regulatory environment to ensure operational transparency leading to patron confidence and customer satisfaction.

Not sufficiently satisfied to outright accept the extension of provincial regulatory authority into First Nation community, and anticipating further challenges to community territorial sovereignty and governing authority, Chief Arcand stated that the Alexander First Nation:

> ♦ chief and council have consistently and historically exercised ultimate and exclusive jurisdiction over the territory of the Alexander First Nation;
>
> ♦ has existing, inherent, and inalienable rights that include the right of self-determination, the right to control economic development within the Alexander First Nation territory, and the right to promote and preserve peace, order, and good government within its territory;
>
> ♦ entered into a treaty with Canada in 1876, and has had ongoing governmental relationships with Canada since then. This predates Alberta's 1905 entry into Confederation by 29 years;

♦ has the ultimate and exclusive right and jurisdiction to regulate gaming and gaming-related activities within the band's territory due to the significant impact of gaming and gaming-related activities on economic development and peace, order, and good government within its territory;

♦ has a deep and long-running history of initiating, participating in, and regulating gaming activities, which are integral to the culture of the community;

♦ has rights as a sovereign nation that are protected under Section 35 of the Canadian Charter of Rights and Freedoms. As such, the province of Alberta does not have any jurisdictional authority to govern the Alexander First Nation.

As the governing body in and for its territory, the Alexander First Nation chief and council, according to Chief Arcand, "has the power and authority to enact the Alexander First Nation Gaming Law pursuant to which it created the Alexander Gaming Commission, setting guidelines for operation of online Gaming Commission."[57]

Provincial officials responded by informing the AGC that its operations would be deemed an illegal venture, and minister of justice Ron Stevens explained, "the Criminal Code that determines legality relative to this matter has nothing to do with the rulings of the Attorney General in this province or anywhere else. I can tell you that our opinion is and has been for a considerable period of time that First Nation Internet gaming, wherever it might take place in Canada, would be contrary to the Criminal Code."[58] Next, Solicitor General Fred Lindsay sent the AGC a letter demanding First Nations officials "immediately cease and desist any and all activities relating in any way to the issuing of gaming licences or the regulation of Internet gaming."[59] Finally, the Alberta Gaming and Liquor Commission (AGLC) also announced that, if its Internet gambling was deemed illegal, it would take immediate and appropriate action against the Alexander First Nation.

Framing the province's response as an attack on his community's sovereignty and economic independence, Chief Arcand declared, "The government of Alberta desires to ignore … our right to regulate online gaming transacted within our territory, along with all of the positives of our developing economic independence."[60] He further suggested that his community's actions were part of a larger plan to institute a useful economic foundation, which to his mind was an existing treaty right. The Alexander First Nation, according to Arcand, was, as a sovereign nation, responsible for regulating its own territory by virtue of being a party to Treaty 6, signed with the British Crown in 1876, even if members of what would later come to be acknowledged as the Alexander First Nation were not at these negotiations. Instead, they adhered to Treaty 6 on 9 August 1877, which meant they were denied the chance to influence the negotiations' outcome or inform the treaty's final provisions. Instead, by adhering, Alexander's leaders accepted previously formulated provisions.

Several facets of Treaty 6 arguably support Chief Arcand's assertion to territorial sovereignty and the right to pursue internally determined economic development initiatives. One scholar has argued, "[that] the treaty provided for some kind of sharing of the land rather than the outright surrender described in the treaty text is a view which runs through all of the testimony of the Alberta Treaty 6 elders. They held that the Indians only gave up limited rights in the land, namely the surface rights."[61] Another has similarly concluded that First Nations treaties with the British Crown imply colonial acknowledgement of the inherent sovereignty of the tribes, their system of law and rights, and ultimately their right to choose their destiny and relationships, and their way of life.[62] The set of negotiations held in 1876 at Forts Pitt and Carlton was complex, as the minutes for each meeting attest. In each instance, however, Native leaders sought identical concessions from the Crown—specifically, that the treaties guarantee certain rights that were to be enjoyed in perpetuity, including: the retention of their internal sovereignty over their people, lands, and resources both on and off reserve, subject to some shared jurisdiction over the lands known as "unoccupied Crown lands"; Crown promises to provide for First Nations economic development in exchange for the right to use the lands covered by treaty; and promises of revenue sharing between the Crown and First Nations.[63]

The First Nations' desire to remain self-governing and free to pursue economic development strategies was a negotiating point Treaty 6 commissioners responded to by assuring those on hand that they would not be expected to abandon their "present mode of living" and by promising to never "interfere with your hunting and fishing … through the country as you have heretofore done."[64] Governance and economics were also considered interdependent processes, and with this in mind treaty commissioner Alexander Morris assured the chiefs, "What I have offered does not take away your living, you will have it then [following the treaty] as you have it now, and what I offer now is put on top of it."[65] Morris further promised Cree negotiators the enriched life they demanded while further indicating that the Queen "wished to help you in the days that are to come, we do not want to take away the means of living that you have now, we do not want to tie you down; we want you to have homes of your own where your children can be taught to raise for themselves food from the mother earth."[66]

Finally, Morris agreed that future adhesions were possible upon negotiation of a finalized treaty. This suggests that Cree leaders did not consider the treaty a completed document so much as an agreement in principle open to negotiated alteration as changes to regional economic and political circumstances dictated. From the Crown's perspective, however, treaties were considered the most effective means of extinguishing Aboriginal title, thus promoting westward expansion and extending Canadian sovereignty to the prairie region.[67] When First Nations were informed that they would receive protected reserves in exchange for ceding vast tracts of lands, their leaders believed this move would enable their communities to remain economically independent by retaining traditional pursuits, thereby easing the transition into the dominant non-Native society.[68]

Both the British Crown and the Canadian government failed to live up to the promises made during treaty negotiations, specifically Morris's pledges to "not take away your living" and that "you will have it then as you have it now." During the next century, federal Indian policies disrupted Native economies by promoting subsistence economies that led to an inferior standard of living further aggravated by policies promoting Native removal from reserves into the growing cities. Writing in 1973 about the generally poor state of Aboriginal development nationally, David Courchene singled out the Canadian Indian Affairs bureaucracy, specifically "the practices of public policy over the past century [seeking] to destroy that element essential to all people for their survival, man's individual initiative and self-reliance." He added, "a century of pursuit of [such polices] finds Indian people on the lowest rung of the social ladder, not only suffering deprivation and poverty to a greater extent than other Canadians but also suffering from psychological intimidation brought about by their almost complete dependence upon the state for the necessities of life."[69]

Contemporary efforts to improve First Nations' economies included acknowledging constitutionally protected Aboriginal and treaty rights. Still, the federal government regulates the exercise of this right and the courts consistently interpret the economic aspect of Aboriginal rights as historic practices with little room to evolve. Commercial enterprises, including casino operations, often fall outside the existing legal and policy frameworks related to First Nations' economic development. We may then conclude that the combined administrative policies and court decisions function to define the parameters of Aboriginal economic development in a way that undermines economic development projects deemed to exist beyond the traditions of historic Indian hunting, trapping and fishing.[70]

Any evaluation of Arcand's claims is complicated by the lack of minutes detailing historic treaty and adherence negotiations. Unlike with the Kahnawá:ke claims, there exists no historic continuity of treaties reaffirming demands for recognition of the Alexander First Nation's economic independence and right to maintain economic endeavours in disputed territories. Arcand's objective of independent economic development nevertheless represents the reaffirmation of the Royal Commission on Aboriginal Peoples' (RCAP) conclusion that "the principal factor that brought Aboriginal communities to the point of impoverishment over the centuries was the intervention—deliberate or unintended, well-intentioned or self-interested—of non-Aboriginal society."[71] Arcand was also echoing a not-so-recent argument attributing First Nations' poverty to government over-regulation as opposed to inadequate social and financial capital.[72] Arcand went so far as to propose First Nations accept the responsibility for regulating gaming, a proposal the province rejected.

In May 2007, the slowdown in North American online gambling caused by the passage of the UIGEA in the United States compelled AIT to focus its efforts exclusively on supporting non-gaming area businesses.[73] The United Kingdom denied the AGC's application for inclusion on its White List due to the Alexander First Nation's dispute with the province of Alberta related to gaming licences.[74] The Alexander First Nation followed through and opened its state-of-the-art data centre that month, albeit without the presence of online casinos. Offering services to companies reliant on information technologies infrastructure and in need of dependable co-location hosting facilities, AIT employed close to 100 people. Once on the brink of expanding its operations, it has since closed shop due to a lack of clients. Chief Arcand consistently indicated that gaming is an integral part of the band's heritage, something he was willing to defend in court.[75] Yet online gambling never was an exclusive aspect of AIT's operations.

CONCLUSION

As this analysis suggests, the Kahnawá:ke Mohawks and Alexander First Nation have an existing treaty right to operate online gambling. We would define this as a right to pursue hosting online casinos, and as but one aspect of establishing and pursuing economic development ventures. What has yet to be acknowledged by provincial or federal officials is the existence of an Aboriginal right to economic development; whether the treaties, specifically those signed by the Kahnawá:ke Mohawks and Alexander First Nation with the British Crown, acknowledged economic development capacity as a component of self-government; and whether this could potentially extend to reserve-based hosting for online gambling activities. The Supreme Court in 1999 developed legal guidelines to help attempt to clarify treaty arrangements and determine how to implement treaty provisions to the satisfaction of the parties involved. These have not been employed independently to help clarify the Kahnawá:ke Mohawks' and Alexander First Nation's treaty rights.[76] Old ideas continue to influence how we interpret federal gaming legislation, whereby the federal Crown considers First Nations non-state actors bound by the Criminal Code of Canada. Consequently, should Canada come to eventually acknowledge First Nations domestic sovereignty, the *Starnet* decision suggests that federal law would be considered prerogative and therefore binding to First Nations. This tension needs to be resolved. In the meantime, First Nations sovereignty and treaty rights remain as yet acknowledged and are legal/constitutional spheres demanding clarification.

NOTES

1   Valerie Jepson, "Internet Gambling and the Canadian Conundrum," *Appeal: Review of Current Law and Law Reform* 6, 6 (2000), http://appeal.law.uvic.ca/vol6/pdf/jepson.pdf; Robin Kelley, Peter Todosichuk, and Jason Azmier, "Gambling@ Home: Internet Gambling in Canada," *Gambling in Canada Research Report No. 15* (Calgary: Canada West Foundation, 2001); Daniel Shap, "Internet Gambling Law in Canada: An Examination of the Legality of Online Gaming from the Perspective of the Players, Providers and the Parties in Between," *Internet and E-Commerce Law in Canada* 3, 9 (2002): 65–72.

2   The ALC began providing online services in August 2004, and the BCLC did so in October 2004.

3   Roxanne Lynne Doty, "Sovereignty and the Nation: Constructing the Boundaries of National Identity," in *State Sovereignty as Social Construct*, ed. Thomas Biersteker and Cynthia Weber (Cambridge: Cambridge University Press, 1996), 143.

4   See, for example, Joshua S. Bauchner, "State Sovereignty and the Globalizing Effects of the Internet: A Case Study of the Privacy Debate," *Brooklyn Journal of International Law* 689 (2000–01): 689–722.

5   See Henry H. Perritt, "The Internet as a Threat to Sovereignty? Thoughts on the Internet's Role in Strengthening National and Global Governance," *Indiana Journal of Global Legal Studies* 5 (1998): 423–442; Georgios Zekos, "Internet or Electronic Technology? A Threat to State Sovereignty," *Journal of Information, Law and Technology* 3 (1999), http://www2.warwick.ac.uk/fac/soc/law/elj/jilt/1999_3/zekos (last accessed 10 November 2008); Sakia Sassen, "The Impact of the Internet on Sovereignty: Unfounded and Real Worries," in *Understanding the Impact of Global Networks on Social, Political and Cultural Values*, ed. Christoph Engel and Kenneth H. Heller (Baden-Baden: Nomos Verlagsgellschaft, 2000), 195–209; and Timothy S. Wu, "Cyberspace Sovereignty? The Internet and the International System," *Harvard Journal of Law and Technology* 10, 3 (1997): 647–666.

6   Kevin Bruyneel, *The Third Space of Sovereignty: The Postcolonial Politics of U.S.-Indigenous Relations* (Minneapolis: University of Minnesota Press, 2007), 24.

7   Samuel F. Miller, "Prescriptive Jurisdiction over Internet Activity: The Need to Define and Establish the Boundaries of Cyberliberty," *Indiana Journal of Global Legal Studies* 10, 2 (2003): 231.

8   Till Muller, "Customary Transnational Law: Attacking the Last Resort of State Sovereignty," *Indiana Journal of Global Legal Studies* 15, 1 (2008): 19–47.

9   Kenichi Ohmae, *The End of the Nation State: The Rise of Regional Economies* (London: Harper Collins, 1996).

10 Christiana Ochoa, "The Individual and Customary International Law Formation," *Virginia Journal of International Law* 48, 1 (2007): 146–148; Wendy Schoener, "Non-Governmental Organizations and Global Activism: Legal and Informal Approaches," *Indiana Journal of Global Legal Studies* 4 (1997): 537, 545.

11 James H. Mittleman, *The Globalization Syndrome: Transformation and Resistance* (Princeton, NJ: Princeton University Press, 2000).

12 Bear Stearns and Co., Inc., *E-Gaming Revisited —At Odds With The World* (New York: 2000).

13 *R. v. Starnet Communications International Inc.*, [2001], B.C.S.C. 125795-1.

14 See C. Ian Kyer and Danielle Hough, "Is Internet Gaming Legal in Canada: A Look at Starnet," *Canadian Journal of Law and Technology* 1, 1, http://cjit.dal.ca (last accessed 22 November 2003).

15 Kelley, Todosichuk, and Azmier, *Gambling@Home*; D. Shap, "Internet Gambling Law in Canada: An Examination of the Legality of Online Gaming from the Perspective of the Players, Providers and the Parties in Between," *Internet and E-Commerce Law in Canada* 3, 9 (2002): 65–72.

16 Peter W. Hogg, *Constitutional Law of Canada* (Toronto: Carswell, 1998), 370.

17 James [Sakej] Youngblood Henderson, "Treaty Governance," in *Aboriginal Self-Government in Canada: Current Trends and Issues*, 3rd ed., ed. Yale D. Belanger (Saskatoon, SK: Purich Publishing, 2008), 20–38; see also his *Treaty Rights in the Constitution of Canada* (Toronto: Carswell, 2007).

18 Joseph G. Starke, *An Introduction to International Law*, 10th ed. (London: Butterworths, 1989), 202.

19 Taiaiake Alfred, *Peace, Power, Righteousness: An Indigenous Manifesto*, 2nd ed. (Toronto: Oxford University Press, 2008), 79–94; and his "Sovereignty," in *A Companion to American Indian History*, ed. Philip J. Deloria and Neal Salisbury (Malden, MA: Blackwell Publishing Ltd., 2004), 460–474; also Kevin Bruyneel, *The Third Space of Sovereignty*, (Minneapolis: University of Minneapolis Press, 2007), 224–225.

20 Dale Turner, "Vision: Toward an Understanding of Aboriginal Sovereignty," in *Canadian Political Philosophy: Contemporary Reflections*, ed. Ronald Beiner and Wayne Norman (Toronto: Oxford University Press, 2001), 325. See also his *This Is Not a Peace Pipe: Towards a Critical Indigenous Philosophy* (Toronto: University of Toronto Press, 2006).

21 Thomas Biolsi, "Imagined Geographies: Sovereignty, Indigenous Space, and American Indian Struggle," *American Ethnologist* 32, 2 (2005): 240, 241.

22 Turner, "Vision: Toward an Understanding of Aboriginal Sovereignty," 329; also, Russel Lawrence Barsh, "The Nature and Spirit of North American Political Systems," *American Indian Quarterly* (Spring 1986): 181–198; Sakej Youngblood Henderson, "*Ayukpachi*: Empowering Aboriginal Thought," in *Reclaiming Indigenous Voice and Vision*, ed. Marie Battiste (Vancouver: University of British Columbia Press, 2000), 248–278; Marie Battiste and Sakej Youngblood Henderson, *Protecting Indigenous Knowledge and Heritage: A Global Challenge* (Saskatoon: Purich Publishing, 2000); Leroy Little Bear, "Relationship of Aboriginal People to the Land and the Aboriginal Perspective on Aboriginal Title," in *For Seven Generations: An Information Legacy of the Royal Commission on Aboriginal Peoples* [CD-ROM] (Ottawa: Canada Communications Group, 1996), cited in Royal Commission on Aboriginal Peoples, *Treaty Making in the Spirit of Co-Existence: An Alternative to Extinguishment* (Ottawa: Canada Communications Group, 1994).

23 Paul Keal, "Indigenous Sovereignty," in *Re-envisioning Sovereignty: The End of Westphalia?*, ed. Trudy Jacobsen, Charles Sampford, Ramesh Thakur, and Ramesh Chandra Thakur (Aldershot, UK: Ashgate Publishing, 2008), 324.

24 This standard discussion can be found in James B. Waldram, D. Ann Herring, and T. Kue Young, *Aboriginal Health in Canada: Historical, Cultural and Epidemiological Perspectives* (Toronto: University of Toronto Press, 2006). For more specific arguments and examples, see Peter Douglas Elias, "Worklessness and Social Pathologies in Aboriginal Communities," *Human Organization* 55, 1 (1996): 13–24; Arnold De Silva, "Wage Discrimination Against Natives," *Canadian Public Policy* 25, 1 (1999): 65–85; Tina Moffat and Ann Herring, "The Historical Roots of High Rates of Infant Death in Aboriginal Communities in Canada in the Early Twentieth Century: The Case of Fisher River, Manitoba," *Social Science and Medicine* 48 (1999): 1821–1832; and Anatole Romaniue, "Aboriginal Population of Canada: Growth Dynamics Under Conditions of Encounter of Civilizations," *Canadian Studies in Population* 30, 1 (2003): 75–115.

25 For this argument see Frances Widdowson and Albert Howard, *Disrobing the Aboriginal Industry: The Deception Behind Indigenous Cultural Preservation* (Kingston and Montreal: McGill-Queen's University Press, 2008); cf. Tom Flanagan, *First Nations? Second Thoughts* (Kingston and Montreal: McGill-Queen's University Press, 2000).

26 Sharon O'Brien, "Indian Treaties as International Agreements: Development of the European Nation State and International Law," in *Treaties with American Indians: An Encyclopedia of Rights, Conflicts, and Sovereignty*, ed. Donald L. Fixico (Santa Barbara, CA: ABC-CLIO, 2008), 50.

27 See Robert A. Williams, *The American Indian in Western Legal Thought: The Discourses of Conquest* (London: Oxford University Press, 1990). See also Robin Thomas Naylor, *Canada in the European Age, 1453–1919* (Kingston and Montreal: McGill-Queen's University Press, 2006); and James Roger Miller, *Skyscrapers Hide the Heavens: A History of Indian-White Relations in Canada*, 3rd ed. (Toronto: University of Toronto Press, 2001).

28 For this discussion, see James Roger Miller, "Compact, Contract, Covenant: The Evolution of Indian Treaty Making," in *New Histories for Old: Changing Perspectives on Canada's Native Pasts*, ed. Ted Binnema and Susan Neylan (Vancouver: University of British Columbia Press, 2007), 66–91; also John Borrows, *Recovering Canada: The Resurgence of Indigenous Law* (Toronto: University of Toronto Press, 2002).

29 See Robert A. Williams, *Linking Arms Together: American Indian Treaty Visions of Law and Peace, 1600–1800* (New York: Routledge, 1999); see also Emmerich Vattel, *The Law of Nations, The Classics of International Law*, ed. James Brown Scott (Washington, DC: Carnegie Institution of Washington, 1916), 160.

30 For this general discussion, see Makere Stewart-Harawira, *The New Imperial Order: Indigenous Responses to Globalization* (New York: Zed Books, 2005).

31 Francis Paul Prucha, *American Indian Treaties: A History of a Political Anomaly* (Berkeley: University of California Press, 1994), 2.

32 *Simon v. The Queen*, [1985] 2 S.C.R. 387.

33 *R. v. Badger*, [1996] 1 S.C.R. 771.

34 See Alexander Morris, *The Treaties of Canada with the Indians* (Toronto: Fifth House Publishers, 1991); and Arthur J. Ray, Jim Miller, and Frank Tough, *Bounty and Benevolence: A History of Saskatchewan Treaties* (Kingston and Montreal: McGill-Queen's University Press, 2002).

35 James [Sakej] Youngblood Henderson, "Implementing the Treaty Order," in *Continuing Poundmaker's and Riel's Quest: Presentations Made at a Conference on Aboriginal Peoples and Justice*, ed. Richard Gosse, James [Sakej] Youngblood Henderson, and Roger Carter (Saskatoon: Purich Publishing, 1994), 52–62.

36 Online Casino Topic, "Cyber World Group of Golden Palace Casino Charged 2 Million Dollars," http://www.onlinecasinotopic.com/cyber-world-group-of-golden-palace-casino-charged-2-million-dollars-147.html (3 Dec. 2007).

37 Kahnwá:ke Ratitsenhaiens (Mohawk Council of Kahnawá:ke), "Mohawks respond to Internet gaming decisions." Press release, 15 Jan. 2008, http://www.Kahnawa:ke .com/gamingcommission/pr01152008a.pdf (last accessed 12 Nov. 2008).

38 Matthew Dennis, *Cultivating a Landscape of Peace: Iroquois-European Encounters in Seventeenth-Century America* (New York: Oxford University Press, 1993), 69.

39 Francis Jennings, *The Ambiguous Iroquois Empire: The Covenant Chain Confederation of Indian Tribes with English Colonies, from Its Beginnings to the Lancaster Treaty of 1744* (New York: Norton, 1984).

40 Borrows, *Recovering Canada*, 148–150; 159–160.

41 Darlene Johnston, "The Quest of the Six Nations Confederacy for Self-Determination," *University of Toronto Law Review* 44, 1 (1986): 18–19.

42 David Blanchard, "The Seven Nations of Canada: An Alliance and a Treaty," *American Indian Culture and Research Journal* 7, 2 (1983): 3–23. The Supreme Court of Canada in 1990 upheld the status of the Oswegatchie Treaty. See *R. v. Sioui*, [1990] 1 S.C.R. 1025.

43 Although the writings on the Kahnawá:ke First Nation are significant, readers should first consult the following resources, which provide a solid foundation concerning local political and economic beliefs: Gerald R. Alfred, *Heeding the Voices of our Ancestors: Kahnawá:ke Mohawk Politics and the Rise of Native Nationalism* (Toronto: Oxford University Press, 1995); Gerald F. Reid, *Kahnawá:ke: Factionalism, Traditionalism, and Nationalism in a Mohawk Community* (Lincoln: University of Nebraska Press, 2004).

44 Yale D. Belanger, "The Six Nations of Grand River Territory's Attempts at Renewing International Political Relationships, 1921–1924," *Canadian Foreign Policy* 13, 3 (2007): 33.

45 Andy Riga, "Kahnawá:ke Rakes in Profit as Mohawk Wins Online-gambling Bet," *Montreal Gazette*, 19 June 2003, B1.

46 Traditionally the Mohawk, Oneida, Onondaga, Cayuga, and Seneca comprised the Iroquois Confederacy, or "the people of the Longhouse." Following the Tuscarora Wars (1711–13), a number of Tuscarora joined the Oneida, and the Confederacy became known and was formally recognized by the English as the Six Nations at Albany in 1722.

47 Jose A. Brandao and William A. Starna, "The Treaties of 1701: A Triumph of Iroquois Diplomacy." *Ethnohistory* 43, 2 (1996): 228, 232.

48 *R. v. Ireland,* [1990] 1 O.R. (3d) 577.

49 Levi General Deskaheh, letter to King George V. Library and Archives Canada (LAC), Record Group (RG) 10, Vol. 2285.

50 Graeme Hamilton, "'Sovereign' Reserve Hits the Jackpot," *National Post,* 18 July 2005, A3.

51 "Kahnawá:ke Weighs in on Kentucky Issue," http://www.online-casinos.com/news/news7640.asp (last accessed 26 Feb. 2009).

52 Johnston, "The Quest of the Six Nations Confederacy for Self-Determination," 17.

53 See Geoffrey York and Loreen Pindera, *People of the Pines: The Warriors and the Legacy of Oka* (Toronto: Little, Brown, 1991); Alanis Obomsawin, *Kahnesatake: 270 Years of Resistance* (National Film Board of Canada, 1993); Alanis Obomsawin, *Rocks at Whiskey Trench* (National Film Board of Canada, 2000).

54 "Alberta Tribal Commission Offers Online Licences," *Casino City Times,* 3 Nov. 2006. http://online.casinocity.com/article/alberta-tribal-commission-offers-online-licences-68682 (last accessed 10 July 2010)

55 "Band Probed over Internet Gambling," *Alberni Valley Times,* 9 Feb. 2007, A9.

56 See, for example, Yale D. Belanger, "Northern Disconnect: Information Communications Technology Needs Assessment for Aboriginal Communities in Manitoba," *Native Studies Review* 14, 1 (2001): 43–69; and Laura Lamb, "Opportunities and Challenges: What Does the New Economy Have to Offer Aboriginal Economic Development?" *Journal of Aboriginal Economic Development* 6, 1 (2008).

57 "Alexander Gaming Commission Reports that the Alexander Chief and Council Defends its Inherent Right to Build and Operate a Data Center," *NationalTalk,* 3 March 2007, www.nationtalk.ca/modules/news/article.php?storyid=784 (last accessed 24 November 2008).

58 *Alberta Hansard,* Spring Session (5 April 2007), 436.

59 Jason Markusoff, "Gaming, band's heritage: Chief: Alexander First Nations rebukes Alberta's interference," *Edmonton Journal,* 22 March 2007, A6.

60 Ibid.

61 John Leonard Taylor, *Treaty Research Report: Treaty Six (1876)* (Ottawa: Treaties and Historical Research Centre, Indian and Northern Affairs Canada, 1985).

62 See Henderson, "Treaty Governance," 20–38.

63 Norman Zlotkin, "Interpretation of the Prairie Treaties," in *Beyond the Nass Valley: National Implications of the Supreme Court's Delgamuukw Decision,* ed. Owen Lippert (Vancouver: The Fraser Institute, 2000), 185.

64 Ibid., 184.

65 Ibid., 211.

66 Morris, *The Treaties of Canada with the Indians,* 28.

67 Mark Dockstator, *Toward an Understanding of the Crown's Views on Justice at the Time of Entering Into Treaty with the First Nations of Canada* (Saskatoon: Office of the Treaty Commissioner, 2001); and Hugh Dempsey, *Firewater: The Impact of the Whiskey Trade on the Blackfoot Nation* (Calgary: Fitzhenry and Whiteside, 2002).

68 See Morris, *The Treaties of Canada with the Indians*; and Arthur J. Ray, Jim Miller, and Frank Tough, *Bounty and Benevolence: A History of Saskatchewan Treaties* (Kingston and Montreal: McGill-Queen's University Press, 2002).

69 David Courchene, "Problems and Possible Solutions," in *Indians Without Tipis: A Resource Book by Indians and Métis*, ed. D. Bruce Sealy and Verna J. Kikness (Winnipeg: William Clare, 1973), 179.

70 See *R. v. Van der Peet,* [1996] 2 S.C.R. 507; and *R. v. Marshall*, [1999] 3 S.C.R. 456.

71 Royal Commission on Aboriginal Peoples (RCAP), *For Seven Generations: An Information Legacy of the Royal Commission on Aboriginal Peoples.* CD. Ottawa: Libraxus, 1997.

72 Calvin Helin, *Dances With Dependency: Indigenous Success Through Self-Reliance* (Vancouver: Orca Spirit Publishing and Communications, 2006). For the American literature, see, for example, Ronald L. Trosper, "Traditional American Indian Economic Policy," *American Indian Culture and Research Journal* 19, 1 (1995): 65–95; and Russel Lawrence Barsh, *Aboriginal Self-Government in the United States: A Qualitative Political Analysis*, Submitted to the Royal Commission on Aboriginal Peoples (RCAP), 1993.

73 "Alexander First Nation: Strong Local Demand Greets New Edmonton-area Data Centre Facility," *Marketwire*, 16 May 2007, www.marketwire.com/press-release/ Alexander-First-Nation-652329.html (last accessed 24 Nov. 2008).

74 James Kilsby, "DCMS deals blow to First Nation Ambitions with White List Snub," *Gambling Compliance*, www.gamblingcompliance.com/node/11025 (last accessed 23 November 2008).

75 Jason Markusoff, "Alexander First Nation Ignores Solicitor General's Order," *Edmonton Journal*, 21 March 2007.

76 Writing in dissent, Justice McLachlin in *R. v. Marshall* [1999] summarized the prior case law regarding the principles governing the Supreme Court of Canada's treaty interpretation:

> Aboriginal treaties constitute a unique type of agreement and attract special principles of interpretation.
>
> Treaties should be liberally construed and ambiguities or doubtful expressions should be resolved in favour of the aboriginal signatories.
>
> The goal of treaty interpretation is to choose from among the various possible interpretations of common intention the one which best reconciles the interests of both parties at the time the treaty was signed.
>
> In searching for the common intention of the parties, the integrity and honour of the Crown is presumed.
>
> In determining the signatories' respective understanding and intentions, the court must be sensitive to the unique cultural and linguistic differences between the parties.

The words of the treaty must be given the sense which they would naturally have held for the parties at the time.

A technical or contractual interpretation of treaty wording should be avoided.

While construing the language generously, courts cannot alter the terms of the treaty by exceeding what "is possible on the language" or realistic.

Treaty rights of aboriginal peoples must not be interpreted in a static or rigid way. They are not frozen at the date of signature. The interpreting court must update treaty rights [Page 219] to provide for their modern exercise. This involves determining what modern practices are reasonably incidental to the core treaty right in its modern context.

PART II
SOCIO-ECONOMIC AND RESEARCH CONSIDERATIONS

CHAPTER 4

A FRAMEWORK FOR ASSESSING THE SOCIO-ECONOMIC IMPACTS OF GAMBLING

ROBERT J. WILLIAMS

INTRODUCTION

The socio-economic impact of gambling is an important issue with major pol-icy implications. However, assessing that impact is a complicated task beset by many methodological issues and problems.[1] These methodological issues have been the focus of conferences (the Whistler Symposium in British Columbia in 1999; the Social and Economic Costs and Benefits of Gambling conference in Banff, Alberta, in 2006); special issues of the *Journal of Gambling Studies* (June 2003) and the *Managerial and Decision Economics Journal* (June 2004); litera-ture reviews;[2] books;[3] and the guidelines for impact estimation developed by the Social and Economic Impact of Gambling (SEIG) Project team.[4]

Unfortunately, despite all of this work, it is fair to say that a well-agreed-upon framework for assessing the socio-economic impacts of gambling still does not exist. There remain several unresolved issues, a main one being how to quantify the social impacts.[5] As will be discussed in this chapter, on the one hand are traditional cost-benefit frameworks that either ignore social im-pacts or try to re-construe them into purely monetary terms, and thus are insufficient and unsatisfactory. On the other hand are approaches that at-tempt to use non-monetary measures to assess the overall impact (e.g., "global progress," "quality of life"), which tend to be too subjective. The divergent theoretical orientations of people involved in this endeavour make it unlikely that there will ever be total consensus on the appropriate approach to these issues. Rather, some degree of consensus will only be achieved from an ap-proach that is comprehensive, objective, and theoretically neutral. The purpose of the present chapter is to outline a set of methodological principles for conducting socio-economic analyses that meet these conditions and that can be used as an analytical framework for any type of gambling (including First Nations casinos). It combines cost-benefit analysis (CBA) with a meaningful accounting of the social impacts of gambling. The framework outlined has been successfully used by the author in conducting socio-economic analyses of gambling in British Columbia, Ontario, and Alberta.[6]

TABULATE ALL GAMBLING AND GAMBLING-RELATED REVENUE

The first step in a socio-economic impact analysis of gambling is to document exactly how much gambling and gambling-related revenue is being generated. Gambling-related revenue refers to additional revenue from services that support gambling. At gambling venues this includes such things as food and beverage sales, automated teller machine (ATM) fees, and parking. Where the gambling venue has a physically associated hotel or convention centre, it is also appropriate to include a portion of revenue generated from these enterprises. The appropriate proportion is difficult to determine; however, a reasonable assessment would calculate the percentage increase in business once the gambling venue was opened, or the proportion of hotel or convention-centre visitors that also reports patronizing the gambling venue.

DOCUMENT CASH FLOW TO HELP IDENTIFY AREAS OF FOCUS AND THE GEOGRAPHIC PARAMETERS OF THE STUDY

Gambling is an economic activity characterized by a significant transfer of wealth. There are winners and there are losers, and most of the impacts are seen in these two groups. Thus, the next step in a socio-economic analysis of gambling is to document where the money is coming from. The demographics of people who are gambling is particularly important, with the most significant variables of social and economic interest being age, gender, ethnicity, income, and problem-gambling status. The geographic origin of the gamblers is also relevant because it speaks to: (a) whether the revenue is an influx of new wealth or just local money that has been redirected; and (b) the geographic range in which to expect (and therefore measure) impacts. Finally, it is useful to survey gamblers to assess whether their spending patterns have changed as a consequence of their gambling. This information provides some idea about the economic sectors where impacts might be evident.

Next, it is important to clearly document which groups are the primary recipients of gambling revenue (i.e., private operator, different levels of government, charity, local community) as well as the geographic location of each of these groups. It is also essential to document how these groups then disburse or spend the money, so as to identify all the downstream beneficiaries. The geographic origin of the operating expenses for the new type of gambling, and the origin of any equipment purchased, are also relevant to a socioeconomic accounting. In addition to helping identify areas of focus and the geographic parameters of the study, documentation of cash flow provides the starting point for a much more detailed determination of cash flow, which is used for cost-benefit analysis (described later).

ESTABLISH THE GEOGRAPHIC/JURISDICTIONAL PARAMETERS

At the outset, specify the geographic region that is the focus of interest. This could be a specific jurisdiction (First Nations reserve, municipality, state/province, country) or a geographic area within a jurisdiction. However, for a full understanding of the impacts, it is necessary to go beyond these boundaries, as in many cases financial inflow or benefits in one region come at the expense of financial outflow or loss of benefits in adjoining regions. Thus, one should aspire to assess both the micro (community-specific) impacts and the macro (greater-regional) impacts. As mentioned, the geographic origin of the patronage is a good indication of the regional scope of the impacts. Once the boundary of this larger region/jurisdiction is established, it will be important to clearly identify the impacts within the community of interest as well as in the outside region.

USE CONTROL COMMUNITIES/REGIONS

There are a multitude of economic and social forces at work that are responsible for changes in a community. Furthermore, gambling is often a relatively small activity in economic terms. Changes in a community from before a gambling facility to after do not unambiguously establish that the changes are due to the introduction of gambling. A much stronger methodology is a matched control comparison, in which changes in the community receiving the new gambling opportunities are compared against changes in an economically, socially, and demographically similar community not receiving a new form of gambling.

USE LONGITUDINAL DESIGNS WHEN POSSIBLE

Most socio-economic impact studies collect annual statistical "snapshots" of a community's socio-economic indicators and then try to attribute any changes to the introduction of the new gambling activity. For example, a problem gambling increase after one year is held responsible for a corresponding bankruptcy rate increase after one year. However, two data points provide no information concerning whether problem gambling caused the bankruptcies, the bankruptcies caused the problem gambling, or whether they are independent events. Even if one event precedes the other (e.g., there is a problem gambling increase in year one followed by bankruptcy increase in year two), causal attributions are weak unless it can be established that those increased bankruptcies were filed primarily by the problem gamblers.

A related problem with these cross-sectional designs is that there is no way of knowing the exact meaning of stable prevalence rates from Time 1 to Time 2. For example, although severe levels of pathological gambling appear to be reasonably stable over time,[7] moderate problem gambling (which is much more common) is not. Two studies have found that a large majority of moderate problem gamblers are no longer problem gamblers at one-year follow up[8] or seven-year follow up.[9] Thus, stable rates of problem/pathological gambling from Time 1 to Time 2 imply the existence of a large group of newly affected individuals roughly equivalent to the number of individuals who have recovered or remitted (meaning that gambling is producing a cumulatively wider impact on the general population than would have otherwise been known). The ability to make causal attributions for individuals and establish problem gambling *incidence* is strengthened with use of a longitudinal design that documents the temporal sequence of events in "real time" for individuals.

MEASURE "IMPACTS" RATHER THAN "COSTS AND BENEFITS"

One of the problems with cost-benefit analysis is that it requires everything to either be a *cost* or a *benefit*. While many gambling impacts are clearly costs (e.g., increased problem gambling) or benefits (e.g., employment gains), the positive or negative nature of other changes is less clear and somewhat subjective (e.g., changed societal pattern of leisure pursuits, demise of competing industries). Typically, these latter types of impacts are simply omitted from cost-benefit analyses and are therefore lost. It is preferable to comprehensively measure all changes or impacts. In cases where there is no ambiguity about their positive or negative nature, impacts can also be characterized as either costs or benefits.

ASSESS IMPACTS FOR YEARS BEFORE AND AFTER
THE INTRODUCTION OF NEW GAMBLING VENUES/OPPORTUNITIES

The length of time it takes for all economic and social impacts of gambling to manifest themselves is unknown. Much of the economic impact (e.g., revenue and employment) appears to be fairly immediate. However, it may take a few years for competing industries to fail or for increased utilization of roads, sewers, and other infrastructure to result in repairs. Some economic impacts will also reverse themselves in a resilient economy as industry repositions itself. Social impacts may take longer to appear than economic impacts.[10] While some individuals sink rapidly into gambling problems, many others gamble safely for several years before problems develop.[11] There is also evidence that rates of gambling and problem gambling may decline with extended exposure.[12] It is also very important to realize that new gambling venues are always added to existing gambling opportunities (even if they are illegal). Thus, lag effects of these pre-existing opportunities can easily be mistaken for immediate impacts of new facilities. It is important to try to document prior gambling opportunities and socio-economic effects for several years before the opening of the new gambling venue, as well as for several years after.

MEASURE IMPACTS IN A WAY THAT BEST CAPTURES THE IMPACT

The traditional approach to measuring socio-economic impacts is to use *money* as the way of measuring and quantifying all impacts in a cost-benefit analysis approach. While monetary gains or losses provide appropriate measures of the value of many economic activities, many social effects of gambling have limited monetary consequences (e.g., psychic trauma of being a problem gambler, family turmoil, suicide). Furthermore, attempts to apply a monetary value to these variables (e.g., asking people how much money they would pay to not be a problem gambler) fail to recognize that the true nature of the impact is largely non-monetary in nature. A variant of the CBA approach to social costs is illustrated by the work of Douglas Walker[13] and Walker and A.H. Barnett,[14] who define a social cost as "the amount by which that action reduces aggregate societal real wealth." François Vaillancourt and Alexandre Roy use this type of methodology to produce a cost-benefit analysis of gambling in Canada.[15] However, this also is not a satisfactory solution because many social problems associated with gambling (e.g., theft, suicide, unemployment) are not included in these costs because they do not result in a reduction of the aggregate wealth of society; that is, thefts are just transfers of wealth.

The point is that it is important to use a form of measurement that best captures the impact. Money is most appropriate for most economic changes, as well as for social changes with clear monetary costs (e.g., police time, treatment cost). However, most social impacts are best quantified by means of percentage change in the variable or the actual number of people impacted (e.g., percent change in rate of problem gambling, change in crime, or number of new jobs created).

COMPREHENSIVELY ASSESS ALL POTENTIAL ECONOMIC AND SOCIAL CHANGES

Gambling has pervasive socio-economic ripple effects. Despite this, many studies have only measured the most apparent and obvious economic effects, those that are easily quantifiable in monetary terms (direct gambling revenue, employment, government tax revenue, etc.). Examples of this are Arthur Anderson's study of United States casino gambling;[16] Laura Littlepage, Seth Payton, and Chistiana Atibil's study of riverboat gambling in Indiana;[17] Yves Rabeau's study of casino gambling in Quebec;[18] studies of the economic impacts of racinos[19] in Ontario;[20] and the recent analysis of the impacts of gambling in Canada by the Canadian Gaming Association (CGA).[21] These types of studies create a very unbalanced analysis in that the economic impacts are not measured against the social impacts. It would be inappropriate if socio-economic analyses of the effects of alcohol or tobacco just focused on the tax revenues, employment gains, and support to the agricultural sector, and failed to mention the social costs caused by consumption. However, this is a frequent occurrence in the socio-economic analysis of gambling. Hence, it is essential that a wide net be cast to capture and measure all economic *and* social variables that may be impacted by gambling. The main areas to be assessed are as follows.

GOVERNMENT TAXES — Changes in tax revenue at the municipal, state/provincial, and federal levels may occur because of increased tax revenue from businesses offering or benefiting from gambling, and/or decreased tax revenue from businesses suffering because of competition with gambling. These taxes come in the form of licensing fees, property tax, corporate income tax, and goods and services taxes. It is also important to assess (or at least speculate on) whether taxes may have risen if government had not received additional revenue from gambling.

REGULATORY COSTS — There will be government costs (primarily wages) related to ensuring that the new form of gambling operates according to regulation.

CAPITAL INVESTMENT — Any buildings, roads, and infrastructure upgrades that are directly or indirectly due to the introduction of gambling will add to the "wealth" of the community.

INFRASTRUCTURE SUPPORT COSTS — Various levels of government usually incur costs to support the infrastructure needed to service new gambling facilities (i.e., road maintenance, utilities, fire services, police services).

PROPERTY VALUES — Property value changes in the areas proximate to new venues need to be documented, as do changes in average rental costs.

BUSINESS STARTS AND FAILURES — While there is merit in comprehensively investigating the number of new business and commercial bankruptcies, certain businesses should receive particular attention because research has shown them more likely to be impacted by gambling introduction.[22] Specifically, these are other forms of gambling (bingo, horse racing, lotteries); the hospitality industry (hotels, restaurants, lounges); the construction industry; pawnshops; cheque-cashing stores; horse breeding and training operations; tourism (car rental, sightseeing, etc.); and other entertainment industries.

BUSINESS REVENUE — Changes in business revenue/sales should be investigated using the same guidelines mentioned in the preceding category.

PUBLIC SERVICES — In jurisdictions where government or charity groups are the primary recipients of gambling revenue, the benefits to the public in the form of enhanced range and amount of public services (e.g., health care, education, social services, infrastructure, arts funding) are usually touted as the main benefit. Documentation of how and where government and/or charity gambling revenues are spent (and the financial value of these services) provides some quantification of this impact.

EMPLOYMENT — Studies should tabulate the number of full and part-time jobs that are directly or indirectly created as a result of gambling introduction. This tabulation should be approached in two ways. The first is simply by counting the number of employees that are now employed in the new establishment(s). For these individuals, it is important to know whether they were previously unemployed (which indicates a "new" job was created) or they simply changed employment from one industry to another; the type of industry in which they were previously employed; where they resided immediately prior to employment (to gauge the employment benefits to the local community); where their residency is now (to determine where the person may be spending his/her wages); and their wages.

This is not a perfect way of establishing the actual number of new jobs created, as people who shifted employment from other industries may have created a new job opening for someone who was unemployed. Hence, the second method of judging employment impacts is to compare the overall rates of employment and unemployment in the area before and after gambling introduction.

LEISURE ACTIVITY — Legal gambling produces a change in people's leisure behaviour as they patronize this new form of entertainment. The percentage of the population that participates needs to be documented, as well as what sorts of things people are engaging in less frequently as a consequence of gambling (some of which will also be evident from changes in business revenue).

SUBJECTIVE WELL-BEING — It is instructive to evaluate whether there are any changes in the general populace's subjective well-being, and/or whether there is any difference in the subjective well-being of people who engage in the new form of gambling as compared with those who do not.

PROBLEM GAMBLING — A potential increase in the rate of problem gambling is generally regarded as the main negative consequence of increased gambling availability. Hence, the population prevalence of problem gambling before and after gambling introduction needs to be determined. Changes in the rate of problem gambling will be associated with coincidental changes in the rate of negative societal consequences that are manifestations/aspects of problem gambling (e.g., bankruptcy, divorce, suicide). Nonetheless, it is useful to independently assess changes in these associated variables so as to establish how prevalent and financially costly each of these things are. Ascertainment of "problem gambling" is not an exact science, and there will be people who experience significant negative consequences deriving from their gambling who are not identified as problem gamblers. Thus, changes in the following areas should also be documented.

> **Treatment/Prevention.** The number of people receiving treatment for problem gambling, and the estimated costs of providing problem gambling-related treatment and prevention.

> **Finances.** The estimated amount of "abused dollars" (total amount of money borrowed, obtained from selling posses-

sions, or obtained illegally), as well as the number of personal bankruptcies attributable to problem gambling.

Mental Health. The number of people who report developing a significant mental health problem due to problem gambling, as well as the number of suicides attributable to problem gambling.

Family. The number of people directly or indirectly affected by problem gambling (e.g., number of problem gamblers times the size of the average household in which a problem gambler resides). Also, the number of people who report domestic violence, who have separated or divorced, or who have had child welfare services become involved because of problem gambling. The financial costs of these consequences also need to be estimated.

Work. The projected number of work days lost, the number of people who have lost their jobs, the number of people who have received unemployment or welfare benefits, and the financial costs of these consequences.

Crime. The number of people committing a crime, being convicted of a crime, and being incarcerated because of problem gambling. The financial costs of these consequences also need to be estimated.

CRIME RATE — Change in the rate of overall gambling-related crime should also be evaluated. The introduction of legal gambling may result in a decrease in the rate of illegal gambling as well as potential increases in rates of property crime and fraud. The estimated cost or savings of this changed crime rate should be determined.

PUBLIC ATTITUDES — Impact analysis should include examination of public satisfaction with the availability of legal gambling, the benefit or harm it has, and how gambling revenue is distributed.

CONDUCT A COST-BENEFIT
ANALYSIS OF MONETARY "COSTS" AND "GAINS"

There are three primary ways in which a new economic activity (such as gambling) can produce beneficial economic effects:

1) The economic activity brings in **assets or money from outside** the jurisdiction. For gambling, this occurs when the primary patronage base is from outside the jurisdiction, or when outside agencies (e.g., casino developers, private businesses, government) make capital investments in the community.

2) The economic activity **increases intrinsic value**. For gambling, this can occur when the new gambling venue increases the value of neighbouring property, or when manufactured gambling equipment (e.g., electronic gambling machines) can be sold for more than the sum of its parts.

3) The economic activity produces **increased utilization of existing money**. Money that sits dormant has very little economic utility. It has much greater potential value if it is spent on gambling, this gambling revenue is then spent on employee wages, and these wages are then used to buy local goods and services. In general, money has increased economic value as the number of people that use the money and the speed of the cash flow from one person to the next increase. Increased utilization of existing money is more likely to occur if gambling patronage comes from individuals who are not financing their gambling by reducing their spending on other activities. (The income class of the patronage potentially speaks to this.) Evidence of increased utilization of existing money is seen if the increased revenue and employment in the gambling industry (and supporting or complementary industries) occurs without there being offsetting declines in the revenue and employment in competing industries.

Whether a net beneficial economic effect is actually present or not is seen by adding up all the unambiguous monetary gains and losses in gambling revenue, taxes, capital investment, infrastructure support costs, property value changes, changes in business revenue, public services, employment wages, problem gambling costs, and crime rate as a function of whether these gains or losses occur in the community of interest or the outside community.

Even if there is not a clear economic gain, an economic benefit still exists if the gambling activity *prevented assets or money from leaving the jurisdiction, prevented a decrease in intrinsic value, or prevented decreased utilization of existing money.* This prevention of loss is often difficult to assess, as it requires a projection of what the situation would have been like if the gambling had not been introduced. Nonetheless, the loss of gambling revenue to neighbouring jurisdictions is often the main justification for the introduction of gambling, and this potential economic cost/benefit must also be estimated.

CREATE A LIST OF OTHER ECONOMIC AND SOCIAL IMPACTS

When it is unclear whether a monetary change is a cost or benefit, then it should simply be reported as an impact (e.g., a change in business starts or failures, changes in business revenue).

Similarly, non-monetary aspects of social impacts need to be measured and reported in a manner that best captures the impact (e.g., nature and amount of enhanced public services, percent change in employment, changing patterns of leisure activity, changes in subjective wellbeing, percent change in prevalence and aspects of problem gambling, percent change in crime, nature of and change in public attitudes). As part of this list of impacts it is also important to document the transfer of wealth that occurs within different demographic groups (i.e., net revenue gain/loss as a function of age group, gender, ethnic group, income group, and problem gambling status[23]).

Obviously, these different social impacts do not lend themselves well to aggregation into a singular index or combination with a monetary one. Nonetheless, there are several approaches that have attempted to do so. These include the General Progress Indicator,[24] the United Nations' Human Development Index, the Economist Intelligence Unit's Quality of Life Index, and the Community Well-Being Index. These approaches represent advancements over approaches that either ignore or inappropriately re-construe social impacts in monetary terms. However, the marked differences in the details of these approaches attest to the fact that determining what indicators contribute to societal "well-being" is a very value-laden task that is not well agreed upon. Another problem is that these approaches aspire to combine impacts into a single index (usually just by adding up the number of beneficial indicators and subtracting the detrimental ones). This is problematic because it makes all impacts equivalent in value and/or requires a subjective judgement about the relative value/weight of one impact against the others.

Hence, the best approach is simply to provide a comprehensive, non-aggregated list of the economic and social impacts.

CREATE A PROFILE OF IMPACTS THAT INCLUDES THE NET MONETARY COST/BENEFIT

The next step is to create a comprehensive profile of impacts that includes the net monetary cost/benefit along with a list of all the other economic and social impacts. This profile constitutes the primary result of the study.

An overall judgement about whether the social/economic benefits outweigh the social/economic costs is a subjective determination dependent on: (a) how each of these impacts is construed (positive, negative, or neutral), and (b) the relative importance one assigns to different impacts (i.e., importance one places on increased employment versus increased problem gambling). If one wishes to assess how a particular community feels about these impacts, then a representative group of community members can be given this impact profile and asked to judge whether they consider the overall impact to be positive or negative.

REPORT THE LIMITATIONS AND PARAMETERS OF THESE RESULTS

The final step is to clearly recognize and report that the results obtained are very much a function of the context in which the study was conducted. More specifically:

IMPACTS ARE SOMEWHAT SPECIFIC TO THE TYPE OF GAMBLING STUDIED — Different types of gambling have different impact profiles, in terms of their potential for causing problem gambling, the number of jobs they produce, and their likelihood of cannibalization of other industries. Hence, it is necessary to qualify results as being specific to the type of gambling studied. If multiple forms of gambling are being assessed, then some attempt needs to be made to ascertain the independent impacts of each form.

IIMPACTS ARE SOMEWHAT SPECIFIC TO THE JURISDICTION STUDIED — Jurisdictions differ widely in their revenue-distribution models, pre-existing availability of gambling, strength of policy and educational initiatives to prevent problem gambling, baseline unemployment rates, and so on. Hence, it is important to recognize that the results found may be specific to the particular jurisdiction studied.

IMPACTS ARE SOMEWHAT SPECIFIC TO THE TIME PERIOD STUDIED — The time period during which impacts are studied is critical, as gambling availability and gambling policy can change rapidly within a jurisdiction. Furthermore, there is good evidence that populations with extended exposure to gambling may develop problems at a rate that differs from that in populations that have more recently been introduced to it.[25] Hence, it is also important to qualify results as being specific to the time period studied.

CONCLUSION

As mentioned in the introduction, socio-economic analysis of gambling is a very important task that is both complicated and contentious. There is some arbitrariness in decisions regarding the best way to organize the impacts. There is also some difference of opinion about the best way to measure and aggregate these impacts. However, there is no difference of opinion on the need for any socio-economic analysis to be comprehensive and scientifically rigorous. This is the underlying essence of the present framework.

NOTES

1   Robert J. Williams and Rhys Stevens, "The Devil is in the Details: Overview of the Main Methodological Issues in Analysis of the Socioeconomic Impacts of Gambling" (presentation, Alberta Gaming Research Institute 5th Annual Conference in Banff, Alberta, 21 April 2006), http://gaming.uleth.ca/agri_downloads/4001/Williams_Stevens.pdf.

2   Mark Anielski and Aaron Braaten, *The Social and Economic Impacts of Gambling* (literature review prepared for the Social and Economic Impacts of Gambling [SEIG] Project, Edmonton, AB, 2005); Rhys Stevens and Robert J. Williams, *Socio-economic Impacts Associated with the Introduction of Casino Gambling: A Literature Review and Synthesis,* Alberta Gaming Research Institute, 2004, http://www.uleth.ca/dspace/handle/10133/407.

3   Earl L. Grinols, *Gambling in America: Costs and Benefits* (New York: Cambridge University Press, 2004); Douglas M. Walker, *The Economics of Casino Gambling* (New York: Springer, 2007).

4   Mark Anielski, *Socio-economic Impacts of Gambling (SEIG) Framework: An Assessment Framework for Canada,* Inter-Provincial Consortium for the Development of Methodology to Assess the Social and Economic Impact of Gambling, Anielski Management Inc., 2008, http://www.gamblingresearch.org/contentdetail.sz?cid=3420.

5   Douglas M. Walker, "Problems in Quantifying the Social Costs and Benefits of Gambling," *American Journal of Economics and Sociology* 66 (2007): 609–645; Williams and Stevens, "The Devil is in the Details."

6   Blue Thorn Research, Population Health Promotion Associates, PFIA Corporation, and Robert J. Williams, *Socioeconomic Impacts of New Gaming Venues in Four British Columbia Lower Mainland Communities: Final Report,* 2007, http://www.hsd.gov.bc.ca/gaming/reports/docs/rpt-rg-impact-study-final.pdf. There are many important logistical issues associated with how and where to collect the data that are beyond the scope of this paper (e.g., the need for multiple forms of data collection such as population surveys, patron surveys, annual report data).

7   David C. Hodgins and Nicole Peden, "Natural Course of Gambling Disorders: Forty-month Follow-up, *Journal of Gambling Issues* 14 (2005), http://www.camh.net/egambling/issue14/jgi_14_hodgins.html; Wendy S. Slutske, "Natural Recovery and Treatment-seeking in Pathological Gambling: Results of Two U.S. National Surveys," *American Journal of Psychiatry* 163 (2006): 297–302.

8   Jaime B. Wiebe, Brian Cox, and Agata Falkowski-Ham, *Psychological and Social Factors Associated with Problem Gambling in Ontario: A One Year Follow-up Study,* Ontario Problem Gambling Research Centre, October 2003, http://www.gamblingresearch.org/download.sz/social%20psychological%20factors%20final%2report.pdf?docid=3829.

9   Max Abbott, Maynard Williams, and Rachel Volberg, *Seven Years On: A Follow-up Study of Frequent and Problem Gamblers Living in the Community* (Wellington, New Zealand: Department of Internal Affairs, 1999).

10 Jan McMillen, *Study of the Social and Economic Impacts of New Zealand Casinos* (Sydney: Australian Institute for Gambling Research, 1998); Jan McMillen, *Comparative Study of the Social and Economic Impacts of the Brisbane and Cairns Casinos 1996–98 1–3* (Australian Research Council, 2000).

11 National Research Council, *Pathological Gambling: A Critical Review* (Washington, DC: National Academy Press, 1999).

12 Howard J. Shaffer, Richard A. LaBrie, and Debbie LaPlante, "Laying the Foundation for Quantifying Regional Exposure to Social Phenomena: Considering the Case of Legalized Gambling as a Public Health Toxin," *Psychology of Addictive Behaviors* 18 (2004): 40–48.

13 Douglas M. Walker, "Methodological Issues in the Social Cost of Gambling Studies," *Journal of Gambling Studies* 19, 2 (2003): 149–184; Walker, *The Economics of Casino Gambling*.

14 Douglas M. Walker and A. H. Barnett, "The Social Costs of Gambling: An Economic Perspective," *Journal of Gambling Studies* 15, 3 (1999), 181-182.

15 François Vaillancourt and Alexandre Roy, *Gambling and Governments in Canada, 1969–1998: How Much? Who Plays? What Pay-off?* Special Studies in Taxation and Public Finance (Ottawa: Canadian Tax Foundation, 2000).

16 Arthur Anderson, *Economic Impacts of Casino Gaming in the United States* (Washington, DC: American Gaming Association, 1997).

17 Laura Littlepage, Seth Payton, and Chistiana Atibil, *Riverboat Gambling in Indiana: An Analysis of the Impacts* (Indianapolis: Center for Urban Policy and the Environment, 2004).

18 Yves Rabeau, *Updated Evaluation of the Economic Impact of the Societé des Casinos du Quebec's Activities* (Montreal: Université du Québec à Montreal, 2004).

19 Racinos are horse-race tracks that have added electronic gambling machines.

20 George L. Brinkman and Alfons J. Weersink, *Contribution of the Horseman Component of the Harness Horse Industry to the Ontario Economy* (Guelph, ON: Department of Agricultural Economics and Business, University of Guelph, 2004); Econometric Research Limited, *The Economic Impacts of Slot Machines on Horse Racing and Breeding in Ontario: Benchmarking the Industry 1992-2004*, The Ontario Ministry of Public Infrastructure Renewal, 2005, http://www.pir.gov. on.ca/english/aboutpir/publications/gaming_benchmarking_industry.pdf.

21 Canadian Gaming Association, *National Gaming Impact Study: Preliminary Results*, HLT Advisory Inc., 2008, http://www.canadiangaming.ca/english/home/ index.cfm?id=226&.

22 Grinols, *Gambling in America;* Stevens and Williams, *Socio-economic Impacts*.

23 See Robert J. Williams and Robert T. Wood, "The Proportion of Gaming Revenue Derived from Problem Gamblers: Examining the Issues in a Canadian Context," *Analyses of Social Issues and Public Policy* 4 (2004): 1-13.

24 Mark Anielski, *The Alberta GPI Accounts: Gambling* [Report #15], Pembina Institute, 2002, http://www.pembina.org/pdf/publications/15.%20Gambling%20 FINAL.doc; Anielski, *Socio-economic Impacts*; Karen Hayward, *The Costs and Benefits of Gaming: A Literature Review with Emphasis on Nova Scotia* (Glen Haven, NS: GPI Atlantic Research Reports, 2004), http://www.gpiatlantic.org/pdf/ gambling/gambling.pdf.

25 See, for example, Shaffer, LaBrie, and LaPlante, *Laying the Foundation*, 40–48.

CHAPTER 5

GAMBLING RESEARCH IN CANADIAN ABORIGINAL COMMUNITIES: A PARTICIPATORY ACTION APPROACH

HAROLD J. WYNNE

THE GROWTH OF GAMBLING IN CANADA

In the past decade, the gambling industry has become the fastest-growing sector in the Canadian economy. According to Statistics Canada, "net revenue from government-run lotteries, video-lottery terminals (VLTS), casinos, and slot machines not in casinos rose from $2.7 billion in 1992 to $13.6 in 2007."[1] The gambling GDP index rose from 100 to 460 points between 1992 and 2007, outpacing all other Canadian non-gambling industries, which rose just 60 points during the same period. Gambling-related employment also surpassed employment in non-gambling sectors over the past fifteen years, rising from 100 to 400 points, versus 100 to 130 points, according to Statistics Canada.

The provision and regulation of gambling is the purview of provincial governments in Canada. Enabling gambling is an effective way for provincial governments to raise capital for the delivery of health care, education, recreation, social services, infrastructure, and other pubic goods and services without having to increase taxes.[2] The *Canadian Gambling Digest,* published annually by an interprovincial partnership of government gambling providers and regulators, shows that all provinces receive a significant amount of their total annual revenue from gambling sources.[3] In the 2006–07 fiscal year, the percentage of total provincial revenue derived from gambling averaged 2.4 percent for all ten provinces.

Gambling has also grown dramatically in Aboriginal communities across Canada. Yale Belanger reports that, since 1996, there has been a proliferation of casinos on First Nations lands in every province—British Columbia (1), Alberta (5), Saskatchewan (6), Manitoba (2), and Ontario (3).[4] Since their inception in 1996, First Nations casinos have generated billions of dollars in gambling revenues, which benefit the communities.[5] For example, revenues from Casino Rama in Ontario have been used to fund a daycare and seniors' home and to otherwise create some 3,000 jobs in the casino's hotel, restaurant, and entertainment facilities.

HORNS OF A DILEMMA

Although gambling provides welcome revenues for Aboriginal and other Canadian communities, this financial benefit comes with a significant social cost. This social cost results from the reality that some people cannot control their gambling behaviour and, consequently, become problem gamblers. Problem gamblers usually experience severe negative consequences of their uncontrolled gambling, and these consequences or costs often extend to the gamblers' family, friends, co-workers, and community at large.

The prevalence of problem gambling is much greater in Canadian Aboriginal populations than in provincial populations in general. In the 2002 Canadian Community Health Survey—Mental Health and Well-Being (CCHS 1.2) undertaken by Statistics Canada, it was discovered that off-reserve Aboriginal gamblers (18 percent) were significantly more likely to be at-risk for developing a gambling problem than were non-Aboriginal gamblers (6 percent).[6] The 2002 Saskatchewan Health Gambling and Problem Gambling Prevalence Survey also showed that Aboriginal gamblers in Saskatchewan were significantly more likely than non-Aboriginal gamblers to be both at-risk for developing a gambling problem (29 percent versus 13 percent) or to be problem gamblers (10 percent versus 1 percent).[7] Similar results were found in the 2002 Alberta prevalence survey, where a greater percentage of Aboriginal gamblers were at risk (23 percent versus 1 percent) or were problem gamblers (8 percent versus 1 percent).[8] These troubling findings have been confirmed in virtually every other Canadian problem-gambling prevalence survey conducted.

Decision makers see the opportunity for Aboriginal communities to raise substantial revenues from casinos, VLTs, bingos, lotteries, and other gambling activities, but at the same time they recognize that many community members and their families may suffer from the consequences of problem gambling. This places them on the horns of a dilemma: should a casino be built in the community to garner much-needed revenue, given that there will likely be a significant social cost associated with an increase in problem gambling amongst the people? This dilemma is not easily resolved.

GAMBLING POLICY AND RESEARCH

The introduction and expansion of gambling within Canadian provinces and Aboriginal communities is fundamentally a public policy issue. Public policy has been defined by many scholars, with one of the earliest and most succinct definitions being offered by Thomas Dye, a pioneer in the policy sciences field. According to Dye, public policy is whatever governments choose to do or not to do.[9] This definition begs the question, how do governments decide what to do or not to do? Irrespective of how public policy decisions *should* be made, policy making is invariably a political process wherein power elites often make decisions based on their own special interests or those of constituent groups. One can argue that this is essentially how policies that led to gambling expansionism in both Aboriginal and other Canadian communities have been made. That is, chiefs and band councils or provincial governments decide that a casino will be built, VLTs will be introduced, or lottery products will be expanded to garner new revenues for public coffers. These gambling policy decisions have typically been made without the benefit of social and economic impact studies that estimate the costs and benefits of gambling initiatives, and without consulting people in the community.

Information gathering is of central importance to developing effective gambling policies. Undoubtedly, a great deal of information is compiled by chiefs, band councils, and provincial government politicians before decisions are made to site a new casino, expand a VLT program, or develop a community gaming centre. However, most of this information is finance-related and focuses on the benefits that are expected to accrue from the new gambling venture. In contrast, typically very little information about the potential social costs of the gambling initiative is gathered and weighed before decisions are made. It has only been within the past few years that there has been any interest on the part of Canadian provincial governments in consulting the people or conducting social and economic impact assessments prior to introducing or expanding gambling opportunities.[10] To date, no Aboriginal community in Canada has ever conducted a thorough socio-economic impact gambling assessment prior to introducing a gambling initiative.

GAMBLING RESEARCH IN ABORIGINAL COMMUNITIES

Over the past decade, gambling studies have emerged as an important area of academic inquiry.[11] Up to the mid-1990s, there were only a handful of academic researchers studying gambling, and these pioneers were mainly psychologists and mental health therapists interested in the social issue that was variously identified as compulsive, problem, or pathological gambling, or gambling addiction.[12] Since these early years, there has been an explosion of academic interest in studying gambling and problem gambling. Once the veritable private domain of psychologists, the field has captured the interest of academics and researchers from other disciplines, who have accepted the challenge of contributing to the knowledge base.

University academics have their own gambling research agendas, and these are heavily influenced by the availability of funding and the priorities of the funding agency. In Canada, many university professors rely on funding from two major research institutions established to specifically fund gambling research—namely, the Ontario Problem Gambling Research Centre (OPGRC) and the Alberta Gaming Research Institute (AGRI).[13] At $4 million, the OPGRC has the largest annual gambling research budget in the world; the AGRI budget is also substantial at $1.5 million a year. An analysis of the research projects funded by the OPGRC and AGRI is illustrative of the general lack of academic interest and support for studying gambling in Aboriginal communities in Canada. Of the six gambling research funding priorities listed on the OPGRC website, none make reference to the importance of research in Ontario Aboriginal communities. As a result, of seventy-four major research projects and 108 minor grants awarded by the OPGRC between 2000 and 2008, only three have focussed on studying gambling in Aboriginal communities in Ontario. Similarly, although the AGRI website states that the socio-cultural domain and research on Aboriginal issues is a priority, only four of the forty-nine research projects funded between 2001 and 2008 have examined gambling in Aboriginal populations or communities.

Coupled with the apparent general lack of academic interest and agency support for studying gambling in Aboriginal communities in Canada is the problem that those who do conduct research inevitably develop agendas that reflect their own interests. The issue here is that gambling research on Aboriginal populations that is of interest to a university professor may be of marginal interest or usefulness to Aboriginal leaders, who may have a greater need to address other issues, such as the impact of gambling within their communities. This raises three fundamental questions related to setting the gambling research agenda in Aboriginal communities: (1) who should set the gambling research agenda in Aboriginal communities; (2) what knowledge garnered through gambling research is most important; and (3) who should ultimately conduct and own the research? In my view, it is crucial that Aboriginal leaders and researchers assume joint responsibility for establishing the gambling research agenda that will ultimately be implemented in the community. The agenda-setting process must involve collaboration between Aboriginal leaders and university academics, or other researchers who have the expertise to develop research plans for undertaking projects in the most rigorous manner possible. This collaboration between the Aboriginal community and researcher should include, as a first step, an exploration of the gambling research needs of the community. What do the chief and band council need to know about gambling and problem gambling in the community? Why does the community need this information, and how will it be used? What is already known or suspected about the role and impact of gambling? These preliminary questions can help focus the research agenda on specific projects, provide the rationale for undertaking these, and help set priorities for the sequencing of projects to ensure that knowledge builds progressively.

I would argue that setting a gambling research agenda and conducting studies in Aboriginal communities is ideally a partnership between the community and the researcher. There must be some mutual benefit in this joint venture. For instance, the community may gain information that helps maximize the benefits of gambling while minimizing the harmful effects associated with problem gambling. The university professor may gain funding for her research interests, opportunities to publish articles in scholarly journals, tenure promotions, and a general satisfaction knowing she has helped make conditions better in the community. Finally, I would advocate that the Aboriginal community and researcher share in the ownership of the research agenda and projects facilitated therein. While research contracts will inevitably establish ownership in a legal sense, the Aboriginal community and researcher should endeavour to agree that they jointly own the research process and outcome, as this implies that both parties have a responsibility for ensuring that the research makes a positive difference to the community.

PARTICIPATORY ACTION RESEARCH (PAR)

Different research approaches in the social sciences have evolved from fundamentally different paradigms. Two main paradigms that continue to guide enquiry in the social sciences are positivism (sometimes referred to as functionalism) and interpretive sociology.[14] Positivism has clearly been the most ubiquitous and influential paradigm in the social sciences, and its roots may be traced to the writings of Auguste Comte, Herbert Spencer, and Emile Durkheim.[15] Interpretive sociology has its origins in the philosophy of Immanuel Kant and the writings of German idealists including Wilhelm Dilthey, Max Weber, and Edmund Husserl.[16]

Modern quantitative research is grounded in the positivist paradigm. This approach assumes there is an objective reality in the social world that can be discovered and explored using systematic, rigorous scientific methods of observation. There is reliance on numbers as a proxy for reality and on empiricism as the process of observation and experimentation; these lead to findings that are verifiable, generalizable, and immutable. Given the central importance of numerical data, the science of statistics is the fundamental analytical tool used to extract meaning from observations. In contrast, qualitative research has been defined as a situated activity that locates the observer in the real world.[17] Qualitative research, as a set of interpretive activities, privileges no single methodological practice over another and is multidisciplinary in focus.[18] One important methodology that has emerged from within the qualitative research domain is participatory action research (PAR), which underpins the approach described in this chapter to researching gambling in Aboriginal communities in Canada.

Participatory action research has been described in qualitative research literature by other names, including participatory research, critical action research, classroom action research, action learning, action science, soft systems approaches, and industrial action research.[19] There are essentially two key concepts that define PAR. The first is *action*. The focus of PAR is not on the research itself but on the research as a means to an end, which is to take action to improve a situation, typically a social, health, or economic problem faced by a community. The second concept is the *participation* in the research-action process of those people who are directly affected by the problem or situation being studied. Based on these concepts, my definition of PAR is as follows:

> Participatory action research (PAR) is a process through which group members and researchers form a working partnership based on the principles of democracy and empowerment to (a) identify and research social, health, education, economic or other problems facing the group; and (b) plan and implement actions to facilitate positive change.

This is an operational definition of PAR, as it contains elements that can guide or operationalize the research process.

First, the definition identifies who must be directly involved in the research process: namely, group members and researchers. Group members may be citizens, teachers and students in a school, members of an Aboriginal community, workers in a factory, health care providers, members of the gay and lesbian community, new immigrants, unemployed auto workers, senior citizens, or members of any other social group interested in researching a problem that affects the group. Researchers may include sociologists, anthropologists, psychologists, educators, economists, health professionals, private consultants, government officials, and others who have special knowledge about the problem domain and the expertise to design and implement research plans that explore the problem and facilitate action solutions.

Second, the definition describes a context that is predicated on the principles of democracy and empowerment. This means that joint decision making must occur in a democratic forum, with both researchers and group members able to nominate projects for the research agenda, decide which projects will proceed, and determine how information will be used and action strategies for change implemented. Furthermore, group members must be empowered so they may become full participants in the research process. A democratic milieu will help accomplish this; however, group members must also be given knowledge about the general nature of problem and research/action planning approaches to resolution so they feel empowered and comfortable enough to participate. Beyond this, group members who work alongside researchers must be given knowledge about research planning, data collection and analysis, interpretation of findings, formulation of conclusions, and development of action strategies so they may be full participants in the research process. The knowledge and experience these group members gain will help build capacity within the group to continue with research projects and monitor action plan outcomes once the PAR project winds down.

Third, the definition identifies what must be the focus of the research; that is, social, health, education, economic, or other problems that are adversely affecting the group. The first task of the researcher-group partners is to arrive at a shared understanding of the problem that brought them together. Problems may include lack of job opportunities, health issues such as diabetes, addictions including problem gambling, persecution for religious beliefs, low morale within teaching staff, impact of an oil pipeline, or lack of community sanitation systems. From a shared understanding of the problem, the research process can be focussed to provide the information needed by the partners to design and implement changes to improve the situation.

Finally, this operational definition of PAR reminds the researcher-group partners that the ultimate goal of the research process is to deliver information that can be used to plan and implement actions to facilitate positive change. The focus of the PAR approach is not on the research itself, but rather on ensuring that the research generates the type of information that is needed to remedy the problem that brought the researcher-group together in the first place.

The PAR approach is iterative and invariably involves a cycle of revisitation of the original problem, with new information gleaned through ongoing research, and monitoring and evaluating the outcomes of action plans that are implemented to improve conditions. In this sense, although the group and researcher will likely disengage at some point, the PAR process is never ending, as most social problems are never truly solved. At the very least, once the PAR process is nominally completed, it is prudent to have a mechanism in place to keep an eye on the problem that precipitated the need for research and action in the first place.

PAR EXPERIENCES IN CANADIAN ABORIGINAL COMMUNITIES

Since the early twentieth century, Aboriginal people in Canada have been studied ad infinitum by university professors from a host of disciplines, government officials, church leaders, business consultants, health care providers, and others who have ostensibly been concerned about social, health, economic, and other conditions in Aboriginal communities. Even when this research was motivated purely by an interest in improving community conditions, the approach was often misguided and paternalistic. Outside researchers typically objectified Aboriginal people, their communities, and their socio-health problems by viewing them as subjects to be studied through a microscope using a top-down approach. Most of these outsiders rode into the community, looked around and gathered some information, and then rode out again. Elder James Ross of Fort MacPherson, Northwest Territories, quipped, "They remind us of ducks. We see them first in the late spring after break-up and they go south before freeze-up in the fall."[20] Whatever information these researchers found was usually analyzed and interpreted in offices outside the community. Conclusions and recommendations for action were also crafted in the outside world and often thrust upon the community—if there was any action taken at all—without explanation or concern for implementation or monitoring outcomes. Overall, it may be argued that the collective socio-health research experience in Canadian Aboriginal communities has been unsatisfactory, from the peoples' perspective, in facilitating the real social change that is in many instances so desperately needed.

Against this dismal backdrop, there have been some positive examples of PAR approaches that have been successfully undertaken in Canadian Aboriginal communities, and it is instructive to synthesize what may be learned from these. The first example describes a ten-year (1971–1982) community development project in Big Trout Lake, Ontario, directed at the problem of developing a sanitation and water supply system for the community.[21] At the time, about 700 Nishnawbe-speaking indigenous people lived on the Big Trout Lake Indian Reserve. In 1972 the Department of Indian Affairs and Northern Development (DIAND) hired an engineering firm to develop a water and sewer system. However, the plan was to only provide a wastewater collection system to service the Hudson Bay complex, nursing station, school, Anglican Church, and band council hall. No native homes were to be included on the sewer line, even though none of these homes had running water or flush toilets. Without addressing the community's concern that services would not be extended to their homes, the DIAND commenced construction of the project in 1976 by inadvertently blowing up some unmarked graves near the local cemetery. Appalled, the band council stopped the project and forbade DIAND contractors from entering their land, passing a strongly worded resolution that made it clear to DIAND that construction would only resume after several conditions had been met. With the help of a staff member from the regional Economic Development Bureau, the band council itself funded and implemented a PAR approach to come up with a research-based solution for completing this project. This approach included the agreement that "the community would direct the research as well as being involved in carrying it out, from formulating the problem to deciding on the course of action."[22] The band employed a team whose members included a sanitary engineer, technical advisor, chemical limnologist, environmental health specialist, and a participatory research specialist (team leader), and this team worked together with a larger team of Big Trout Lake residents as the Community Assessment Committee. During the period between 1976 and 1981, this team of consultants met with DIAND, the Department of Environment, and other federal department officials many times to try to resolve issues that were impediments to the construction proceeding; however, at every turn the band was stalled and thwarted by the federal government bureaucracy. Ted Jackson and Gerry McKay concluded their narrative by stating, "as of this writing the concrete results of this project have been rather limited"; specifically, "there is no community-wide waste and water system in place."[23] Notwithstanding this lack of concrete success, they do enumerate a number of positive outcomes associated with the PAR process itself.

A second instructive PAR experience describes Nin.da.waab.jig, a "cooperative research program" on resource management between the University of Windsor and Walpole Island Indian Reserve.[24] Although a land claim research unit on the reserve already existed, the band and university entered into an agreement to collaborate on research projects of mutual benefit. This is an important case study as it illustrates how a mutually beneficial research relationship can be developed between an Aboriginal community and university. The agreement itself is illuminating as it describes how the community and university collaborate:

> 1) Particular research projects might be suggested either by the band or the university researchers, subject to approval by the band council.
>
> 2) Research funds would be sought by the university from outside sources; however, the band might be asked to provide support in the form of work space and other resources, where appropriate. The band council, at its own discretion, could seek funding to support such projects.
>
> 3) Band members would be encouraged to work on projects as co-researchers or field assistants and to participate in related workshops, courses, and training sessions. Where a project involved the hiring of field workers, an attempt would be made to employ band members and university students as teams in equal proportions.
>
> 4) The results of research on the reserve would be made available to the band. Any potentially sensitive matters would be discussed with band representatives before publication, and the band council would determine any potentially sensitive matters.[25]

This agreement contains two main PAR elements—namely, collaborative research agenda-setting and band-researcher joint participation in research projects. Although an action-oriented focus on community problems was not formally included in the agreement, Hedley identified some problems the group agreed were candidates for research projects (e.g., problems of fall ploughing in relation to soil quality and erosion); presumably, research was intended to lead to action to remedy these. It is not clear from the article which research projects were ultimately undertaken or if any action resulted from these.

The final example of an Aboriginal community PAR project is a study of gambling and problem gambling in five Aboriginal communities in Ontario.[26] The Ontario Ministry of Health and Long Term Care (OMHLTC) was concerned about the high problem-gambling prevalence rate in the Ontario Aboriginal population, so they provided funding to the Ontario Problem Gambling Research Centre (OPGRC) to study the issue. Working under the aegis of the OPGRC, John McCready and I developed a research strategy predicated on a PAR approach that empowered five Aboriginal communities to control the research and action planning process in their communities. The five Aboriginal communities—Moosonee, North Bay, Welland/Niagara, Ottawa, and Thunder Bay—set about to research gambling and problem gambling in their populations and take action at the local level; however, they also worked in collaboration with one another to offer mutual support and discern what could be learned from this experience across all five communities.

When the research phase was completed, each Aboriginal community was ready and prepared to enter the "action planning phase" to develop and implement strategies to mitigate problem gambling. However, at this point the researchers and community advisory committees disengaged and, in the end, only some communities were successful in garnering resources from the provincial OMHLTC for problem-gambling program initiatives.

KNOWLEDGE GAINED FROM PAR EXPERIENCES

In developing a PAR approach to researching gambling in Aboriginal communities, it is useful to distil what has been learned from these previous experiences described above. The Big Trout Lake experience addressing the problem of a sanitation and water supply system is the first case in point. On the surface, it may appear as if this PAR project was unsuccessful, as it did not result in the desired outcome, which was the actual construction of a water and sewer system for the community. However, this fact in itself provides some knowledge, including: (a) regardless of the amount of effort a group invests, success in achieving a goal may be thwarted by power bases outside the group; (b) even if the ultimate goal is not achieved, there are often successes along the way; and (c) whether goals are met or not, empowerment through PAR raises group consciousness and builds capacity that leaves the community better able to address the problem in the future. Jackson and McKay identified other positive PAR outcomes at Big Trout Lake, notwithstanding that the ultimate construction goal was not achieved, and these included: (a) *new* knowledge was produced; (b) the community learned to control this new knowledge and information they now "owned" and use this to benefit the community; (c) the community was empowered by maintaining control over the money and the consultants; (d) consultants became politicized and supportive of First Nation self-determination goals; (e) the PAR project required different types of consultants, so a natural cross-fertilization of disciplines occurred; (f) the band and researchers both had uses for the information generated, so an accommodation was struck to facilitate joint-use and dissemination; and (g) products of the PAR project—in this case the "users-making-choices" manual—were appropriated by others outside the community.[27]

The research relationship between the University of Windsor and Walpole Island Indian Reserve also sheds light on important elements of the PAR process.[28] Limitations of the experience are especially enlightening, and these include: (a) when the research group contracts to do projects with outside agencies, there may be constraints on the problem selection and research design; (b) externally imposed demands on researchers—especially university professors—may lessen the time they have to complete ongoing Aboriginal community research projects; and (c) an Aboriginal community-university cooperative research program may become institutionalized, bureaucratized, and inwardly-focussed—and thus less devoted to researching community problems in the PAR tradition.

Finally, the PAR project that studied gambling and problem gambling in five Ontario Aboriginal communities also included experiences that are instructive.[29] First, while the impetus for studying problem gambling in the Ontario Aboriginal population came from the Ontario provincial health department, a PAR approach was utilized that allowed the Aboriginal communities to plan and carry out the research themselves. This demonstrates that even when research to address Aboriginal community problems is externally funded, control can be transferred to the community using a PAR approach. Second, researchers with expertise in studying problem gambling and utilizing the PAR process, and experience working with Aboriginal communities, were retained to work directly with local communities to help the people successfully complete the research. This underscores the importance of engaging researchers who are knowledgeable about the community problem under study, who have expertise and experience utilizing the PAR approach, and who have experience working with Aboriginal people. Third, intra- and inter-community participation and communications were facilitated through an advisory committee structure that operated at both local and regional levels. This demonstrates the merit of establishing an organizational structure that provides a forum for community-member participation and management of the PAR process. Fourth, Aboriginal community and advisory committee members, through workshops and on-going interaction with the researchers, were given knowledge about the nature and characteristics of problem gambling and how to develop research plans and gather and analyze data. This educational process empowers the group, as members feel more knowledgeable about their community problem and how to operationalize a PAR project to address it. Finally, the advisory committees in each community hired project coordinators and research assistants, and these people were trained by the researchers to conduct community surveys, facilitate focus group sessions, conduct key informant interviews, develop problem-gambler case studies, analyze both statistical and qualitative data, and write final reports. Hiring and training community members to work on the PAR project demonstrates a commitment to full participation and collaboration between the researcher and Aboriginal community. Moreover, it provides community entry that researches may not gain on their own and builds capacity and confidence within the community to undertake similar PAR projects in the future.

Two problems experienced in this Ontario Aboriginal community gambling research project are also noteworthy. The first is associated with hiring local project coordinators and research assistants in the communities. The arrival of this new gambling study generated interest in each community, and some people aspired to be involved as paid project coordinators or assistants. Staff recruitment and hiring was left up to each community advisory committee, and, in most cases, this process went smoothly and the most appropriate people were employed. However, in other communities, research jobs were hotly contested and perceived conflicts-of-interest led to hard feelings and, conceivably, the best people not being hired. This experience shows that hiring community members to work within the PAR project is not a straightforward exercise, and hiring practices should be carefully considered while the research is being planned. The second problem is related to the lack of action planning as a follow-up to the research process. Although the Ontario health ministry provided funding for the research, they failed to follow this up with funding for a subsequent action planning stage. The assumption was that each Aboriginal community—armed with its research findings about problem gambling—would petition the health ministry for program funds to improve the situation. The researchers were discharged and no longer available to help the communities develop action plans and lobby for funding; consequently, virtually no action was taken in the Aboriginal communities to mitigate problem gambling as a direct result of this PAR project. This demonstrates that a lack of funding and premature disengagement of researchers from the PAR project may result in the community being left to its own devices. The researcher and Aboriginal community should discuss this potentiality at the outset, with measures being taken to ensure that action plans are formulated before the PAR project winds down.

To reflect, much has been learned from PAR experiences in Canadian Aboriginal communities. Even when PAR outcomes are not achieved, as with the sanitation and water supply system in Big Trout Lake, or with establishing action plans to deal with problem gambling in Ontario Aboriginal communities, the experience can result in other successes along the journey. For instance, awareness of community problems is raised and the people feel a sense of empowerment and confidence that they can control a research process directed at improving local conditions. New knowledge is gained and, when ownership is vested in the community, this knowledge can be used for community benefit. PAR experiences in Aboriginal communities have also contributed insights into cultural sensitivity and community entry, mutually beneficial community-researcher agreements, collaboration to identify and illuminate the community problem(s) under study, joint development of research and action plans, and methodological approaches that are at the same time rigorous and participatory. Armed with these contributions from others and my experience as a team member in the Ontario Aboriginal problem-gambling study, I offer for consideration the following PAR approach to conducting gambling research in Canadian Aboriginal communities.

PAR APPROACH TO GAMBLING RESEARCH

The knowledge gained from Aboriginal community PAR projects has been presented in some detail, as researchers and Aboriginal leaders who wish to undertake PAR projects to study gambling have much to gain from reflecting on these experiences. For instance, there is much to learn from the Big Trout Lake experience about the community–government agency relationship and the merit of community ownership of the PAR process. This raises the question, what are the implications of a provincial addictions agency or gambling research foundation funding the Aboriginal gambling research? Similarly, the University of Windsor–Walpole Island Indian Reserve agreement demonstrates the need for a reciprocal relationship that is beneficial to both the researcher and Aboriginal community. Given that much of the gambling research funding is only available to university professors who have a need to publish, the question is, how can this imperative be reconciled with the community's need to participate in the research and share ownership of the information that results? Finally, I have also recounted some of what I learned from my experience working with five Ontario Aboriginal communities on the PAR project to study gambling and problem gambling. This includes: the importance of ensuring community owner-ship of the project even if funding is provided by the provincial government; the merit of having researchers with expertise in the problem, the PAR process, and working in Aboriginal communities; the utility of community advisory commit-tees in facilitating democracy and empowerment; the need to impart knowledge to community participants about the problem and PAR process; the importance of carefully hiring community members to work on the PAR project; and the need to ensure that action will result from the research process.

In addition to this experiential knowledge, it is useful to have a framework that can serve as a heuristic device for guiding the PAR process in Aboriginal com-munities. The model presented in Figure 1 is an attempt to synthesize what has been learned from these PAR experiences, and the description that follows focuses on problem gambling as the problem the Aboriginal community seeks to address.

FIGURE 1: Participatory Action Research Model

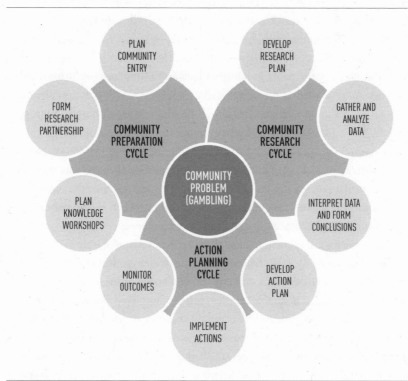

THE THREE CYCLES — Central to the PAR model are three overlapping cycles of activity: community preparation, community research, and action planning. Each of these activity cycles is distinct; however, for the PAR process to proceed, all three must be successfully completed. The PAR process begins with the community preparation cycle. First, an interest in examining the indicated community problem—in this example, problem gambling—must be articulated by someone (i.e., chief and band council, university professor, addictions treatment agency, government department). Once the prospective presence of problem gambling has been raised, Aboriginal community leaders must be approached to validate that this is, indeed, an issue they are at least prepared to consider studying through the PAR process. To begin the process, preparations must then be made to formalize the relationship between the researcher and Aboriginal community, to prepare and sensitize the researcher(s) for entering and working in the community, and to impart knowledge about problem gambling and the PAR research process to community members.

The second cycle is the PAR research process itself. Once the Aboriginal community and researcher have committed to proceeding with the project, the first step is to develop a research plan that defines the problem and presents a methodology for examining problem gambling. The research plan is implemented through data collection and analysis activities. The final task is for the researcher and Aboriginal participants to interpret data and formulate conclusions. These findings are then used as the input for the final cycle, which is action planning. The action planning process involves developing a research-based action plan that includes initiatives specifically designed to mitigate problem gambling. Once the action plan has been developed mounting the specific initiatives identified, such as problem gambling treatment and prevention, programs must then be operationalized. Finally, the action planning cycle recognizes the importance of monitoring the outcomes of these program initiatives, to ensure that they are having the desired effect of mitigating problem gambling.

There is a logical sequence to the three action cycles; that is, the community preparation stage proceeds the research cycle, which in turn comes before action planning. Each cycle can stand on its own; however, for the entire PAR process to be effective, it is important that each be completed. For example, if only the community preparation cycle is undertaken, the researcher and Aboriginal community might be prepared and willing to study problem gambling, but this good intention will never be accomplished because of a failure to proceed beyond this stage. This may happen when there is a willingness to study problem gambling in Aboriginal populations but no funding available to proceed. The presence of only the community research cycle is an example of the way that university professors have traditionally studied problems in Aboriginal communities. That is, the research is an academic exercise that is located *in* the community but is not *of* the community, as Aboriginal people have not been full participants, nor has there been any thought given to taking action in the community based on the researchers' findings. Finally, if only the action planning cycle is present, there is the danger that well-intentioned initiatives may be mounted only to fail because they are not predicated on sound research or full participation of community members. There are many examples of Canadian federal government programs that have been parachuted into Aboriginal communities only to fail because they were ill-conceived and not advised by community-based research.

The community problem is always the focus in each of the three cycles, and it serves as the ultimate touchstone for each. That is, the community preparation cycle focuses on a willingness and preparedness to study the problem; the community research cycle posits a plan and gathers data to help understand the problem; and the action planning cycle makes sure this information precipitates action to address the problem and effect positive change. Although there is an implicit sequencing in the three cycles, these should be viewed as an interconnected group with the focus shifting back and forth between the cycles, as need dictates. For example, the researcher may discover that initial perceptions of the prevalence of problem gambling in the community are overstated and that the co-morbid condition of alcoholism is more problematic. This may cause the group to re-enter the community preparation cycle to discuss and formulate a different definition of the community problem. In a similar vein, it is possible that an action taken to mount a treatment program is not successful in attracting problem gamblers, and this may result in revisiting the research cycle to identify peoples' preferences for treatment modalities. In the final analysis, one should view the PAR model as being dynamic, and the researcher and Aboriginal community PAR participants must feel comfortable moving within and among the three cycles as part of the process.

COMMUNITY PREPARATION CYCLE — There are specific tasks within each of the three cycles that must be undertaken by researchers and Aboriginal community participants as they proceed with the PAR project. In the community preparation cycle, the tasks include: (a) forming a research partnership; (b) planning community entry; and (c) planning knowledge workshops. As a preliminary step, an individual or group must raise the possibility that a problem exists in the Aboriginal community and that something should be done about it. The chief and band council, a member of a community women's group, a government department such as Indian and Northern Affairs Canada, or a university professor in a native studies program may express this concern. If there is initial agreement that this problem and remedial action are a priority, the first task in the community preparation cycle is to establish a partnership between researcher(s) and Aboriginal community members who will come together and assume responsibility for the research and action response. The research partnership should be clearly based on the principles of democracy and empowerment, the full participation of community members, and the joint ownership of the PAR process and information outcomes. If there is consensus that a formal agreement will establish these principles and clarify the roles of various stakeholders, then this should be considered. Furthermore, the partnership should consider mechanisms to facilitate community participation, such as establishing a research advisory committee that provides an opportunity for the people to be heard. Similarly, special provisions should be made to involve community elders in the PAR process in a way that respects their status and wisdom. Finally, the partnership should ensure that financial and other resources would be available to sustain the process beyond the research cycle to the action planning cycle, so that program initiatives may be implemented to improve conditions.

The second task in the community preparation cycle is to develop a concrete plan for entering the community. This refers to both introducing the PAR project to the community and sensitizing non-community researchers to cultural values, norms, attitudes, and nuances they must respect. For instance, community members may wonder why Aboriginal people and their community have been singled out for a study of problem gambling. Does this mean there is a problem-gambling epidemic? The partners must anticipate these types of questions, and responses must be carefully considered and communicated. Beyond this, outsiders working on the PAR project must be sensitized about how to behave when they are in the community so as to be accepted by the people. Here, it is useful for community leaders to develop a list of behavioural "dos and don'ts" and discuss this with researchers and other outsiders who may be working on the PAR project.

The final task in the community preparation cycle is to plan knowledge workshops that inform the people about gambling, the issue of problem gambling, and the purpose of the research project, which is to study this issue in their community and, if warranted, take action to help lessen problem gambling. This knowledge must not be imparted in a condescending manner; that is, the attitude of the presenters should not be that they have come to "educate" the ignorant community people. The purpose of the knowledge workshops is not just to inform but also to empower the people by sharing what is known about problem gambling and making people feel comfortable studying this social problem themselves and actually doing something about it. The second type of information that needs to be delivered through knowledge workshops is directed at community members who will be hired as employees of the PAR research project. A hiring strategy should be carefully developed by the partners and, once the PAR employees have been selected, the researchers should undertake a formal training process to provide information on research planning; design and methodology; data collection, analysis, and interpretation; action planning; program development and implementation; monitoring and evaluating outcomes; report writing; and any other skill areas that are required.

COMMUNITY RESEARCH CYCLE — The community research cycle is central to the PAR process. Without credible and trustworthy information about gambling and problem gambling in the community, actions that may be taken to deal with the problem are more likely to be ill-advised and ineffective. The researchers who are in partnership with the Aboriginal community must have the expertise to structure the research problem and develop an appropriate research plan that will provide the results necessary to inform action strategies. The research planning process begins with a restructuring of the community problem first articulated through the community preparation cycle. For instance, the partners may have started out to study the prevalence of problem gambling in the Aboriginal community; however, through the research planning process, it may be discovered that this focus needs to be broadened to encompass a study of gambling in general; problem gambling as a subset of all gambling; and co-morbidity issues, such as alcohol and drug abuse, that may be associated with gambling. There also may be a need to study treatment preferences and the types of problem-gambling prevention strategies that may work. Clearly, it is not possible to study all these areas at once, which suggests that it would be useful to establish a research agenda that sequences a series of gambling studies over time, with one building on another.

The research plan may include a multi-study agenda, with the PAR process beginning with the first study, perhaps a gambling and problem-gambling prevalence study. The specific plan for this study will identify research questions that guide the inquiry and methods for gathering and analyzing data, which will be the second important task in the community research cycle. Required data addressing the research questions must be identified, along with the best methods for collecting these. Much of the data will be perceptual; for instance, in a prevalence study people in the community will be asked to report on their gambling activities and answer questions that may identify them as problem gamblers. They may also be asked to comment on the negative consequences they have experienced from problem gambling. Community research assistants, through face-to-face interviews, will typically gather these perceptual data, and the truthfulness of this information will be dependent on the type of questions posed and the demeanour and skill of the interviewers. The data gathering and analysis task is of central importance to the entire PAR process. Comprehensive, credible, and trustworthy information is crucial to ensure that the correct action strategies are designed and implemented.

The final task in the community research cycle is to interpret the data that have been gathered and formulate conclusions. In most non-PAR gambling studies, the researcher analyzes the statistical and qualitative data, interprets the meaning, and posits conclusions. This process is different in a PAR project, as not only do the community members on the research team have an opportunity to view and interpret the data and draw conclusions, but the community itself can also participate in this process. For example, when the data are gathered and analyzed, a knowledge workshop might be organized to present the findings about gambling and problem gambling to the community. Part of this workshop process may also be to ask members, first, whether these findings seem truthful to them, and second, what these results mean and what may be concluded.

The communication of research results could also be expanded to sister Aboriginal communities as a form of triangulation to discover whether other Aboriginal people have the same experiences associated with gambling and problem gambling in their communities. By sharing the interpretation process with others outside the research team and enjoining them to help formulate conclusions, the research will be more rigorous, and it is conceivable that new knowledge will also be discovered.

ACTION PLANNING CYCLE — The ultimate goal of the PAR process is to develop action strategies to address the community problem under study. This takes place in the final component in the PAR model: the action planning cycle. The action planning cycle relies on information provided from the community research cycle as the main input in the development of an action plan. The task of action planning requires experience and a special skill set that gambling researchers do not necessarily have; consequently, the partners should determine whether they need to add someone with program development expertise to the research team. The process of action planning involves: (a) determination of action alternatives based on research information; (b) establishment of an inventory of community resources that may be used to support action initiatives (e.g., organizations, expertise, leaders, funding, volunteers, facilities); (c) development of an improvement strategy; (d) identification of accountability for implementing the strategy; (e) development of performance indicators to measure outcomes of action initiatives; (f) implementation of the improvement strategy and specific action initiatives; and (g) observation of the progress of action initiatives and evaluation of outcomes.

The second PAR task in the action planning cycle is to implement action initiatives. Up to this stage, the action plan is still largely a paper and pencil exercise. There are numerous examples of problem-gambling action plans that have been submitted to provincial governments and other agencies but have failed to receive the funding needed for implementation. In some cases, Aboriginal action plans to address problem gambling were deemed not to have sufficiently demonstrated the need or articulated an appropriate program response strategy to mitigate problem gambling. In other instances, there was simply not enough funding available, as other program needs took priority. Clearly, funding is a necessary ingredient in the implementation of problem-gambling action plans in Aboriginal communities; however, by going through the process of inventorying community resources, it is sometimes possible to find alternatives to total reliance on outside funding agencies. The program developer may find creative ways to accomplish this implementation (e.g., relying on other organizations for office space and administrative support; developing fundraising campaigns; negotiating free advertising from newspapers, radio, and television; training community para-professional problem-gambling counsellors; and relying on tele-health technology to connect to outside counselling services). It is important to reiterate that the partners must make a strong commitment during the community preparation cycle to seeing the research result in action, regardless of how difficult it may be to garner the resources needed to implement action initiatives.

The final task in the action planning cycle is to monitor outcomes from the various action initiatives that have been implemented. Although a problem-gambling treatment or prevention program may have been successfully implemented, there is no guarantee that it is functioning as expected to address the problem. During the program development process, it is essential to identify key performance indicators that may ultimately be monitored and measured to determine whether the initiative is effectively meeting its goals and resulting in the outcomes desired. Just as gambling researchers may not have action planning or program development skills, they may also not have the expertise to develop effective evaluation plans. Consequently, the partners should ask themselves during the community preparation cycle whether it would be prudent to add an evaluator to the research team to undertake this final PAR task. Outcomes should be monitored on a continuous basis, with adjustments to action initiatives being made as these are warranted. Beyond this, there should be summative evaluations undertaken at regular intervals to assess the overall impact of the action on mitigating problem gambling in the community. Finally, the information gleaned from both monitoring and evaluation exercises should be communicated to Aboriginal community members, preferably through knowledge workshops where the people can come and hear first-hand what impact the research and action taken has had on addressing the issue of problem gambling.

FINAL COMMENT

Many Aboriginal communities in Canada experience both significant benefits and costs from casinos and other gambling opportunities. Gambling revenues provide clear advantages to the community when these are invested in housing, employment, recreation, social services, health, infrastructure, and other human service areas. Regrettably, we anticipate these benefits come with a significant social cost that is attributable to problem gambling, which causes individual and family breakdown that ultimately leaves the community worse off. The dilemma facing Aboriginal leaders is how to establish gambling policies that maximize the benefits from gambling revenues while mitigating the costs associated with problem gambling. The quality of these gambling policy decisions is dramatically enhanced when they are based on credible and trustworthy information gained through community-based research. This chapter introduces the merit of using a PAR approach to acquiring the knowledge needed to inform gambling policy decisions.

The PAR approach to studying gambling in Aboriginal communities is empowering, as the people are directly involved in all aspects of the research process and in taking action to mitigate problem gambling. Moreover, the PAR process ensures that the information gathered is grounded in the experience of Aboriginal people, who participate in interpreting information, forming conclusions, and taking action that will ultimately lead to positive change. However, the PAR process is not without its challenges. For instance, Michael Robinson points to three challenges to the growing acceptance of using PAR in Aboriginal communities: first, the greater time commitment and cost of PAR when compared to individual positivistic research methods; second, the need to train a young generation of PAR practitioner/trainers to replace the first Canadian generation of PAR disciples; and third, the need to overcome the traditional academic recognition and reward system.[30] To be sure, these are challenges to PAR. Perhaps they are best overcome through partnerships between Aboriginal communities and Canadian universities that are dedicated to building PAR capacity and interest in both the community and academic setting.

NOTES

1   Statistics Canada, *Gambling, Perspectives on Labour and Income* (Ottawa: Statistics Canada, Sept. 2008).

2   François Vaillancourt and Alexandre Roy, *Gambling and Government in Canada, 1969–1998: How Much? Who Pays? What Pay-off?* Special Studies in Taxation and Public Finance (Ottawa: Canadian Tax Foundation, 2000).

3   Canadian Partnership for Responsible Gambling, *Canadian Gambling Digest: 2006–2007*, 2008, www.cprg.ca.

4   Yale D. Belanger. "First Nations Gaming as a Self-government Imperative? Ensuring the Health of First Nations Problem Gamblers." *International Journal of Canadian Studies* 41 (2010): 1-24.

5   Ibid.

6   Katherine Marshall and Harold Wynne, "Fighting the Odds," *Perspectives* (Ottawa: Statistics Canada, catalogue no. 75-001-XIE, 2003).

7   Harold Wynne, *Gambling and Problem Gambling in Saskatchewan: Final Report* (Ottawa: Canadian Centre on Substance Abuse, 2002). http://www.health.gov.sk.ca/adx/aspx/adxGetMedia.aspx?DocID=317,94,88,Documents&MediaID=166&Filename=gambling-final-report.pdf. (last accessed 11 July 2010).

8   Garry Smith and Harold J. Wynne, *Measuring Gambling and Problem Gambling in Alberta Using the Canadian Problem Gambling Index (CPGI): Final Report*, Alberta Gaming Research Institute (2002), 23, http://hdl.handle.net/1880/1626.

9   Thomas Dye, *Understanding Public Policy*, 2nd ed. (Englewood Cliffs, NJ: Prentice-Hall, 1975).

10   Harold Wynne and Howard Shaffer, "The Socioeconomic Impact of Gambling: The Whistler Symposium," *Journal of Gambling Studies* 19, 2 (2003): 111–121.

11   Gerda Reith, "Situating Gambling Studies," in *Research and Measurement Issues in Gambling Studies*, ed. Garry Smith, D. Smith, and R. Williams (Burlington, MA: Elsevier, 2007).

12   Robert Wildman, *Gambling: An Attempt at an Integration* (Edmonton: Wynne Resources, 1997).

13   Ontario Problem Gambling Research Centre, http://www.gamblingresearch.org; Alberta Gaming Research Institute, http://www.abgaminginsitute.ualberta.ca.

14   Gibson Burrell and Gather Morgan, *Sociological Paradigms and Organizational Analysis* (London: Heinemann Educational Books, 1980).

15   Auguste Comte, *The Positivist Philosophy*, trans. Henri Martineau, vol. I (London: Chapman, 1853); Herbert Spencer, *The Study of Sociology* (London: Kegan Paul and Tench, 1873); Emile Durkheim, *The Rules of Sociological Method* (New York: Free Press, 1938).

16   Wilhelm Dilthey, *Selected Writings*, ed. Hans P. Rickman (London: Cambridge University Press, 1976); Max Weber, *The Methodology of the Social Sciences* (Glencoe, IL: Free Press, 1949); Edmund Husserl, "Phenomenology," *Encyclopedia Brittanica*, 14th ed. (1929).

17 Norman Denzin and Yvonna Lincoln, "The Discipline and Practice of Qualitative Research," in *The Handbook of Qualitative Research*, ed. Norman Denzin and Yvonna Lincoln (Thousand Oaks, CA: Sage, 2000).

18 Denzin and Lincoln, "The Discipline and Practice of Qualitative Research, 2;" Uwe Flick, *An Introduction to Qualitative Research: Theory, Method and Application* (London: Sage, 1998), 229.

19 Stephen Kemmis and Robin McTaggart, "Participatory Action Research," in *The Handbook of Qualitative Research*, ed. Norman Denzin and Yvonna Lincoln (Thousand Oaks, CA: Sage, 2000).

20 Michael Robinson, "Shampoo Archaeology: Towards a Participatory Action Research Approach in Civil Society," *Canadian Journal of Native Studies* 16, 1 (1996): 125–138.

21 Ted Jackson and Gerry McKay, "Sanitation and Water Supply in Big Trout Lake: Participatory Research for Democratic Technical Solutions," *Canadian Journal of Native Studies* 2, 1 (1982): 129–145.

22 Ibid., 133.

23 Ibid., 144.

24 M.J. Hedley, "Community Based Research: The Dilemma of Contract," *Canadian Journal of Native Studies* 6, 1 (1986): 91–103.

25 Ibid., 93.

26 Harold Wynne and John McCready, *Examining Gambling and Problem Gambling in Ontario Aboriginal Communities: Final Summary Report* (submitted on behalf of the Ontario Federation of Indian Friendship Centres and the Métis Nation of Ontario to the Ontario Problem Gambling Research Centre, April 2005); John McCready, *Examining Gambling and Problem Gambling in Ontario Aboriginal Communities: Final Summary Report* (submitted on behalf of the Ontario Federation of Indian Friendship Centres and the Métis Nation of Ontario to the Ontario Problem Gambling Research Centre, April 2005).

27 Jackson and McKay, "Sanitation and Water Supply in Big Trout Lake."

28 Hedley, "Community Based Research."

29 Wynne and McCready, *Examining Gambling and Problem Gambling in Ontario Aboriginal Communities.*

30 Robinson, "Shampoo Archaeology," 131.

CHAPTER 6

EXPLORING GAMBLING IMPACTS IN TWO ALBERTA CREE COMMUNITIES: A PARTICIPATORY ACTION STUDY

GARRY J. SMITH, CHERYL L. CURRIE, AND JAMES BATTLE

INTRODUCTION

Aboriginal Canadians, generally speaking, have not enjoyed the same level of health and well-being, economic independence, or social standing as other Canadians.[1] A recent initiative to assuage these inequities has been the development and operation of First Nations gambling establishments. While games of chance were part of the Aboriginal cultural landscape before European contact, large-scale commercial gaming facilities within First Nations communities are a relatively new phenomenon in Canada.[2] Traditionally, Aboriginal peoples regarded gambling for monetary gain as potentially dangerous for both individuals and communities, and gambling was discouraged if it seriously disadvantaged First Nation community members.[3] Today, gambling occurs in a markedly different socio-political and economic context with different meanings and consequences for Aboriginal peoples. The rapid increase of legalized gambling in Canada since the 1980s has been associated with increasing rates of problem gambling across the country, particularly for Aboriginal Canadians.[4] Compounding this dilemma is the lack of infrastructure for problem-gambling treatment and prevention in many First Nations communities.[5]

High levels of self-destructive and addictive behaviours are commonly found among disadvantaged individuals and communities, and in Canada it is clear that the Aboriginal population is particularly economically and socially disadvantaged.[6] In 2001, Canada ranked eighth on the Human Development Index, while Aboriginal Canadians ranked thirty-third.[7] The socio-economic disparities between Aboriginal and non-Aboriginal Canadians that led to this difference in ranking (e.g., average household income, rates of unemployment) are especially apparent for those First Nations people living within First Nations communities.[8] Currently, Canada's First Nations live on reserved lands that total 0.2 percent of Canada's landmass.[9] The allocation of First Nations lands by the Canadian government proceeded on the assumption that no meaningful development would take place in these communities.[10] As a consequence, the bulk of lands set aside for First Nations are typically of poor quality and too small for most forms of development.[11] Winona LaDuke argues that, in the process of colonialism, First Nations became peripheral to the colonial economy, and a set of relations developed characterized by dependency and underdevelopment. These circumstances have fostered the formation of stereotypes about Aboriginal people that have led to social discrimination and the internalization of these beliefs by Aboriginal peoples themselves.[12]

First Nations casino development has been proposed as a venture that can create jobs, stimulate economic development, and provide revenue for social programs and community infrastructure. However, the need for economic growth in First Nations communities needs to be balanced with the reality that the fiscal benefits of gambling expansion are not guaranteed, as they are influenced heavily by prevailing economic conditions and competition from existing casinos.[13] Increased problem gambling and resulting negative social impacts may also engender costs that outweigh financial gains.[14]

At the community level, elevated levels of suicide have been found among visitors and residents of gambling destinations (e.g., Las Vegas, Atlantic City).[15] At the individual level, problem gambling has been associated with increased suicide risk, financial instability, relationship breakdowns, substance abuse, and crime.[16] Evidence also suggests that close to 60 percent of revenue from electronic gaming machines is derived from players who have difficulty controlling their gambling, and 39 percent of overall gaming revenue is derived from problem gamblers.[17] Given that the highest rates of problem gambling in Canada occur in provinces with high concentrations of electronic gaming machines and permanent casinos, some question the logic of placing casinos in communities that may be more vulnerable to these negative impacts.[18]

Thus, legalized gambling on First Nations lands has been a contentious public policy issue. While casino gaming on First Nations lands continues to expand in Canada, the overall socio-economic impacts of these ventures remain largely unknown.[19] Yale Belanger underscores the dearth of information about the impacts on the economic health of host communities and their members, political stability, cultural continuity, the incidence and prevalence of problem gambling, and the surrounding First Nations communities as particularly troublesome.[20]

The Alberta provincial government developed a First Nations Gaming Policy in 2001. The policy outlines the process to apply for and operate casino facilities on First Nations lands. Several key concessions were made by the Alberta government in order to expedite First Nations casinos. For example, host First Nations are designated as their own charities and may employ charity workers rather than using volunteers; there is a more favourable split of slot machine revenues for First Nations casinos; and the province-wide smoking ban in public buildings does not apply to First Nations casino sites. Since the implementation of the Alberta First Nations Gaming Policy, a number of First Nations communities have expressed interest in having a casino. At present, five Alberta First Nation casinos are operating, including the Enoch Cree band's River Cree Casino, situated just west of the Edmonton city limits, the Tsuu T'ina Grey Eagle Casino in Calgary, the Alexis Eagle River Casino in Whitecourt, the Stoney Nakoda Casino in Morley, and the Dene Casino in Cold Lake.

Samson Cree Nation, located 100 kilometres south of Edmonton, has been approved for casino development but remains undecided about whether to proceed. Although Alberta First Nations are not required to conduct socio-economic impact studies before proceeding with casino development, the Samson Cree community sought information from researchers at the University of Alberta to assist in its decision. The purpose of this study was to provide a starting point for further assessment of the socio-economic impacts that gambling expansion may have on Samson Cree Nation (population 5268). A second community, Ermineskin Cree Nation (population 2633), with no plans for casino development and located adjacent to Samson Cree, was also examined, for the purposes of comparison. Each First Nation selected community-based members to join the research team. Our primary objectives were to work collaboratively with these communities to: (1) select salient indicators of the socio-economic impacts of gambling that could help First Nation communities make informed decisions about gambling expansion; (2) pilot selected measures of these constructs within a small sample of members from each community; and (3) collect data on community perceptions of on-reserve gambling expansion.

METHOD

PROCEDURE — Permission to collect data from residents and use community facilities was obtained from each chief and band council. Data collection was facilitated by community-based members of the research team, who recruited participants, arranged data collection areas, and informed respondents of interview times. Recruitment posters were displayed in each community one week before data collection began. Research assistants from the partner First Nations and the University of Alberta were trained to collect data. The survey took approximately forty-five to sixty minutes to complete; when finished, participants were provided with a twenty-five-dollar honorarium. Participants were encouraged to comment either verbally or in writing on the survey in general or the measures therein. Interest in the survey was high across both communities, and our quota of fifty interviews took only two days rather than the scheduled three.

Data collection in the Ermineskin Cree Nation took place in the Elders' Centre. Five interviewers at separate tables in one large room conducted one-on-one interviews simultaneously. Due to the complexity of some measurement items, the research team decided to read questions to participants in a face-to-face interview format for seven of the eleven measures (including the gambling, alcohol, and nicotine modules; the self-esteem inventory; the health survey; and the demographic and treatment/historical questions). Participants completed the remaining items by hand in the interview room, with researchers available to answer questions. Participants wanting to complete surveys on their own were allowed to do so. As well, all questionnaires were read to participants who requested it or appeared to have difficulty reading the survey. In Ermineskin four participants requested that their questionnaires be completed in an interview format and seven requested to complete the entire survey package by hand.

Data collection in Samson Cree was administered in a large, partitioned-off area of the community bingo hall. As our research team completed the required number of interviews in Ermineskin quicker than expected, we arrived in Samson a day early. Community members were accommodating, calling participants who had volunteered for the subsequent day and announcing our arrival at a community meeting that morning. As a result, news of our early arrival spread quickly and all interviews were completed in the community that day. With fewer interviewers present and many community members wanting to take the survey, it was determined that participants would be read the consent form, but asked to complete all but the treatment/historical questionnaire (deemed the most complicated) on their own. As a result, nineteen of the twenty-three Samson Cree participants completed the entire survey package by hand (with the exception of the consent form). Participants were seated at separate tables while research assistants circled the room answering questions and checking with participants as they completed items. In Samson, four participants asked for the entire survey to be completed in interview format.

SAMPLE — Fifty adults from the First Nation communities of Ermineskin Cree Nation (n = 27) and Samson Cree Nation (n = 23) participated in this pilot. All participants self-identified as First Nations members with full treaty status. In Ermineskin, 40 percent of respondents were male; half were married, 23 percent divorced, separated, or widowed, and 27 percent never married. The average age was 36 years (SD: 13.6, $range$: 18–60 yrs), Almost one-quarter (23 percent) had completed one or more years of university or college, and 62 percent had not completed high school. Most were employed full time, 4 percent employed part time, 23 percent students, 15 percent unemployed, and 4 percent disabled. Over half (52 percent) had lived outside of the community for a year or more at some point in their lives. The average time was 15 years (SD: 10.4, $range$: 3–35 yrs). Annual income was the only demographic information that Ermineskin respondents were hesitant to share. Overall, 70 percent answered this question; of those, 40 percent reported an annual income of less than $20,000, and the rest of the sample reported annual incomes between $20,000 and $59,000.

In Samson Cree, 43 percent of respondents were male; more than half married, 19 percent divorced or separated, and 24 percent never married. The average age was 39 years (SD: 11.7, $range$: 20–63 yrs). Regarding education, 15 percent had completed one or more years of university or college, another 15 percent had a high school diploma, while the remaining 70 percent had not completed high school. More than half were employed full time, 5 percent worked part time, 5 percent were students, 19 percent unemployed, 14 percent homemakers, and 5 percent retired. One-quarter (26 percent) of respondents had lived away from the community for a year or more at some point in their lives. The average time was 11 years (SD: 5.0, $range$: 5–16 yrs). Similar to Ermineskin respondents, Samson participants were reluctant to share household incomes. Less than half (43 percent) provided this information; of those, 60 percent reported an annual income of less than $20,000, while the rest reported an annual income between $20,000 and $89,000.

MEASURES — The impact of gambling on a community can be viewed from multiple perspectives. The goal of our research team was to select socio-economic indicators of gambling impacts that would help these communities make informed decisions about gambling expansion. Across several meetings, it was determined that information about the interpersonal, intrapersonal, and community impacts of gambling currently and historically would be of use in community decision making about gambling expansion. Measures related to these constructs were then considered and selected by the research team, and additional open-ended questions were created to supplement validated measures.

Demographic and Historical Information. Demographic information was collected, including gender, age, education, employment, and household income, as well historical information about years lived in the community, attendance at residential schools, family history of addictive behaviours, and personal histories of treatment for addictive problems.

Gambling. The Canadian Problem Gambling Index (CPGI) was used to assess gambling behaviour. Problem gambling was assessed using the Problem Gambling Severity Index (PGSI), a nine-item subset of the CPGI.[21] The PGSI measures gambling behaviours (five items) and consequences (four items) in the general population. The maximum score is 27. Scores of 8 or more define severe risk, scores of 3 to 7 moderate risk, scores of 1 to 2 qualify as low risk, and a score of 0 denotes non-risk gambling. Respondents who fall into the moderate to severe risk categories are typically classified under the umbrella term "problem gamblers." The PGSI has been used in twelve Canadian studies across ten provinces and six international studies in Australia, Norway, and Iceland.[22] A comparison of the PGSI screen to the Victorian Gambling Screen and the South Oaks Gambling Screen concluded that the PGSI demonstrated the best psychometric properties among the three screening instruments for assessing problem gambling.[23] In the present study, PGSI scores ranged from 0 to 22 ($M = 4.52$, $SD = 4.57$). Internal consistency for the composite PGSI score was excellent ($\alpha = 0.88$). The ten-item Gambling Fallacies Scale was also included to assess respondents' awareness of and resistance to common gambling fallacies (e.g., "to win at gambling you need to think positively"). The measure has been shown to have strong one-month test-retest reliability, internal consistency, and concurrent and predictive validity.[24] In the present study, the internal consistency of the measure could not be assessed due to participants having left some questions blank.

Alcohol and Drug Use and Dependence. The Composite International Diagnostic Interview Short Form (CIDI-SF) scales assess alcohol and drug dependence separately. These seven-item scales classify respondents as probable or non-probable cases based on a score of four or more and are intended for use in epidemiological and cross-cultural studies.[25] The scales map reported symptoms onto DSM-IV diagnostic criteria and indicate whether the diagnostic criteria for dependence are satisfied (cases—coded as 1) or not satisfied (non-cases—coded as 0).[26] CIDI-SF scores for alcohol dependence ranged from 0 to 7 in the present sample ($M = 2.6$, $SD = 2.70$). The internal consistency of scores for alcohol dependence in the present study was excellent ($\alpha = 0.91$). Drug dependence scores ranged from 0 to 5 ($M = 2.4$, $SD = 2.01$). The internal consistency of CIDI-SF scores for drug dependence was acceptable ($\alpha = 0.79$). Information was also collected about alcohol use and binge-drinking behaviour during the twelve months preceding the survey, as was information about the use of cannabis, illicit amphetamines (e.g., speed, crystal meth), hallucinogens (e.g., LSD, mescaline, ecstasy, PCP, angel dust, peyote), solvents (e.g., amylnitrate, freon, nitrous oxide, gasoline, spray paint), cocaine/crack, and heroin. Information was collected separately on the use of prescription sedatives (e.g., Seconal, Halcion, Methaqualone), tranquilizers (e.g., Librium, Valium, Ativan), opioids (e.g., Demerol, Darvon, Percodan, Codeine, Morphine), and amphetamines (e.g., Preludin, Dexedrine, Ritalin) in the twelve-month period preceding the survey.

Smoking. The Fagerstrom Test for Nicotine Dependence (FTND) is a six-item measure that computes a nicotine dependence score ranging from 0 to 10.[27] Scores of 5 or more define moderate to severe dependence, scores of 1 to 4 low dependence, and scores of 0 non-dependence. In the present study, FTND scores ranged from 0 to 8 ($M = 4.21$, $SD = 2.29$). The internal consistency was acceptable ($\alpha = 0.76$). As well, participants were asked additional questions about smoking behaviour while gambling in the past twelve months.

Health. The SF-8 Health Survey (SF-8) is a generic eight-item assessment that generates a health profile describing health-related quality of life (HRQOL). HRQOL refers to the impact of an illness on functional health and well-being as reported by the individual with the condition. Numerous studies have demonstrated the construct- and criterion-related validity of the SF-8.[28] In the present study, there were few missing items on completed surveys and the internal consistency of the scale was good ($\alpha = 0.84$).

Self-Esteem. The Culture Free Self-Esteem Inventory (CFSEI-2) is a forty-item measure that examines three components of self-esteem: general, social, and personal. Scores range from 0 to 32. Scores above 24 indicate high to very high self-esteem, scores of 15 to 24 intermediate self-esteem, and scores of 0 to 14 low to very low self-esteem. In the present study, the internal consistency of the measure could not be assessed due to the large number of questions that were not completed.

Community Cohesion. The ten-item Lubben Social Network Scale (LSNS) measures perceived support from family, friends, and neighbours. This measure is typically used with older adults and has documented that a feeling of social integration contributes to well-being in a number of ways. This study focussed on differences in network size between categories of gamblers living in two First Nations in Alberta in order to assess the social integrating or disintegrating impact of gambling on community members. The Family Cohesion Scale and a modified version of the York Ethnicity Scale were also used to examine differences in family and community cohesion between problem and non-problem gamblers. Unfortunately, participants declined to answer many questions on these scales; as a result, only limited information could be derived from them.

ANALYTIC STRATEGY — Frequencies, cross-tabulations, and measures of central tendency were used to examine various interpersonal, intrapersonal, and community variables measured across the two communities. Given the small sample size, characteristics and opinions of problem gamblers were collapsed across communities to protect personal identities. The quantity of questions left blank on various measures, and comments made by respondents about measures, were also examined to judge the suitability of the measures used.

RESULTS
GAMBLING PARTICIPATION — Overall, all but one participant had gambled in the past twelve months. Participation in gambling activities was high and varied between communities (Table 1).

TABLE 1: Past-year Gambling Activities among Ermineskin and Samson Cree Respondents

GAMBLING ACTIVITY	ERMINESKIN PERCENT	SAMSON PERCENT
LOTTERY OR RAFFLE TICKETS	88.9	83.3
INSTANT-WIN TICKETS	63.0	75.0
BINGO	61.5	85.0
SLOT MACHINES, VLT'S	77.8	52.4
CASINO TABLE GAMES	38.5	15.0
HORSE RACING	14.8	0.0
CARDS FOR MONEY WITH FRIENDS	70.4	47.4
BETS ON A SPORTING EVENT	40.7	35.0
BETS ON TRADITIONAL ABORIGINAL GAMES	25.9	10.0

More than half of all respondents (53 percent) reported gambling with family members, 36 percent with friends, 29 percent with spouses, and 11 percent alone. In the past year, the largest amount of money participants claimed to have lost gambling in one day ranged from $5 to $700; the median response was $100. More than one-third (38 percent) travelled outside their community to gamble at least once per month, with the majority (68 percent) driving less than thirty minutes. One-quarter of respondents indicated that if a casino opened in their area, they would frequent it once a week or more. When asked why they gambled, 41 percent reported it was to make money, 38 percent to socialize, 35 percent to relax, and 33 percent for excitement (more than one response permitted).

When participants were asked to name the forms of gambling that they thought caused the most problems for community members, the top three were slot machines/VLTs, bingo outside the community, and instant-win tickets. Playing cards with friends was viewed as the least problematic form of gambling (Table 2).

TABLE 2: Gambling Activities Perceived to be Causing Problems for Community Members

GAMBLING ACTIVITY	ERMINESKIN AGREE (PERCENT)	SAMSON AGREE (PERCENT)
PLAYING SLOT MACHINES/VLT'S OUTSIDE COMMUNITY	88.9	90.0
PLAYING BINGO OUTSIDE COMMUNITY	77.8	75.0
PLAYING BINGO INSIDE COMMUNITY	55.6	75.0
PLAYING CARDS AT CASINO	51.9	55.0
INSTANT WIN TICKETS	59.3	55.0
BETTING ON SPORTING EVENTS	40.7	40.0
PLAYING CARDS WITH FRIENDS FOR MONEY	14.8	0.0

PROBLEM GAMBLING — Respondents who indicated they had gambled in the past twelve months ($n = 49$) were screened for problem gambling using the Problem Gambling Severity Index (PGSI); of these, forty-six completed the screen in full. More than half of the Ermineskin participants and two-thirds of Samson Cree respondents qualified as problem gamblers (Table 3).

TABLE 3: Ermineskin and Samson Gamblers by Gambler Sub-types

GAMBLING CATEGORY	ERMINESKIN PERCENT	SAMSON PERCENT	OVERALL PERCENT
NON-PROBLEM	18.5	10.5	15.2
AT-RISK	29.6	21.1	26.1
PROBLEM GAMBLING	51.9	68.4	58.7

To protect personal identities, the characteristics of problem gamblers were collapsed across the two communities. Problem gamblers were more likely to be female, married, and live in households earning less than $20,000 per year (Table 4). Only 11 percent of problem gamblers had sought help for their problem; they cited a lack of resources for problem-gambling treatment within or around their community or not knowing where to seek help.

TABLE 4: Demographic Characteristics of Problem Gamblers (PG) and Non-problem Gamblers

CHARACTERISTICS	PG (N=27)	NON-PG (N=19)
MEAN AGE	36 YEARS	37 YEARS
FEMALE	68.0%	50.0%
LOW INCOME[a]	53.3%	35.7%
MARRIED	59.3%	38.9%
COMPLETED HIGH SCHOOL	30.8%	38.9%
EMPLOYED FULL TIME[b]	55.6%	50.0%

a. Defined as an annual household income of <$20,000 per year
b. Defined as working ≥ 30 hours per week

GAMBLING AND OTHER ADDICTIVE BEHAVIOURS

Almost 90 percent of participants smoked cigarettes in the past year and nearly two-thirds (64 percent) reported smoking more when they gambled. When asked why they smoked while gambling, the most frequent response involved controlling their emotions:

> "I get anxious so I have to smoke."
> "It makes it easier to concentrate—it calms my nerves."
> "I smoke more due to stress and worrying when I gamble."

In terms of alcohol use, abstinence among participants was high, with 27 percent reporting no alcohol consumption in the past year, a finding consistent with other Canadian studies.[29] When asked why they abstained from alcohol or had significantly cut down, 43 percent commented that alcohol was impacting their happiness and outlook on life, 43 percent stated it was negatively affecting their family and home life, 40 percent stated they had a problem with alcohol, and 37 percent reported that alcohol was damaging their physical health (more than one response permitted).

The prevalence of problem gambling was lower among participants who had been abstinent from alcohol in the past twelve months compared to those who were not (41.7 percent vs. 63.6 percent). Among current drinkers, 39 percent binge drank regularly (five or more drinks on one occasion once a month or more), 42 percent binge drank less frequently or not at all, and 19 percent declined to answer. Fifty-four percent of current drinkers met the criteria for alcohol dependence, 23 percent did not, and 23 percent declined to answer. The prevalence of problem gambling among participants with alcohol-use problems did not differ from those without these problems. This may be due to the small sample size and amount of incomplete information collected, given the known comorbidity between gambling and alcohol-use problems in large random samples across the general population.[30]

Almost half of respondents (48 percent) reported using cannabis, hallucinogens, inhalants, crystal meth, cocaine, or crack in the past year. The most frequently used substance was cannabis (42 percent), while 11 percent reported using cocaine or crack, 6 percent hallucinogens, 2 percent crystal meth and 2 percent inhalants. As well, 44 percent reported using psychoactive prescription drugs in the past year, with 38 percent reporting opioids, 28 percent sedatives, 6 percent tranquilizers, and 2 percent amphetamines. Information about prescription misuse was not collected.

Problem gamblers were less likely to use prescription drugs, with 35 percent of problem gamblers reporting past-year prescription drug use, compared to 61 percent of non-problem gamblers. In contrast, problem gamblers were somewhat more likely to use illicit drugs, with 48 percent of problem gamblers reporting past-year illicit drug use, compared with 39 percent of non-problem gamblers. Overall, 22 percent of the survey participants met criteria for drug dependence, 35 percent did not, and 43 percent declined to answer. Of the problem gamblers, 35 percent of were drug dependent, compared to 40 percent of non-problem gamblers.

GAMBLING AND GENERAL HEALTH — Overall, 78 percent of participants reported their general health as being good, very good, or excellent. There were no significant health differences between the two communities. Thirty percent of problem gamblers rated their health as very good to excellent, as compared to 42 percent of non-problem gamblers.

SELF-ESTEEM — The mean score on the Culture Free Self-Esteem Inventory was 20.9, indicating average self-esteem levels across both communities. The average self-esteem level in Samson was lower ($M = 18$) than Ermineskin ($M = 23$). This sample size was limited to thirty-nine participants, as some declined to answer some or all questions. The mean self-esteem score for problem gamblers did not differ from non-problem gamblers. This may be due to the small sample size, given the known association between low self-esteem and problem gambling in general populations.[31]

HISTORICAL AND CURRENT IMPACTS OF GAMBLING — More than half of all respondents reported having been negatively affected by a family member's gambling as a child. There was a trend in the data showing that respondents who had problem gambling mothers and fathers also had a parent with alcohol problems while growing up (Table 5). Among problem gamblers, 58 percent reported one or both parents had a gambling problem, and 86 percent reported that as children one or both parents had an alcohol problem.

TABLE 5: Childhood Experiences of Parental Alcohol and Gambling Problems

CHILDHOOD EXPERIENCES	ERMINESKIN PERCENT	SAMSON PERCENT	CHILDHOOD EXPERIENCES	ERMINESKIN PERCENT	SAMSON PERCENT
GAMBLING PROBLEM			**ALCOHOL PROBLEM**		
MOTHER	23.0	33.0	MOTHER	0.0	0.0
FATHER	0.0	6.7	FATHER	41.7	21.2
BOTH PARENTS	26.9	13.3	BOTH PARENTS	33.3	63.2

As adults, 36 percent of respondents were currently negatively impacted by their parents gambling, 32 percent by another relative's gambling, and 25 percent by a friend's gambling. Participants from both communities were concerned about the adverse effect that gambling was having on families, and there was a strong belief that excessive gambling was contributing to community dysfunction:

> "People borrowing money off you, even co-workers, is very negative. Especially when they make their own."

> "I have to help out on the mortgage and bank loans."

> "Gambling affects children more than anyone. It takes parents and teachers away from doing their jobs. It puts money in places that should be put into their kids. I don't think gambling is good. I don't want to see a casino built in our community."

> "They don't think it will affect the family, but it does."

"People lose their children to child welfare due
to addictions and bingo."

When asked about the impact of their own gambling behaviour, 39 percent reported their gambling was negatively impacting others, one-third reported it was not, and 28 percent declined to answer. Children, parents, and friends were the groups most impacted by a respondent's gambling behaviour. While participants were hesitant to comment on the detrimental effects their gambling might have on their families, two participants shared these remarks:

"It takes my time away from grandchildren."

"I've had the idea of leaving my children."

Findings from this exploratory study suggest that respondents who met criteria for problem gambling generally felt less integrated with their communities as compared to non-problem gamblers (Table 6), although further research with larger sample sizes is needed to determine the impact of problem gambling on community cohesiveness and family relations within First Nations communities.

TABLE 6: Perceptions of Problem and Non-problem Gamblers about their Community

PERCEPTION	NON-PROBLEM GAMBLERS AGREE (PERCENT)	PROBLEM GAMBLERS AGREE (PERCENT)
I AM GLAD TO BE A MEMBER OF THIS FIRST NATIONS COMMUNITY	93.0	77.0
BEING A PART OF THIS FIRST NATIONS COMMUNITY IS AN IMPORTANT PART OF MY SELF-IMAGE	87.0	73.0
I FEEL THAT I REALLY BELONG	80.0	62.0
BEING A MEMBER OF THIS FIRST NATIONS COMMUNITY HAS VERY LITTLE TO DO WITH HOW I FEEL ABOUT MYSELF	40.0	62.0
I DON'T FEEL A SENSE OF BEING CONNECTED WITH OTHER MEMBERS OF MY FIRST NATIONS COMMUNITY	20.0	46.0

OPINIONS ABOUT GAMBLING AND GAMBLING EXPANSION

Most participants stated that gambling was a social activity for community members and predicted that an on-reserve casino would give their band a sense of pride (Table 7).

TABLE 7: Views about the Impact of Gambling on Community Well-being

VIEWS ABOUT GAMBLING	ERMINESKIN AGREE (PERCENT)	SAMSON AGREE (PERCENT)
GAMBLING IS A POPULAR SOCIAL ACTIVITY HERE	85.0	74.0
HAVING A CASINO IN OUR FIRST NATION WOULD GIVE PEOPLE WHO LIVE HERE A SENSE OF PRIDE	46.0	61.0
I WOULD LIKE TO SEE A CASINO OPENED HERE	48.0	55.0
GAMBLING IS A GOOD WAY FOR MY FIRST NATION TO RAISE MONEY	56.0	55.0
GAMBLING IS WRONG	67.0	68.0
MANY PEOPLE HERE HAVE A PROBLEM WITH GAMBLING	96.0	85.0
PEOPLE IN MY FIRST NATION HAVE ATTEMPTED SUICIDE DUE TO PROBLEMS WITH GAMBLING	38.0	50.0
MY FIRST NATION SHOULD HOLD PUBLIC CONSULTATIONS BEFORE INTRODUCING NEW FORMS OF GAMBLING	96.0	86.0

However, some respondents held contrary views about a new casino, based on the harm that gambling was already doing in the community, and overall, participants were conflicted about whether or not they wanted a casino, as highlighted by one participant:

> "There's nothing to be proud about having a casino. But I can see how if we had Enoch's casino, I would probably feel pride."

When asked if they had anything further to share about potential gambling impacts, the following positive comments were made:

> "I am thrilled about a casino coming. I will get a job as a card dealer. I am so good with cards in fact, I probably won't even be allowed to gamble there because I am too good and I know my stuff. I will work there though and make good money."

> "I think a casino will be good. It will be good for people who want to work."

> "A casino will be good because it will provide money for the kids in this community—like scholarships for school and sports will come from the casino."

> "I'm happy about the casino because it means I will have a job."

Some respondents were concerned that, despite employment opportunities, the ultimate economic impact of a casino would be negative:

> "The community is not ready for a casino. There are not enough educated people around.

> "The people living here have been so sheltered. They haven't had enough experience outside the reserve in the white society. They don't know how to budget. They will go to the casino and just spend everything."

> "Gambling is a source of violence and it is raising the crime rate in our community so I'm against the casino."

DISCUSSION

The purpose of this study was to provide a starting point for assessing the socio-economic impacts that gambling expansion may have on a First Nation approved for casino development in Alberta, with information collected from a neighbouring Aboriginal community for the purposes of comparison. We worked collaboratively with these communities to select the appropriate indicators and measures of gambling's likely socio-economic impacts in these First Nations communities.

The majority of participants in the study engaged in multiple forms of gambling and were motivated by the opportunity to make money, socialize, relax, and garner excitement. Some of the most popular activities (VLTs and slot machines, bingo, and instant-win tickets) were also those deemed to be causing the biggest problems for community members. Approximately one-half of all study participants met the criteria for problem gambling. These individuals were frequently female, married, and living in low-income homes, and few had sought help for their problem.

Most participants reported smoking while gambling, often to control the emotions associated with the activity. More than one-quarter reported abstinence from alcohol over the past year, and gambling problems were lower among these individuals. More than half of those who reported past-year alcohol consumption were alcohol-dependent. The use of illicit and psychoactive prescription drugs was frequently reported, and almost one-quarter of the sample met criteria for drug dependence. Interestingly, problem gamblers were somewhat less likely to use prescription drugs, and more likely to use illicit drugs, than non-problem gamblers. Further studies with larger, random samples are needed to determine if this pattern is a finding of interest or a spurious result.

More than half the participants had been negatively impacted as children by gambling. Frequently, participants' mothers had gambling problems while their fathers had alcohol problems. Among problem gamblers, most had parents with alcohol problems while young and more than half had parents with gambling problems. As adults, many participants were currently impacted by the gambling behaviours of their parents and other relatives, and there was a general belief that gambling was contributing to community dysfunction. While participants were hesitant to comment on the impact their own gambling was having on the community, some noted negative impacts on friends, children, grandchildren, and other relatives. These findings also suggest that respondents who were problem gamblers felt less integrated within their communities, although further studies with larger samples are needed to determine the extent of these impacts.

On the whole, there was ambiguity about gambling expansion in their First Nation community. On the one hand, participants cited it as an important social activity; on the other hand, and in the same breath, they noted the social damages it was causing. Similarly, building a new casino was viewed as bringing jobs, money for community development, and a source of community pride, but also as an enterprise that could increase crime, debt, and family breakdown.

MEASUREMENT

One of the goals of this exploratory study was to test measures for several constructs related to the socio-economic impacts of gambling in these First Nations communities. We found instruments used to assess problem gambling (the CPGI) and nicotine dependence (the Fagerstrom Nicotine Dependence Scale) to be well received, with few participants leaving questions blank or commenting negatively about these scales. However, participants were more hesitant to answer questions about alcohol and drug misuse. The Composite International Diagnostic Instruments for Alcohol and Drug Dependence (short forms) were used to assess alcohol and drug use problems. Almost half of the surveys administered had one or more questions left blank. This is not surprising, given the stigma associated with alcohol and drug misuse in many First Nations communities due to the emphasis placed on abstinence and the stereotyping of Aboriginal people regarding the abuse of these substances. In fact, it is suspected that only about half of all alcohol use is reported on surveys in First Nations communities.[32] Because research shows a strong correlation between alcohol, drugs, and gambling problems, it would seem important to include questions about other addictive behaviours in future studies, while recognizing the sensitivity that some respondents have to these questions.[33] Given the large number of questions left blank on measures used in this study, it may be worthwhile to pilot test (or develop) other measures of alcohol and drug misuse in these First Nations communities.

Participants were also reluctant to answer questions about gambling fallacies, with three-quarters of the sample leaving one or more of these questions blank, thus making it impractical to calculate scale scores. An accurate gauge of gambling misperceptions is needed for community leaders to plan effective problem-gambling prevention strategies. Hence, it is suggested that questions about gambling misperceptions be developed in consultation with First Nations community members and used in future impact studies. Given that many participants voiced concerns about inappropriate questions on the Family Environment Scale, this measure is not recommended for use in future studies within these First Nations. Respondents also noted some discomfort in answering questions related to feelings of self-esteem.

Finally, as this was an exploratory study, questions were asked about household income and the amount of money spent gambling. Getting accurate information about the amount of money individuals spend on gambling is a complex and difficult process. In particular, retrospective gambling expenditures provide an inaccurate picture of the amount individuals spend per month on gambling, no matter how the questions are worded; participants tend to underestimate the amount spent.[34] Nevertheless, the legitimacy of gambling and its expansion in First Nations communities depends in part on the impact gambling is having on the community and, in particular, the extent to which revenue is derived from vulnerable individuals. Thus it is important to gauge the amount of money individuals in First Nations community spend on gambling relative to their household income, as well as changes to these spending patterns after a casino is introduced. We suggest future impact studies use prospective diaries as outlined by Robert Williams and Robert Wood, with participants recording when they gambled, game(s) played, and their net win/loss for each gambling session.[35]

LIMITATIONS

Given that this was a pilot study with a restricted, non-random sample, findings cannot be generalized to these communities as a whole, and results provide only basic information on the sources and magnitude of variation among the measures used. As well, the mode of survey administration was not consistent across participants. Unfortunately, the sample size did not allow an examination of possible bias between surveys that were self-administered versus those administered in face-to-face interviews. Research suggests that information about sensitive topics (e.g., alcoholism) is best collected using self-administered surveys.[36] However, literacy rates must also be considered. In the present pilot, 16 percent of participants requested the entire survey package read to them, presumably due to literacy concerns.

COMMUNITY RECOMMENDATIONS AND FUTURE RESEARCH

This pilot should be followed up by a large-scale study to help Samson Cree make critical decisions about gambling expansion in their community, establish benchmarks for future studies, and assist in preparations for the negative impacts that may accompany large-scale gaming expansion, if it occurs. The authors suggest that future research continue the tradition of working collaboratively with First Nations and utilize the new tools developed for assessing gambling-related costs and benefits.[37] In the interim, the authors suggest several policy and prevention strategies for these communities that may reduce current gambling problems and allow preparations for future expansion, if it occurs, including:

1. INTRODUCING PROBLEM GAMBLING PREVENTION

a) **Responsible Gambling Education in the Community:** Develop campaigns to educate residents about responsible gambling and emphasize the need to set time and monetary limits on play. Such campaigns should be introduced well before a community casino becomes operational.

b) **Responsible-Gambling Education Onsite:** Consider installing an onsite responsible-gambling booth in a high traffic area of the casino and staff the booth with trained treatment specialists.

c) **Smart Cards:** Research suggests most responsible gambling features on electronic gaming machines are ineffective.[38] Smart card technology allows players to track their own time and spending. This may reduce problem gambling and should be explored in more detail.

d) **Identification Required to Enter Casinos:** It is difficult for casino operators to effectively monitor the entry of self-excluded patrons and youth. Requiring scanned identification to enter a First Nations casino, a practice already in place in Europe, could improve the community's ability to prevent excluded patrons and youth from entering these venues.

2. IMPROVING ACCESS TO PROBLEM-GAMBLING TREATMENT

As Williams and Wood have argued, the amount of money spent on treatment of problem gambling should be proportionate to the amount that comes from people with gambling addictions.[39] This study found that problem gambling was already troublesome for more than one-half the respondents, despite there being no electronic gaming machines (EGMS) or casinos on the reserve, thus indicating that an on-reserve casino would likely increase problem gambling among both Samson and Ermineskin residents. If a casino is introduced, it will be critical to accurately gauge and monitor the percentage of problem gamblers in the community to ensure that sufficient resources are available to treat these individuals. These resources might include:

> ♦ establishing a Gamblers Anonymous chapter and free problem-gambling hotline for residents;

> ♦ allowing residents to screen themselves for gambling problems from the privacy of their homes by including the PGSI nine-item screen in community newsletters;

> ♦ providing residents access to free, confidential problem-gambling counselling services within driving range of the community; and

> ♦ considering not allowing band members with gambling problems to play at an on-reserve casino.

CONCLUSIONS

This study sought to provide a starting point for the possible socio-economic impacts that gambling expansion may have on Samson Cree First Nation and its neighbouring community, Ermineskin Cree Nation, and to test several measures that may be used to examine these impacts in more detail. Broader and more in-depth studies are needed to assist these communities in making informed decisions related to gambling expansion.[40]

NOTES

1   Royal Commission on Aboriginal People, *The Report of the Royal Commission on Aboriginal Peoples* (Ottawa: Indian and Northern Affairs, 1996).

2   M.A. Salter, "Games, Goods and Gods: An Analysis of Iroquoian Gambling," *Canadian Journal of Applied Sports Science* 4 (1979): 160–164.

3   Karen Campbell, "Community Life and Governance: Early Experiences of Mnjikaning First Nation with Casino Rama" (master's thesis, University of Manitoba, 1999); Thomas D. Peacock, Priscilla Day, and Robert Peacock, "At What Cost? The Social Impact of American Indian Gaming," *Journal of Health and Social Policy* 10, 4 (1999): 23–24.

4   David N. Crockford and Nady el-Guebaly, "Psychiatric Comorbidity in Pathological Gambling: A Critical Review," *Canadian Journal of Psychiatry*, 43, 1 (1998): 43–50; Jill Oakes, Cheryl C. Currie, and David Courtney, *Gambling and Problem Gambling in First Nations Communities* (Winnipeg, MB, and Guelph, ON: University of Manitoba and Ontario Problem Gambling Research Centre, 2004); D. Wardman, Nady el-Guebaly, and David Hodgins, "Problem and Pathological Gambling in North American Aboriginal Populations: A Review of the Empirical Literature," *Journal of Gambling Studies* 17, 2 (2001): 81–99.

5   Harold Wynne and John McCready, *Examining Gambling and Problem Gambling in Ontario Aboriginal Communities* (Guelph, ON: Ontario Problem Gambling Research Centre, 2005).

6   Deborah S. Hasin et al., "Prevalence, Correlates, Disability, and Comorbidity of DSM-IV Alcohol Abuse and Dependence in the United States: Results From the National Epidemiologic Survey on Alcohol and Related Conditions," *Archives of General Psychiatry* 65, 7 (2007): 830–842; Katherine M. Keyes and Deborah Hasin, "Socio-economic Status and Problem Alcohol Use: The Positive Relationship between Income and the DSM-IV Alcohol Abuse Diagnosis," *Addiction* 103, 7 (2008): 1120–1130; Jam Van Oers et al., "Alcohol Consumption, Alcohol-related Problems, Problem Drinking, and Socio-economic Status," *Alcohol* 1 (1999): 78–88; John Welte et al., "Alcohol and Gambling Pathology among U.S. Adults: Prevalence, Demographic Patterns and Comorbidity," *Journal of Studies of Alcohol and Drugs* 62, 5 (2001): 706.

7   Martin Cooke, Daniel Beavon, and Mindy McHardy, *Measuring the Well-Being of Aboriginal People: An Application of the United Nations' Human Development Index to Registered Indians in Canada, 1981–2001* (Ottawa: Indian and Northern Affairs Canada, 2004).

8   Ibid.

9   Katherine L. Frolich, Nancy Ross, and Chantelle Richmond, "Health Disparities in Canada Today: Some Evidence and a Theoretical Framework," *Health Policy* 79 (2–3), 12 (2006): 132–143.

10 Geoffrey York, *The Dispossessed: Life and Death in Native Canada* (Toronto: Lester and Orpen Dennys, 1989).

11 Ibid.

12 Winona LaDuke, *The Winona LaDuke Reader: A Collection of Essential Writings* (Stillwater, MN: Voyageur Press, 2002); Frolich, Ross, and Richmond, "Health Disparities in Canada Today."

13 John Kiedrowski, *Native Gaming and Gambling in Canada* (Ottawa: Indian and Northern Affairs, 2001).

14 Robin Kelly, *First Nations Gambling Policy in Canada* (Calgary, AB: Canada West Foundation 12, 2001).

15 David Phillips, Ward Welty, and Marisa Smith, "Elevated Suicide Levels Associated with Legal Gambling," *Suicide and Life-Threatening Behavior* 27, 3 (1997): 373–378.

16 Stephen Newman and Angus Thompson, "A Population-based Study of the Association between Pathological Gambling and Attempted Suicide," *Suicide and Life-Threatening Behavior* 33, 1 (2003): 80–87.

17 Robert J. Williams and Robert T. Wood, "The Proportion of Gaming Revenue Derived from Problem Gamblers: Examining the Issues in a Canadian Context," *Analyses of Social Issues and Public Policy* 4, 1 (2004): 33–45; Robert J. Williams and Robert T. Wood, *Demographic Sources on Ontario Gaming Revenue* (Ontario: Ontario Problem Gambling Research Centre, 2004).

18 Brian J. Cox et al., "A National Survey of Gambling Problems in Canada," *Canadian Journal of Psychiatry* 50, 4 (2005): 213–217.

19 Kiedrowski, *Native Gaming and Gambling in Canada*.

20 Yale D. Belanger, *Gambling with the Future: The Evolution of Aboriginal Gaming in Canada* (Saskatoon: Purich Publishing, 2006).

21 Jacqueline Ferris and Harold Wynne, *Canadian PG Index: Final Report* (Ontario: Canadian Centre on Drug Abuse, 2001).

22 John McCready and Edward Adalf, *Performance and Enhancement of the Canadian PG Index (CPGI): Report and Recommendations* (Canada: Healthy Horizons Consulting, 2006).

23 Jan McMillen and Michael Wenzel, "Measuring Problem Gambling: Assessment of Three Prevalence Screens, *International Gambling Studies* 6, 2 (2006): 147–174.

24 Robert J. Williams, "Reliability and Validity of Four Scales to Assess Gambling Attitudes, Gambling Knowledge, Gambling Fallacies and Ability to Calculate Gambling Odds" (Unpublished technical report available from the author, University of Lethbridge, AB, 2003).

25 E.E. Walters et al., *Scoring the World Health Organization's Composite International Diagnostic Interview Short Form (CIDI-SF)*, 2002, http://www3.who.int/cidi/CIDISFScoringMemo12-03-02.pdf.

26 Ibid.

27 Megan E. Piper, Danielle E. McCarthy, and Timothy B. Baker, "Assessing Tobacco Dependence: A Guide to Measure Evaluation and Selection," *Nicotine and Tobacco Research* 8 (2006): 339–351.

28 J. Ware, M. Kosinski, J. Dewey, B. Gandek. *How to Score and Interpret Single-Item Health Status Measures: A Manual for Users of the SF-8 Health Survey*. Boston: QualyMetric, 2001

29 Government of the Northwest Territories Bureau of Statistics, *NWT Alcohol and Drug Survey* (2003); T. Kue Young, *The Health of Native Americans: Toward a Biocultural Epediomology* (New York: Oxford University Press, 1994).

30 Brian R. Rush et al., "Influence of Co-ocurring Mental and Substance Use Disorders on the Prevalence of Problem Gambling in Canada," *Addiction* 103 (2008): 1847–1856; Nancy M. Petry, Frederick S. Stinson, and B.F. Grant, "Comorbidity of DSM-IV Pathological Gambling and Other Psychiatric Disorders: Results From the National Epidemiologic Survey on Alcohol and Related Conditions," *Journal of Clinical Psychiatry* 66 (2005): 564–574; Nady el-Guebaly et al., "Epideomological Associations between Gambling Behavior, Substance Use and Mood and Anxiety Disorders," *Journal of Gambling Studies* 22 (2006): 275–287.

31 Henry R. Lesieur and Richard J. Rosenthal, "Pathological Gambling: A Review of the Literature," *Journal of Gambling Studies* 7, 1 (1991): 5–39.

32 Peter Bjerregaard and T. Kue Young, *The Circumpolar Unit: Health of a Population in Transition* (Copenhagen, Denmark: Munksgaard, 1998).

33 Rush et al., "Influence of Co-occurring Mental and Substance Use Disorders"; Petry, Stinson, and Grant, "Comorbidity of DSM-IV Pathological Gambling and Other Psychiatric Disorders"; el-Guebaly et al., "Epidemiological Associations between Gambling Behavior, Substance Use and Mood and Anxiety Disorders."

34 Williams and Wood, "The Proportion of Gaming Revenue Derived from Problem Gamblers."

35 Ibid.; Williams and Wood, *Demographic Sources of Ontario Gaming Revenue.*

36 Kirsten E.E. Schroder, Michael P. Carey, and Peter Vanable, "Methodological Challenges in Research on Sexual Risk Behavior: II. Accuracy of Self-reports," *Annals of Behavioral Medicine* 26 (2003): 104–123.

37 Anielski Management Inc., *The Socio-economic Impact of Gambling (SEIG) Framework* (Inter-Provincial Consortium for the Development of Methodology to Assess the Social and Economic Impact of Gambling, 2008), http://www.mgcc. mb.ca/forms/seig_framework.pdf.

38 Garry Smith and Harold Wynne, *VLT Gambling in Alberta: A Preliminary Analysis* (Alberta: Alberta Gaming Research Institute, 2004), https://dspace.ucalgary.ca/ handle/1880/1632.

39 Williams and Wood, "The Proportion of Gaming Revenue Derived from Problem Gamblers; Williams and Wood, *Demographic Sources of Ontario Gaming Revenue.*

40 The authors gratefully acknowledge the contributions of Sharon Gladue and Terrie Quinney, who served as community-based members of our research team; Daniel McKennitt, Nicole Cardinal, Amelia Denby, and Cayley Webber, who served as research assistants; and the Alberta Gaming Research Institute, which funded this pilot work.

CHAPTER 7

FIRST NATIONS GAMING AND URBAN ABORIGINAL PEOPLES IN ALBERTA: DOES AN ECONOMIC "FIT" EXIST?

YALE D. BELANGER

INTRODUCTION

Legalized gambling in Canada is "not only an individual choice and consumer activity, but also a public policy instrument and component of state infrastructure."[1] Most provinces permit some form of gambling, and many have become reliant on a proven and reliable revenue stream, regardless of concerns about gambling's social and economic utility, to grow provincial treasuries, improve overall employment rates, and stimulate depressed economies.[2] This increased popularity is reflected in the growing numbers of gamblers and amplified revenues directed toward state-focussed activities, which have led to the popular belief that gambling revenues equal net societal benefit.[3] The numbers are striking. In 2008 the Canadian Gaming Association reported that national gaming revenues more than doubled between 1995 and 2006 ($6.4 billion to $15.3 billion). Gaming and its associated businesses produced 135,000 jobs, resulting in $11.6 billion in labour income for 2006.[4] These data include the fifteen for-profit and two charitable First Nations[5] casinos operating nationally, which in 2007 generated an estimated $804 million in gross revenues.[6] All First Nations casinos the following year reported a net profit, with Alberta and Ontario First Nations emerging as the financial leaders, followed by Saskatchewan, Manitoba, and British Columbia.

Each province hosting reserve casinos has in place a revenue-distribution model assigning First Nations proscribed access to accumulated gaming revenues (e.g., for community infrastructure and education programs) that is exclusively focused on developing reserve communities. Conspicuously absent from these funding arrangements are urban Aboriginal populations and band members living off-reserve. The question of whether First Nations governments receiving gaming revenues should allocate a portion of these funds to band members living off-reserve engenders potentially divisive debates. Currently in Alberta, First Nations revenue recipients are entitled to manage their gaming-related funding, once released by provincial officials, as they see fit. Complicating our understanding of where urban Aboriginal populations fit into existing gaming revenue models, and of the rights of off-reserve band members to a portion of these revenues for development purposes, is a complex and frequently contradictory legal/jurisdictional environment outlining the legal standing of bands and their members, and the provincial and federal governments' responsibilities for urban Aboriginal populations.

A recent set of Supreme Court of Canada decisions added a further dimension by suggesting that province–First Nation gaming agreements disregarding urban populations are discriminatory in scope, as are those First Nations willingly withholding revenues from urban members. This raises several important questions: Could urban Aboriginal people sue their band councils for formal recognition in the form of access to revenues, or are the provinces partially culpable? Have these agreements opened both First Nations and the provinces to lawsuits? If the bands are politically responsible to their members, should the urban population be allocated a portion of gaming revenues? Does this issue fall under the heading of discretionary spending, meaning it is acceptable for First Nations and the provincial government to withhold funds from urban Aboriginal populations until they have improved reserve economies and local infrastructure? Could the provinces distance themselves from the issues by arguing that the First Nations are responsible for their citizens, and that band members seeking redress must pursue resolution through litigation with their home communities?

The purpose of this chapter is to provide public policy makers and students of First Nations gaming the context needed to begin evaluating these questions. Currently there is no positive obligation of bands or the federal government toward registered Indians, and the federal government cannot influence provincial treasury board spending. Meanwhile, urban Aboriginal populations remain a provincial responsibility. But what about enumerated band members living in the cities? Should they, as community members, be entitled to a portion of those revenues? If so, should this not be outlined in the gaming agreements? Does this failure to acknowledge off-reserve populations represent First Nations' discrimination against their registered members? First Nations leaders assert that their communities are most in need of gambling revenue streams for local development initiatives, thus rationalizing retention of revenues. The multiple agreements' emphases on reserve development would suggest also that provincial officials have accepted Aboriginal people as "reserve people" to avoid accepting urban populations as a provincial responsibility (i.e., as reserve members they remain a band council responsibility even if living in the city). It must be noted that despite the provincial jurisdiction for gambling, and a responsibility for urban Aboriginal peoples, the gaming agreements are limited to Indian reserves and bands. In an attempt to produce clarity, this chapter is presented as a case study, examining this issue's potential impact in Alberta while helping to describe whether urban Aboriginal populations can anticipate access to this revenue stream.

FIRST NATIONS PARTICIPATION IN THE PROVINCIAL GAMING INDUSTRIES

In the 1990s, First Nations leaders in Alberta offered gaming, specifically reserve casinos, as an effective means of offsetting devastating economic trends and producing "economic stability, thereby engendering political stability and the agency required to compete with neighbouring non-Native communities."[7] As the industry evolved, reserve casinos came to embrace two unique features First Nations leaders prized. One, they were local businesses that can generate general operating revenue and on-site employment. Two, the business model required start-up capital financed by partners willing to initially absorb the bulk of the financial risk. Like provincial governments that utilize gambling revenues to improve local services and infrastructure, First Nations who actively lobbied for permission to place casinos on reserves rationalized their actions as a "legislative blessing… based on the premise that the social good of the activity outweighs any negative consequences."[8]

Despite pursuing reserve casinos with the goal of securing local control of economic development, thus augmenting community sovereignty, the Canadian courts stated in a series of decisions that First Nations did not have an inherent right to establish reserve casinos outside the scope of provincial jurisdiction.[9] Each province may establish its own regulatory environment to govern gaming and gambling practices, a responsibility attributable to a 1985 agreement that transferred jurisdiction for lotteries and other forms of gaming from federal to provincial jurisdiction. The changes to the Criminal Code of Canada prohibited all forms of lotteries, bingos, and other games of chance unless otherwise licenced by the province. First Nations gambling ventures are subsequently regulated in one of three ways: (1) a community applies for a licence as any other charitable organization would; (2) a community negotiates an agreement with the host province to operate a casino, which may be on- or off-reserve, depending on the province; or (3) a licence to conduct gambling events is obtained from a provincially approved licensing body.[10]

As criminologist Colin Campbell points out, however, "in the federal-provincial negotiations which led to the 1985 amendment and the corresponding transfer of jurisdiction over gambling, it is apparent that First Nations' interests were not considered," and that by disregarding these interests non-Native governments were able to "consolidate jurisdiction over new forms of gambling and the revenues they would generate for private sector groups, for charities, and for provinces." Moreover, "the failure of Canadian legislators to consider First Nations' interests dramatically underscores the lack of foresight."[11] Existing law specifies that a provincial legislature has the authority to enact laws in the gaming area, subject only to Parliament's paramountcy in the case of a clash between federal and provincial legislation.[12] Considering the provincial proclivity to deny responsibility for urban Aboriginal peoples and its concomitant authority to determine which communities it will negotiate gaming agreements with, the initial reserve orientation of provincial–First Nations gaming agreements is not surprising.

FIRST NATIONS ENTRY INTO THE ALBERTA GAMING INDUSTRY

Alberta historically advocated for expansion of gambling provisions, instituting two minor sweepstakes in the 1970s and partnering with Manitoba, Saskatchewan, and British Columbia in 1974 to establish the Western Canada Lottery Foundation. In 1989 the Alberta Lottery Fund was founded, followed by the first test run of video lottery terminals (VLTs) at summer fairs in Edmonton and Calgary. Both were considered successful experiments, leading to the introduction of a provincial VLT program in 1992. A spike in demand for VLTs led to the provincial casino industry's growth. In 1994, three permanent casinos were sited in Calgary and Edmonton. By 1995, eleven were operating in Alberta (see Appendix A for details).[13] Small-scale casino operations soon transformed into larger, more sophisticated complexes as legislation was altered to double the number of casino slot machines, permit liquor to be served on the gaming floor, and allow casinos to open on Sundays.[14]

First Nations' entry into the provincial gaming industry dates to 1993, when provincial officials granted the Tsuu T'ina First Nation (southwest of Calgary), and the Enoch Cree First Nation (west of Edmonton) licences to hold super-bingos guaranteeing jackpots exceeding $10,000. The Tsuu T'ina made a $100,000 profit for the bingo held in 1993, leading to calls for the creation of an independent First Nations Gaming Commission.[15] First Nations leaders developed a policy model that initially ensured all bands would benefit equally from any reserve casino developments. They also sponsored a chiefs' summit in November 1993, which was attended by several provincial ministers and officials, the minister of Indian and Northern Affairs Canada (INAC), and all provincial First Nations chiefs. Although little came from the meeting, a second summit held in March 1995 witnessed the minister of Family and Social Services, Mike Cardinal, encourage First Nations leaders to "take a leading role" to determine "if a casino industry will exist." If this support was not sufficient, he added, "I think Native leaders should propose what they'd like to see in Alberta and then we'll negotiate."[16]

The third summit, held in November 1995, led to the Understanding on First Nations–Canada Relations, signed by minister of Indian Affairs Ron Irwin and the chiefs of Alberta, to which recently elected premier Ralph Klein and minister Cardinal later appended their signatures. The agreement was somewhat surprising, considering that two months earlier the First Nations Gaming Congress, representing all Alberta bands, demanded $100 million from the provincial government in exchange for halting casino construction. Later that December, however, Tsuu T'ina band members voted 73 percent in favour of a casino proposal, prompting a January 1996 meeting between Premier Klein, Alberta Lotteries Review Committee chair Judy Gordon, and Chief Roy Whitney and the Tsuu T'ina band council. At that time all parties agreed that final arrangements about "casino size, location, construction dates, and revenue-sharing possibilities still needed to be discussed."[17]

The next year a provincial First Nations gaming policy was announced (First Nations were minimally consulted) permitting the construction and operation of four reserve casinos. With the exception of their location in reserve communities, the First Nations casinos were expected to operate as would other provincial charity casinos: half of the profits would be assigned the operator with the other half going to a First Nations charity. First Nations leaders were stunned, especially those negotiating with provincial officials. The Enoch and Louis Bull nations, for example, two communities that had plans in place to develop large destination-type casinos, ended their relationships with a Las Vegas developer when informed of the charity casino model. Their leaders reasoned that the charity model would hinder the developer and the nations' ability to produce the revenues needed to substantiate capital investment. Tsuu T'ina officials also temporarily halted their casino plans. Enoch chief Ron Morin challenged the province to revamp the revenue model to increase the First Nations share. "If you take a look at what First Nations had when we came into this province," Morin opined, "all of the oil and gas that has been produced, the revenues that non-First Nations people have got, those haven't been totally shared with us." He cryptically added, "I don't think I have to give a history lesson in Canada as to what First Nations agreed to share."[18] Several First Nations threatened to challenge the proposed provincial First Nations gaming policy by building and operating their own casinos and bingo halls. Enoch officials even struck a deal with a new corporate partner.[19] Little immediate gain was made during the 1990s, however.

In 1999 it appeared that the First Nations casino process would be indefinitely stalled with the implementation of a moratorium on provincial casino construction. A twenty-month review of licensing policies followed in response to concerns about unsustainable industry growth and lobbying by provincial groups demanding government accountability concerning gambling's social impact. In 2001, a report containing sixty-one recommendations led to the creation of new provincial gaming policies intended to "reflect this government's continued commitment to maintaining the unique charitable gaming model of this province."[20] On 1 March 2002, the moratorium was lifted, opening the door to First Nations seeking participation in the provincial gaming industry.

Anticipating the final report, in 2001 provincial officials announced the First Nations Gaming Policy, which was an altered version of the original policy that jettisoned the previous revenue-distribution model. Under the new policy, 30 percent of slot-machine revenue was to be divided between the casino operator and the host First Nation, which needed to register as a charitable entity prior to any funds being released. The remaining 70 percent was to be divided between existing lottery programs and the First Nation Development Fund (FNDF), for the benefit of all provincial First Nations.[21] Urban Aboriginal, Métis, and Inuit populations were not permitted FNDF access; however, they were entitled to apply to the Alberta Lottery Fund (ALF) for program support. A systematic eight-step application process was established, thereby ensuring controlled and managed growth of the provincial casino industry (see Appendix B). The Alberta Gaming and Liquor Commission (AGLC) as of 2006 was vetting applications from seven First Nations according to the terms and conditions established for other provincial charitable casinos. The eight-step proposal process considers various criteria, ranging from site selection, to community support, to practical business plans evaluating alternate viewpoints. Following acceptance of a casino proposal as reflected by a community referendum, a band council resolution confirms community support.

As the review of applications proceeded, provincial officials worked with provincial First Nations, Alberta's satellite INAC office, and Alberta Community Development at establishing the framework for the FNDF. Funded by provincial revenues from electronic gambling in casinos on First Nations land, it was anticipated that the FNDF would provide opportunities for investment in social and economic development on reserves, as well as social, health, education, and infrastructure spending.[22] The River Cree Resort and Casino located at the Enoch Cree Nation, west of Edmonton, opened in 2006, followed in succession by the Cold Lake First Nation's Casino Dene and the Tsuu T'ina First Nation's Grey Eagle Casino in 2007. In 2008, the Eagle River Casino and Travel Plaza in Whitecourt and the Stoney Nakoda Casino on Stoney Nakoda First Nation (near Morley) opened.[23]

DISTRIBUTION OF ALBERTA GAMBLING REVENUE

Established in 1989 for traditional lottery programs, the ALF is made up from the government's share of net revenues from VLTs, slot machines, and ticket lotteries. Traditional casinos in Alberta are privately operated and provide space and services to charitable groups licenced by the AGLC to conduct short-term charity casinos. This requires approximately 180 charities per casino per year. Charitable and religious organizations must meet AGLC eligibility requirements to obtain a casino event licence. Licenced charities initially receive all proceeds from table games. From this, they pay casino facility operators a fixed fee for service to a maximum ranging from 50 percent of the proceeds in major casinos to 75 percent of the proceeds in minor casinos. Slot-machine revenues are divided as follows: 15 percent is assigned to the operator; 15 percent to the charity; and 70 percent to the ALF.

The ALF relies on a percentage of revenues produced at First Nations casinos: 30 percent of First Nation casino-generated slot revenues help fund provincial programs. An additional 15 percent of slot revenues are immediately set aside to pay the casino operator (in Alberta four of the five casino operations are non-Native businesses). The remaining 55 percent of slot revenues are distributed according to the flowchart below (see Figure 1). Fifteen percent is directed to the host First Nation in anticipation of issues directly attributable to casino placement, including the impact that increased traffic would have on reserve infrastructure, and the need for funding of local programs to deal with increased problem gaming.[24] The remaining 40 percent of slot revenues are assigned to the FNDF. All provincial First Nations may access FNDF revenues according to an application process structured to ensure allocated funds are spent according to previously negotiated terms of usage. For table games, whose revenues are less than slot revenues but still significant, splits are determined on a casino-by-casino basis, taking into account the operator's fee. The operator's portion will range from 50 percent to 75 percent, while the charity's portion will range from 25 percent to 50 percent.

FIGURE 1: First Nations Casino Slot-Machine Revenue Distribution (APRIL 2007)

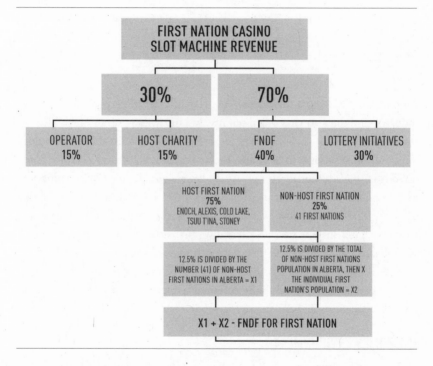

Aboriginal Relations provides grants from the FNDF Grant Program to assist First Nations with proscribed economic, social, and community development projects; education; health; and infrastructure (see Table 1). The FNDF is not unlike traditional trust funds managed by the federal government for the benefit of "Indians": the province of Alberta holds the monies in trust for the respective First Nation and owes these monies only "notionally."[25] Aboriginal Affairs will release these funds only when a First Nation satisfies program officers' expectations that they will be expended for First Nations use and benefit, according to the controlled categories. For example, FNDF monies cannot be used to finance the development or acquisition of a casino or dedicated gaming facility or gaming equipment; to meet any operating or development costs—including but not limited to debt servicing costs and repair and maintenance costs—associated with any gaming activity or dedicated gaming facility; or to subsidize any rates or pay for special promotions for any gaming activity or dedicated gaming facility. Per capita distributions of FNDF monies are also not permissible.[26] In all, 921 projects have been funded by the FNDF to date (May 2010).

TABLE 1: First Nations Development Fund[27]

	N/A	2006/2007	2007/2008	2008/2009	2009/2010	TOTAL
FDNF	$378,392	$13,498,220	$56,312,274	$103,267,322	$104,834,495	$278,290,703
GRANT COUNT	2	53	245	286	335	921

Alberta's First Nations have become important players in the provincial gaming industry, and the FNDF has doled out nearly $158 million (as of May 2010) for reserve projects that have improved local well-being, and the industry employs hundreds of Aboriginal individuals. The AGLC, through the ALF, has also benefitted from the additional revenue, which largely goes to non-Native communities, although First Nations and non-status Indians, Métis, and Inuit may also apply for funding. Importantly, each of the proscribed community development pathways has a specific reserve orientation that suggests that the FNDF is a reserve-based policy expressly intended for "Indians, and lands reserved for the Indians."[28] Urban First Nation band members are not mentioned, nor are provisions aimed at ensuring gambling revenues are spent according to per capita formulas benefiting all band members, urban residents included.

THE POLICY ENVIRONMENT

Through its gaming agreements, Alberta and its First Nations have excluded urban Aboriginal peoples, and First Nations have chosen also to restrict urban band members' access to gaming revenues. Answering why this occurs is difficult. It is, however, possible to provide the context to understand how and why the system operates as it does. Federal Indian policies are characterized by variability in policy formulation, overlap and gaps in policy areas in different cities, and a mismatch between policy areas and community needs of urban Aboriginal peoples.[29] One policy analyst has observed that the majority of existing programs were produced in the absence of policy, suggesting they were little more than makeshift measures, part of a practice that has resulted "in urban Native programming that is largely disjointed and at times incoherent."[30] Despite federal acknowledgement of the need for coordination and collaboration between different levels of government to mitigate the difficulties being experienced by urban Aboriginal populations, there are no signs indicating that "basic issues of jurisdiction and responsibility are being addressed."[31]

Aboriginal peoples are a constitutional category according to section 91(24) of the British North America Act, 1867. The federal government has exclusive legislative jurisdiction over "Indians, and lands reserved for the Indians."[32] Prior to the first noteworthy movement of Indians from reserves to the cities in the 1950s, the federal government, through its Indian Affairs department (1880–1935) and Indian Affairs branches (1936–1966), delivered Indian-specific social benefits and services.[33] These and similar policies were ad hoc in scope and expected to lapse upon Indian assimilation into Canadian society.[34] The Métis and Inuit were largely ignored. However, beginning with the Indian integration-into-the-family allowance and the pension regime in 1945, followed by the federal grant of citizenship in 1960, the provinces were unwittingly drawn into the management of Indian Affairs. They were forced to adopt augmented responsibility for Indians. Note that the provinces continue to resist accepting any responsibility for Aboriginal people, whom they believe are exclusively a federal responsibility.

Legally, band members living on-reserve are considered federal responsibilities, whereas band members living off-reserve are acknowledged to be provincial citizens. Bands are considered federal entities under the Indian Act, and they are located on reserves originally established to segregate First Nations from Canadian society.[35] At the time these reserves were established, assimilation was the primary goal, and urban immigration was aggressively championed. Once abandoned, the reserves would be decommissioned and the lands turned over to provincial jurisdiction. Although actively promoted as a means of improving their socio-economic standing, Indian emigration was considered to result in those Indians voluntarily abdicating their rights to federal programming. A model delineating use of reserve resources for band members living in the city was never developed, and Canadian political orthodoxy presumes that an Indian's "home" cannot be sited in multiple centres (read "cities"), even if these sites fall within pre-colonial homelands.[36] First Nations leaders similarly suggested that band members willingly residing off-reserve were rejecting their traditional culture, thus abdicating any and all claims to local resources. Yet cities are often acknowledged by First Nations as extensions of traditional lands that inform the construction of identities both uniquely urban and informed by reserve social and political norms.[37] This has led to increasing numbers of urban Aboriginal peoples demanding recognition of their political communities as imbued with distinctive rights.[38] Urban Aboriginal leaders are seeking what the United Nations proclaimed an indigenous right to "full and effective participation in all matters that concern: a self-determining people" according to "the principle of free, prior and informed consent."[39]

Provincial officials suggest this policy environment is strictly a federal concern. As a result, a jurisdictional void has developed in which the provinces and, gradually, more First Nation councils refuse to accept responsibility for urban Aboriginal peoples.[40] In an era of heightened funding competition, a progressively more politicized and polarized climate has evolved as First Nations and urban Aboriginal peoples compete for a common pool of federal funding and access to limited provincial programming. It should be noted that funding competition is but one of a variety of socio-political and socio-economic forces driving a wedge between urban and reserve First Nations. For the purposes of this chapter, however, funding competition remains our focus, specifically how historic attempts to ensure First Nations urban immigration led to entrenched attitudes, both conscious and unconscious, that urban Aboriginal peoples had severed political and economic ties with their home First Nations. Such attitudes continue to influence First Nations leadership's decision making processes related to gaming revenue allocation to community members.

Challenging these attitudes is a recent set of Canadian court decisions that potentially force a policy reconceptualization of who urban Aboriginal peoples are and what roles First Nations will be expected to play in their development.

THE SUPREME COURT AND THE URBAN ABORIGINAL COMMUNITY

In 2002, the Federal Court in Canada v. Misquadis ruled that Human Resources and Skills Development Canada (HRSDC) had discriminated against the urban Aboriginal community. The court determined that Aboriginal political organizations can represent urban Aboriginal interests, and that the HRSDC needed to help fund the infrastructure required for urban service delivery and to establish representative governance. It also defined off-reserve Aboriginal people as a group of self-organized, self-determining, and distinct communities, analogous to reserve communities.[41] Significantly, Misquadis reinforced the political connection between on- and off-reserve Aboriginal people expressed in the Supreme Court's Corbière (1999) decision, which compelled First Nations to permit off-reserve members to vote in Indian Act sanctioned elections and referenda.[42] Further to this, the recent Esquega (2007) decision ruled that reserve residence was not required for band councillors.[43] Several key issues emerged from these decisions: (1) the First Nations franchise was extended to band members living in cities, as were, potentially, the corresponding First Nations political obligations for urban band members; (2) the urban Aboriginal community was for the first time formally recognized as a political community; and (3) it was implicitly suggested that outside funding was needed to aid urban Aboriginal development.

At the core of each of the three decisions was the issue of "Aboriginality-residence," in particular its potential to discriminate against individuals living off-reserve. In Corbiere, the Supreme Court ruled that First Nations members living off-reserve were entitled to vote in band elections. The court determined that the Indian Act's voting provisions violated section 15(1) of the Canadian Charter of Rights and Freedoms and were thus rendered invalid. Aboriginality -residence, in the court's opinion, was an analogous ground of discrimination, since the decision to live off-reserve was and remains profound and frequently compelled rather than voluntary. It is also associated with numerous negative policy outcomes. Justices McLachlan and Bastrache concluded that "the complete denial to off-reserve members of the right to vote and participate in band governance treats them as less worthy and entitled, not on the merits of their situation, but simply because they live off-reserve."[44] They went on to state that the distinction between reserve and off-reserve members for the purposes of voting presumed those individuals living off-reserve were "persons who have chosen to be assimilated by the mainstream society."[45] Madame Justice L'Huereux-Dubé noted this tension and concluded that traditionally "people have often been only seen as 'truly Aboriginal' if they live on reserves."[46]

Each case challenged the popular belief that First Nations band members who moved to cities were abandoning their home community and local political issues. In the Esquega decision, not only did the litigants seek to retain their franchise, and as such their First Nation citizenship, they also demanded the opportunity to run for office without being handicapped by residency requirements. The federal court in Misquadis (2002) also debunked the notion that urban Aboriginal peoples lack legitimacy and accountability. The court determined that HRSDC (formally HRDC) discriminated against the urban Aboriginal community by failing to ensure its benefits were provided to all Aboriginal peoples equally. This case is significant for both off-reserve and non-status Indians as it provides legal recognition of Aboriginal communities "outside the constructs of bands and reserves under the Indian Act [while affirming] the rights of individuals in these communities to be given equal respect and consideration in application of the law."[47] It also highlights the disparity of how the courts, the federal government, and First Nations are interpreting these issues. Interestingly, the Canadian courts have insinuated themselves into the self-determination dialogue, arguably becoming agents of Aboriginal self-determination in the process. This issue, while not the subject of this chapter, demands additional study. Importantly, in insinuating themselves in the issue, the courts have extended First Nations citizenship, as well as the attendant citizenship rights, beyond reserve boundaries.

FIRST NATIONS CITIZENSHIP AND PROGRAM FUNDING

Urban Aboriginal development has in recent years become a hot topic, even if it historically baffled federal officials oblivious to a six-decade period of urban Aboriginal growth. The debate is further inflamed by the courts' acknowledgment that urban Aboriginal communities are imbued with rights to the resources needed to fuel local development. That acknowledgement also has the potential to pressure First Nations to formally recognize urban band members, possibly resulting in their redirecting a portion of gaming revenues to the cities. An interesting tension has developed that exposes the strengths and weaknesses of each community seeking additional development resources. For instance, although both locales lack the opportunities and infrastructure available to non-First Nations communities, each is unique in its strengths. Whereas the city offers better educational opportunities, recreational options, and access to employment, First Nations are established political agents that are considered self-governing, which includes the right to determine citizenship criteria.[48]

With his conclusion that urban Aboriginal peoples are a political community, Justice Lemieux legally erased the view that urban émigrés were no longer interested in their home communities' political development. A legal reconceptualization of what home or, more appropriately, political home means is thus necessary, given that "political communities are organic and not fixed in time, and over the past several decades they have not only persisted among Aboriginal peoples in rural and reserve environments but also taken on urban identities specific to the city as a home-place, whether singly or intertwined with reserve/rural communities elsewhere."[49] The criteria for First Nations citizenship are then also up for discussion. Citizenship embraces democratic engagement, individual property, taxpayers' rights, and governing obligations of elected officials, things federal officials historically did not believe existed in communal societies exhibiting constrained individualism and limited individual labour power, all of which ultimately undermined personal productivity.[50] The black-and-white world of federal Indian policy made it impossible for one person to be both Indian and a Canadian citizen, and this impossibility undermined any attempts to discuss First Nations citizenship.

Such exclusion likely perplexed Aboriginal peoples, whose communities traditionally embraced plurality of citizenship models that promoted inter- and intra-community movement.[51] More importantly, these citizenship regimes attained international political standing when European crowns negotiated treaties and instituted diplomatic accords with First Nations.[52] As legal scholar James Henderson argues, these constitutionally protected Aboriginal orders preserve sui generis and treaty citizenship and are immune from Canada's unilateral bestowment of Canadian citizenship.[53] This interpretation suggests that, when Canada made all Indians non-consensual citizens in 1960, it infringed upon constitutionally protected Aboriginal rights to freely determine political associations. Henderson further counters the belief that the right to Canadian citizenship replaces the Aboriginal–sovereign compact, and that actions such as this reinforce societally entrenched dichotomies that imply citizenship is a "take it or leave it" proposition.[54]

Citing the Supreme Court, Henderson states that such "constitutional recognition affirms Aboriginal choices, not to be confined by or to British concepts of subjecthood or Canadian concepts of citizenship."[55] The sui generis existence of Aboriginal rights suggests they are easily extended to the city by virtue of indigenous nations practising governance within their traditional territories. This extension is occurring at a time when the Canadian courts have been charged with extending "constitutional equality before and under the law to these sui generis Aboriginal orders and treaty federalism."[56] In his discussion of the nature of Aboriginal rights, legal scholar Brian Slattery explains that the courts recognize two forms of Aboriginal rights: generic rights and specific rights. The latter "are rights whose nature and scope are defined by factors pertaining to a particular Aboriginal group," which means they vary from group to group, whereas the former "are rights of a uniform character whose basic contours are established by common law of Aboriginal rights."[57] Generic Aboriginal rights include, but are not limited to, the right to conclude treaties, the right to customary law, the right to honourable treatment by the crown, the right to an ancestral territory, the right of cultural integrity, and the right to self-government.[58]

Consequently, it is difficult to conceptualize Aboriginal citizenship when one considers customary law that promotes plurality of citizenship based on relational citizenship models. Such definitions defy simple dichotomies and advance a more holistic ideal of citizenship. This holistic vision is grounded in the values of self-determination and choice, which oppose legal classifications that seek to impose physical and ideological boundaries and thus corrupt culturally specific citizenship theories. According to Henderson's reading, urban band members remain First Nations citizens and should be able to access privileges of community programming that support local development—that is, unless the community, in an act of self-determination, decides that band members living in the cities have willingly abdicated their rights to community resources. Ironically, such actions would suggest to individuals considering moving to the city that they do not have an individual Aboriginal right to freely determine political associations, and that First Nations citizenship is in fact a "take it or leave it" proposition.

DISCUSSION

Highlighting the discriminatory aspect of disenfranchisement by virtue of urban habitation led to the extension of the First Nations franchise to non-resident citizens, and with it a say in the community's daily governance. But, as Julie Tomiak has observed, "a major challenge for Indigenous people who reside in urban areas is the lack of clarity with regard to the roles and responsibilities of different levels of government, Aboriginal governments, and local institutions."[59] The current provincial failure to acknowledge urban band members' claims to gaming revenues is based on several assumptions. First, First Nations individuals abdicate their rights to reserve resources in favour of urban residency. Second, ongoing jurisdictional disputes between the federal and provincial governments over responsibility for urban Aboriginal peoples leave those peoples in a bureaucratic stasis, with limited access to federal programs. Finally, the gaming agreements between province and First Nations, and their criteria, are limited to Indian reserves and bands, and as such are considered federal responsibilities. This enables provincial officials to officially deny responsibility for urban Aboriginal populations. The issues in each case are attributable to the dilemma of indigenous politics, which is that social and legal positioning are relied on to create social and legal boundaries.[60] Unpopular decisions denying programming to urban Aboriginal populations are based on a refusal to accept urban Aboriginal peoples as communities with rights. The aforementioned court decisions and Henderson's citizenship discussion appear to buttress the belief that the right to community citizenship should be extended to band members living in the city, even if it is currently possible to discriminate against this individual choice.

Thorny issues of who precisely is responsible for assisting with urban Aboriginal development remain unresolved. Within the context of the larger discussion concerning First Nations gaming revenues, the question of how these monies should be utilized remains unanswered. We must also consider an added dimension, which is the general First Nations rejection of urban band members' claims to gaming revenues, or (to place it in legal terms Canadian officials would value) their refusal to appreciate their fiduciary obligation to citizens of the nation. Early First Nations casino advocates expressed an interest in improving reserve employment levels and generating gambling revenues to improve social programs and housing, reduce overcrowding and poor health, and bolster deteriorating infrastructure.[61] At no time during this early stage in the dialogue were non-reserve populations mentioned. This may be attributed to a provincial lack of knowledge of urban Aboriginal populations, their relocation and employment habits, and whether they would ever consider the city home. First Nations did not highlight the fact that they were confronting significant out-migration of band members to the cities (see Table 3). Little to no public attention was directed to the plight of off-reserve members during negotiations in the early 2000s. Rather, the focus was exclusively on reserve populations and reserve social issues as First Nations engaged in an act of self-determination to improve the lack in economic growth and governance that could be traced to inadequate federal funding arrangements.

TABLE 3: Urban Aboriginal Populations

CITY	1996	2001	2006	PERCENT GROWTH OVER 10 YEARS
EDMONTON	32,825	40,930	52,100	40.9
CALGARY	15,195	21,915	26,575	46.8

Currently, First Nations governance is financed through the Indian Government Support Programs, which include Band Support Funding, Professional and Institutional Development, Tribal Council Funding, Band Advisory Services, and Band Employee Benefits. Each is funded through federal procurements and is based on a distribution formula that provides First Nations with funding support for local governance and the administration of programs and services related to the transfer of direct program administration from Indian and Northern Affairs

Canada. The formula calculates funding levels based on, among other criteria, on- and off-reserve populations, but it does not stipulate how money is to be utilized for urban band members' programming. This enables First Nations to retain full funding allocations at the expense of band members living outside the community. In addition, First Nations spending through core federal programs is capped annually below inflation and population growth rates, creating necessarily rigid spending practices that also negatively impact off-reserve residents. The resulting First Nations per capita payment is half the amount for average Canadians (between $7,000 and $8,000, compared to between $15,000 and $16,000 for average Canadians). For instance, core INAC program budgets in 2005 were capped at 2 percent growth for ten years after a five-year period in which INAC funding increased by only 1.6 percent while the status First Nation population increased by 11.2 percent. First Nations budgets have dropped by almost 13 percent since 2000. The amount of lost funds (the difference between the 2 percent received and the needed 6 percent) amounted to more than $10 billion. Gathering Strength, Canada's response to the Royal Commission on Aboriginal Peoples (RCAP), provided roughly $2.3 billion, leaving a shortfall of over $7.9 billion. Individual community losses range from $1.5 million to $13.9 million.[62]

Like federal funding arrangements, the existing Alberta–First Nation gaming agreement does not dictate how a First Nation is to utilize released revenues. It simply decrees that upon a band council resolution (BCR) being passed, "dollars distributed from [the FNDF] would be available for economic and community development, addictions programs, education, health and infrastructure projects."[63] Urban Aboriginal populations, specifically band members, are not mentioned. Existing application procedures suggest that FNDF revenue could be directed to urban initiatives. The main hurdle is the need for a BCR. The urban community of band members would have to persuade their representative band council to submit an application to fund an off-reserve project, something that has not yet occurred in Alberta. A band council member or employee would have to devote precious resources toward developing an application package that includes the band council description of the project in question, a detailed budget and project funding overview, and a funding allocation sheet. Once the monies are released, a band council member or employee would then be responsible for liaising with the urban community of band members regarding spending practices, and for collecting the necessary paperwork in anticipation of submitting annual FNDF accounting reports to Aboriginal Affairs.

Arguably, such costs would be borne by the First Nation, and the project would marginally benefit reserve residents. Should the band's chief and council refuse, urban members could rightfully argue that the governing elite was discriminating against non-reserve band members. Indeed, the above-mentioned set of Canadian court decisions suggests that First Nations band councils are responsible for an electorate that has chosen to live outside the community. These decisions further suggest that urban band members are a First Nation's responsibility, especially if that First Nation claims the city as falling within its traditional territories where citizens are residing. Ignoring urban band members' concerns will inevitably lead to confrontations over civic membership. Despite the Canadian courts' decision that urban members remain First Nations citizens by virtue of an extended franchise, First Nations in Alberta have refused to acknowledge this through program funding vis-à-vis the distribution of gambling revenues. First Nations have instead adopted a political, legalistic model whereby "becoming a citizen depends on how one is constituted as a subject and who exercises or submits to power relations."[64] Adherence to what could best be described as a neoliberal approach to citizenship challenges historically embedded forms of relational citizenship and instead embraces a vision of common humanity among individuals sharing corresponding aspirations, mutually supportive social actions, and the need to belong.

CONCLUSION

This chapter has argued that First Nations and the provincial government, vis-à-vis the gaming agreements, remain to a degree politically responsible for urban band members (urban citizens). This analysis reflects the Misquadis decision, which expressed its distaste for federal treatment of urban Aboriginal people as "less worthy of recognition, and viewed as being disorganized and less accountable than other [read 'reserve'] Aboriginal peoples."[65] This chapter also concurs with Justice Lemieux's conclusion that urban Aboriginal peoples "have the right to be free from any kind of discrimination, in the exercise of their rights," which in this case was the right to deliver programs "based on their indigenous... identity" tied to the city. Impressed by the evidence presented demonstrating urban organization, Justice Lemieux concluded that urban Aboriginal people had the right to federal aid to design, implement, and fund training programs to meet urban Aboriginal needs.[66] Does this entail First Nation contributions, in particular an allocation of gaming revenues from a provincially sanctioned development model ostensibly implemented for the benefit of all Alberta's First Nations individuals? Additional research is necessary here to expand upon this chapter's conclusions, but I would suggest at this point that it does.

The implications of the courts' decision have yet to be fully tested. For example, notifying First Nations leaders of their fiduciary obligation for urban band members undermines the spirit of self-determination. This is troubling. So, too, is the courts' influence in these matters. The cases represent the opening salvo in what is quite likely to become a drawn-out and contentious debate regarding urban Aboriginal peoples' rights, and the role that both the provinces and the First Nations are expected to play in their development. One must also remain cognizant of the disparate nature of equal treatment programs, and how they often lead to the institution of political and economic asymmetry between First Nations and urban Aboriginal communities.[67] Although additional research is needed, for now urban band members remain First Nations citizens who are morally entitled to community resources, suggesting that it is appropriate for urban Aboriginal band members to expect access to a portion of First Nations gaming revenues for urban initiatives.

APPENDIX A: Location of Current and Planned Casinos/Racinos, Alberta (as of Nov. 2007)

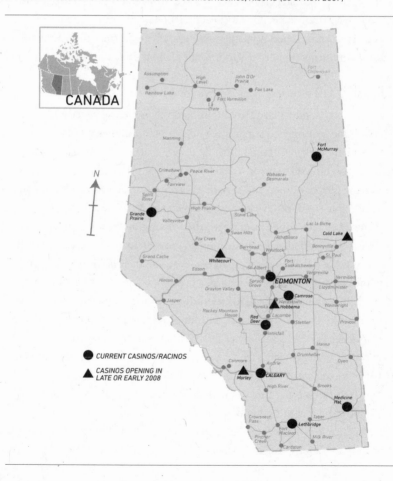

Approved on 19 January 2001, the First Nations gaming policy allows for the operation of reserve casinos according to Alberta's charitable gaming model. Under the policy established for the Alberta Gaming and Liquor Commission (AGLC), reserve casinos are required to adhere to the terms and conditions established for other charitable casinos in the province. The eight-step proposal process for funding applications is as follows:

1. An interested group or individual expresses formal interest in developing a casino in a community.

2. The AGLC issues a notice of expressed interest for a traditional casino or a First Nations casino, as the case may be, depending on the location of the community. The AGLC places an advertisement in a local newspaper, advising interested parties that the AGLC will accept expressions of interest from other groups or individuals for this licence. This process allows all interested parties in a specified area an opportunity to make an application for a casino facility licence in that area and to be considered at the same time as the original applicant. The AGLC will advise all municipal and band councils in the surrounding community of the interest in the proposed facility.

3. The AGLC conducts an initial assessment to determine if the responses have merit and meet basic criteria related to market demand and benefit to charitable groups. At this stage, the AGLC does not require municipal land use, zoning, or development approval for an expression of interest to be deemed valid. Applicants are expected to defer seeking appropriate municipal approvals until advised in writing by the AGLC.

4. The board of the AGLC considers community support—or the lack thereof—as expressed through the municipal or band council, and may conclude the process if, in the board's view, the council does not support the concept of a new casino facility in the community. If the council is silent and there is no demonstrated opposition, the board, at its discretion, may decide to continue the application process.

5. The AGLC accepts detailed proposals from applicants who have expressed an interest in the development of a casino in the community under consideration. The proposals must include a business plan, and the applicant must demonstrate to the commission that the proposal has taken into consideration factors that may affect the community and adjacent communities. The applicants are also required to issue a public notice of their application for a casino facility licence. The AGLC will advise all councils in the surrounding community of any proposals received.

6. A selection committee evaluates proposals using stringent criteria, and the best proposal is selected.

7. A thorough due diligence investigation is conducted into the proponents and other key persons or organizations associated with the selected proposal.

8. If all requirements for a gaming facility have been met (federal and provincial legislation, regulation, and policies, and municipal requirements, permits, licences, or authorizations), the AGLC will make a recommendation to the board respecting the issuance of a casino facility licence to the successful applicant.

NOTES

1   James F. Cosgrave and Thomas R. Klassen, "Introduction: The Shape of Legalized Gambling in Canada," in *Casino State: Legalized Gambling in Canada*, ed. James F. Cosgrave and Thomas R. Klassen (Toronto: University of Toronto Press, 2009), 3.

2   Rhys Stevens, *Socio and Economic Costs and Benefits of Gambling* (Alberta: Alberta Gaming Research Institute, 2006), http://www.abgaminginstitute.ualberta.ca/pdfs/Costs_Benefits_Intro.pdf (last accessed 16 May 2009).

3   Garry J. Smith and Harold J. Wynne, *A Review of the Gambling Literature in the Economic and Policy Domains* (Edmonton: Alberta Gaming Research Institute, 2000).

4   See Canadian Gaming Association, *Economic Impact of the Canadian Gaming Industry: Key Findings Report* (Toronto: HLT Advisory, 2008), v, vi, 17.

5   The term First Nations represents "band," and is not a synonym for Aboriginal peoples, as it does not include Inuit or Métis. The term First Nations people generally applies to both status and non-status Indians, although where distinctions occur they will be identified in this chapter. Aboriginal people is a constitutionally entrenched term describing Canada's Indian, Inuit, and Métis peoples. Because of the historic time period framing this analysis, the term Indian is used in legislation or policy; it also appears in discussions concerning such legislation or policy, as will proper names of communities used historically and today.

6   Albert Warson, "First Nations Gaming: After 11 Years, More Casinos and More Control over Operations," *Canadian Gaming Business* (June/July 2007): 25, quoting Clint Davis, Bank of Montreal. Five First Nations casinos opened in 1996: one in Ontario and four in Saskatchewan. First Nations in Nova Scotia (1998), British Columbia (2001), Manitoba (2002), and Alberta (2006) have since become prominent, and in certain cases dominant, players in their host provincial gaming industries. First Nations in Nova Scotia do not operate casinos. Rather, they have the authority to operate VLTs within reserve boundaries. They have to pay a weekly $56 per machine administrative fee to the Atlantic Lottery Corporation. Revenues raised through the individual gaming agreements remain with the First Nations.

7   Yale D. Belanger, *Gambling with the Future: The Evolution of Aboriginal Gambling in Canada* (Saskatoon: Purich Publishing, 2006), 13. See also Daniel Salée, "Quality of Life of Aboriginal People in Canada: An Analysis of Current Research," *IRPP Choices* 12, 6 (2006).

8   Garry Smith and Harold Wynne, *A Review of the Literature in the Economic and Policy Domains* (Edmonton: Alberta Gaming Research Institute, 2000), 32.

9   See St. Marys Indian Band v. Canada (Minister of Indian Affairs and Northern Development), [1995] 3 F.C. 461, 127 D.L.R. (4th) 686, 100 F.T.R. 148, [1996] 2 C.N.L.R. 214 (Fed. T.D.); and R. v Gladue, ([986] 30 C.C.C. (3d) 308, [1987] 4 C.N.L.R. 92 (Alta. Prov. Ct.).

10 For a detailed discussion of the evolution of First Nations casino gaming in Canada, and the timeline of events in Alberta leading to the first reserve casinos, see Belanger, *Gambling with the Future*; and Warren Skea, "Time to Deal: A Comparison of the Native Casino Gambling Policy in Alberta and Saskatchewan" (PhD diss., University of Calgary, 1997).

11 Campbell, "Canadian Gambling Legislation," 250.

12 R. v. Furtney, [1991] 3 S.C.R., 91.

13 Ibid.

14 See Stevens, *Casinos in Alberta*.

15 Monte Stewart, "Natives Seeking Own Gaming Commission," *Calgary Herald*, 29 Aug. 1993, A4.

16 "Klein Nod Given to Reserve Casinos Already, says MLA," *Edmonton Journal*, 17 March 1995, A7.

17 "Tsuu T'ina Open to Some Changes," *Calgary Herald*, 30 Jan. 1996, A6.

18 Tom Arnold, "Natives Seek Bigger Chunk of Gaming Profits," *Edmonton Journal*, 21 Nov. 1996, A7.

19 "Native Casinos are a Big Gamble," *Edmonton Journal*, 2 April 2000, A14.

20 Government of Alberta News Release, quoting Alberta Minister of Gaming Ron Stevens, "Government Approves Policies to Effectively Manage Growth of Gaming: Community Support Required for New Casinos; VLT cap to remain," 22 Oct. 2001, http://www.gaming.gov.ab.ca/news/20011022.asp (last accessed 2 June 2005).

21 Robin Summerfield, "Natives Praise New Gaming Policy: Casino Revenues to Benefit Bands and Charities," *Calgary Herald*, 20 Jan. 2001, B1.

22 *Benefiting Albertans* (Alberta: Alberta Gaming and Liquor Commission, 2003).

23 Specific dates are as follows: River Cree Resort and Casino on the Enoch Cree Nation, west of Edmonton, opened on 26 October 2006. The Cold Lake First Nation's Casino Dene opened 26 September 2007, followed by the Tsuu T'ina First Nation's Grey Eagle Casino, which opened just west of Calgary on 19 December 2007. The Eagle River Casino and Travel Plaza in Whitecourt opened 31 January 2008. Finally, the Stoney Nakoda Casino on Stoney Nakoda First Nation (near Morley) opened 10 June 2008.

24 Robin Kelley, "First Nations Gambling Policy in Canada," *Journal of Aboriginal Economic Development 2*, 2 (2002): 41–55; and Yale D. Belanger, "The Morality of Aboriginal Gaming: A Concept in the Process of Definition," Journal of Aboriginal Economic Development 2, 2 (2002): 25–36.

25 For this general history, see Dean Neu and Richard Therrien, *Accounting for Genocide: Canada's Bureaucratic Assault on Aboriginal People* (Winnipeg: Fernwood Publishing, 2003).

26 Alberta, *First Nations Development Fund Agreement* (Edmonton: Aboriginal Affairs, 2009), in particular Attachment A.

27 Alberta, *Aboriginal Relations: Business Plan 2009–12* (Edmonton: Alberta Finance and Enterprise, 2008); and information provided by Peter Crossen, Director, First Nations Development Fund, Alberta Aboriginal Relations.

28 *Indian Act* (R.S. 1985, c-15).

29 Katherine A.H. Graham and Evelyn Peters, *Aboriginal Communities and Urban Sustainability* (Ottawa: Canadian Policy Research Networks, 2002), 18.

30 Calvin Hanselmann, *Uncommon Sense: Promising Practices in Urban Aboriginal Policy-Making and Programming* (Calgary: Canada West Foundation, 2002), 11.

31 Graham and Peters, *Aboriginal Communities and Urban Sustainability*, 18.

32 Calvin Hanselmann and Roger Gibbins, "Another Voice Is Needed: Intergovernmentalism in the Urban Aboriginal Context," in *Re-Configuring Aboriginal-State Relations: Canada: The State of the Federation 2003*, ed. Michael Murphy (Kingston: McGill-Queen's University Press, 2005), 79.

33 Responsibility for Indian Affairs at Confederation was vested with Secretary of the State Responsible for Indian Affairs. In 1873, responsibility for Indian Affairs was transferred to the Department of the Interior. The Department of Indian Affairs, a branch office of the Department of the Interior, was created in 1880. It operated until 1935, when it was dissolved as a cost-cutting measure. Responsibility for Indian Affairs transferred to the Department of Mines and Resources and a subdepartment was established: The Indian Affairs Branch (IAB). Responsibility for Indian Affairs was reassigned to the Department of Immigration and Citizenship in 1950, where it remained until an independent Department of Indian Affairs and Northern Development was established in 1966.

34 Hugh Shewell, "Enough to Keep Them Alive." *Indian Welfare in Canada, 1873–1965* (Toronto, University of Toronto Press, 2004).

35 Mark S. Dockstator, "Toward an Understanding of Aboriginal Self-government: A Proposed Theoretical Model and Illustrative Factual Analysis" (PhD diss., York University, 1993); and A. H. Mawhiney, Towards Aboriginal Self-Government (New York: Garland Publishing, 1994)

36 John Borrows, "'Landed' Citizenship: Narratives of Aboriginal Political Participation," in *Citizenship in Diverse Societies*, ed. Will Kymlicka and Wayne Norman (Toronto: Oxford University Press), 326–344.

37 Chris Andersen, "Residual Tensions of Empire: Contemporary Métis Communities and the Canadian Judicial Imagination," in *Reconfiguring Aboriginal-state Relations: Canada: The State of the Federation*, ed. M. Murphy (Montreal and Kingston: McGill-Queen's University Press, 2005), 295–325; and Kathi Wilson and Evelyn Peters, "'You can make a place for it': Remapping Urban First Nations Spaces of Identity," *Society and Space* 23 (2005): 395–413.

38 Audra Simpson, "Paths toward a Mohawk nation: Narratives of Citizenship and Nationhood in Kahnawake," in *Political Theory and the Rights of Indigenous Peoples*, ed. D. Ivison, P. Patton, and W. Sanders (Toronto: Cambridge University Press, 2000), 113–136.

39 See United Nations, *United Nations Declaration on the Rights of Indigenous Peoples. Report of the Human Rights Council*. U.N. Doc. A/61/L.67/2007; and United Nations, *Draft Programme of Action for the Second International Decade of the World's Indigenous People*. Report of the Secretary-General. U.N. Doc. A/60/270/2005.

40 James S. Frideres and René R. Gadazc. *Aboriginal Peoples in Canada*, 8th ed. (Toronto, Prentice Hall, 2008), 368.

41 Misquadis, FCA 370

42 *Corbiere v. Canada* (Minister of Indian and Northern Affairs), [1999] 2 S.C.R. 203.

43 Misquadis, FCA 370

44 *Corbiere* 1999, 221.

45 Ibid., 224.

46 Ibid., 258.

47 Mahmud Jamal. "The Misquadis Case," in *Legal Aspects of Aboriginal Business Development*, ed. Joseph Eliot Magnet and Dwight A. Dorey (Toronto: Butterworths, 2005), 130.

48 Thanks to Darrell Manitowabi for identifying these disparities.

49 Yale D. Belanger and Ryan Walker, "Interest Convergence and Co-production of Plans: An Examination of Winnipeg's 'Aboriginal Pathways,'" *Canadian Journal of Urban Research* 18, 1 (2009): 121.

50 Makere Stewart-Harawira, *The New Imperial Order: Indigenous Responses to Globalization* (London: Zed Books, 2005), 77; and Vic Satzewich and Terry Wotherspoon, *First Nations: Race, Class, and Gender Relations* (Regina: Canadian Plains Research Center, 2000).

51 Russel Lawrence Barsh, "The Nature and Spirit of North American Political Systems," *American Indian Quarterly* 19, 3 (1986): 181–198; Sakej Youngblood Henderson, "Ayukpachi: Empowering Aboriginal Thought," in *Reclaiming Indigenous Voice and Vision*, ed. Marie Battiste (Vancouver: UBC Press, 2000), 248–278.

52 James [Sakej] Youngblood Henderson, "Sui Generis and Treaty Citizenship," *Citizenship Studies* 6, 4 (2003): 415–440; and his "Treaty Governance," in *Aboriginal Self-Government in Canada: Current Trends and Issues*, 3rd ed., ed. Yale D. Belanger (Saskatoon: Purich Publishing, 2008), 20–38.

53 Henderson, "Sui Generis and Treaty Citizenship."

54 Ibid., 418

55 Ibid., 418

56 Ibid., 429

57 Brian Slattery, "A Taxonomy of Aboriginal Rights," in *Let Right Be Done: Aboriginal Title, the Calder Case and the Future of Indigenous Rights*, ed. Hamar Foster, Heather Raven, and Jeremy Webber (Vancouver: University of British Columbia Press, 2007), 114.

58 Ibid., 115.

59 Julie Tomiak, *Urban Aboriginal Self-Governance in Ottawa, Winnipeg and Vancouver: Trends, Problems and Perspectives* (Ottawa: Institute on Governance, 2009), 1.

60 Kevin Bruyneel, *The Third Space of Sovereignty: The Postcolonial Politics of U.S.-Indigenous Relations* (Minneapolis: University of Minnesota Press, 2007).

61 Chris Purdy, "Band Stakes its Future on a Roll of the Dice," *Edmonton Journal*, 23 May 2004, D6.

62 Assembly of First Nations, "Fiscal Imbalance: The Truth about Spending on First Nations," in *Poverty History: The First Nations Plan for Creating Opportunity*, http://www.afn.ca/cmslib/general/FI-FS.pdf (last accessed 17 February 2009).

63 Alberta. "First Nations Development Fund Grant Agreement Form." http://www.docstoc.com/docs/44177340/First-Nations-Development-Fund-Grant-Agreement-Form (last accessed 11 July 2010).

64 Aihwa Ong, "Cultural Citizenship as Subject Making: Immigrants Negotiate Racial and Cultural Boundaries in the United States," in *Race, Identity, Citizenship: A Reader*, ed. Rodolfo D. Torres, Louis F. Miron, and Jonathan X. Inda (London: Blackwell, 1999), 264.

65 Misquadis, para. 126.

66 Ibid., paras. 155, 158.

67 Again, thanks to Darrell Manitowabi for identifying this issue.

PART III
HEALTH

CHAPTER 8

GAMBLING AND PROBLEM GAMBLING IN NORTH AMERICAN INDIGENOUS PEOPLES

ROBERT J. WILLIAMS, RHYS M.G. STEVENS, AND GARY NIXON

INTRODUCTION

The purpose of this chapter is to review what is known about gambling and problem gambling among indigenous peoples of North America. The focus is primarily on current gambling practices, and on health and social issues rather than economic ones. The first part provides a brief review of historical aspects of indigenous gambling. The second part reviews the current situation with specific reference to the meaning of gambling for indigenous people, current patterns of gambling behaviour, and the prevalence and causes of problem gambling within this population.

HISTORICAL ASPECTS

Gambling is a worldwide phenomenon found in virtually all societies. However, this is partly due to the pervasive influence of Western culture, which has a long established tradition of gambling. Prior to European expansion, gambling was found in many, but not all, societies.[1] It tended to be absent or uncommon in most parts of South America, southeast Africa, and Oceania.[2] In contrast, it was prevalent in Europe, southeast Asia, west-central Africa, Central America, and North America.[3] Cross-cultural comparisons have found gambling to be more common in societies that use money; with larger concentrations of people; that are more technically and economically developed; that have socio-economic stratification/inequality; that have greater amounts of leisure time; that do not have religious prohibitions against it; and that experience a higher degree of environmental uncertainty due to their hunting/gathering lifestyle or involvement in frequent warfare (i.e., gambling perhaps provides a way of ritualizing or influencing unpredictable events).[4]

North American indigenous peoples have a particularly extensive historical tradition of gambling. Virtually all tribes engaged in gambling (with the possible exception of a few in the far north), with evidence of this tradition dating back at least 1000 years before European contact.[5] Stewart Culin documented that three main types of gambling games were played, with all three types often present in the same tribe, and with a great deal of similarity in the object and method of play across tribes.[6] The first type involved contests of physical skill, such as archery, spearing moving objects (e.g., hoop and pole), foot races, wrestling, sliding sticks on snow/ice for distance (snow snake), and several different types of ball games, including lacrosse. These games of physical skill were mostly played by men and were played either individually or in teams. It was fairly common for spectators to wager on the outcome. The second type included guessing games requiring guessing which person, or container, or hand was concealing the hidden object (bone, stone, stick), or whether the person was holding an even or odd number of sticks, or which hand held the marked object, or the relative position of the hidden objects. Usually a score was kept by means of stick or pebble counters, with the game ending when one side had won all the counters. The number of players on each side ranged from one to several, with rhythmic chanting or singing and drumming often accompanying team play. Spectators often wagered on the results. The third group of games encompassed dice games, usually played with several two-sided dice made of shells, pits, bone, stone, or wood that were either tossed or contained in a bowl/basket that was struck. Here again, scores were usually kept by means of counters that were exchanged, although sometimes the score was used for the purpose of moving markers in a parcheesi-like circuit game. Both men and women were avid players of guessing and dice games, but they generally did not play together. However, occasionally men played against women, and it was common for spectators to reflect both genders. Only men engaged in these games when they were used for ritualistic or ceremonial purposes, as described below.

Similar to other cultures, North American indigenous peoples believed that supernatural forces influenced the outcomes of unpredictable events. Consequently, as in other cultures, gambling games were sometimes used to divine the future or to ascertain the appropriate course of action. It was also common to do things to try to cultivate favour with these supernatural forces, and for gambling success to be interpreted as evidence of having this spiritual support.[7]

Somewhat unique to indigenous culture is the prominence of gambling in oral tradition and mythology.[8] Common in these mythic stories is the existence of supernatural beings with great gambling skill. Also prevalent is the figure of a "gambling hero" who is able to "out-gamble" one of these superbeings or some enemy of the tribe through superior skill, cunning, or magic.[9] Gambling was also believed to summon and promote the gathering of these supernatural spirits. Consequently, gambling was a frequent part of ceremonies associated with ensuring a good harvest or hunt, producing rain, or marking the changing of the seasons. For similar reasons, gambling games were engaged in to help cure sickness, expel demons, aid in fertility, and to facilitate passage to the afterlife after death.[10]

Gambling games were also an important element of inter-tribal interaction. They provided a forum for nonviolent competition between villages, clans, and tribes (although injuries were not uncommon in some of the physical team competitions), as well as an opportunity for socializing and trade. They also promoted continued tribal interaction, as it was common practice for one tribe to challenge another to a contest and for the loser to re-challenge so as to regain their honour. The remarkable similarity of games across widely diverse and distant tribes provides indirect evidence of their importance in this regard.[11] Per Binde argues that gambling's use for the purposes of inter-tribal competition is in fact the primary reason for gambling's prevalence and intensity in North American indigenous culture.[12]

Gambling was also a popular recreational pastime. However, indigenous oral tradition contains the message that gambling outside of its ritualistic/ceremonial context was frowned upon and could lead to excess. Indeed, several of the situations that required the mythical gambling hero to prevail were said to be brought about by the devastating gambling losses of the tribe. The potential dangers of gambling were also noted by early European observers (e.g., Jesuits), who reported many instances of "reckless" gambling leading to loss of all possessions, as well as occasional assault, murder, and suicide. However, as pointed out by Yale Belanger, the high stakes of gambling would naturally look more reckless to a European observer than to a member of a more communal society with extensive family support systems to fall back on, where there would be plenty of opportunities to win back what was lost, and where it was believed that supernatural rather than human forces were responsible for the outcome.[13] The surprising lack of emotion with which indigenous peoples typically accepted both their wins and losses (as noted by these same European observers) perhaps provides some evidence of this.

It is sometimes implied that another purpose of indigenous gambling was reciprocal exchange and redistribution of wealth.[14] There is no doubt that gambling commonly resulted in a useful redistribution of wealth and also had a levelling economic effect. However, it is doubtful that redistribution was actually a goal or a desired outcome in most situations, especially in the context of the inter-tribal competitions that occurred.

CURRENT SITUATION

European colonialism transformed both the nature and the types of gambling available in North America. In contrast to the more spiritual, ceremonial, or social orientation of traditional indigenous gambling, Western forms of gambling have a predominantly recreational and commercial orientation. The socio-cultural impact this fundamental change has had on indigenous people is somewhat unclear. The new Western forms of gambling (e.g., horse racing, card games) were readily adopted and engaged in. Indeed, as will be documented later in this chapter, North American Aboriginal peoples currently have high rates of participation in almost *all* forms of Western gambling. Furthermore, in the past thirty years many tribes have also become major providers of Western-style gambling in commercial casinos and bingo halls.[15] It is also noteworthy that some of the highest prevalence rates of problem gambling have been reported in Aboriginal populations.[16]

The socio-cultural impact of this change in the nature of gambling is an important issue meriting further scrutiny. More specifically, it would be instructive to know:

a) What is the current meaning of gambling among First Nations people? For example, what do they consider "gambling" to be; what are their motivations for gambling; what are their current attitudes toward gambling; and how their attitudes toward these things differ from those of the non-Aboriginal population?

b) What is the current pattern of gambling behaviour among First Nations people, and how is this different from that among other groups?

c) What are the nature, prevalence, and causes of problem gambling among First Nations people?

The remainder of this chapter reviews the research that speaks to these issues, with a focus on recent research the first author (Robert Williams) has conducted. There are some important methodological considerations to be aware of when discussing this research. The first is that none of these studies contain a large, representative sample of First Nations people. Rather, what is available are several large, general-population samples containing a small number of First Nations peoples, which then have to be combined to produce sufficient numbers for analysis. There are often methodological complications when combining studies from different time periods and with different response rates, administration format, etc. On the other hand, these studies have a high degree of methodological consistency in that they were all conducted by the first author in a relatively circumscribed time period (2004–2008) using the same question wordings and roughly the same procedures. Furthermore, the advantage of combining different studies is that it may level out methodological differences, potentially making the results more generalizable.

A second issue is that indigenous North American people comprise a diverse array of tribes with different historical traditions, different current socioeconomic situations, and different availabilities of gambling. Combining them into one group obscures potentially important inter-tribal differences.[17] That being said, these tribes do have similar gambling traditions and also share a common experience with European colonization and exposure to Western forms of gambling. Furthermore, as described below, the obtained results are fairly consistent between different geographic regions, implying the similarities are stronger than the differences.

A final methodological issue is that non-Aboriginal researchers using a Western "lens" have conducted these studies.[18] However, it is also the case that there is some cross-cultural validity to the constructs examined, and there is also some research done by First Nations investigators that provides a validity check to these findings.[19]

CURRENT MEANING OF GAMBLING

DEFINITION OF GAMBLING — *Gambling* is usually defined as "wagering money or something of material value on something with an uncertain outcome in the hope of winning money or something of material value."[20] Nonetheless, despite this common definition, people differ in what things they choose to characterize as gambling. Examining these differences is potentially instructive in understanding the meaning of gambling to different groups.

In three separate studies, the first author provided a comprehensive list of eighteen gambling-like activities and asked people to indicate whether they considered each activity gambling or not. These activities included such things as buying insurance, paying money to enter tournaments or contests for cash prizes, taking physical or emotional risks, spending money on games at fairs to win prizes, and stock market speculation, as well as more stereotypic gambling games such as electronic gambling machines (EGMs), casino table games, and lottery tickets. The first study involved a telephone survey of a random sample of 2088 Canadian adults between 2006 and 2007 that included sixty-seven people who indicated the primary ethnic or cultural origin of their ancestors was Aboriginal, Métis, or Inuit.[21] The second study was an online survey of 10,755 North Americans (89 percent from United States) in 2007 that included 84 people who similarly identified their ancestry to be Aboriginal, Métis, or Inuit.[22] The third study was a door-to-door survey of a random sample of 120 adults from the Kainai (Blood) Reserve in southern Alberta[23] in 2005.[24] This last study used a participatory action research approach, whereby the first author and his colleagues created research capacity in the First Nations community and the community conducted the survey themselves.[25]

FIGURE 1: Percentage of People Indicating that They Consider the Activity to be Gambling, as a Function of Aboriginal (n = 271) versus Non-Aboriginal (n = 12,692) Status

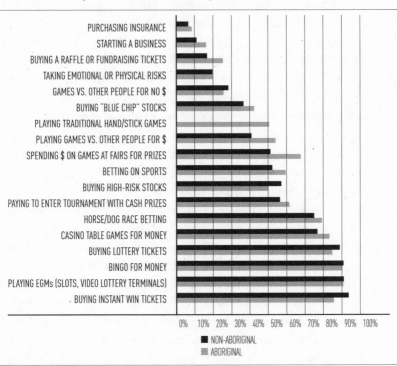

NOTE: Results for traditional hand/stick games is based only on results from the Blood Tribe Survey (n = 120)

Data analysis revealed a high degree of consistency in the sentiments expressed among the three different Aboriginal samples as well as between the two different non-Aboriginal samples. A few small differences were observed, likely attributable to the somewhat different populations being sampled as well as the different survey administrations (phone, online, face-to-face). The samples were combined to level out these differences and to increase overall sample size. The results from the aggregated sample are presented in Figure 1, which shows the percentage of people who identify each activity as gambling as a function of Aboriginal or non-Aboriginal status.

As seen in Figure 1, the Aboriginal and non-Aboriginal results are quite similar. Both groups see gambling on a continuum, with some things being endorsed by less than 10 percent of people (e.g., buying insurance), some things having moderate endorsement (e.g., high-risk stocks), and some things being endorsed by over 90 percent of people (e.g., EGMs). Furthermore, the rank order is almost identical, with current Western/commercial forms of gambling being seen as the most "gambling-like" by both Aboriginal and non-Aboriginal people. There are a few interesting and potentially important differences, however. A chi-square test found that Aboriginal people are significantly ($p < .01$) more likely to identify the following activities as gambling compared to non-Aboriginal peoples:[26] buying raffle/fundraising tickets (25 percent versus 17 percent), playing games against other people for money (54 percent versus 41 percent), and spending money on games at fairs for prizes (68 percent versus 51 percent). It is quite plausible that the identification of these activities as gambling may be related to the extensive Aboriginal cultural tradition of gambling in these types of contexts.

As an activity, traditional hand/stick games were listed only in the Blood Tribe survey (as non-Aboriginals would be unfamiliar with these activities). A quite interesting finding was that there was almost an even split between people who believe these activities are gambling (50.5 percent) and those who do not consider it gambling (49.5 percent). Information arising from focus groups conducted as part of this study shed some light on this. What emerged from these groups was the fact that these types of traditional games were often just played for "fun" and only *sometimes* played for money or material goods (the survey question did not specify whether money or goods were involved).[27] However, even if money or goods had been specified in the survey question, it seems clear that First Nations and Inuit people still would not consider their traditional gambling games to fit well into current connotations of "gambling." As evidence of this, it was also found that only 20.5 percent of the sample endorsed the statement that "gambling[28] is a part of traditional Native cultural practices," and only 19.0 percent believed "gambling is a part of traditional Native religious or spiritual practices." (There were no non-Aboriginals surveyed in the Blood Tribe survey.)[29]

MOTIVATIONS FOR GAMBLING — Investigating reported motives for gambling is another way of ascertaining gambling's meaning for different groups of people. For example, it has been suggested that gambling for some First Nations people may be serving as a form of escape from their frustrating circumstances.[30] An alternative theory is that they may be trying to consciously or unconsciously emulate the gambling hero in indigenous mythology and, consequently, that prestige may be a more important motivation than winning money or seeking entertainment.[31]

People's motivations for gambling were investigated in two different studies. The first was an online survey in 2006 of 4123 randomly selected adults in southeastern Ontario, including a sample of 197 individuals who identified their primary ancestry as First Nations, Métis, or Inuit.[32] The second was a telephone and online sample in 2008 of 9532 adults in Alberta that included a sample of 249 Aboriginal people.[33] In each study, people were asked, "What is the main reason that you gamble?" and they were provided with the following response options: excitement/entertainment/fun; to win money; for escape or to distract myself; to socialize; to support worthy causes; to feel good about myself; or "other." These choices were derived from a content analysis done on earlier studies that used an open-ended format for the same question. As before, the samples were combined to improve overall representativeness and sample size.

The results of this investigation are shown in Figure 2. As can be seen, there are again more similarities than differences between the Aboriginal and non-Aboriginal groups. In both cases, the most popular reason for gambling was for excitement/entertainment/fun, with winning money and socializing being less popular second and third choices. Gambling to "escape or distract myself" was endorsed by less than 4 percent of both groups, and gambling to "feel good about myself" was endorsed by less than 1 percent of both groups. Chi-square tests found no significant differences in motivations between the groups. Consistent with different cultural traditions, there was a trend for Aboriginal peoples to gamble more for entertainment/excitement/fun ($p = .02$), and for non-Aboriginals to consider winning money to be somewhat more important ($p = .03$).

FIGURE 2: Main Reason for Gambling, as a Function of Aboriginal (n = 446) versus Non-Aboriginal (n = 13,209) Status

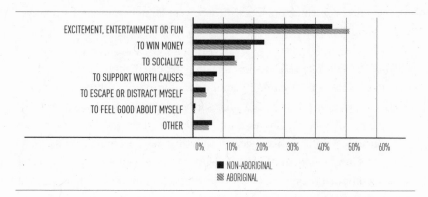

ATTITUDES TOWARD GAMBLING — A final measure of gambling's meaning concerns people's attitudes toward it: more specifically, whether they consider it immoral, and whether they think the harms outweigh the benefits or vice versa. Six studies were used for this analysis. This includes the aforementioned telephone survey of 2088 Canadian adults in 2006-07;[34] the online survey of 10,755 North Americans in 2007;[35] the southern Alberta Blood Tribe door-to-door survey of 120 Aboriginal people in 2005;[36] the online survey of 4123 Ontario adults in 2006;[37] the telephone and online sample of 9532 adult Albertans in 2008;[38] as well as a telephone survey of 7947 randomly selected adults from the British Columbia lower mainland conducted in 2004, 2005, and 2006 that surveyed 158 individuals of Aboriginal ancestry.[39] The total combined sample consisted of 875 Aboriginal individuals and 33,690 non-Aboriginals. Results are seen in Figure 3.

FIGURE 3a: Current Attitudes toward Gambling, as a Function of Aboriginal (n = 875) versus Non-Aboriginal (n = 33,690) Status

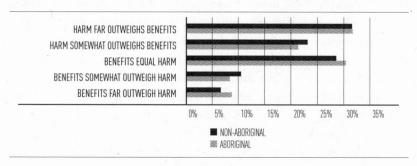

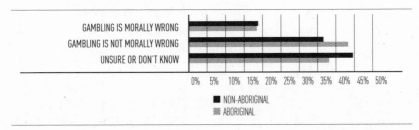

FIGURE 3b: Current Attitudes toward Gambling, as a Function of Aboriginal (n = 875) versus Non-Aboriginal (n = 33,690) Status

As in the previous analyses, the Aboriginal results in this analysis are quite similar to the non-Aboriginal results. The majority of both groups thought that the harm of gambling outweighed the benefits. More specifically, 56 percent of non-Aboriginals and 53 percent of Aboriginal people believed the harms either far or somewhat outweighed the benefits, compared to 18 percent of non-Aboriginals and 17 percent of Aboriginal individuals who believed the benefits either far or somewhat outweighed the harm. There was no significant difference in Aboriginal versus non-Aboriginal opinion on this issue. The large majority of people also did not believe that gambling was morally wrong, although a significant portion of people were unsure of its morality. While the Aboriginal profile here was similar to the non-Aboriginal profile, there was a significantly greater percentage of Aboriginal people who believed that gambling is *not* morally wrong relative to non-Aboriginal people (43 percent versus 37 percent). Similarly, significantly fewer Aboriginal people are "unsure" of gambling's morality compared to non-Aboriginal people (38 percent versus 45 percent). These results almost certainly speak to the much greater historical (and current) religious denunciation of gambling in Western than in First Nations and Inuit societies.

GAMBLING BEHAVIOUR — Existing research suggests that overall prevalence rates of Aboriginal gambling may be roughly equivalent to rates among non-Aboriginal peoples, but that there are some differences in frequency of participation, expenditures, and game preference.

A large-scale study of Alberta students in grades 5 to 12 (n = 1961) found that 88 percent had gambled in the past year.[40] A much smaller-scale Alberta adolescent study also found a very high rate of past-year gambling.[41]

Rachel Volberg and Max Abbott found that the lifetime prevalence of gambling among North American Indian adults in North Dakota in 1992 was equivalent to that among the general population, but their overall weekly frequency of gambling and gambling expenditures were higher (particularly for bingo and card games).[42] Jason Blankenship et al. found that North American Indian people in New Mexico in 1998 had lower rates of past-month sports betting, but higher rates of involvement in casino gambling, lottery play, EGMs, and instant-win tickets.[43] Harold Wynne found a slightly lower rate of past-year gambling participation for Aboriginal people (82 percent) compared to other ethnic/racial groups (87-89 percent) in Saskatchewan in 2001.[44] Garry Smith and Harold Wynne found a similar result in 2001 in Alberta (84 percent of Aboriginals reported past-year gambling, versus 83 to 96 percent of those of British, German, French, and Ukrainian backgrounds).[45] David Patton et al. found that Aboriginal individuals in Manitoba in 2001 had significantly higher rates of involvement in keno, bingo, EGMs, casinos, instant-win tickets, and sports lotteries, but lower rates of purchasing raffle and fundraising tickets.[46] They also spent significantly more money on most of these forms of gambling than did non-Aboriginal population. Rachel Volberg and Bo Bernhard found North American Indian people in New Mexico to have a somewhat higher rate of past-year gambling compared to non-Aboriginals (73 percent versus 67 percent), with this increased prevalence being notably higher for casino gambling and bingo.[47] A proportionally higher rate of bingo play has also been reported for Aboriginal people in Alberta,[48] Montana,[49] Ontario,[50] and Quebec.[51]

In a series of prevalence studies of individuals aged fifteen and older in the Northwest Territories[52] (where Aboriginal people comprise roughly 50 percent of the population) it was found that the past-year prevalence of gambling among Aboriginal people was significantly higher than among non-Aboriginals in the three time periods studied (84 percent versus 75 percent in 1996, 80 percent versus 67 percent in 2002, 72 percent versus 68 percent in 2006). The intensity of Aboriginal involvement in gambling was also higher than that of non-Aboriginal involvement in all three time periods, as evidenced by engagement in more forms of gambling, two to three times higher expenditure, and roughly twice as many regular gamblers. Types of gambling engaged in were also different, with lottery tickets being the favourite form for non-Aboriginals in all years, whereas card games were the favourite form for Aboriginal people in 1996, and bingo in 2002 and 2006. The largest and most consistent differences between Aboriginal people and non-Aboriginals occurred for bingo (54 percent versus 14 percent in 1996; 64 percent versus 17 percent in 2002; 56 percent versus 9 percent in 2006) and lottery tickets (49 percent versus 80 percent in 1996; 42 percent versus 72 percent in 2002; 52 percent versus 74 percent in 2006).

Mélanie Anctil and Serge Chevalier conducted face-to-face interviews with a representative sample of 920 Cree (age twelve or older) living in the James

Bay area of Quebec (Iiyiyiu Aschii) in 2003.[53] Compared to the general Quebec adult (18+) population, Cree adults (18+) had gambled proportionally less (72 percent) in the past year than did inhabitants of Quebec (81 percent). Bingo and video lottery terminals (VLTs) were played at a significantly higher rate (45 percent versus 9 percent for bingo; 25 percent versus 8 percent for VLTs), and regular lotteries played as a significantly lower rate (39 percent versus 65 percent), but there were no differences for playing slot machines in casinos, cards, or instant lotteries. In terms of gender and age differences, women played bingo significantly more and people age eighteen to twenty-nine played VLTs more.

Five studies were used in the present analysis to assess gambling behaviour. These included all of the above-mentioned studies used to assess gambling attitudes, with the exception of the North American online survey. This latter survey was excluded as there was some over-selection for gamblers, and the actual prevalence of gambling is of interest in the present analysis. Because this survey contains the only United States sample, excluding it also means that the results obtained herein reflect Canadian prevalence rates only. Another difference in the aggregated sample is that the sample size was larger in the Canadian 2006-07 survey (i.e., $n = 8496$, with 131 Aboriginal people),[54] as everyone in this survey received the gambling participation questions, whereas only a random sample of 25 percent received the attitude and gambling definition questions. Thus, the total sample for the present analysis consisted of 859 Aboriginal people and 29,363 non-Aboriginals.

The first finding of note is that past-year participation in gambling was significantly higher in Aboriginal people (84.6 percent) compared to non-Aboriginal people (75.1 percent). Furthermore, as shown in Figure 4, Aboriginal people have greater involvement in all forms of gambling, with the exception of lotteries and high-risk stocks. As can be seen, the relative popularity of different games is roughly the same for Aboriginal versus non-Aboriginal people, with lotteries, raffles, and instant-win tickets being most popular, and Internet gambling, horse/dog race betting, and high-risk stocks being the least popular. Only the Blood Tribe survey asked about traditional hand/stick games, with results indicating that only about 20 percent of people had participated in these traditional games in the past year (i.e., it was the seventh most popular out of the twelve forms of gambling).

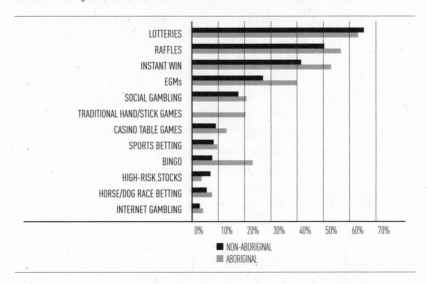

FIGURE 4: Past-year Participation in Different Forms of Gambling, as a Function of Aboriginal (n = 859) versus Non-Aboriginal (n = 29,363) Status

Consistent with prior research, there were significant differences in game preference, with greater Aboriginal participation in bingo (23.2 percent versus 7.6 percent), EGMs (40.0 percent versus 27.2 percent), casino table games (13.2 percent versus 9.1 percent), and instant-win tickets (52.9 percent versus 41.7 percent), and significantly lower participation in high-risk stocks (3.5 percent versus 7.0 percent). Bingo's much greater popularity is likely attributable to the fact that, historically, Western churches (particularly the Roman Catholic and Anglican) spent considerable time with indigenous people in their efforts to convert them to Christianity. Because these same religions routinely used bingo for fundraising, they also introduced large numbers of Aboriginal people to one of the few legal forms of gambling that existed prior to the modern era of gambling expansion. Bingo parlours were also the first type of commercial gambling operations offered by tribal governments in the United States in the late 1970s. (Conflict over the legality of these expanding bingo operations precipitated the Indian Gaming Regulation Act of 1988). The reason for the higher rate of EGM and casino table-game play among Aboriginal people is less clear, however. It is quite plausible this is also due to familiarity and exposure, as there are many tribes that now commercially provide these forms of gambling.

Not only is their overall gambling participation higher, but Aboriginal gambling involvement is also more extensive. Figure 5 illustrates the statistically higher number of gambling games engaged in by Aboriginal gamblers

(M = 2.92) relative to non-Aboriginal gamblers (M = 2.40). Expenditures are also significantly higher. In Aboriginal individuals, the self-reported mean, median, and modal "typical month" gambling expenditures were $119.87, $41.63, and $21.40 respectively, compared to $71.07, $19.00, and $5.00 for non-Aboriginals.

FIGURE 5: Number of Different Forms of Gambling Engaged in by Gamblers, as a Function of Aboriginal (n = 859) versus Non-Aboriginal (n = 29,363) Status

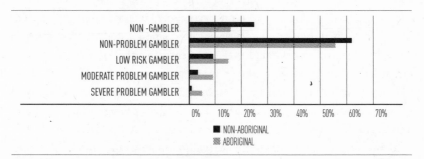

PROBLEM/PATHOLOGICAL GAMBLING

PREVALENCE AND NATURE — *Problem gambling* is usually defined as "difficulties in limiting money and/or time spent on gambling which leads to significant adverse consequences for the gambler, for others, or for the community."[55] *Pathological gambling* is generally considered a more severe form of problem gambling.

A literature review by D. Wardman, Nady el-Guebaly, and David Hodgins in 2001[56] identified three studies that provided an estimate of problem/pathological gambling prevalence among Aboriginal adolescents.[57] Obtained rates were between 10 percent and 28 percent. However, these figures have to be considered tentative because of uncertainty concerning whether the assessment instruments used are valid for adolescents (i.e., the South Oaks Gambling Screen (SOGS)[58] and the SOGS-Revised for Adolescents (SOGS-RA).[59]

The Wardman et al. review also identified five studies that provided estimates for Aboriginal *adults* using the SOGS.[60] It was found that Aboriginal adults had rates of problem gambling 2.2 to 5.0 times higher than non-Aboriginals and rates of pathological gambling that were 4.1 to 15.7 times higher. These studies mostly used non-representative samples (e.g., alcohol treatment seekers, casino patrons). The only reasonably representative samples were that of: (a) Volberg and Abbott, who estimated that the past-year problem and pathological gambling prevalence rate was 12.4 percent among North American Indian people in North Dakota in 1992;[61] and (b) Don Cozzetto and Brent Larocque, who obtained a 10-14 percent prevalence rate of pathological gambling on two North Dakota reservations.[62] In the past few years there have been other studies that have also documented higher rates of problem/pathological gambling among Aboriginal people. In 2000, Darlene Auger and David Hewitt found that 24 percent of 500 Aboriginal adults in Alberta met SOGS criteria for problem or pathological gambling.[63] In 2001, Wynne found that 19.8 percent of the 91 Aboriginal adults surveyed in Saskatchewan were either Canadian Problem Gambling Index (CPGI) moderate or severe problem gamblers.[64] A comparable study in Alberta in 2001 found a combined rate of 14.5 percent among the 62 Aboriginal individuals surveyed.[65] In a national study of Canadians in 2002,[66] Statistics Canada found that 11.2 percent of the 217 off-reserve Aboriginal gamblers were moderate or severe problem gamblers as assessed by the CPGI.[67] Anctil and Chevalier conducted face-to-face interviews with a representative sample of 920 Cree (age twelve or older) living in the James Bay are of Quebec (Iiyiyiu Aschii) in 2003 and found that 9.2 percent were CPGI moderate or severe problem gamblers (with a trend for the rates to be higher in women and among those ages eighteen to twenty-nine).[68] Joseph Westermeyer et al. found significantly higher lifetime rates of pathological gambling among United States North American Indian veterans (10 percent) compared to United States Hispanic veterans.[69]

While it seems clear that the overall rates of problem/pathological gambling are higher in Aboriginal people, the actual rate in the general population of Aboriginal people has not been established. Thus, the same studies used to establish gambling prevalence described in the previous section were also used to estimate the Canadian prevalence rate of problem/pathological gambling in the present analysis. It is important to note that all the studies in the present analysis used the CPGI as opposed to the SOGS. The CPGI has some major advantages over other instruments, in that it was developed for general population surveys as opposed to clinical settings.[70] It also does not have some of the false positive problems of the SOGS.[71] Of particular concern to Aboriginal prevalence research is the fact that the SOGS's heavy emphasis on financial problems results in significantly more people with low incomes being identified as problem gamblers than with the CPGI.[72] One disadvantage of the CPGI is that people who score in the lower boundary of problem gambling on the CPGI (i.e., a score of 3 or 4) sometimes do not correspond well to clinical judgments of "problem gambling" and may represent a different type of false positive problem.[73]

Figure 6 displays the prevalence rates for each of the categories of gamblers. In the non-Aboriginal sample, 24.9 percent were Non-gamblers; 61.8 percent Non-problem Gamblers; 9.1 percent Low Risk Gamblers; 3.2 percent Moderate

Problem Gamblers; and 1.0 percent Severe Problem Gamblers (equivalent to "pathological gamblers"). The rates in the Aboriginal sample were as follows: 15.4 percent Non-gamblers; 55.7 percent Non-problem Gamblers; 15.0 percent Low Risk Gamblers; 9.1 percent Moderate Problem Gamblers; and 4.8 percent Severe Problem Gamblers. Thus, the combined rate of problem plus pathological gambling in the Aboriginal sample (13.9 percent) was 3.3 times higher than the rate in the non-Aboriginal sample (4.2 percent), with this ratio being particularly high for severe problem gambling (4.8 times higher).

FIGURE 6: Past-year Gambling Categorization on the Canadian Problem Gambling Index, as a Function of Aboriginal (n = 859) versus Non-Aboriginal (n = 29,363) Status

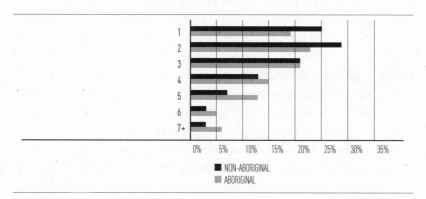

There are some important caveats to these findings. One issue concerns the fact that there were marked differences in the rates between the different sub-samples used: 48.8 percent (Blood Tribe in southern Alberta); 19.4 percent (Alberta); 11.8 percent (southeastern Ontario); 11.4 percent (Canada); and 6.4 percent (British Columbia lower mainland). There are two reasons for this. The first is that real differences exist in prevalence rates between different Aboriginal groups. It is likely no coincidence that the highest rate is found in the on-reserve population in southern Alberta (Blood Tribe), while the lowest rate is found among urban Aboriginal people in the British Columbia lower mainland. The second reason is due to differences in administration format. Problem/pathological gambling rates are lowest in the telephone interviews (BC lower mainland; Canada; Alberta telephone subsample), intermediate in the self-administered online surveys (southeastern Ontario; Alberta online subsample), and highest in the door-to-door interviews administered by First Nations research assistants. Problem gambling rates obtained by telephone surveys underestimate the true rate[74] due to the fact that a considerable percentage of Aboriginal people do not have residential telephone service, with evidence indicating these particular individuals have significantly higher rates of poverty, unemployment, health problems, and substance use.[75] The self-administered surveys (used in Alberta and southeastern Ontario) were in a format that tends to produce more valid results (i.e., higher rates).[76] However, these surveys were also administered online, thus requiring access to and some fluency with a computer. Hence, it seems likely that these studies also produced underestimated rates of problem/pathological gambling. For Aboriginal people, it seems clear that door-to-door surveys will likely achieve the most representative sampling (as in the Blood Tribe survey). Furthermore, there is good evidence that the face-to-face interview format tends to produce more valid results than telephone interviews because of the more honest and candid responses in the former.[77] This may be particularly true when the interviewer is of the same ethnic/racial ancestry. However, it must be remembered that the previously mentioned Blood Tribe prevalence rate of 48.8 percent can really only be used as a rough estimate perhaps of the "upper rate" of problem/pathological gambling among Aboriginal people, as this sample consists primarily of *on-reserve* individuals in just *one* tribe and location.

A final consideration concerns whether Aboriginal people believe the definition used to identify people as problem/pathological gamblers to be the same as the one they themselves would use. This was investigated in the Blood Tribe survey in couple of different ways. The first was by asking people, "In your opinion, what are the main signs and symptoms of problem gambling?" A total of 48 percent of the total responses were in the general category of financial problems (i.e., "spending all your money on gambling," "poverty," "debt," "being broke," "selling things," "borrowing money to gamble"). The next most commonly reported category of signs or symptoms (19 percent of all responses) concerned loss of control (i.e., "gambling all the time," "preoccupied with gambling," "can't stop gambling"). The third most commonly given sign or symptom (14 percent of responses) concerned family issues (i.e., "never home," "no time for family," "marriage/family problems," "family violence," "kids left alone"). Reports of mental health problems constituted 12 percent of all responses (i.e., "stress," "anxiety," "depression," "suicide," "no self esteem," "anger," "irritable"). The remaining 7 percent of responses reflected a variety of other signs and symptoms ("alcohol abuse," "isolation," "physical illness," "fantasy replaces reality," "loss of family and moral values").[78] In general, these results indicate that the construct of problem/pathological gambling has some cross-cultural validity, as these self-identified signs or symptoms of problem/pathological gambling are very consistent with the core features assessed by the standard assessment instruments (CPGI, SOGS). Further evidence of this is seen in the fact that one of the survey questions also asked people to estimate the percentage of adults on the Blood Reserve that they believed had a gambling problem. The average estimate of 56.6 percent (range of 0 percent to 100 percent) is very close to the 48.8 percent assessed by the CPGI.[79]

In summary, considering the above evidence as well as the previously mentioned problems with the lower boundaries of the CPGI,[80] our best estimate is that the true, current, overall average rate of problem/pathological gambling in Aboriginal people is probably somewhere between 10 percent and 20 percent, but that the range among different groups may vary from 7 percent to 45 percent.

REASONS FOR HIGHER RATES
OF PROBLEM/PATHOLOGICAL GAMBLING

There have been many suggestions as to why Aboriginal people have higher rates of problem/pathological gambling. These include poverty, higher exposure to gambling, cultural stress, and greater acceptance of "magical thinking."[81] However, in the absence of longitudinal research, there is no unambiguous evidence concerning the etiology of problem gambling in the general population, let alone in First Nations people.[82] However, it is quite likely that many of the same variables known to be responsible for the development of other addictions (and psychopathology more generally) are also causally related to the development of problem gambling. The bio-psychosocial model is the best explanatory model of addictions[83] and is also widely accepted as an appropriate model for problem/pathological gambling.[84] This model posits that there is a multitude of biological, psychological, social, and environmental factors that both contribute to and provide protection from the development of addictions, and also that the pattern of contributing factors will often be different for different people.[85]

The variables known to be causally related to addictions, and which are found in North American Aboriginal people, are as follows:

> ♦ *Greater rates of gambling participation.* As mentioned earlier, North American indigenous people have a particularly strong cultural tradition and acceptance of gambling, which is probably related to their greater overall participation in and frequency of gambling. Unfortunately, however, it is well established that greater rates of participation in any potentially addictive product has a direct relationship to greater overall rates of problems associated with that activity.[86]

♦ *Conducive cultural beliefs.* Traditional indigenous cultural beliefs reveal that supernatural forces influence gambling outcomes and that these supernatural forces can be influenced by human actions.[87] However, most modern forms of gambling (e.g., EGMs, bingo, lotteries, instant-win tickets) have been specifically designed to have completely random outcomes and also to deceptively convey the impression that skill and choice may influence what happens. Furthermore, unlike social or traditional forms of gambling, the longer you play any of these modern forms, the more you are guaranteed to lose. Today, beliefs that human skill and choice can somehow influence gambling outcomes are known as "gambling fallacies," and they have a strong association with problematic gambling.[88] Number and overall level of gambling fallacies were measured in most of the studies used in the present analysis. In all cases, the average number of fallacies was higher in the Aboriginal group relative to the non-Aboriginal group. As an example, in the Blood Tribe Survey, when asked "why do some people win more than others," only 32.5 percent endorsed the statement "it is just random chance."[89]

♦ *Disadvantageous social conditions.* Poverty, unemployment, lack of education, health problems, cultural stress/disenfranchisement, and societal marginalization/discrimination are inter-connected factors causally related to the high rates of mental health and drug and alcohol problems in most indigenous peoples.[90] As an illustrative example, despite the very high rate of problem gambling on the Blood Reserve, problem gambling was only identified as the fifth most pressing issue that needed to be dealt with, after "economic development and jobs," "drug and alcohol problems," "better education," and "violence."[91] Having a mental health problem or abusing drugs or alcohol is known to strongly predispose people to additional addictions such as problem gambling.[92] This constellation of addictions, mental health problems, and social problems then reinforce one another's existence, making it much more difficult to recover from any of them.[93] These problems are also known to have perpetuating inter-generational impacts.[94]

♦ *Younger age.* The highest rate of problem gambling is almost always found in people younger than thirty.[95] This was also the case in all of the studies used in the present analysis. Because the average age of First Nations people is significantly younger than that of non-Aboriginal people, this is another factor contributing to their higher rates.

♦ *Greater availability compared to non-Aboriginal populations?* Greater availability of a product is typically related to greater use of the product, which is then related to greater overall harm associated with the product. This has been established for alcohol, drugs, firearms, *and* gambling.[96] While it is not clear whether Aboriginal people have greater overall availability of gambling opportunities compared to non-Aboriginals, it is plausible, considering the large number of North American indigenous communities that are actual providers of commercial gambling.[97]

CONCLUSION

The purpose of this chapter was to review what is known about gambling and problem gambling among Aboriginal peoples, with specific reference to the meaning of gambling, current patterns of gambling behaviour, and the nature, prevalence, and causes of problem gambling within this population. In general, it is evident North American indigenous people have become strongly Westernized in their understanding and motivations for gambling, as well as in their pattern of play. This is a sentiment that has been expressed before,[98] and also appears to be true of indigenous people in other parts of the world.[99] North American Aboriginal people tend to see gambling in the same way non-Aboriginal people do. That is, as a commercial and recreational activity typified by forms such as EGMs, bingo, lottery tickets, casino table games, instant-win tickets, and horse/dog racing, and as something distinct from their historical practices. Their primary motivation for gambling is the same as it is for non-Aboriginal people, which is for excitement/entertainment/fun, with winning money being a secondary concern. Attitudes are also very similar, with both Aboriginal and non-Aboriginal people strongly believing that the harms of gambling outweigh the benefits, and that gambling is not an immoral activity. Finally, the relative popularity of different gambling games is roughly the same for Aboriginal versus non-Aboriginal people, with lotteries, raffles, and instant-win tickets tending to be the most popular, and Internet gambling, horse/dog race betting, and high-risk stocks being the least popular. Participation in traditional gambling games appears to be much less common.

While the similarities definitely outweigh the differences, there *do* exist some important differences. For one, Aboriginal people are significantly more likely to correctly recognize that things such as raffles and wagering money against other people in a social setting are forms of gambling. It is quite plausible this is because of their more extensive cultural tradition of gambling in these types of contexts. While gambling for the purposes of entertainment/excitement/fun tends to be a more important reason than winning money for all people who gamble, entertainment/fun has a tendency to be even more important for Aboriginal people compared to non-Aboriginal people. Here again, this speaks to different cultural traditions. Opinion about the morality of gambling is also different, with a significantly higher percentage of non-Aboriginal people believing it to be immoral, which is almost certainly due to its greater religious denunciation in Western society. There are also significant differences in game preference, with greater Aboriginal participation in bingo, EGMs, casino table games, and instant-win tickets, and significantly lower participation in high-risk stocks. The higher rate of bingo, EGM, and casino table-game play may well be due to greater familiarity and exposure, as well as the influence of Western churches (in the case of bingo). Overall gambling participation is also significantly higher, as is the number of games engaged in and the amount of money spent. While this is likely partly due to a greater cultural tradition of gambling, it also points to the area where there is an unambiguous difference between Aboriginal and non-Aboriginal people: rates of problem and pathological gambling. The best estimate is that the current overall average rate of problem/pathological gambling is in the 10 percent to 20 percent range, and is at least four times higher than that found in non-Aboriginal populations. This is attributable to the many more risk factors for problem gambling, such as greater participation in gambling, different beliefs about the forces and factors influencing the outcome of gambling, younger average age, and a range of disadvantageous social conditions (e.g., poverty, unemployment, poor education, cultural stress) that are conducive to the development of addictive behaviour. Rectifying disadvantageous social conditions is essential to helping ameliorate these high problem/pathological gambling rates.[100]

NOTES

1 Per Binde, "Gambling across Cultures: Mapping Worldwide Occurrence and Learning from Ethnographic Comparison," *International Gambling Studies* 5, 1 (2005): 1–27.

2 The following works point to evidence of gambling among indigenous Australians prior to European contact: Jan McMillen and Katie Donnelly, "Gambling in Australian Indigenous Communities: The State of Play," *Australian Journal of Social Issues Vol. 43, 3 (Spring 2008)*, 397-426; John M. Cooper, "Games and Gambling," in *Handbook of South American Indians*, ed. Julian H. Steward (Washington, DC: Smithsonian Institution, 1949), 503–524; Stewart Culin, *Games of the North American Indians* (New York: Dover, 1907), 31; Alfred Louis Kroeber, *Anthropology: Race, Language, Culture, Psychology, Prehistory* (New York: Harcourt, Brace and World, 1948), 552–553; John A. Price, "Gambling in Traditional Asia," *Anthropologica* 14, 2 (1972): 157–180; Frederic L. Pryor, "The Friedman-Savage Utility Function in Cross-cultural Perspective," *Journal of Political Economy* 84, 4, Part 1 (1976): 821–834; Thomas Q. Reefe, "The Biggest Game of All: Gambling in Traditional Africa," in *Sport in Africa: Essays in Social History*, ed. William J. Baker and James A. Mangan (New York: Africana, 1987), 48.

3 John M. Cooper, *Temporal Sequence and the Marginal Cultures* (Washington, DC: Catholic University of America, 1941); John M. Cooper, "Games and Gambling," in *Handbook of South American Indians*, ed. Julian H. Steward (Washington, DC: Smithsonian Institution, 1949), 503–524; Stewart Culin, *Games of the North American Indians* (New York: Dover, 1907), 31; Alfred Louis Kroeber, *Anthropology: Race, Language, Culture, Psychology, Prehistory* (New York: Harcourt, Brace and World, 1948), 552–553; John A. Price, "Gambling in Traditional Asia," *Anthropologica* 14, 2 (1972): 157–180; Frederic L. Pryor, "The Friedman-Savage Utility Function in Cross-cultural Perspective," *Journal of Political Economy* 84, 4, Part 1 (1976): 821–834; Thomas Q. Reefe, "The Biggest Game of All: Gambling in Traditional Africa," in *Sport in Africa: Essays in Social History*, ed. William J. Baker and James A. Mangan (New York: Africana, 1987), 48.

4 Binde, "Gambling across Cultures," 1–27; Pryor, "The Friedman-Savage Utility Function," 821–834.

5 Binde, "Gambling across Cultures," 1–27; Culin, *Games of the North*, 31.

6 Culin, *Games of the North*, 31

7 Per Binde, "Gambling and Religion: Histories of Concord and Conflict," *Journal of Gambling Issues* 20 (June 2007): 145–166, http://www.camh.net/egambling/issue20/pdfs/03binde.pdf; Culin, *Games of the North*, 34.

8 Culin, *Games of the North*; Kathryn Gabriel, *Gambler Way: Indian Gaming in Mythology, History, and Archaeology in North America* (Boulder: Johnson Books, 1996), 17–21.

9 Gabriel, *Gambler Way*, 18.

10 Culin, *Games of the North*, 34; Michael A. Salter, "An Analysis of the Role of Games in the Fertility Rituals of the Native North American," *Anthropos* 69 (1974): 494–504; Michael A. Salter, "Play in Ritual: An Ethnohistorical Overview of Native North America," in *Play and Culture: 1978 Proceedings of the Association for the*

Anthropological Study of Play, ed. Helen B. Schwartzman (West Point, NY: Leisure Press, 1980), 70–82.

11   Yale D. Belanger, *Gambling with the Future: The Evolution of Aboriginal Gaming in Canada* (Saskatoon: Purich, 2006), 31.

12   Binde, *Gambling across Cultures*, 1–27.

13   Belanger, *Gambling with the Future*, 34.

14   Per Binde, "Gambling, Exchange Systems, and Moralities," *Journal of Gambling Studies* 21, 4 (2005): 445–479; Virginia McGowan et al., "Sacred and Secular Play in Gambling among Blackfoot Peoples of Southwest Alberta," in *Proceedings of the 11th National Association for Gambling Studies Conference, Sydney, 2001* (Alphington, Australia: National Association for Gambling Studies, 2001), 241–255; Michael A. Salter, "Games, Goods, and Gods: An Analysis of Iroquoian Gambling," *Canadian Journal of Applied Sport Sciences* 4 (1979): 160–164.

15   Belanger, *Gambling with the Future*, 70–71; Mark. R. Dixon and Kim Moore, "Native American Gambling: The Quest for the New White Buffalo," in *Gambling: Behavior Theory, Research and Application*, ed. Patrick Ghezzi et al. (Reno, NV: Context Press, 2006), 231–247.

16   D. Wardman, Nady el-Guebaly, and David Hodgins, "Problem and Pathological Gambling in North American Aboriginal Populations: A Review of the Empirical Literature," *Journal of Gambling Studies* 17, 2 (2001): 81–100.

17   The same point about within-group diversity needs to be made about the comparison group of North American "non-Aboriginal" populations used in these analyses.

18   Jan McMillen, "Cross-cultural Comparisons," in *Research and Measurement Issues in Gambling Studies*, ed. Garry Smith, David C. Hodgins, and Robert J. Williams (Burlington, MA: Elsevier, 2007), 465–483; Peter D. Steane, Jan McMillen, and Samantlia Togni, "Researching Gambling with Aboriginal People," *Australian Journal of Social Issues* 33, 3 (1998): 303–315.

19   Kainaakiiski Secretariat, *Gaming Research Report: Final Report Prepared for the University of Lethbridge* (Lethbridge, AB: Author, 2005).

20   This definition has come to be generally accepted by gambling researchers.

21   Robert J. Williams and Robert T. Wood, "Prevalence of Gambling and Problem Gambling in Canada in 2006/2007," in submission process. A potential limitation of the data is that there are some theoretical problems in lumping Aboriginal, Métis, and Inuit together, as their cultural and historical experiences are different.

22   Robert T. Wood and Robert J. Williams, *Internet Gambling: Prevalence, Patterns, Problems and Policy Options: Final Report,* Ontario Problem Gambling Research Centre (2009), http://www.gamblingresearch.org.

23   The Kainai are part of the Blackfoot Nation. This particular reserve is the largest in Canada by land area.

24   Kainaakiiski Secretariat, *Gaming Research Report*; Robert J. Williams et al., "Using Participatory Action Research to Study Canadian Aboriginal Gambling" (presentation, 6th European Conference on Gambling Studies and Policy Issues, Malmo, Sweden, 30 June 2005), http://www.easg.org/media/file/conferences/malmo2005/presentations/Donderdag/14.15-15.45/2/robert_williams.pdf

25 Stephen Kemmis and Robin McTaggart, "Participatory Action Research," in *The Handbook of Qualitative Research*, ed. Norman K. Denzin and Yvonne S. Lincoln (Thousand Oaks, CA: Sage, 2000), 567–605; Harold J. Wynne, "Participatory Action Approaches for Conducting Research on Aboriginal Gambling," chapter 5 of this volume.

26 Because of the very large sample sizes in the present study, a significance level of $p < .01$ is used to denote "significance" throughout this chapter.

27 It also emerged from the focus groups that some of the associated elements (e.g., singing) were sometimes an equally or more important part of the competition/activity than the game itself or any betting that occurred.

28 The fact that *gambling* is an English word rather than an Aboriginal word undoubtedly contributes to its association with Western forms and its distinction from traditional Aboriginal gambling practices.

29 Kainaakiiski Secretariat, *Gaming Research Report*; Williams et al., *Using Participatory Action Research*, http://www.easg.org/files/malmo2005/presentations/Donderdag/14.15-15.45/2/robert_williams.pdf (site discontinued).

30 Virginia M. McGowan and Gary Nixon, "Blackfoot Traditional Knowledge in Resolution of Problem Gambling: Getting Gambled and Seeking Wholeness," *Canadian Journal of Native Studies* 24, 1 (2004): 7–35.

31 McGowan et al., *Sacred and Secular Play*, 249; McGowan and Nixon, *Blackfoot Traditional Knowledge*, 7–35; Gary Nixon and Jason Solowoniuk, "Introducing the Hero Complex and the Mythic Iconic Pathway of Problem Gambling," *International Journal of Mental Health and Addiction* 7, 1 (2009): 108–123.

32 Robert J. Williams et al., *The Quinte Exhibition and Raceway Impact (QERI) Study*, The Ontario Problem Gambling Research Centre, ongoing, 2006–2011, http://www.qeri.ca.

33 Robert J. Williams et al., *The Social and Economic Impacts of Gambling in Alberta (SEIGA) Project*, The Alberta Gaming Research Institute, ongoing, 2008–2010, http://www.abgaminginstitute.ualberta.ca/social_and_economic_Alberta.cfm.

34 Williams and Wood, *Prevalence of Gambling*.

35 Wood and Williams, *Internet Gambling*.

36 Kainaakiiski Secretariat, *Gaming Research Report*.

37 Williams et al., *The Quinte Exhibition and Raceway*.

38 Williams et al., *The Social and Economic Impacts*.

39 Blue Thorn Research et al., *Socioeconomic Impacts of New Gaming Venues in Four British Columbia Lower Mainland Communities: Final Report*, Gaming Policy and Enforcement Branch, Ministry of Public Safety and Solicitor General, Government of British Columbia (2007), http://www.pssg.gov.bc.ca/gaming/reports/docs/rpt-rg-impact-study-final.pdf.

40 David Hewitt and Darlene Auger, *Firewatch on Aboriginal Adolescent Gambling* (Edmonton: Nechi Training, Research and Health Promotions Institute, 1995).

41 Bob Adebayo, "Gambling Behavior of Students in Grades Seven and Eight in Alberta, Canada," *Journal of School Health* 68, 1 (1998): 7–11.

42 Rachel A. Volberg and Max W. Abbott, "Gambling and Problem Gambling among Indigenous Peoples," *Substance Use and Misuse* 32, 11 (1997): 1525–1538.

43 Jason Blankenship et al., "Gambling Trends in the State of New Mexico: 1996–1998," *International Journal of Mental Health and Addiction* 7, 1 (2009): 203–216.

44 Harold J. Wynne, *Gambling and Problem Gambling in Saskatchewan*, Saskatchewan Health (2002), 32, http://www.health.gov.sk.ca/adx/aspx/adxGetMedia.aspx?DocI D=317,94,88,Documents&MediaID=166&Filename=gambling-final-report.pdf.

45 Garry Smith and Harold J. Wynne, *Measuring Gambling and Problem Gambling in Alberta Using the Canadian Problem Gambling Index (CPGI): Final Report*, Alberta Gaming Research Institute (2002), 23, http://hdl.handle.net/1880/1626.

46 David Patton at al., *Gambling Involvement and Problem Gambling in Manitoba: Final Report*, Addictions Foundation of Manitoba (2002), 92–93, http://www.afm. mb.ca/pdf/FinalGamblingReport_Full_.pdf.

47 Rachel A. Volberg and Bo Bernhard, *The 2006 Study of Gambling and Problem Gambling in New Mexico*, Gemini Research (2006), 46–51, http://hdl.handle. net/1880/44211.

48 David Hewitt, *Spirit of Bingoland: A Study of Problem Gambling among Alberta Native People* (Edmonton: Nechi Training and Research and Health Promotions Institute/AADAC, 1994), 11; Darlene Auger and David Hewitt, *Dreamchaser: Aboriginal Adult Gambling Prevalence Study* (Edmonton: Nechi Institute, 2000).

49 Paul E. Polzin et al., *Final Report on the Economic and Social Impacts of Legal Gambling in Montana. Report to the Montana Gambling Study Commission* (Helena: Montana Legislative Services Division, 1998).

50 Harold J. Wynne and John McCready, *Examining Gambling and Problem Gambling in Ontario Aboriginal Communities: Final Report* (Guelph: Ontario Problem Gambling Research Centre, 2005), 41.

51 Gina Muckle et al., *Qanuippitaa? How are we? Alcohol, drug use and gambling among the Inuit of Nunavik: Epidemiological profile*, Institut national de santé publique du Québec and Nunavik Regional Board of Health and Social Services (2007), 7–10, http://www.inspq.qc.ca/pdf/publications/657_esi_alcool_drogues_ gambling.pdf. The study of 521 Inuit in Nunavik (northern Quebec) in 2004 found that the past-year rate of gambling (60 percent) was lower than in the general Quebec population, but that weekly involvement (31 percent) and average reported yearly expenditure were significantly higher. Past-year involvement in bingo and card/dice games was significantly higher than the general Quebec population (36 percent versus 9 percent for bingo; 24 percent versus 11 percent for card/dice games), but there was no significant difference in instant lottery involvement.

52 Northwest Territories Health and Social Services, *The 2006 Northwest Territories Addictions Report* (2008), 34–39, http://www.hlthss.gov.nt.ca/pdf/reports/mental_ health_and_addictions/2008/english/2006_nwt_addictions_report.pdf.

53 Mélanie Anctil and Serge Chevalier, *Lifestyles Related to Alcohol Consumption, Drugs, and Gambling. Canadian Community Health Survey, Cycle 2.1 Iiyiyiu Aschii*, Cree Board of Health and Social Services of James Bay and Institut national de santé publique du Québec (2008), 12–16, http://www.inspq.qc.ca/pdf/ publications/832_cree_alcohol_drugs_gambling_an.pdf.

54 Williams and Wood, *Prevalence of Gambling.*

55 Penny Neal, Paul Delfabbro, and Michael O'Neil, *Problem Gambling and Harm: Towards a National Definition*, Office of Gaming and Racing, Victorian Government Department of Justice (2005), 3, http://www.gamblingresearch.org. au.

56 Wardman, el-Guebaly, and Hodgins, *Problem and Pathological Gambling*, 81–100.

57 Hewitt and Auger, *Firewatch*; Robert B. Peacock, Priscilla A. Day, and Thomas D. Peacock, "Adolescent Gambling on a Great Lakes Indian Reservation," *Journal of Human Behavior in the Social Environment* 2, 1/2 (1999): 5–17; Darryl Zitzow, "Comparative Study of Problematic Gambling Behaviours between American Indian and Non-Indian Adolescents in a Northern Plains Reservation," *American Indian and Alaska Native Mental Health Research* 7, 2 (1996): 14–26.

58 Henry R. Lesieur and Sheila B. Blume, "The South Oaks Gambling Screen (SOGS): A New Instrument for the Identification of Pathological Gamblers," *American Journal of Psychiatry* 144 (1987): 1184–1188.

59 Ken C. Winters, Randy D. Stinchfield, and Jayne Fulkerson, "Toward the Development of an Adolescent Gambling Problem Severity Scale," *Journal of Gambling Studies* 9, 1 (1993): 63–84; Robert Ladouceur et al., "Is the SOGS an Accurate Measure of Pathological Gambling among Children, Adolescents and Adults?" *Journal of Gambling Studies* 16, 1 (2000): 1–24.

60 Don A. Cozzetto and Brent W. Larocque, "Compulsive Gambling in the Indian Community: A North Dakota Case Study," *American Indian Culture and Research Journal* 20, 1 (1996): 73–86; Christopher Elia and Durand F. Jacobs, "The Incidence of Pathological Gambling among Native Americans Treated for Alcohol Dependence," *The International Journal of the Addictions* 28, 7 (1993): 659–666; Volberg and Abbott, *Gambling and Problem Gambling*, 1525–1538; Rachel A. Volberg and Precision Marketing, Inc., *Gambling and Problem Gambling among Native Americans in North Dakota*, (Fargo: North Dakota Department of Human Services Division of Mental Health, 1993); Darryl Zitzow, "Comparative Study of Problematic Gambling Behaviors between American Indian and Non-Indian Adults in a Northern Plains Reservation," *American Indian and Alaska Native Mental Health Research* 7, 2 (1996): 27–41.

61 Volberg and Abbott, *Gambling and Problem Gambling*, 1525–1538.

62 Cozzetto and Larocque, *Compulsive Gambling*, 73–86.

63 Auger and Hewitt, *Dreamchaser.*

64 Wynne, *Gambling and Problem Gambling in Saskatchewan.*

65 Smith and Wynne, *Measuring Gambling and Problem Gambling in Alberta.*

66 Statistics Canada, *Canadian Community Health Survey Mental Health and Well-being: Master File Documentation. Cycle 1.2* (Ottawa: Author, 2003), http://www. statcan.gc.ca/imdb-bmdi/document/5015_D4_T1_V1-eng.pdf.

67 Jackie Ferris and Harold Wynne, *The Canadian Problem Gambling Index: Final Report*, Canadian Centre on Substance Abuse (2001), http://www.ccsa.ca/2003%20 and%20earlier%20CCSA%20Documents/ccsa-008805-2001.pdf.

68 Anctil and Chevalier, *Lifestyles Related to Alcohol Consumption, Drugs, and Gambling.*

69 Joseph Westermeyer et al., "Lifetime Prevalence of Pathological Gambling among American Indian and Hispanic American Veterans," *American Journal of Public Health* 95, 5 (2005): 860–866.

70 Ferris and Wynne, *The Canadian Problem Gambling Index*.

71 Max W. Abbott and Rachel A. Volberg, "The New Zealand National Survey of Problem and Pathological Gambling," *Journal of Gambling Studies* 12, 2 (1996): 143–160; Ferris and Wynne, *The Canadian Problem Gambling Index*; Ladouceur et al., *Is the SOGS an Accurate Measure*, 1–24.

72 Martin Young and Matthew Stevens, "SOGS and CPGI: Parallel Comparison on a Diverse Population," *Journal of Gambling Studies* 24, 3 (2008): 337–356.

73 Robert J. Williams and Rachel A. Volberg, "Impact of Survey Description, Administration Format, and Exclusionary Criteria on Population Prevalence Rates of Problem Gambling," *International Gambling Studies* 9, 2 (2009): 101–117.

74 As evidence of this phenomenon more generally, the following Swedish national survey found that the rates of probable pathological gambling were three times higher for people who could not be contacted by telephone, but who did complete the survey by mail: Sten Rönnberg et al., *Gambling and Problem Gambling in Sweden: Report No. 2 of the National Institute of Public Health Series on Gambling*, National Institute of Public Health (1999), 30–31, http://www.spelinstitutet.se/.

75 Earl S. Ford, "Characteristics of Survey Participants with and without a Telephone: Findings from the Third National Health and Nutrition Examination Survey," *Journal of Clinical Epidemiology* 51, 1 (1998), 55–60; David Pearson et al., "Differences in Sociodemographic, Health Status, and Lifestyle Characteristics among American Indians by Telephone Coverage," *Preventive Medicine* 23, 4 (1994): 461–464.

76 Roger Tourangeau and Ting Yan, "Sensitive Questions in Surveys," *Psychological Bulletin* 133, 5 (2007): 859–883.

77 Edith de Leeuw and Johannes van der Zouwen, "Data Quality in Telephone and Face to Face Surveys: A Comparative Meta-analysis," in *Telephone Survey Methodology*, ed. Robert M. Groves et al. (New York: Wiley, 1988), 283–299; Williams and Volberg, *Impact of Survey Description*, 101–117.

78 Kainaakiiski Secretariat, *Gaming Research Report*.

79 Ibid.

80 Williams and Volberg, *Impact of Survey Description*, 101–117.

81 Namrata Raylu and Tian Po Oei, "Role of Culture in Gambling and Problem Gambling," *Clinical Psychology Review* 23, 8 (2004): 1087–1114.

82 Major longitudinal studies designed to shed light on this issue are underway in both Ontario and Alberta. See Williams et al., *The Quinte Exhibition and Raceway*, http://www.qeri.ca; Nady el-Guebaly et al., "Designing a Longitudinal Cohort Study of Gambling in Alberta: Rationale, Methods, and Challenges," *Journal of Gambling Studies* 24, 4 (2008): 479–504.

83 G. Alan Marlatt et al., "Addictive Behaviours: Etiology and Treatment," *Annual Review of Psychology* 39 (1988): 223–252.

84 Mark Griffiths and Paul Delfabbro, "The Biopsychosocial Approach to Gambling: Contextual Factors in Research and Clinical Interventions," *The Electronic Journal of Gambling Issues* 5 (October 2001), http://www.camh.net/egambling/archive/pdf/EJGI-issue5/EJGI-issue5-feature.pdf.

85 For a more detailed elucidation of this model for problem gambling, see Robert J. Williams, Beverly L. West, and Robert I. Simpson, *Prevention of Problem Gambling: A Comprehensive Review of the Evidence 2008*, Ontario Problem Gambling Research Centre (2008), 5–8, http://hdl.handle.net/10133/414.

86 Ingeborg Lund, "The Population Mean and the Proportion of Frequent Gamblers: Is the Theory of Total Consumption Valid for Gambling?" *Journal of Gambling Studies* 24, 2 (2008): 247–256; Brian R. Rush, Louis Gliksman, and Robert Brook, "Alcohol Availability, Alcohol Consumption and Alcohol-related Damage. The Distribution of Consumption Model," *Journal of Studies on Alcohol* 47, 1 (1986): 1–10.

87 Kathryn Shanley, "Lady Luck or Mother Earth? Gaming as a Trope in Plains Indian Cultural Tradition," *Wicazo Sa Review* 15, 2 (2000): 93–101.

88 Jackie Joukhador, Alex Blaszczynski, and Fiona MacCallum, "Superstitious Beliefs among Problem and Nonproblem Gamblers: Preliminary Data," *Journal of Gambling Studies* 20, 2 (2004): 171–180; Jackie Joukhador, Fiona MacCallum, and Alex Blaszczynski, "Differences in Cognitive Distortions between Problem and Social Gamblers," *Psychological Reports* 92, 3, Pt. 2 (2003): 1203–1214; Tony Toneatto et al., "Cognitive Distortions in Heavy Gambling," *Journal of Gambling Studies* 13, 3 (1997): 253–266.

89 Kainaakiiski Secretariat, *Gaming Research Report*.

90 Deborah Chansonneuve, *Addictive Behaviours among Aboriginal People in Canada*, Aboriginal Healing Foundation (2007), www.ahf.ca/pages/download/28_13222; Laurence A. French, *Addictions and Native Americans* (Westport, CT: Praeger, 2000), 35–43; McMillen and Donnelly, *Gambling in Australian*, 397–426.

91 Kainaakiiski Secretariat, *Gaming Research Report*.

92 Nancy M. Petry, "Gambling and Substance Use Disorders: Current Status and Future Directions," *The American Journal on Addictions* 16, 1 (2007): 1–9; Nancy M. Petry, Frederick S. Stinson, and Bridget F. Grant, "Comorbidity of DSM-IV Pathological Gambling and Other Psychiatric Disorders: Results from the National Epidemiologic Survey on Alcohol and Related Conditions," *Journal of Clinical Psychiatry* 66, 5 (2005): 564–574; Brian R. Rush et al., "Influence of Co-occurring Mental and Substance Use Disorders on the Prevalence of Problem Gambling in Canada," *Addiction* 103, 11 (2008): 1847–1956.

93 Williams, West, and Simpson, *Prevention of Problem Gambling*, 5–8.

94 Chansonneuve, *Addictive Behaviours*, 12–17; Sandra L. Momper and Aurora P. Jackson, "Maternal Gambling, Parenting, and Child Behavioral Functioning in Native American Families," *Social Work Research* 31, 4 (2007): 199–209; Thomas D. Peacock, Priscilla, A. Day, and Robert B. Peacock, "At What Cost? The Social Impact of American Indian Gaming," *Journal of Health and Social Policy* 10, 4 (1999): 23–34.

95 Harold J. Shaffer and Matthew N. Hall, "Updating and Refining Meta-analytic Prevalence Estimates of Disordered Gambling Behavior in the United States and Canada," *Canadian Journal of Public Health* 92, 3 (2001): 168–172.

96 Lisa M. Hepburn and David Hemenway, "Firearm Availability and Homicide: A Review of the Literature," *Aggression and Violent Behavior* 9, 4 (2004): 417–447; Rush, Gliksman, and Brook, *Alcohol Availability, Alcohol Consumption*, 1–10; Williams, West, and Simpson, *Prevention of Problem Gambling*, 1–72.

97 A study currently underway in Alberta is specifically comparing the prevalence of gambling and problem gambling in Aboriginal communities that host casinos versus communities that do not. See Williams et al., *The Social and Economic Impacts*, http://www.abgaminginstitute.ualberta.ca/social_and_economic_Alberta.cfm.

98 Peacock, Day, and Peacock, *At What Cost*, 23–34.

99 Martin Young et al., "The Changing Landscape of Indigenous Gambling in Northern Australia: Current Knowledge and Future Directions," *International Gambling Studies* 7, 3 (2007): 327–343; Matthew Stevens and Martin Young, *Reported Gambling Problems in the Indigenous and Total Australian Population*, Office of Gaming and Racing, Department of Justice (2009), http://www.gamblingresearch.org.au/.

100 Chansonneuve, *Addictive Behaviours*, 33; E. Jane Costello et al., "Relationships between Poverty and Psychopathology: A Natural Experiment," *JAMA* 290, 15 (October 2008): 2023–2039; McMillen and Donnelly, *Gambling in Australian*, 397–426; Stevens and Young, *Reported Gambling Problems*.

CHAPTER 9

GAMBLING BEHAVIOURS AMONG ABORIGINAL PEOPLES: INDIGENOUS AND CRITICAL SOCIO-ECOLOGICAL PERSPECTIVES

SHARON YANICKI, DAVID GREGORY, AND BONNIE LEE

OVERVIEW

In this chapter, an indigenous world view and a critical socio-ecological perspective offer an expanded framework to understand gambling among Aboriginal peoples. Taken together, this framework shifts attention to the collective and the environment in contrast to the individualistic framing implicit in current gambling research. The framework is used to explore and identify the social inequities that may underlie current patterns of gambling among Aboriginal peoples and invites holistic understanding of person-environment interactions.[1]

Social and cultural meanings of gambling as well as a focus on equity, population health, and human and socio-economic development contributing to unhealthy gambling behaviours are considered. Health inequities are differences in the health status of individuals and populations that are unfair, unjust, and potentially modifiable and avoidable.[2] We consider the possibility that patterns of gambling among Aboriginal peoples may be socially constructed because of social inequities. Relevant to the framework are the historical, spiritual, socio-economic, and political conditions of everyday life.[3] These influence the continuum of gambling behaviours among individuals, groups, and populations.

The purpose of this chapter is twofold: (a) to present a theoretical framework to inform research and knowledge development on the gambling behaviours of Aboriginal peoples, and (b) to examine opportunities for future health promotion interventions. To begin, we briefly outline the components of this combined framework and apply it to explore the current context of Aboriginal gambling. Then, we identify gaps in current knowledge and highlight opportunities for further research.

THE MEDICINE WHEEL

> Everything is connected to everything else. Therefore, every
> aspect of our healing and development is related to all
> others (personal, social, cultural, political, economic, etc.).
> When we work on any one part, the whole circle is affected.[4]

Indigenous knowledge and concepts of health provide a holistic context for understanding Aboriginal gambling.[5] The Royal Commission on Aboriginal Peoples in 1996 suggested that indigenous knowledge is "a cumulative body of knowledge and beliefs, handed down through generations by cultural transmission, about the relationships of living beings (including humans) with one another and their environment."[6] The Medicine Wheel distils a cumulative body of knowledge on the nature of health.

Health, well-being, the individual, the community, and the nation are traditionally represented in the sacred symbol of the circle of life, or the Medicine Wheel.[7] The Medicine Wheel represents a view of health that is based on balance across the physical, emotional, mental, and spiritual dimensions of health and well-being.[8] In indigenous views, the individual, community, and environment are inextricably linked.[9] Thus the Medicine Wheel represents a key point of departure from Euro-western models which privilege the individual as the primary unit of consideration.

How does the Medicine Wheel add to an understanding of Aboriginal gambling? Heeding the advice of the Assembly of First Nations[10], an indigenous view of health, and a focus on the community are central[11] to understanding the health of Aboriginal peoples. By placing the Medicine Wheel at the heart of the framework, indigenous knowledge is honoured and resonates with an ecological and holistic understanding of health (see Figure 1). This world view demands a shift toward a collective, contextual focus.[12] While it is acknowledged that the Medicine Wheel is not embraced by, or part of the worldview, of all Aboriginal peoples, the principles of holism and balance central to this view of health may be considered more universal.

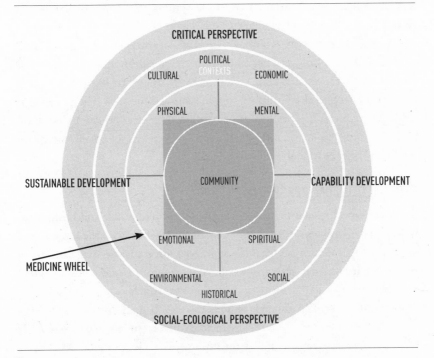

CRITICAL PERSPECTIVE

POLITICAL

CULTURAL   CONTEXTS   ECONOMIC

PHYSICAL | MENTAL

SUSTAINABLE DEVELOPMENT   COMMUNITY   CAPABILITY DEVELOPMENT

EMOTIONAL | SPIRITUAL

MEDICINE WHEEL

ENVIRONMENTAL   SOCIAL

HISTORICAL

SOCIAL-ECOLOGICAL PERSPECTIVE

SOURCES: Assembly of First Nations, *First Nations Public Health: A Framework for Improving the Health of Our People and Our Communities*, 86; Hancock, "Health, Human Development and the Community Ecosystem."

The importance and relevance of the Medicine Wheel has only been recently recognized by mainstream health and treatment services. As Ann Dapice noted, "The traditional Medicine Wheel is both culturally grounded and supported by scientific research."[13] The Medicine Wheel has been used to guide programs in addictions as well as to promote healing, health, and well-being for First Nations peoples.[14] For example, it has been successfully incorporated as a strategy for the treatment of substance abuse in First Nations communities. The Medicine Wheel is considered a promising framework for supporting the health of Aboriginal peoples in Canada.[15]

A CRITICAL PERSPECTIVE

Critical social theory (CST) is a conceptual foundation for our proposed framework[16] Contemporary CST has been strongly influenced by the writings of Jürgen Habermas and Paulo Freire.[17] As a systematic approach to knowledge development and critique, CST seeks to uncover the social inequities and hidden power relationships that constrain human potential.[18] Ideological[19] and cultural critiques[20] are used to expose oppression.[21] New possibilities are sought by comparing "what is" to "what ought to be."[22]

A critical perspective questions negative stereotypes about Aboriginal peoples and gambling, and examines underlying assumptions that may implicitly support the status quo. Our framework questions the designation of Aboriginal peoples as a vulnerable population and the view that gambling is defacto a high risk activity in this population. A critical perspective seeks to promote equity in social conditions and therefore has an emancipatory intent,[23] and may be a catalyst for social change.[24]

SOCIO-ECOLOGICAL PERSPECTIVES

Socio-ecological models have been applied in public health and health promotion for many years; these models are decidedly not new. The holistic perspective of the Medicine Wheel is congruent with a socio-ecological view of person-environmental interactions. Socio-ecological models presume that multiple levels of social relations (e.g., inter-personal, organizational, community, and societal levels) and multiple contexts (e.g., historical, social, economic, political, cultural, and environmental) interact to influence health. Cultural contexts are deeply embedded within socio-ecological models[25] yet this focus is limited within gambling literature.[26] The *Youth Gambling Risk Prevention Model* provides an example of a socio-ecological model applied to gambling.[27] Although Carmen Messerlian and her colleagues considered multiple levels of social interaction influencing youth gambling behaviours, their model did not address Aboriginal gambling.

Multi-level, multi-sectoral interventions are thought to have synergistic effects on promoting health.[28] Community-level interventions may include community development initiatives supporting health, education, and social and economic development on reserve.[29] Societal-level interventions may include public policies, advertising bans, counter-marketing, and price controls to limit youth gambling initiation.[30] For example, combining public policies that restrict underaged access to video lottery terminals along with school-based initiatives to promote access to recreation could have combined synergistic effects that exceed the effects of a single intervention.

SUMMARY OF THE FRAMEWORK AND KEY ASSUMPTIONS – What understanding is privileged through the lens of this framework? First, and importantly, the Medicine Wheel,[31] a holistic view of health and the community are central to this perspective.[32] Second, a critical perspective [33] and a socio-ecological view of social relations, person-environmental interactions, and health are the focus.[34]

♦ Multiple strata of social relations[35] and multiple contexts are thought to influence patterns of behaviour and health outcomes.[36]

♦ Exposure to risk conditions[37] such as poverty, low socio-economic status, unsafe living conditions, and social exclusion may limit human development and opportunities for wellbeing.[38]

♦ Social inequities underlie many health inequities, as the social determinants of health have a substantive impact on population health.[39]

A paradigm shift is occurring within the field of gambling research.[40] Gambling is more than an individual behaviour and needs to be understood as a population health matter,[41] and not all gambling behaviours are unhealthy. [42] Consistent with Korn and Shaffer, we view gambling as existing along a continuum of behaviour from the absence of gambling, to recreational or healthy gambling, to pathological or unhealthy gambling.[43] Our framework adds a critical focus on social inequities and a socioecological focus on contextual factors.

HISTORICAL AND CONTEMPORARY UNDERSTANDING OF ABORIGINAL GAMBLING

HISTORICAL AND CULTURAL CONTEXTS – Gambling has been reported as a cultural practice since the beginning of recorded history.[44] Gambling has been defined as "risking something of value" on the outcome of an event that is less than certain or a game determined by chance.[45] Traditional gaming among indigenous peoples is well documented, yet little research considers this broad historical and cultural context.[46] *Traditional games,* described among First Nations people in Canada as a part of traditional ceremonies,[47] included the stick game, the moccasin game, the peace bowl game, and the hoop and arrow game.[48] One Aboriginal respondent described the peace bowl game as:

part of our mid-winter ceremonies... You are supposed to bring something that is very near and dear to your heart, be it moccasins, rattles, dress clothes, anything. The teams are divided up into clans ... the prizes get handed out to the

winning teams ... they say that if you lose something you
will get it back in the Spirit world.[49]

Traditional games involved competition between clans, an exchange of valued
goods, risk, and a sense of ultimate spiritual balancing of losses.[50] Gambling
within this ceremonial context may have provided a spiritual lesson, teaching
one not to be too attached to what one prizes. Traditional games may also have
served a social function by creating economic parity between tribes in periods
of economic stress.[51]

While some Aboriginal peoples suggest that Europeans introduced contemporary gambling behaviours, others see their gambling as having roots in
traditional Aboriginal gaming practices.[52] The cultural meanings, practices,
and historical contexts of gaming may influence current gambling behaviours; however, new meanings also continue to emerge over time. Culture can
be defined as a relational, dynamic process that is enacted within the context
of history, gender, experience, and social status.[53] In contrast to traditional
gaming, contemporary Aboriginal gambling may differ in both meaning and
social purpose[54] which needs to be continuously deciphered.

CONTEMPORARY ABORIGINAL GAMBLING – Contemporary Aboriginal gambling
behaviour has been described as predominantly a matter of risk and luck,
and as a coping strategy.[55] Traditional gaming was considered to be a matter
of skill, intellect, and experience.[56] Differences in the meaning and function
of gambling over time reflect a shift from communal values to individualistic
and capitalistic values. Therefore, Aboriginal gambling cannot be understood
simply as a risky behaviour or an individual addiction, but is best understood
within broader contexts.

Aboriginal gaming and gambling practices have changed over time.[57] Aboriginal gambling for money is a more recent phenomenon.[58] Contemporary
Aboriginal gambling behaviours may be influenced by family gambling practices, cultural acceptability, accessibility, and public policies. In this chapter,
we explore gambling behaviours among Aboriginal peoples (referred to subsequently as *Aboriginal gambling*)[59] from this broader lens.

TOWARD A MORE HOLISTIC UNDERSTANDING
OF ABORIGINAL GAMBLING

The gambling literature has predominantly focused on individual disordered
gambling[60] and the concomitant bio-psychosocial attributes of individuals,[61]

from mental health, addictions, economic, and moral perspectives.[62] An individualistic lens is apparent in classification systems for disordered gambling (see Table 1). Rather than viewing risk factors[63] as intrinsic, biological, or cultural characteristics of individuals and groups, a more contextual understanding of gambling behaviours is needed.

TABLE 1: A Comparison of Two Classifications of the Levels of Gambling-related Behaviours

SHAFFER'S		SOUTH OAKS GAMBLING SCREEN	
CLASSIFICATION	DESCRIPTION	CLASSIFICATION	DESCRIPTION
LEVEL 0	NON-GAMBLERS	SCORE OF 0	NO PROBLEMS WITH GAMBLING BEHAVIOR
LEVEL 1	RECREATIONAL GAMBLERS, NO ADVERSE CONSEQUENCES	SCORE OF 1	NO PROBLEMS WITH GAMBLING BEHAVIOR
LEVEL 2	GAMBLERS EXPERIENCING SOME NEGATIVE CONSEQUENCES (DOES NOT MEET DIAGNOSTIC CUT FOR DISORDERED GAMBLING	SCORE OF 2	AT-RISK GAMBLING BEHAVIOR (GAMBLING FREQUENTLY WITH ONE PROBLEM OR GAMBLING LESS FREQUENTLY WITH TWO OR MORE PROBLEMS)
LEVEL 3	GAMBLERS WITH SERIOUS AND CO-OCCURRING CONSEQUENCES CONSISTENT WITH DIAGNOSTIC CRITERIA FOR DISORDERED GAMBLING	SCORE OF 4 OR HIGHER	PROBLEM GAMBLING (GAMBLING DAILY OR GAMBLING WEEKLY WITH TWO OR MORE PROBLEMS)
LEVEL 4	GAMBLERS WHO SEEK HELP FOR THEIR PROBLEM, REGARDLESS OF THE EXTENT OF THEIR DISTRESS OR THE EXTENT OF CONSEQUENCES EXPERIENCED	LEVEL 4	

SOURCES: Shaffer, "A Public Health Perspective on Gambling." AADAC, *Gambling among Alberta Youth*; Christiane Poulin, "Problem Gambling among Adolescent Students," 53–78. Note: Results for traditional hand/stick games is based only on results from the Blood Tribe Survey (n = 120)

Our expanded framework brings attention to the interaction of risk conditions with bio-psychosocial risk factors in the social construction[64] of gambling behaviour. A focus on individual risk factors and vulnerability has been more common than a focus on exposure to risk conditions and protective factors in the gambling literature.

ASSET-BASED AND DEFICIT-BASED LANGUAGE AND GAMBLING

The language used to describe phenomena suggests some of the underlying assumptions involved. Korn and Shaffer used positive terms to focus attention on gambling as a range of behaviour including *healthy gambling or* non-problematic gambling,[65] while Shaffer later used the term *recreational gambling* (Level 1).[66] Complex person-environment interactions are shaped by the social determinants of health.[67] Clearly disordered gambling has negative impacts on

TABLE 2: Adverse Effects of Disordered Gambling on Individuals, Families, and Communities

AUTHOR	TITLE AND TOPIC	EFFECTS ON INDIVIDUALS AND FAMILIES	EFFECTS ON COMMUNITY
LESIEUR AND BLUME	'THE SOUTH OAKS GAMBLING SCREEN (SOGS)' - EFFECTS OF PROBLEM GAMBLING	MARITAL CONFLICT SEPARATION AND DIVORCE FINANCIAL PROBLEMS/DEBT (BORROWS FROM OTHERS) EMOTIONAL DIFFICULTIES MEDICAL PROBLEMS DEPRESSION AND SUICIDE OCCUPATIONAL EFFECTS LEGAL ISSUES (ILLEGAL ACTS SUPPORTING GAMBLING)	UNPAID DEBT LOST TIME AT SCHOOL LOST TIME AT WORK CIVIL AND CRIMINAL COURT APPEARANCES
AMERICAN PSYCHIATRIC ASSOCIATION	'DIAGNOSTIC AND STATISTICAL MANUAL OF MENTAL DISORDERS' - PATHOLOGICAL GAMBLING	LYING TO HIDE GAMBLING FINANCIAL BAILOUTS ANTISOCIAL BEHAVIOR TO OBTAIN MONEY (FORGERY, FRAUD, THEFT, OR EMBEZZLEMENT) LOSS/JEOPARDIZATION OF SIGNIFICANT RELATIONSHIP, EDUCATIONAL OR CAREER OPPORTUNITY	ILLEGAL ACTIVITIES
FERRIS AND WYNNE	'THE CANADIAN PROBLEM GAMBLING INDEX' - PROBLEM GAMBLING	BORROWING LYING FINANCIAL PROBLEMS CRITICISM BY OTHERS FEELINGS OF GUILT FAMILY PROBLEMS (FAMILY GAMBLING PROBLEM, ALCOHOL/DRUG PROBLEM) CO-MORBIDITIES (GAMBLING PROBLEM, ALCOHOL/DRUG PROBLEM) SELF-MEDICATION (GAMBLING, ALCOHOL/DRUGS) STRESS/DEPRESSION/SUICIDE	
WYNNE AND MCCREADY	'EXAMINING GAMBLING AND PROBLEM GAMBLING IN ONTARIO ABORIGINAL COMMUNITIES'	FAMILY DEBT AND POVERTY SENSE OF HELPLESSNESS SUICIDE NEGLECT OF CHILDREN MARITAL BREAKUP CHILDREN FEELING ASHAMED/LOW SELF-ESTEEM CHILD/SPOUSAL ABUSE OR ABANDONMENT THEFT AND FRAUD FREQUENTLY TALKING ABOUT GAMBLING	NON-PAYMENT OF BILLS SEPARATION FROM THE COMMUNITY
OAKES, CURRIE AND COURTNEY	'PROBLEM GAMBLING IN FIRST NATIONS COMMUNITIES' - PROBLEM GAMBLING IN ONTARIO TREATY 3	IMPACT ON CHILDREN, FAMILIES, AND SOCIAL RELATIONSHIPS LOST MONEY AND TIME GAMBLING AS A SUBSTITUTE ADDICTION	IMPACT ON THE COMMUNITY AND TRADITIONS

SOURCES: Lesieur and Blume, "The South Oaks Gambling Screen (SOGS)": 1987, 1184–1188; *American Psychiatric Association, Diagnostic and Statistical Manual of Mental Disorders*; Ferris and Wynne, *The Canadian Problem Gambling Index*; Oakes, Currie, and Courtney, *Problem Gambling in First Nations Communities*; Wynne and McCready, *Examining Gambling and Problem Gambling in Ontario Aboriginal Communities*.

individuals, families and communities (See Table 2), however, healthy gambling also deserves our attention. Prevention strategies and the promotion of health are both keys to addressing gambling as a population health matter. From an epidemiological perspective,[68] higher rates of problem[69] and pathological[70] gambling have been reported among Aboriginal peoples, and thus Aboriginal peoples have been described as a vulnerable population.[71] From a critical perspective, we posit that individualism risks attributing pathology as intrinsic to individuals and groups. A focus on individuals risks ignoring the influence of multiple forms of social inequities across multiple socio-ecological contexts and at multiple socio-ecological levels of interaction that shape patterns of gambling behaviour.

The deficit-based language of "vulnerable" populations, and the accompanying epidemiological prevalence data focused on population groups, may imply there are intrinsic reasons for vulnerability to problem gambling among Aboriginal people. It could lead to the interpretation that Aboriginal people are not capable of exercising reasoned decision making with respect to gambling, individually or as a collective, or the paternalistic assumption that Aboriginal peoples as vulnerable populations need to be protected from the potentially harmful consequences of exposure and easy access to gambling.

In contrast, we question the social conditions that contribute to an inequitably higher prevalence of problem gambling among Aboriginal peoples. Our focus is on identifying and addressing the environmental and contextual factors that sustain differential rates of disordered gambling. Vulnerability cannot simply be attributed to individual and/or population characteristics or attributes.[72] In the next section, we explore the risk and protective factors, risk conditions, and socio-ecological contexts that may influence patterns of healthy and unhealthy gambling among Aboriginal peoples.

GAMBLING PARTICIPATION AND RISK – Gambling is not a risky behaviour in and of itself, since the majority of Canadians report gambling at least occasionally and do not report negative consequences.[73] Gambling participation rates are high, and 76 percent of Canadians reported gambling during 2002 based on the national *Canadian Community Health Survey*.[74] Similarly, high rates of participation in gambling have been reported for Aboriginal peoples. Wynne and McCready reported Aboriginal gambling participation rates of between 48 percent and 93 percent in five Aboriginal communities studied in Ontario.[75]

PSYCHOSOCIAL RISK FACTORS AND GAMBLING – A body of evidence supports the assertion that Aboriginal peoples have disproportionately experienced many psychosocial risk factors.[76] Social exclusion and social isolation are associated with poorer health status.[77] Social exclusion engenders "experiences of ... powerlessness and voicelessness, a lack of recognition and sense of belonging ... [and] despair."[78] Could these conditions predispose some Aboriginal people to higher rates of gambling problems?

DIFFERENTIAL VULNERABILITY OR SOCIAL DETERMINANTS OF HEALTH – Several epidemiological studies have identified a higher prevalence of problem gambling for Aboriginal adults.[79] In a review of Aboriginal gambling in North America, Wardman and colleagues reported prevalence rates of problem gambling between 10.1 and 21.0 percent for Aboriginal adolescents, and between 6.6 and 22 percent for Aboriginal adults.[80] Rates of problem gambling among the general population of Aboriginal peoples ranged from 2.2 to 15.69 times higher than those of the non-Aboriginal population.[81]

An Alberta study identified a higher risk of problem gambling (three times higher) among Aboriginal adolescents in comparison with other Canadian youth.[82] As a result of such studies, Aboriginal peoples in Canada have been described as a vulnerable group for problem gambling.[83] However, the relationship between social determinants of health and problem gambling remains largely unexamined in prevalence studies. Significant disparities in income, education, and employment underlie comparisons between Aboriginal peoples and the general population of Canada as a whole.[84]

DIFFERENTIAL EXPOSURE TO GAMBLING OR RISK CONDITIONS – Environmental conditions that create easy access to gambling and normalize gambling as a form of recreation could lead to higher rates of gambling, especially among vulnerable groups.[85] In the United States, the *National Council on Problem Gambling* reported that pathological gambling[86] was more prevalent in areas where gambling was more available.[87]

Gambling trends in Canada, which include the increased availability of legalized forms of gambling,[88] increased casino development on reserves,[89] and an increased potential for early exposure and involvement of Aboriginal youth in gambling,[90] raise concerns about the potential impact of casino development on First Nations reserves. Canadian studies examining the impact of casino openings and local rates of pathological gambling have had mixed results. One study on the opening of a casino in Windsor, Ontario, failed to find an increased prevalence of pathological gambling.[91] A similar study in Niagara Falls, Ontario, reported increased rates.[92] A recent study based on the national *Canadian Community Health Survey* reported that the highest rates of problem gambling in Canada occurred in areas with both permanent casinos and higher concentrations of video terminals.[93]

Aboriginal peoples are also disproportionately affected by exposure to a variety of risk conditions in Canadian society. Ronald Labonte described poverty, low socio-economic status, and unsafe environments as risk conditions.[94] Many Aboriginal peoples and their children have higher rates of poverty than non-Aboriginal Canadians.[95] Grace-Edward Galabuzi also described multiple forms of social exclusion for Aboriginal people (including social, cultural, and political marginalization from participation in community life).[96] A history of colonialism, displacements, limited autonomy and paternalism have resulted in a legacy of poorer population health status for Aboriginal peoples in Canada.[97] Social exclusion, marginalization, oppression, and displacement can also be considered risk conditions for poor population health predisposing Aboriginal peoples to unhealthy gambling.

Naomi Adelson claimed that "health disparities are directly and indirectly associated with social, economic, cultural and political inequities."[98] Several recent international reports suggest that health inequities are a consequence of social inequities.[99] Aboriginal people living on-reserve reported higher rates of problem gambling than those living in other rural locations.[100] Wardman and colleagues speculate that living on-reserve might be associated with problem gambling because of stressful living conditions, unemployment, a lack of educational opportunities, limited recreation, and the need for income.[101]

Social breakdown and social dislocation have also been considered as possible causes of addiction, which has been described as "both a response to social breakdown and an important factor in worsening the resulting inequalities in health."[102] Social dislocation is the main precursor of addictions, including gambling addiction.[103] Social dislocation arises from an inability to fully participate in society and societal failure to integrate members into dominant society. Thus, it can be hypothesized that the socio-ecological contexts of everyday living (including social inequities, socio-economic deprivation, social breakdown, and social dislocation) may be related to the higher prevalence rates of problem gambling among Aboriginal peoples. An examination of the socioenvironmental contexts of Aboriginal gambling may illuminate the multilevel relational factors, social conditions and contexts that protect communities or increase the risk of disordered gambling.

HEALTHY GAMBLING AND PROTECTIVE FACTORS — A critical socio-ecological framework focuses on promoting health equity, not just the prevention of problem gambling. Therefore, a key question is "What factors are associated with the development of healthy versus unhealthy gambling behaviours?" Protective factors have recently been described in studies of youth gambling behaviours and drug and alcohol use by the Alberta Alcohol and Drug Abuse Commission (AADAC) and Alberta Health Services - Alberta Alcohol and Drug Abuse Commission (AHS-AADAC).[104] Table 3 described the risk and protective factors associated with youth gambling behaviour in Alberta.

TABLE 3: Top Five Risk and Protective Factors Associated with Patterns of Youth Gambling in Alberta

RISK AND PROTECTIVE FACTORS, ADAPTED FROM AADAC AND AHS-AADAC, THE ALBERTA YOUTH EXPERIENCE SURVEY (TAYES)	HAZARDOUS AND PROBLEM GAMBLING, BASED ON THE SOUTH OAKS GAMBLING SCREEN (REVISED FOR ADOLESCENTS)	HAZARDOUS AND PROBLEM GAMBLING BASED ON THE SOUTH OAKS GAMBLING SCREEN (REVISED FOR ADOLESCENTS)
RISK FACTORS		
INTRAPERSONAL:		
AGE (INCREASES WITH AGE)	X	
GRADE (HIGHER IN GRADES 10-12)		X
GENDER (HIGHER IN MALES)		X
SUBSTANCE USE DURING THE YEAR		X
INTERPERSONAL:		
PEER RISK BEHAVIOR	X	X
HISTORY OF FAMILY SUBSTANCE ABUSE	X	
FAMILY DISCORD	X	
INSTITUTIONAL:		
SCHOOL DISCONNECTION	X	
SIGNS OF LEAVING SCHOOL EARLY	X	
PROTECTIVE FACTORS		
INTERPERSONAL:		
PARENTAL MONITORING (HIGH)	X	X
SOCIAL SKILLS	X	
INSTITUTIONAL:		
CONNECTION AT SCHOOL	X	
COMMUNITY:		
AVAILABILITY OF PRO-SOCIAL ACTIVITIES	X	
PARTICIPATION IN PRO-SOCIAL ACTIVITIES	X	

SOURCES: AHS-AADAC, *Gambling among Alberta Youth*; AADAC, *The Alberta Youth Experience Survey* 2008.

The AADAC's *Alberta Youth Experience Studies* (TAYES) provides support for the hypothesis that youth with a higher number of protective factors were more likely to be resilient and less likely to report problem gambling or substance abuse. Protective factors were identified at multiple socio-ecological levels (interpersonal, institutional, and community). The most commonly identified protective factors were high parental monitoring, social skills, connection to school, as well as the availability of and participation in pro-social activities.[105] Pro-social activities involved youth participation in clubs, recreation and sports as opposed to participation in gangs or deviant groups.

BOX 1: Case Example: Saskatchewan Indian Gaming Authority

The Saskatchewan Indian Gaming Authority (SIGA), a not-for-profit corporation that operated four First Nations casinos in 2007, was first established in 1996. SIGA reported sustained revenue increases in the last seven out of ten years of operation. SIGA also reported meeting their employment targets of 73 percent First Nations employees in 2007. Annual revenues in 2007 were $130 million, and net profits were $45.8 million, making siga one of Saskatchewan's top fifty companies.

SIGA's revenue-sharing agreement with the province of Saskatchewan distributed net profits as follows: 50 percent to the First Nations Trust Fund, 25 percent to the Community Investment Program, and 25 percent to the Saskatchewan government, and administered through four Community Development Corporations. Thus, First Nations bands across the province of Saskatchewan shared in casino revenues directly through the trust fund as well as indirectly through community development funds, which supported hundreds of Aboriginal non-profit community organizations. SIGA reported that the community investment fund supported First Nations organizations providing sports and recreation (20 percent), education and health services (23 percent), First Nations tradition and culture (17 percent), services for elders and youth (20 percent), and arts, community events, employment, and business tourism (20 percent).

SOURCE: SIGA, *Saskatchewan Indian Gaming Authority Inc. Annual Report 2006–2007.*

Protective factors have also been examined on First Nations reserves in relation to youth suicide in British Columbia. Aboriginal self-governance and cultural continuity were identified as important protective factors.[106] Cultural continuity involved First Nations community efforts to restore and preserve Aboriginal culture. To our knowledge, this approach, of examining protective factors, or protective conditions and contexts, has not yet been applied to research on Aboriginal gambling. Further research is needed to identify the factors and processes that support or maintain healthy or non-problematic gambling behaviours among some Aboriginal peoples. Interventions could then be tested on upstream (population-based) strategies to reduce risk conditions and strengthen protective factors within the community. A greater impact on the health of a population can be achieved by universal strategies to improve the health of the population (adjusting the population mean) for a given health behaviour than by targeted strategies to prevent and treat the disorder in a targeted group.[107]

DISCUSSION

The holistic view of health and community-level focus applied in the framework presented here is consistent with an expanding body of evidence on the social determinants of health. In 1986 the Ottawa Charter marked a shift from individually oriented strategies for health promotion to a socio-environmental model of health that focuses on the determinants of health and the interaction of people within their environment.[108] Many determinants of population health status have since been defined, including socio-economic status, culture, food security, housing shortages, distribution of income, social exclusion, and unemployment.[109]

EQUITY AND SOCIAL DETERMINANTS OF ABORIGINAL HEALTH – The health of Aboriginal peoples has also been greatly influenced by the impact of colonization, migration, cultural continuity, globalization and loss of traditional territory.[110] A growing body of evidence suggests that socio-economic factors are among the most significant determinants of health.[111] Viewing health with a focus on populations and multiple levels of social interaction helps to identity new opportunities for health promotion.[112]

Public health professionals and social scientists have focused on the social and environmental contexts in which gambling occurs, in addition to the biological, emotional, cognitive, and behavioural determinants of individual gambling problems.[113] A population health promotion approach seeks to maintain a larger proportion of "healthy" gamblers.[114] Theory-driven by a population health focus considers the determinants of gambling behaviour,[115] suggesting the possibility of prevention (primary, secondary, and tertiary) and the promotion of "balanced attitudes, behaviours and policies" that "protect vulnerable populations."[116] Both the potential benefits and harms of gambling on populations can be considered,[117] and to explore this, the socio-economic and political contexts affecting First Nations communities need to be considered.

POLITICAL AND SOCIO-ECONOMIC CONTEXTS – Social policies have a significant impact on health and opportunities for human and socio-economic development.[118] The need for First Nations economic development is increasingly becoming more urgent. The Assembly of First Nations reported that federal funding for health programs was capped at 3 percent in 1997, a rate below inflation.[119] The combination of population growth, restricted funding, and high morbidity has resulted in an estimated shortfall of 14 percent in health budgets for the 2007–08 fiscal year. Compounding this problem are significant budget cuts in funding for First Nations economic development. It is not surprising, then, that casino development has been considered as a source of sustainable development.[120]

The development of Aboriginal casinos marked a substantial difference from traditional gaming.[121] The First Nations gaming industry views gambling as a form of recreation, a matter of individual choice, and a source of economic development.[122] Gambling affords employment and may potentially reduce high rates of poverty on reserves.[123] Typically, First Nations gaming-industry reports make use of quantitative data and address the socio-economic impact of casino development. In addition to numeracy, however, the meaning of gambling, its cultural and social impacts, and the voices of Aboriginal peoples warrant consideration.

As First Nations seek opportunities for on-reserve economic development, gambling and casinos have increasingly been viewed as sources of revenue for infrastructure, increased local employment, and the diversification of local economies.[124] In Canada, the Federal Government had historically regulated gambling; however, control over gambling came under provincial jurisdiction in 1985, following an amendment to the *Criminal Code of Canada*. Since 1985, a diverse range of provincial policy approaches to Aboriginal gambling has emerged.[125] Most provinces have signed agreements with their First Nations bands. Some provinces have established First Nations Development Funds and other similar trust-fund models to allocate a portion of on-reserve gambling revenues to social and economic development initiatives. Typically, these monies are shared among First Nations bands within the province.[126] See Box 1 for a case example of First Nations gambling in Saskatchewan in 2007.

A critical socio-ecological framework seeking to uncover social inequities asks, "Is there a role for gambling in supporting equity, capability development, and sustainable development?"

CAPABILITY DEVELOPMENT –

> If people cannot imagine a condition other than the one in which they now live, then they are trapped. It is only when we are able to see ourselves in terms of our potential, and within healthier and more sustainable conditions, that we can begin

to move towards creating those conditions within ourselves
and in our relationships with the world around us.[127]

From the perspective of the Medicine Wheel, individual capability development is just as important as community economic development. In fact, the two are closely linked. *Development* refers to reaching one's full potential to live a flourishing life and discovering one's opportunities for well-being.[128]

Amaryta Sen argued that capability development must be understood in relation to the conditions of everyday living and what one can "do" and "be".[129] Participation in community life is central to having: (a) opportunities to develop capabilities; and (b) the freedom to live a life one has reason to value.[130] Capability deprivation results from poverty, social exclusion, a lack of freedom to choose, and an inability to participate in activities one has reason to value.[131] Absolute capability deprivation can result in capability failure—an inability to meet basic needs.[132] Capability deprivation may have an important influence on patterns of gambling among Aboriginal people.

Aboriginal peoples experience disproportionately higher rates of poverty, with one in four First Nations children living in poverty, in comparison to one in six Canadian children.[133] Reducing health inequities is a moral imperative.[134] Children growing up in poverty experience barriers to participation in society, report lower school achievement, and have reduced life chances.[135] Additionally, health inequities have significant impacts on Aboriginal peoples' quality of life.[136] Capability failure within Aboriginal populations can be viewed as a social consequence of physical and social environments that do not support basic human needs, fail to provide opportunities for optimal human development, and fail to support human freedom of choice.[137] Consistent with a holistic understanding of health, individual capability development[138] and "good health" at a population level are critical for sustainable development.[139]

SUSTAINABLE DEVELOPMENT – The interaction of persons, health, the environment, and the economy are fundamentally connected.[140] The United Nations defines sustainable development as meeting "the needs of the present without compromising the ability of future generations to meet their own needs."[141] This definition is consistent with Canada's national Sustainable Development Strategy.[142] Sustainable development commonly addresses: economic development, social development, and the environmental impacts of development.[143]

A healthy and sustainable community requires a flourishing environment, a vibrant and just society, and a prosperous economy; thus a healthy population is both a "precondition and an outcome of sustainable development."[144] Such interactions are consistent with the Public Health Agency of Canada's conceptualization of the relationships between public health and sustainable development.[145] Dean and Hancock suggested that sustainable development requires: (a) a viable environment to support human life; (b) sustainable economic activity; and (c) equity in human relations and access to resources.[146]

From a critical perspective capability deprivation involves a societal failure to provide social and environmental conditions that support optimal human development, the ability to meet basic needs, and opportunities for full participation in society. Economic development could potentially create increased opportunities for capability development through training, employment, and increased participation in community life. Clearly, human capability development is linked to economic development and the potential for creating sustainable development within First Nations communities.

There is an urgent need for economic development to improve the everyday living conditions on First Nations reserves and to reduce health disparities. How this challenge is best addressed, whether by casino development or other forms of economic development, remains a question for First Nations leaders and communities. Governments also bear a responsibility to provide equitable access to the resources required to support a minimally acceptable standard of living for all citizens.

Casinos may act as a tangible symbol of infrastructure development and employment on reserves to support social and economic development. This could potentially instil a sense of pride, hope for the future, and a sense of ownership within First Nations communities. Non-Aboriginal gamblers regularly patronize First Nations casinos. Given the presence of Aboriginal employees, these casinos may create new opportunities for the development of positive social relationships between First Nations communities and non-Aboriginal peoples through informal contacts. Positive social contacts may create a new image of First Nations communities as thriving centres with sustainable businesses. Such developments may also challenge existing stereotypes regarding Aboriginal people, challenge the tenets of racism and discrimination, and create a shift in social attitudes. Our framework seeks to promote research that will help to inform these developments and guide emancipatory action.

POTENTIAL CONTRIBUTIONS OF THE FRAMEWORK – The Medicine Wheel and a holistic view of health provide a new lens through which to understand Aboriginal gambling. Gambling behaviours can be considered within a dynamic balance of contextual factors. The inclusion of the Medicine Wheel provides a shared indigenous perspective from which to consider the influence of gambling behaviours on the health of Aboriginal populations. This framework does not presume that Aboriginal gambling behaviours are homogeneous across population groups or settings; rather, it supports an exploration of dynamic interrelated factors. It can be expected that First Nations vary in levels of community well-being and in levels of human, social, and economic development, and that urban Aboriginal gambling contexts vary from reserve contexts.

The framework fosters exploration of multiple levels of interaction within the socio-ecological environment from the micro level (intrapersonal and family-level factors) to the macro level (interpersonal, community, and societal public-policy interactions).[147] At the macro level, there is a clear need for research to explicate the patterns of gambling behaviours within and between Aboriginal populations. Additionally, increased understanding of the influence of contextual factors on Aboriginal gambling may support opportunities to maintain healthy gambling behaviour and reduce disordered behaviour.

The framework highlights the interrelationships between human, social, and economic development and Aboriginal gambling. While First Nations leaders have pursued casino development mainly as a strategy for economic viability, it is recognized that there are associated risks and benefits.[148] Thus, community assets (protective factors and resiliency) and human-capability development concomitantly exist with risk factors and differential vulnerability for gambling at a population level. The need for sustainable development in First Nations communities whether on reserve or in urban settings is evident and pressing. Casino development, within the context of First Nations' self-governance, may support sustainable economies for economically depressed reserve communities; however, other forms of economic development may present lower risks to community health and well-being.[149] Community-based, mixed methods research could address some of the critical questions surrounding Aboriginal gambling and sustainable development that are of most concern to Aboriginal peoples. Such research is predicated on full partnerships between researchers and First Nations peoples.[150]

The framework can be used to reveal underlying power relationships and explore the social inequities and contextual factors that may sustain health inequities. We suggest that the higher prevalence of problem gambling among

Aboriginal peoples may be socially constructed by exposure to risk conditions.[151] Similarly, according to Sen's capability framework, the potential impact of casino development should be considered in relation to the pressing need for sustainable development in First Nations communities.[152]

The application of the Medicine Wheel and a critical socio-ecological perspective brings to light several new areas of investigation:

♦ The concept of "differential vulnerability" is considered at a population level.

♦ The complex socio-ecological contextual factors that may influence Aboriginal gambling behaviour at a population level are explored.

♦ Human, social, and economic development factors critical to sustainable development are examined.

♦ Such topics of investigation raise questions for research about Aboriginal gambling and the potential interventions within a socio-ecological context.

OPPORTUNITIES FOR FUTURE RESEARCH

A holistic perspective on gambling seeks to understand complex dynamic relationships between person and environment. This is both a benefit and a criticism of the application of socio-ecological models in health promotion.[153] Mixed methods research, partnerships, and the engagement with and participation of Aboriginal people/First Nations communities are all suggested approaches that can address questions from this perspective. There is a need for epidemiological research examining the patterns of Aboriginal gambling within populations, yet there is also a need to understand the social construction of these patterns within the contexts in which they occur. The complexity of cultural meanings embedded within traditional and contemporary Aboriginal gambling requires qualitative research methods and attention to multiple contexts,[154] while an exploration of complex, dynamic processes within open systems requires both qualitative and quantitative research methods.[155]

Little research has explored effective prevention strategies for problem gambling among Aboriginal people. Participatory Action Research (PAR) is one approach to research that engages communities in defining the research questions, building community capacity to undertake research, utilizing cultural knowledge, and applying research to take action at a community level.[156] This participatory approach is commensurate with the framework (see chapter 5 and 6, this volume).

A PAR study in five Aboriginal communities in Ontario engaged community members in the design and research process to insure locally relevant information was obtained in community surveys, focus groups, and case studies.[157] Focus group participants identified several strategies to address the higher rates of at-risk and problem gambling in their communities. The prevention strategies suggested were: early intervention and prevention programs for youth, school-based education, and information kits and media campaigns to raise awareness of the issue of problem gambling within the Aboriginal community.[158] There was a perception that problem gamblers were generally unaware of treatment services, and that treatment should be adapted to Aboriginal culture to reduce stigma.[159]

The following are examples of mixed methods research questions:

> a) How are Aboriginal gambling behaviours understood within the context of the social, emotional, physical, and spiritual dimensions of health? How is this understood from the perspective of gamblers? How is this understood from a critical perspective?

> b) Do patterns of Aboriginal gambling change with perceived changes in human, social-economic, and empirical measures of economic development as a result of First Nations casinos?

Based on the levels of social interaction within ecological models,[160] questions are raised for Aboriginal gambling, including those regarding:

> a) Intrapersonal factors. How are personal factors associated with problem gambling influenced by changes in the social and economic environment on-reserve?

> b) Interpersonal relations. How do First Nations casinos influence patterns of social relations (risk and resiliency factors) and health behaviours, including Aboriginal gambling behaviours?

c) Institutional factors. How do health promotion interventions at the organization level within First Nations communities influence gambling behaviours?

d) Community factors. Do community development investments from casino development and First Nations self-governance influence Aboriginal gambling behaviours (e.g., healthy gambling and problem gambling)?

e) Public policies. Are First Nations creating policies to promote healthy or responsible gambling? How do variations in provincial public policies influence casino development and provincial Aboriginal gambling?

Based on the capability framework, several key issues need to be addressed:[161]

a) How does First Nation casino development impact conditions of everyday living?

b) How does casino development influence capability development and the ability of First Nations people to meet their basic needs with dignity?

c) How does strengthened self-governance for Aboriginal peoples (e.g., control and management of First Nations casino development on reserves) influence the freedom of Aboriginal peoples to live lives they have reason to value?

d) Does the potential revenue and opportunity for investment in First Nations communities provided by casino development promote capability development?

e) Can the potential social and economic benefits of casino development reduce the long-term social costs of childhood poverty on First Nations reserves?

f) What is the balance of the social benefits and costs of problem gambling that may accompany economic development for individuals, families, and communities?

This line of questioning considers human development to be just as important to measure as economic development in the First Nations casino industry.

CONCLUSIONS

The Medicine Wheel and a critical socio-ecological perspective offer a framework supporting a new way of thinking about Aboriginal gambling based on a confluence of theoretical perspectives. This model privileges a holistic understanding of Aboriginal gambling that has been underrepresented within the current literature. The framework honours indigenous knowledge and its potential explicatory power. The framework raises several key points of departure from previous public health models.

First, by exploring the root causes of population-based differences in vulnerability to disordered gambling, new insights are raised. Second, human, social, and economic development need to be considered as components of the broader issue of Aboriginal gambling. While the major focus of other models has been at the individual level or on prevention of disordered gambling, this framework shifts focus to the potential of "whole of community" and population-level interventions to influence gambling behaviours. Third, mixed methods community-based research, partnerships, and participatory action research are proposed to better understand Aboriginal gambling. Health inequities within Aboriginal populations, whether related to differential exposure to risk conditions or capability deprivation, urgently need to be addressed. A critical socio-ecological perspective seeks to create more equitable social arrangements. To accomplish this emancipatory end, participatory research in partnership with Aboriginal peoples is a preferred methodology for developing a holistic understanding of Aboriginal gambling behaviours, identifying opportunities for sustainable development, and promoting a balanced perspective on gambling.

NOTES

1 In the framework presented here, the person (individuals, families and community) is considered holistically and the focus is at the community level.

2 Margret Whitehead, "The Concepts and Principles of Equity and Health: Discussion Paper," World Health Organization, Regional Office for Europe (1993), http://whqlibdoc.who.int/euro/-1993/EUR_ICP_RPD_414.pdf.

3 World Health Organization [WHO] Commission on Social Determinates of Health, *Closing the Gap in a Generation: Health Equity through Action on the Social Determinants of Health—Final Report* (Geneva: World Health Organization, 2008), http://whqlibdoc.who.int/publications/2008/9789241563703_eng.pdf.

4 Michael Bopp and Judy Bopp, *Recreating the World: A Practical Guide to Building Sustainable Communities* (Calgary: Four Worlds Press, 2001).

5 Marie Battiste, and James [Sakej] Youngblood Henderson. *Protecting Indigenous Knowledge and Heritage: A Global Challenge.* (Saskatoon: Purich Publishing Ltd 2000). 44. Battiste suggested that indigenous ecological knowledge is "empirical, experimental, and systematic," but that it differs from Western science in that it is highly localized and social.

6 Royal Commission on Aboriginal Peoples, *Report of the Royal Commission on Aboriginal Peoples*, vol. 4 (Ottawa: Canada Communication Group, 1996).

7 Assembly of First Nations, *First Nations Public Health: A Framework for Improving the Health of our People and our Communities*, 2006, http://www.afn.ca/cmslib/general/FNPB-IH.pdf; Ann N. Dapice, "The Medicine Wheel," *Journal of Transcultural Nursing* 17, 3 (2006): 251–260; Marcy Burka-Charles, *Best Practices in Aboriginal Health Programming Project: Final Report* (Calgary: Calgary Health Region and Alberta Regional Health Authorities, 2008).

8 Burka-Charles, "'Best' Practice in Aboriginal Health Programming."

9 Ibid.; Royal Commission on Aboriginal Peoples, *Report of the Royal Commission on Aboriginal Peoples*, vol. 4.

10 Assembly of First Nations, *First Nations Public Health.*

11 Assembly of First Nations, *First Nations Public Health*; Marcy Burka-Charles, "'Best' Practice in Aboriginal Health Programming: Literature Review" (Calgary: Aboriginal Health Program, Calgary Health Region; Society of Obstetricians and Gynaecologists of Canada, January 2001), http://www.sogc.org/guidelines/public/100E-PS3-January2001.pdf, (accessed 25 Oct. 2008); Battiste and Youngblood Hederson, *Protecting Indigenous Knowledge and Heritage*; Linda Hunter et al., "Aboriginal Healing: Regaining Balance and Culture," *Journal of Transcultural Nursing* 17, 1 (2006): 13–22.

12 David A. Korn and Howard J. Shaffer, "Gambling and the Health of the Public: Adopting a Public Health Perspective," *Journal of Gambling Studies* 15, 4 (1999): 289–365.

13 Dapice, "The Medicine Wheel."

14 Assembly of First Nations, *First Nations Public Health*; Ashifa Jiwa, Len Kelly, and Natalie St. Pierre-Hansen, "Healing the Community to Heal the Individual: Literature Review of Aboriginal Community-based Alcohol and Substance Abuse

Programs," *Canadian Family Physician* 54, 7 (2008): 1000–1007; Burka-Charles, "'Best' Practice in Aboriginal Health Programming: Literature Review."

15 Jiwa, Kelly, and St. Pierre-Hansen, "Healing the Community to Heal the Individual."

16 Judy E. Mill, Marion N. Allen, and Raymond A. Morrow, "Critical Theory: Critical Methodology to Disciplinary Foundations in Nursing," *Canadian Journal of Nursing Research* 33, 2 (2001): 109–127.

17 Jürgen Habermas, *The Theory of Communicative action*, vol. 1 (Boston: Beacon Press, 1984); Paulo Freire, *Pedagogy of the Oppressed*, 30th anniversary ed. (New York: Continuum, 2007).

18 Raymond A. Morrow and David D. Brown, *Critical Theory and Methodology*, vol. 3 (Thousand Oaks, CA: Sage Publications, 1994).

19 Patricia E. Stevens, "A Critical Social Reconceptualization of Environment in Nursing: Implications for Methodology," *Advances in Nursing Science* 11, 4 (1989): 56–68; *ideologies* represent systematic distortions or misrepresentations that are rarely challenged or examined. These ideologies are sustained through social reproduction and dominance in society.

20 Morrow and Brown, *Critical Theory and Methodology*; cultural description carried out from the perspective of critical hermeneutics provides cultural critique and a key point of departure distinguishing critical ethnography from traditional ethnography.

21 Habermas, *The Theory of Communicative Action*.

22 Ibid.; Morrow and Brown, *Critical Theory and Methodology*.

23 Annette J. Browne and Colleen Varcoe, "Critical Cultural Perspectives and Health Care Involving Aboriginal Peoples," *Contemporary Nurse* 22, 2 (2006): 155–167.

24 Habermas, *The Theory of Communicative Action*; Morrow and Brown, *Critical Theory and Methodology*; Freire, *Pedagogy of the Oppressed*.

25 Nancy Edwards, Judy Mill, and Anita R. Kothari, "Multiple Intervention Research Programs in Community Health," *Canadian Journal of Nursing Research* 36, 1 (2004): 40–54.

26 Lorne Tepperman and David Korn, *At Home with Gambling: An Exploratory Study, Final Report* (Toronto: University of Toronto and Ontario Problem Gambling Research Centre, 2002).

27 Carmen Messerlian, Jeffrey L. Derevensky, and Rina Gupta, "Youth Gambling Problems: A Public Health Perspective," *Health Promotion International* 20, 1 (2005): 69–79.

28 Edwards, Mill, and Kothari, "Multiple Intervention Research Programs in Community Health."

29 SIGA, *Saskatchewan Indian Gaming Authority Inc. Annual Report 2006–2007.*

30 Edwards, Mill, and Kothari, "Multiple Intervention Research Programs in Community Health"; Lawrence W. Green, L. Richard, and L. Potvin, "Ecological Foundations of Health Promotion," *American Journal of Health Promotion* 10, 4 (1996): 270–281.

31 Assembly of First Nations, *First Nations Public Health: A Framework for Improving the Health of our People and our Communities*, 2006, http://www.afn.ca/cmslib/general/FNPB-IH.pdf; Ann N. Dapice, "The Medicine Wheel," *Journal of Transcultural Nursing* 17, 3 (2006): 251–260.

32 WHO, *The Ottawa Charter for Health Promotion* (1986), http://www.euro.who.int/AboutWHO/Policy/20010827_2.

33 Habermas, *The Theory of Communicative Action*; Freire, *Pedagogy of the Oppressed*.

34 Trevor Hancock, "Health, Human Development and the Community Ecosystem: Three Ecological Models," *Health Promotion International* 8, 1 (1993): 41–47.

35 Messerlian, Derevensky, and Gupta, "Youth Gambling Problems," 69–79.

36 Kenneth R. McLeroy et al., "An Ecological Perspective on Health Promotion Programs," *Health Education Quarterly* 15, 4 (1988): 351–377; James F. Sallis and Neville Owen, "Ecological Models," *Health Behaviour and Health Education: Theory, Research and Practice*, ed. Karen Glanz, Barbara K. Lewis, and Frances M. Rimer (San Francisco: Jossey-Bass, 1997); Green, Richard, and Potvin, "Ecological Foundations of Health Promotion"; Hancock, "Health, Human Development and the Community Ecosystem."

37 Ronald Labonte, *Health Promotion and Empowerment: Practice Frameworks* (Toronto: Centre for Health Promotion and ParticipACTION, 1993). *Risk factors* include *psychosocial risk factors* such as low self-esteem and a lack of power, and *behavioural risk factors* such as health behaviours associated with higher risk of disease—in this case disordered gambling.

38 Amartya Sen, *Inequality Reexamined* (Cambridge, MA: Harvard University Press and the Russell Sage Foundation, 1995); Amartya Sen, *Social Exclusion: Concept, Application, and Scrutiny*, Office of Environment and Social Development, Asian Development Bank (2000), http://www.adb.org/documents/books/social_exclusion/default.asp.

39 WHO Commission on Social Determinants of Health, *Closing the Gap in a Generation*.

40 Howard J. Shaffer, "A Public Health Perspective on Gambling: The Four Principles," *American Gaming Associaton Responsible Gambling Lecture Series* 2, 1 (2003): 27.

41 Alex Blaszczynski, Robert Ladouceur, and Howard J. Shaffer, "A Science-based Framework for Responsible Gambling: The Reno Model," *Journal of Gambling Studies* 20, 3 (2004): 301–317; Korn and Shaffer, "Gambling and the Health of the Public"; Jill Oakes, Cheryl Currie, and David Courtney, *Gambling and Problem Gambling in First Nations Communities: OPGRC Final Report* (Winnipeg, MB, and Guelph, ON: University of Manitoba and Ontario Problem Gambling Research Centre, 2004), 1–143.

42 Korn and Shaffer, "Gambling and the Health of the Public"; Oaks, Currie, and Courtney, *Gambling and Problem Gambling in First Nations Communities*.

43 Korn and Shaffer, "Gambling and the Health of the Public."

44 Ibid.

45 Korn and Shaffer, "Gambling and the Health of the Public," 292; Tepperman and Korn, *At Home with Gambling: An Exploratory Study, Final Report*, 1–131.

46 Royal Commission on Aboriginal Peoples, *Report of the Royal Commission on Aboriginal Peoples: Part 5, Section 2—Economic Disparities, Government Expenditures and the Cost of the Status Quo,* Indian and Northern Affairs Canada (1996), http://www.ainc-inac.gc.ca/ap/rrc-eng.asp (accessed 15, July 2010). The term *Aboriginal peoples* refers to First Nations peoples, Métis, and Inuit populations within Canada that are descendants of the original peoples of North America. Specifically, the term *First Nations* replaces the term *treaty Indian.* The term *Aboriginal peoples* is also used to refer to both status and non-status Indians, as described in the *Indian Act* by the Government of Canada.

47 Tepperman and Korn, *At Home with Gambling,.*

48 Tepperman and Korn, *At Home with Gambling;* Gabriel M. Yanicki, "Old Man's Playground: Contexts of Rediscovery and Interpretation" (honours thesis, Archeology, University of Calgary, 1999).

49 Tepperman and Korn, *At Home with Gambling.* 81.

50 Tepperman and Korn, *At Home with Gambling.*

51 Wardman, el-Guebaly, and Hodgkins, "Problem and Pathological Gambling in North American Aboriginal Populations. A review of the empirical literature." *Journal of Gambling Studies* 17, 2 (2001): 81–100.

52 Tepperman and Korn, *At Home with Gambling.*

53 Browne et al., "Critical Cultural Perspectives and Health Care Involving Aboriginal Peoples."

54 Tepperman and Korn, *At Home with Gambling.*

55 Oakes, Currie, and Courtney, *Gambling and Problem Gambling in First Nations Communities,* 20.

56 Ibid.

57 Tepperman and Korn, *At Home with Gambling.*

58 Peter D. Steane, Jan McMillen, and Samantlia Togni, "Researching Gambling with Aboriginal People," *Australian Journal of Social Issues* 33, 3 (1998): 303–315.

59 In the literature, *Aboriginal gambling* is omnipresent. We take issue with this phrase as it essentializes the complexity and diversity of Aboriginal peoples as a singular or monolithic cultural entity. In this chapter, however, we use the term as a referent for *the gambling behaviour of Aboriginal peoples.*

60 Shaffer, "A Public Health Perspective on Gambling."

61 Ibid.

62 David A. Korn, "Examining Gambling Issues from a Public Health Perspective," *Electronic Journal of Gambling Issues* 6, 24 (2002): 1–18.

63 Labonte, *Health Promotion and Empowerment.*

64 *Social construction* refers to the impact of social relations and social structures on human behaviour and individual choices. From this perspective, while individuals are considered active agents on their own behalf, they are either constrained or enabled by their socio-ecological contexts.

65 Korn and Shaffer, "Gambling and the Health of the Public."

66 Shaffer, "A Public Health Perspective on Gambling."

67 Dennis Raphael, *Poverty and Policy in Canada: Implications for Health and Quality of Life* (Toronto: Canadian Scholar's Press, 2007); Dennis Raphael, "Strengthening the Social Determinants of Health: The Toronto Charter for a Healthy Canada. In *Social Determinants of Health, Canadian Perspectives*, ed. Dennis Raphael (Toronto: Canadian Scholars Press, 2004).

68 See Korn and Shaffer, "Gambling and the Health of the Public." for a summary of the epidemiological perspective.

69 Problem gambling is an identified mental health disorder affecting a subgroup of the population and is associated with a variety of negative consequences (See Table 1). *Problem gambling* is defined as persistent and maladaptive behaviour and an addiction in the Canadian Problem Gambling Index based on the presence of five of ten diagnostic criteria. The CPGI is a validated instrument that allows for the differentiation of levels of gambling as non-problem, low, risk, moderate risk, and problem gamblers. Jackie Ferris and Harold Wynne, *The Canadian Problem Gambling Index: Final report*, Canadian Centre on Substance Abuse (2001), http://www.ccsa.ca/2003%20and%20earlier%20CCSA%20Documents/ccsa-008805-2001.pdf (accessed 3 Nov. 2008):

70 American Psychiatric Association, *Diagnostic and Statistical Manual of Mental Disorders* (IV-Text Revision), American Psychiatric Publishing, 2008, http://0-www.psychiatryonline.com.darius.uleth.ca/resourceTOC.aspx?resourceID=1 (accessed 1 Nov. 2008). *Pathological gambling*, an American term, was first defined by the American Psychiatric Society in 1980 as a disorder of impulse control involving maladaptive gambling behaviours that impaired personal functioning, as well as family and occupational roles. With more recent revisions of the *Diagnostic and Statistical Manual of Mental Health* [DSM-IV, 2000; code 312.31] the diagnostic criteria also include some similarities to the Canadian diagnostic criteria for problem gambling.

71 Korn, "Examining Gambling Issues from a Public Health Perspective," 1–18.

72 This view is intrinsic to Labonte's socio-environmental model of health, Sen's capability framework, and the critical socio-ecological model.

73 HLT Advisory Inc., and Canadian Gaming Association, *Economic Impact of Canadian Gaming Industry*, Canadian Gaming Association (2008), http://www.canadiangaming.ca/media_uploads/pdf/60.pdf (accessed 2 Nov. 2008).

74 Katherine Marshall, & Harold Wynne, *Fighting the odds*. (75-001-XIE). Statistics Canada 2003 http://www.statcan.gc.ca/studies-etudes/75-001/archive/2003/5018524-eng.pdf (accessed 21 July 2010).

75 Harold J. Wynne and John McCready, *Examining Gambling and Problem Gambling in Ontario Aboriginal Communities: Five Communities' Final Research Reports* (first of two project final reports, Ontario Federation of Indian Friendship Centres and the Métis Nation of Ontario to the Ontario Problem Gambling Research Centre, 2005).

76 Royal Commission on Aboriginal Peoples, *Report of the Royal Commission on Aboriginal Peoples: Part 5, Section 2*; Chandrakant P. Shah, "The Health of Aboriginal Peoples," both in *The Social Determinants of Health: Canadian Perspectives*, ed. Dennis Raphael (Toronto: Canadian Scholar's Press, 2004).

77 Sen, *Social Exclusion*; Grace-Edward Galabuzi, "Social Exclusion"; and Shah, "The Health of Aboriginal Peoples."

78 Galabuzi, "Social Exclusion,"238.

79 David Hewitt and M. Hodgson. *Spirit of Bingoland: A Study of Problem Gambling Among Alberta Native People* (Edmonton: Nechi Training and Research and Health Promotions Institute, 1994); David A. Korn, Roger Gibbins, and Jason Azmier, "Framing Public Policy towards a Public Health Paradigm for Gambling," *Journal of Gambling Studies* 19, 2 (2003): 235–256;

80 Wardman, el-Guebaly, and Hodgins, "Problem and Pathological Gambling in North American Aboriginal Populations."

81 Ibid.

82 See David Hewitt, D. Auger, and M. Hodgson, *Firewatch on Aboriginal Adolescent Gambling* (Edmonton: Nechi Training Research and Health Promotions Institute, 1995).

83 Korn, "Examining Gambling Issues from a Public Health Perspective."

84 Galabuzi, "Social Exclusion"; Shah, "The Health of Aboriginal Peoples."

85 David A. Korn, "Expansion of Gambling in Canada: Implications for Health and Social Policy." *Canadian Medical Association Journal* 163, 1 (2000); Rachel A. Volberg, "The Prevalence and Demographics of Pathological Gamblers: Implications for Public Health," *American Journal of Public Health* 84, 2 (1994): 237–241.

86 Ferris and Wynne, *The Canadian Problem Gambling Index*

87 John W. Welte et al., "The Relationship of Ecological and Geographic Factors to Gambling Behavior and Pathology," *Journal of Gambling Studies* 20, 4 (2004): 405–423.

88 Jeffrey L. Derevensky and Rina Gupta, "Adolescents with Gambling Problems: A Synopsis of our Current Knowledge," *Electronic Journal of Gambling Issues* (2004), http://jgi.camh.net/doi/full/10.4309/jgi.2004.10.3 (accessed 15 July 2010).

89 See Yale D. Belanger, "First Nations Communities and Casino Gaming: Themes, Trends and Ideas," *Research Reveals* 5, 1 (2005): 1–4; and his *Gambling with the Future: The Evolution of Aboriginal Gaming in Canada* (Saskatoon, SK.: Purich Publishing, 2006).

90 Hewitt, Auger, and Hodgson, *Firewatch on Aboriginal Adolescent Gambling*; and Harvey Skinner, Sherry Biscope, Martha Murray, and David A. Korn, "Dares to Addiction: Youth Definitions and Perspectives on Gambling," *Canadian Journal of Public Health* 95, 4 (2004): 264–267.

91 Richard Govoni, G. Ron Frisch, Nicholas Rupcich, and Heather Getty, "First Year Impacts of Casino Gambling in a Community," *Journal of Gambling Studies* 14, 4 (1998): 347–358.

92 Welte et al., "The Relationship of Ecological and Geographic Factors."

93 Brian J. Cox, Nancy Yu, Tracie O. Afifi, and Robert Ladouceur, "A National Survey of Gambling Problems in Canada," *Canadian Journal of Psychiatry* 50, 4 (2005): 213–217.

94 Labonte, *Health Promotion and Empowerment*.

95 Assembly of First Nations, *First Nations Public Health*; Royal Commission on Aboriginal Peoples, *Report of the Royal Commission on Aboriginal Peoples: Part 5, Section 2*; Naomi Adelson, "The Embodiment of Inequity: Health Disparities in Aboriginal Canada," *Canadian Journal of Public Health* 96, suppl. 2 (2005): S45-61; Grace-Edward Galabuzi, "Social Exclusion"; Chandrakant P. Shah, "The Health of Aboriginal Peoples."

96 Galabuzi, "Social Exclusion."

97 Adelson, "The Embodiment of Inequity."

98 Ibid., section 45.

99 Jennie Popay et al., *Understanding and Tackling Social Exclusion: Final Report*, Social Exclusion Knowledge Network (Lancaster: WHO Commission on Social Determinants of Health, 2008); WHO Commission on Social Determinants of Health, *Closing the Gap in a Generation*.

100 See Hewitt and Hodgson, *Spirit of Bingoland*.

101 See Wardman et al., "Problem and Pathological Gambling in North American Aboriginal Populations."

102 Richard Wilkinson and Michael Marmot, *Social Determinants of Health: The Solid Facts* 2 (2005), WHO Regional Office for Europe (2003), http://www.euro.who.int/document/e81384.pdf (accessed 11 Sept. 2005).

103 Bruce K Alexander, *The Roots of Addiction in Free Market Society* (Vancouver: Canadian Centre for Policy Alternatives, 2001).

104 Alberta Alcohol and Drug Abuse Commission (AADAC), *Gambling among Alberta Youth: Alberta Youth Experience Survey 2005*, Feb. 2007; Alberta Health Services-Alberta Alcohol and Drug Abuse Commission (AHS-AADAC), The Alberta Youth Experience Survey (TAYES) Technical Report 2008, Jan. 2009, http://www.albertahealthservices.ca/Researchers/if-res-tayes-2008-technical-report.pdf (accessed 11 January 2011).

105 AHS-AADAC, *Gambling among Alberta Youth*.

106 Michael Chandler and Christopher Lalonde, "Transferring Whose Knowledge? Exchanging Whose Best Practices? On Knowing about Indigenous Knowledge and Aboriginal Suicide," in *Aboriginal Policy Research: Setting the Agenda for Change*, ed. Jerry White, Paul Maxim, and Dan Beavon (Toronto: Thompson Educational Publishing, 2004).

107 Geoffrey Rose, *The Strategy of Preventive Medicine* (Oxford: Oxford University Press, 1993).

108 WHO, *The Ottawa Charter for Health Promotion*.

109 Adelaide, International Symposium on the Social Determinants of Indigenous Health, 2007; WHO Commission on the Social Determinants of Health, *Social Determinants of Indigenous Health: The International Experience and its*

Policy Implications, 2007, http://www.who.int/social_determinants/resources/indigenous_health_adelaide_report_07.pdf (accessed18 July 2010); Assembly of First Nations, *First Nations Public Health*; Dennis Raphael, "Strengthening the Social Determinants of Health."

110 National Aboriginal Health Organization (NAHO), "Broader Determinants of Health in an Aboriginal Context" http://www.naho.ca/publications/determinants.pdf (accessed 18 July 2010).

111 Michael Marmot and Richard G. Wilkinson, eds., *Social Determinants of Health* (Oxford: Oxford University Press, 1999); Raphael, "Strengthening the Social Determinants of Health"; WHO Commission on Social Determinants of Health, *Social Determinants of Indigenous Health*; WHO Commission on Social Determinants of Health, *Closing the Gap in a Generation*.

112 Nancy Hamilton and Tariqu Bhatti, "Population Health Promotion: An Integrated Model of Population Health and Health Promotion." Health Canada, http://www.hc-sc.gc.ca/hppb/healthpromotiondevelopment/pubc/php/php.htm.

113 Max Abbott and Dave Clarke, "Prospective Problem Gambling Research: Contribution and Potential," *International Gambling Studies* 7, 1 (2007): 123–144.

114 Korn and Shaffer, "Gambling and the Health of the Public."

115 Korn, "Examining Gambling Issues from a Public Health Perspective."

116 David A. Korn, Roger Gibbins, and Jason Azmier, "Framing Public Policy towards a Public Health Paradigm for Gambling," *Journal of Gambling Studies* 19, 2 (2003): 235–256.

117 Korn and Shaffer, "Gambling and the Health of the Public"; Shaffer, "A Public Health Perspective on Gambling."

118 Labonte, *Health Promotion and Empowerment*; Raphael, *Poverty and Policy in Canada*; Judith Green and Ronald Labonte, eds., *Critical Perspectives in Public Health* (New York: Routledge, 2008); Hancock, "Health, Human Development and the Community Ecosystem"; Hancock, "People, Partnerships and Human Progress."

119 Assembly of First Nations, *First Nations Public Health*.

120 cf. Yale D. Belanger. "First Nations Gaming as a Self-government Imperative? Ensuring the Health of First Nations Problem Gamblers." *International Journal of Canadian Studies* 41 (2010): 1-24.

121 Tepperman and Korn, *At Home with Gambling*.

122 Blaszczynski, Ladouceur, and Shaffer, "A Science-based Framework for Responsible Gambling"; National Indian Gaming Association, *The Economic Impact of Indian Gaming in 2006* (Washington, DC: National Indian Gaming Association, 2006); Saskatchewan Indian Gaming Authority [SIGA], *Saskatchewan Indian Gaming Authority Inc. Annual Report 2006–2007: Sharing success*, 31/04/2007, http://www.SIGA.sk.ca/06SIGA1008_AR_lo.pdf (accessed 11 Nov. 2008).

123 Belanger, "First Nations Communities and Casino Gaming."

124 Belanger, "First Nations Communities and Casino Gaming."

125 Robin Kelley, *First Nations Gambling Policy in Canada* (Calgary: Canada West Foundation, 2001).

126 Ibid.

127 Bopp and Bopp, *Recreating the World: A Practical Guide to Building Sustainable Communities.*

128 Sen, *Inequality Reexamined*; Sen, *Social Exclusion.*

129 Sen, *Social Exclusion*

130 Sen, *Inequality Reexamined*; Sen, *Social Exclusion.*

131 Sen, *Social Exclusion.*

132 Ibid.

133 Assembly of First Nations, *First Nations Public Health.*

134 Canadian Nurses Association, "Social justice: A means to an end and an end in itself." 2007 (accessed 15 July 2010) http://www.cna-nurses.ca/CNA/ documents/pdf/publications/Social_Justice_e.pdf; WHO Commission on Social Determinants of Health, *Closing the Gap in a Generation.*

135 Clyde Hertzman, *Working Papers Series—Perspectives on Social Inclusion: Leave No Child Behind!*, Laidlaw Foundation (May 2002), http://www.laidlawfdn.org/ page_1069.cfm (accessed 10 Sept. 2005).

136 Raphael, *Poverty and Policy in Canada*; Royal Commission on Aboriginal Peoples, *Report of the Royal Commission on Aboriginal Peoples: Part 5, Section 2*; Burka-Charles, "'Best' Practice in Aboriginal Health Programming: Literature Review."

137 Sen, *Social Exclusion. Capability failure* is the inability to achieve basic capabilities required to meet one's basic needs, achieve full participation in society, and lead a minimally decent standard of living in comparison to one's society and peers.

138 Sen, *Social Exclusion.*

139 WHO, *Sustainable Development and Health: Concepts, Principles and Framework for Action for European Cities and Towns.* European Sustainabile Development and Health Series: Book 1, 1997, http://www.euro.who.int/__data/assets/pdf_ file/0016/43315/E53218.pdf (accessed 15 July 2010).

140 Kathryn Dean and Trevor Hancock, *Supportive Environments for Health*, World Health Organization Regional Office for Europe (1992), http://whqlibdoc.who. int/euro/-1993/EURO_HPR_1.pdf (accesed 14 Nov. 2008).

141 United Nations, *Report of the World Commission on Environment and Development* (96th Plenary Meeting), United Nations General Assembly, 11/12/1987, http:// www.un.org/documents/ga/res/42/ares42-187.htm, (accessed 27 Oct. 2008).

142 Public Health Agency of Canada [PHAC], *Sustainable Development Strategy 2007–2010, Sustainable Development in Public Health: A Long Term Journey Begins*, Public Health Agency of Canada (2006), http://www.phac-aspc.gc.ca/ publicat/sds-sdd/index-eng.php (accessed 27 Oct. 2008).

143 WHO Commission on Social Determinants of Health, "*Social Determinants of Indigenous Health*".

144 PHAC, *Sustainable Development Strategy 2007–2010*, 10.

145 PHAC, *Sustainable Development Strategy 2007–2010*.

146 Dean and Hancock, *Supportive Environments for Health*.

147 Messerlian, Derevensky, and Gupta, "Youth Gambling Problems."

148 Belanger, "First Nations Communities and Casino Gaming."

149 See Jonathon B. Taylor and Joseph P. Kalt, *American Indians on Reservations: A Databook of Socioeconomic Change Between the 1990 and 2000 Censuses* (Cambridge, MA: The Harvard Project on American Indian Economic Development, 2005).

150 David Gregory, Mary J. McCallum, Ruth Grant Kalischuk, and Brenda Elias, "The Swampy Cree Tribal Council and Aboriginal Governance: A Case Study of Nursing Education in Northern Manitoba," *Canadian Journal of Nursing Research* 40, 2 (2008): 132–149.

151 Labonte, *Health Promotion and Empowerment*.

152 Sen, *Social Exclusion*.

153 Green, Richard, and Potvin, "Ecological Foundations of Health Promotion"; 4ean and Hancock, *Supportive Environments for Health*.

154 Steane, McMillen, and Togni, "Researching Gambling with Aboriginal People," 305.

155 Green, Richard, and Potvin, "Ecological Foundations of Health Promotion"; Kothari et al., "Socioecological Models."

156 Meredith Minkler and Nina Wallerstein, *Community Based Participatory Research for Health* (San Francisco: Jossey-Bass, 2003).

157 Wynne and McCready, *Examining Gambling and Problem Gambling in Ontario Aboriginal Communities*.

158 Ibid.

159 Ibid.

160 Green, Richard, and Potvin, "Ecological Foundations of Health Promotion"; McLeroy et al., "An Ecological Perspective on Health Promotion Programs"; Sallis and Owen, "Ecological Models"; Alberta Alcohol and Drug Abuse Commission, *AADAC 2007: Environmental Scan Summary* (2007), http://www.aadac.com/documents/environmental_scan2007_summary.pdf (accessed 12 Oct. 2008).

161 See Sen, *Social Exclusion*.

PART IV

CHALLENGES AND FIRST NATIONS GAMING

CHAPTER 10

FIRST NATIONS APPROACH TO SECURING PUBLIC TRUST: SIGA'S CORPORATE RESPONSE TO THE DUTCH LERAT AFFAIR, 2000–2004*

YALE D. BELANGER

INTRODUCTION

Formed in 1996, the Saskatchewan Indian Gaming Authority (SIGA) has ranked consistently as one of the top fifty most profitable companies in Saskatchewan, citing twenty-seven consecutive quarters of growth and rising revenues as of 2008. It won the Saskatchewan Business Magazine Business of the Year award in 2007 and consistently generates annual gambling revenue in the neighbour-hood of $120 million. At its six casinos SIGA employs more than 1700 people, nearly 63 percent of whom are of Aboriginal descent. Acknowledging the need to promote social responsibility, the Federation of Saskatchewan Indian Na-tions (FSIN), the political body that established SIGA, channels 5 percent of net gambling revenues into the First Nations Addictions Rehabilitation Founda-tion (FNARF) "to ensure that effective and accessible education, prevention and treatment programs about problem gambling are available to First Nation people." SIGA revenues remain a source of funding for the provincial treasury, the province's First Nations communities, and the Community Development Corporations. This success was threatened in 2000 after SIGA chief executive officer (CEO) Dutch Lerat was reputed to have misappropriated more than $360,000. Enhanced provincial scrutiny of all gaming operations followed, as did a forensic audit. To make matters worse, the entire episode received signifi-cant print media attention and was played out provincially and nationally in the court of public opinion. The final auditor's report was critical of the province and SIGA's operations; however, most of the issues identified were remediable. Nevertheless, SIGA's administrators anticipated a potential public crisis of faith and recognized the need to secure the public's trust to ensure continued economic growth.

The effects of the SIGA scandal, or the "Dutch Lerat Affair," as it was branded, led many to publicly question SIGA's accountability, a practice that undermined its corporate image. Since a corporation's image is the link between corporate reality and public perception, how people view a company is vital to that company's success. As SIGA depended appreciably on non-Native patrons, SIGA's management team and board of directors were forced to regroup in 2000 to fashion a policy to counter this negative publicity. Within months, it unveiled a new corporate governance model intended to bolster its reputation as an accountable corporation. This chapter examines the steps taken to improve corporate accountability. First, I will provide a brief history of provincial reserve casinos, followed by an overview of the Dutch Lerat Affair. The second section will discuss the importance of corporate identity and corporate reputation to secure the public's trust and guarantee continued economic success. The third section will develop a thematic analysis drawn from 367 print media articles (2000–2004) to ascertain and evaluate SIGA's and the FSIN's response to the Dutch Lerat Affair.

REALIZING FIRST NATIONS GAMING IN SASKATCHEWAN: THE SETTING

On 1 March 1996, the Gold Eagle Casino opened in North Battleford, Saskatchewan. Less than a week later, the Northern Lights Casino opened in Prince Albert, followed by the Bear Claw Casino on the White Bear Reserve in November and the Painted Hand Casino in Yorkton one month later. FSIN-owned and regulated by SIGA, the FSIN's charitable corporation, these were Canada's first First Nations owned casinos. From 1996 to 2007, these four casinos grossed over $900 million in gambling revenues, producing $281 million net profits. Nearly two-thirds of this amount ($185,328,953) was generated in the last five fiscal years.[1] Two more casinos have since opened, giving SIGA six operations: the Dakota Dunes Casino, located at the Whitecap Reserve (twenty kilometres south of Saskatoon), opened 10 August 2007, followed by the Living Sky Casino in Swift Current on 14 February 2009.

In 1993, the FSIN approached then premier Roy Romanow (NDP) to discuss reserve casino construction. Since taking the reins in 1991, Romanow had been considered pro-business and compassionate towards First Nations issues, leading Chief Roland Crowe to comment, "This historical relationship meant that the Native leadership felt comfortable initiating a discussion regarding a Native casino gambling policy with the NDP government, which demonstrated an impressive level of trust in the Romanow government."[2] Following more than a decade's research and years of FSIN lobbying for the overhaul of provincial gaming policies to permit casinos and high-stakes gambling, Romanow was nevertheless reluctant to yield to these demands. From the premier's perspective, the FSIN's inability to speak on behalf of many of the province's First Nations, tribal councils, and individual band councils appeared to render the organization less than effective. Seeking to establish a working relationship with the province that would lead to new gaming policies benefitting its member communities, the FSIN cited a corresponding desire to stimulate economic development.

Working behind the scenes with First Nations leaders helped satisfy Romanow's concerns about organizational stability, as did market research confirming the positive role gaming could play in helping to expand the province's hospitality and tourism industry.[3] In February 1993, the NDP government published an internal document promoting the expansion of provincial gaming policies. The document made specific mention of First Nations people and their involvement in a proposed "joint-venture framework" with the provincial government.[4] Preliminary discussions with the chiefs of several tribal councils occurred on the topic of their potential involvement in casino projects. The measured pace of negotiations was attributed to the increasingly confrontational approach toward First Nations leaders adopted by the minister in charge of gaming, Janice MacKinnon. Following her removal in March 1993, a government negotiating team was created consisting of Dave Innes, vice-president of the Saskatchewan Liquor and Gaming Authority; Victor Taylor, assistant deputy minister of the Saskatchewan Indian and Métis Affairs Secretariat; and Andrew Thomson, chief of staff to the minister of the Saskatchewan Liquor and Gaming Authority. Negotiations were initially held with the chiefs of Prince Albert, the Battlefords, Saskatoon, the Touchwood File Hills, Qu'Appelle, Meadow Lake, and Yorkton, along with the Agency Chiefs (representing Big River, Pelican Lake, and Witchekan Lake).[5]

Setting to work, First Nations leaders and Romanow's people developed the base principles leading to two agreements signed in 1995: the Gaming Framework Agreement (hereinafter Framework Agreement), and the Casino Operating Agreement (hereinafter Operating Agreement). At the heart of the Framework Agreement was the revenue-sharing formula, including a set of guidelines delineating how the revenues were to be spent by recipient First Nations. Specifically, 37.5 percent of net revenues would go to the provincial government, 37.5 percent to the First Nations Trust, and the residual 25 percent would be allocated to four provincial Community Development Corporations (CDCs). Each CDC was established to aid in distributing one-quarter of the net profit share pursuant to the Framework Agreement in an effort to: (1) stimulate First Nations economic development; (2) fund reserve justice and health initiatives; (3) finance reserve education and cultural development; (4) improve community infrastructure; and (5) develop senior and youth programs and other charitable purposes. Each CDC was recognized as a corporate body with a board of directors.[6] During the first full year of operations (1997–98), the SIGA casinos generated $57.6 million, realizing a total profit of $20.3 million.[7] On the surface it appeared as though the needed checks and balances were in place to ensure smooth operations, and during the first three years everything seemed to be proceeding smoothly. Towards the end of 1999, however, whispers of financial impropriety began to circulate the provincial legislature. By the summer of 2000, the public's perception of and trust in SIGA and the provincial First Nations gaming industry were being significantly challenged.

In May 2000, the *Saskatoon Star-Phoenix* broke the story concerning potential mismanagement of SIGA funds, specifically the FSIN's failure to comply with provincial demands for full disclosure of financial statements related to the distribution of casino revenues. Driven by various complaints about SIGA's and the FSIN's spending, the Saskatchewan Liquor and Gaming Authority (SLGA) intervened.[8] The provincial minister responsible for gaming, Doreen Hamilton, singled out SIGA administration for what she claimed was its inability to control spending. This scrutiny centred on SIGA CEO and board of directors (board) chairman Dutch Lerat, in particular for his receipt of an estimated $360,000 in unauthorized debit and credit card purchases. Lerat's gaming registration was suspended and an interim CEO was appointed in June. In addition to publicly questioning SIGA's effectiveness, Minister Hamilton threatened to fire the association's primary officers. She also stated that any FSIN resistance to her demands would force the shutdown of all casinos.

Provincial auditor Fred Wendel reviewed SIGA's books and indicated that his "audit found improper and questionable use of public money. The problems are serious and the government needs to correct the problems quickly."[9] Wendel initially concluded that Lerat had taken $360,000 in unauthorized debit and credit card advances above his $150,000 salary. He owed SIGA $811,906 for unsupported expense claims and a number of suspect business trips. Critical of SIGA, Wendel was also distressed at the limited research conducted prior to SIGA's initiating of a $12-million advertising campaign. An additional $1.7 million originally destined for Saskatchewan's First Nations Fund, Métis organizations, and the province was also unaccounted for. Finally, SIGA had paid $875,000 to Saskatchewan Indian Gaming Licensing (SIGL), a body that had no authority to grant licences.[10] Wendel took careful aim at the Saskatchewan government's role, given their wilful disregard of a 1999 provincial auditor report that recommended the SLGA work with SIGA "to establish proper conflict of interest guidelines; ensure inspections and audits are completed as planned or document why the plan was changed; receive an external auditor's report within 90 days of the adequacy of SIGA's internal controls and receive and approve SIGA's budget on a timely basis, with procedures in place for approaching changes to the budget." Wendel concluded that improper spending would have been prevented had the SLGA "fully acted on the recommendations we made in our 1999 spring report to the Legislative Assembly."[11] The quickly negotiated Framework Agreement was cited as the basis of the difficulties: it was ill-suited to offer checks and balances in the face of unbridled spending.

CORPORATE IMAGE AND CONSUMER TRUST

The Dutch Lerat Affair preceded a period of larger corporate disgrace epitomized by the Enron accounting scandal of 2001. SIGA administrators presented the issue as inadequate accounting of irregular spending easily resolved once identified. Having originally depicted Dutch Lerat as a spendthrift, the print media quickly reversed course, labelling Lerat and SIGA corrupt and incapable of properly managing a multi-million-dollar corporation. This blow to SIGA's corporate image and reputation signalled to the provincial gaming industry that SIGA was on the cusp of a crippling monetary setback, which would have grave ramifications for the provincial gaming industry.

Corporate image is public reality; it is the general impression that a society of people has of an organization. For SIGA, which was and remains largely dependent on non-Native patrons for its financial success, creating a favourable corporate image is necessary to advance positive attitudes (political and societal) about the organization.[12] These attitudes often reflect an individual's direct experience with an organization, specifically its ability to provide a valued service to its customers.[13] The print media play an influential role in framing public opinion, which suggests that multiple forces inform public attitudes about corporations. Over time, these interactions provide the public with the subjective data from which a corporate reputation develops.[14] Whereas "an image reflects a set of associations linked to a brand or company name that summarizes a brand or firm's identity," reputation "reflects an overall judgment regarding the extent to which a firm is held in light esteem or regard, not the specific identity it has."[15] According to this philosophy, a company with a poor reputation will generate less attention, and ultimately fewer customers, than a firm with a good reputation. The link between a positive corporate image and company performance is generally accepted.[16]

Keeping one's reputation strong requires effective management of the corporate image, because that image influences "stakeholders' perceptions and preferences of companies as employment and investment opportunities, as community members, and as suppliers of products and/or services."[17] Strong corporate governance can effectively enhance the integrity of the financial reporting process, which aids managers in securing consumer trust.[18] Two theoretical frameworks inform our understanding of corporate governance. The first is drawn from agency theory and postulates that managers will act according to their own self-interests, even if it is detrimental to the shareholders. As a result, suitably various mechanisms are adopted to observe managerial performance, including independent scrutineers (members of the board) who monitor management.[19] The second framework considers governance as an agent of regulatory requirements and largely symbolic; it provides limited oversight and generally endorses management's decisions.[20] In both cases, overseers are put in place to ensure adherence to financial reporting criteria and accountability. Multiple definitions of this last term abound, but in the main, *accountability* is "not essentially concerned with discretionary or voluntary disclosure, but rather with the institutionalization of legal rights for stakeholders to information concerning corporate behaviour."[21] Strong corporate governance, then, is concerned with establishing the tools needed to counter the anticipated risks associated with individual advancement in an endeavour to advance a strong reputation.

A trustworthy CEO plays an important role in maintaining customer confidence should questions arise regarding unorthodox management styles or board of director efficiency. For First Nations casino operators, this is critical for several reasons. First, the casinos are largely dependent on non-Native patrons for their financial success. As an example, the Opaskwayak Cree Nation's Aseneskak Casino near The Pas, Manitoba, has consistently suffered from low patronage since opening in 2002. A minimally successful venture based on modest annual profits, it has, as a result, never attained the level of patronage casino advocates and managers desired.[22] Second, public opinion indicates that only 1 percent of Canadians believe First Nations should operate gaming establishments.[23] Thus First Nations casino operators need to combat an already-existing negative feeling. Finally, the public trust is already challenged by regular media reports detailing reserve corruption and political futility, which can shake already tenuous consumer confidence.

Unlike public corporations that are responsible for reporting to one set of shareholders, First Nations businesses are unique: they are often accountable to key stakeholders (the communities) and band councils (the governments). In this regard, First Nations businesses are indeed answerable to a minimum of two and oftentimes multiple stakeholders, each with its own demands and expectations. SIGA faced similar tensions: as the FSIN's charitable arm and gaming regulator, its board of directors was inherently bound to the FSIN as well as to the communities and to various other political agents, such as the province's ten tribal councils. This resulted in intersecting political and economic agendas, and nominal delineation between leadership decisions related to political advancement and those related to corporate surety. Two scholars have written of this and similar models, concluding that "members of tribal council get to make the decisions, hand out the goodies, and reward supporters, but the nation as a whole suffers as *its* power—its capacity to achieve its goals—is crippled by an environment that serves the individual interests of office-holders but not the interests of the community as a whole. Equally crippling is a community attitude ... that sees government not as a mechanism for rebuilding the future but simply as a set of resources that one faction or another can control."[24] The resulting conflict is often an insurmountable and common phenomenon in North American indigenous communities, according to the Harvard Project on American Indian Economic Development. Intended to improve our collective understanding about why some communities flourished economically where others failed, the Harvard Project has identified the policy of legitimate self-rule exercised by Indian tribes to the exclusion of the United States as the central process of nation-building. Among various issues the Harvard Project discovered is that successful tribes are able to separate politics from day-to-day business decisions.

According to the Harvard Project, First Nations seeking business opportunities often find themselves trapped in non-responsive colonial bureaucracies. In Canada, this is attributable to the Indian Act's restrictive provisions regulating reserve economic and political development. The resulting lack of strategic direction can be detrimental for Native leaders directing economic development. A lack of competent bureaucracy often complicates ambitious development programs, making difficult governing and administrative tasks more financially and administratively complex. Those First Nations that choose to not separate political and business interests would be well-advised to attract, develop, and retain skilled personnel, establish effective civil-service systems that protect employees from politics, install robust employee grievance systems, and establish regularized bureaucratic practices so that decisions are implemented and recorded effectively and reliably.[25]

This brief discussion highlights the key components of strong corporate governance and how it can be employed to ensure a positive corporate image, leading to an enhanced public reputation. One researcher laments, however, "Given the importance of the relation between the quality of governance mechanisms and the credibility of the financial reporting system, it is surprising that we know so little about the nature and extend of this relation."[26] This could be said to apply directly to SIGA. Bound by the Framework Agreement and the Operating Agreement, both of which were negotiated with the provincial government, it seemed the proper mechanisms existed to ensure accountable financial reporting. Within three years of opening, however, it was clear that SIGA officials often disregarded an already weak accountability framework, thereby threatening the First Nations gaming industry. As has been suggested by one study, most "fraud firms' governance structures are initially weak."[27] Detecting the fraud is important, but it is also vital to assess how fraud firms respond (e.g., through corporate restructuring) and to determine how new governing models were expected to circumvent what previous governing structures were unable to accomplish.

METHOD

The following analysis is based on newspaper articles, editorials, and op-ed pieces obtained from Canadian newspapers. Most of the stories originated in Saskatchewan, and in most cases were published in the *Saskatoon Star-Phoenix* or the *Regina Leader-Post*. On several occasions stories appeared in other regional newspapers (e.g., the *Kitchener-Waterloo Record*) with additional information not cited by the Saskatchewan-based newspapers. These are occasionally referred to, albeit utilized more for context. The articles used in this study make reference to the Dutch Lerat Affair and SIGA's response to outside challenges to its legitimacy over a four-and-a-half year period: June 2000 to December 2004. A preliminary search of articles for the acronym SIGA turned up 1588 documents on the Canadian Newsstand database; for Dutch Lerat, 523 documents. A combined search generated 367 hits, all of which were used for the following analysis. The research's final phase consisted of a thematic analysis, based on these articles, of subject matter related to both SIGA's response to the fraud and how it countered these actions.[28]

The coding process involved identifying a principal theme or proposition prior to proceeding with data interpretation.[29] This enabled data to be organized and categorized, and from there for central themes to be identified and developed.[30] A comparative overview of newspaper coverage was not conducted, nor was a distinction made between newspaper discourse and the comments of the primary actors. The chapter is concerned with outlining the various ways SIGA attempted to bolster its tarnished corporate image to secure the public's trust.

ANALYSIS

SIGA responded in two ways to buffer criticism in its attempts to secure the public's trust and move forward: (1) by developing an independent corporate response; and (2) by citing Aboriginal rights/inherent right to self-government. Each response involved a variety of actions dealing with the affair (as listed below).

The independent corporate response involved

♦ drafting new internal accountability criteria and calling for audit;

♦ firing Dutch Lerat;

♦ altering SIGA's board of directors selection criteria;

♦ working with the province to rebuild business relationships; and

♦ drawing from tradition to guide contemporary corporate development.

The Aboriginal rights/inherent right to self-government response involved

♦ downplaying the extent of mismanagement;

♦ challenging provincial jurisdiction over reserve casinos;

♦ citing the province's imposed changes as a missed opportunity to learn from mistakes; and

♦ blaming the print media for undermining the FSIN's ability to self-regulate.

INDEPENDENT CORPORATE RESPONSE — SIGA quickly became the focus of unprecedented print media attention highlighting what initially appeared to be financial mismanagement. This soon spiralled into talk of misappropriation of funds and fraudulent activities. All newspapers in the sample contain information and quotes from major players about the need to secure public trust by responding to outside charges in an appropriate manner.

Drafting New Internal Accountability Criteria and Calling for Audit. The first action taken by FSIN president Perry Bellegarde was to announce a new SIGA policy for submitting travel expenses on 16 June 2000. Proper documentation was now required to track spending, including in particular all receipts cataloguing expenses. No maximum spending limit was imposed, although the board would review expenditures on a monthly basis.[31] "As far as we're concerned," claimed Bellegarde, "we have every trust in the system that's there." The issue was simple: a "grey area for [SIGA] financial controls" existed. As part of its self-imposed changes, SIGA adopted the crown corporation schedule for per diems and remuneration.[32] With new monitoring of all spending criteria in place, Bellegarde expressed his confidence that a corporate review and an internal FSIN audit would find no evidence of wrongdoing. This was apparently intended to assuage government fears while impressing upon gaming officials that SIGA employees were exercising due diligence within an imperfect system. Operations were restructured to improve accountability and to reassure the public and government officials, thus reinforcing the public trust.

Firing Dutch Lerat. The following day, 17 June 2000, the provincial minister in charge of gaming (Hamilton) suspended Lerat's gaming registration and ordered the immediate cancellation of his credit and debit cards. Bellegarde was bombarded with questions concerning his continued support of Lerat and how the missing money was spent. Newspaper columns added further fuel to the fire, arguing that "accountability only sure bet," and that SIGA was "setting a new standard in deception." Bellegarde held out for six days before finally terminating Lerat.[33] Lerat's termination suggests that Bellegarde was aware that SIGA's corporate image was taking a hit, thus impugning its reputation. He insisted that Lerat would be forced to pay back the entire amount while occasionally suggesting he could potentially remain on the payroll, citing Lerat's exemplary work—outside of some minor mismanagement issues.

Altering SIGA's Board of Directors Selection Criteria. The day the story broke, Bellegarde admitted the need to realign SIGA's corporate structure. He further acknowledged that having Lerat serve as both CEO and board chair was a conflict of interest. After being asked to resign as the board chair, Lerat did so willingly and immediately. It became evident during this period that the existing SIGA board model was inefficient. Prior to 2000, the ten provincial tribal councils had each elected one representative to the eleven-member board. Tribal councils could change their member without notice, and the operating rules were not clear.[34] Conflict-of-interest guidelines were also non-existent. Meadow Lake tribal council representatives in July "indicated that the whole board should be replaced and Dutch [Lerat] should not be the only one to take the fall. The director of finance for SIGA should be fired as well. He's got a certain amount of responsibility and should have said something."[35] The FSIN responded a few months later by introducing new accountability guidelines, including seventeen internal controls to monitor spending. The tribal councils were also asked to reconsider their appointments to the eleven-person board. During the FSIN election campaign, the need to separate politics and business was broached by Morley Watson, who was seeking to replace Bellegarde. He argued, "Our businesspeople must make the business decisions and our political leaders have to fight the political battles." He added that the board members should be First Nations businesspeople rather than tribal council members or FSIN chiefs.[36] As of the end of the October 2000, five of the eleven SIGA board members had been replaced.[37]

Working with the Province to Rebuild Business Relationship. Returning to the negotiating table to revamp the original Framework Agreement was the first step taken to rebuild the damaged province-FSIN relationship. Of particular concern were: (1) reporting and communication criteria; and (2) criteria outlining SIGA's overall performance objectives. The report demonstrated that both SIGA and the SLGA had failed to properly adhere to provisions detailing auditing and reporting procedures. Cited as the source of the difficulties, the Framework Agreement was loosely configured, making it open to interpretation. It was overhauled and a new framework developed. Signed in 2002, the new agreement created a twenty-five-year partnership that would be reviewed every five years, with the understanding that each party had the authority "to raise any matter for discussion and negotiation during the Review Period by providing the other party with reasonable notice in writing of its intention to do so."[38] The revenue-sharing formula was revamped to assign the First Nations Trust half of net revenues, with the remainder to be divided equally between the province's general revenue fund and the newly reconstituted Community Development Corporations.

The four CDCs' board of directors' structure was jettisoned for a new model, according to which a simple majority representing the host tribal councils would make up the board of directors, along with two other representatives drawn from other tribal councils. A standing committee was also struck to "facilitate and coordinate communication between the Community Development Corporations and the Government concerning the operation of the Community Development Corporations and the distribution of gaming funds to the organizations."[39] To ensure greater accountability, the CDCs were required to hire an auditor to determine whether "the monies received by the Corporation have been fully accounted for and properly disposed of and that the proper rules, policies and procedures are applied."[40] The government retained responsibility for determining SIGA's net profits at the end of each fiscal year, and for distributing those monies according to the revenue-sharing formula. The new Framework Agreement's accountability and management provisions were more rigorous, assuring greater accountability when handling revenues.

Drawing from Tradition to Guide Contemporary Corporate Development. Upon ensuring the public that it had indeed turned over a new leaf, SIGA's *2003–04 Annual Report* outlined a list of five principles it had adopted to guide employee relations and ensure the maintenance of public trust. Drawn from key principles Cree leaders employed during Treaty 6 negotiations with the British Crown in 1876, these ideas reflected a new approach to corporate governance. As the annual report describes, "SIGA will strengthen the lives of Saskatchewan and First Nations people through employment, economic growth and community relations. This will be accomplished through the provision of a distinctive First Nations gaming experience that reflects the traditional aspects of our First Nations culture and hospitality. As a First Nations organization employing First Nations people, SIGA has adopted five principles to encourage balance while incorporating traditional aspects of First Nations culture. While our five guiding principles are presented here in Cree, there are parallel expressions in the Saulteaux, Dene, Lakota, Dakota and Nakota languages." The principles are as follows:

> **Tâpwêwin** (Speaking with precision and accuracy): The principle of Tâpwêwin advocates speaking with precision and accuracy. For SIGA, from a business perspective, it means we are accountable and conduct our business with integrity, honour and discipline.

> **Pimâcihowin** (Making a living): Pimâcihowin stresses the importance of making a living and is today's realization of our First Nations treaty relationship. The financial and

operational success of SIGA provides the means to integrate a holistic approach to improve the quality of life for our people and for all people in the province of Saskatchewan.

Miyo-wîcêhtowin (Establishing good relations and getting along with others): The value of getting along with others is represented by the word Miyo-wîcêhtowin. By conducting our business in a manner that reflects our First Nations hospitality, traditions and customs, we are able to foster good relations with our customers. Guest satisfaction is crucial to our success.

Miskâsowin (Finding one's sense of origin and belonging): Miskâsowin represents the value of finding one's sense of origin and belonging. A fundamental goal of SIGA is to bring about a positive sense of origin and belonging in a predominantly First Nations employee base. This will lead to confident, productive and fulfilled employees.

Wîtaskêwin (Living together on the land): Living together on the land is the fundamental value conveyed by the word Wîtaskêwin. SIGA's vision statement "Sharing Success" speaks to the concept of sharing the land or, in today's terms, sharing resources. This value inspires us to give back to the communities where we live and work.[41]

As discussed above, the FSIN and SIGA responded in what could be described as a responsible manner. Each step appears to have been taken with the intention of countering the poor publicity the Dutch Lerat Affair was generating and ensuring a quick containment of negative publicity. Importantly, it must be noted that these responses could best be described as being informed by economic concerns as opposed to political concerns. Reflecting on the Harvard Project's unease with political and economic amalgamation, the aforementioned responses, while developed by the FSIN's political arm, better reflect the organization's response to a potential economic hit borne of poor publicity and lagging public trust. The following section details the political response.

ABORIGINAL RIGHTS/INHERENT RIGHT TO SELF-GOVERNMENT RESPONSE — On the surface it appeared as though SIGA and the FSIN had taken several positive steps forward through a corporate restructuring process that embraced enhanced accountability. Despite these varied responses, the FSIN concomitantly embraced an Aboriginal rights/self-government discourse that at times appeared to be counterintuitive to the proposed structural and ideological changes that SIGA seemed to be on the verge of implementing.

Downplaying the Extent of Mismanagement. In the same June 2000 meeting in which Lerat stepped down as CEO, the SIGA board announced new controls on expense accounts. It also promised that the misspent monies would be paid back.[42] A SIGA press release initially reported $260,000 was misspent, when in fact the total was $360,000. The reason for the difference: the SIGA board (of which Lerat was the chair) agreed to an unbudgeted annual $50,000 salary increase for Lerat retroactive two years, in keeping with industry standards, followed by a three-year contract reflecting these changes. This raised his annual salary to $500,000 to offset the amount of Lerat's indebtedness to SIGA. This occurred a little more than one month before the original story broke.[43] Bellegarde publicly supported Lerat, claiming his CEO spent appropriately on gifts, contributions to powwows, and travel expenses for himself and others. The province intervened and ordered both the rescission of the pay raise and the cancellation of Lerat's credit cards, while also bringing to a close negotiations between the province and SIGA regarding two new casinos. (Negotiations remained closed until 2002.)

The internal SIGA audit was submitted 14 September 2000, two months before the provincial audit authored by Fred Wendel. It contended the print media was exaggerating the extent of its perceived overspending. Acknowledging Lerat's unauthorized expenditures, the FSIN admitted the board's spending was "out of step with our fiscal reality. Despite rising revenues our profit margin is falling."[44] The SIGA audit concluded that the board misspent an approximate $835,000.[45] This amounted to an average of $47,000 annually for each board member for travel expenses, per diems, and remuneration. The Manitoba Lottery Corporation spent $45,000 total during the same period; likewise, the Saskatchewan Crop Insurance Corporation incurred $87,798 in board expenses.[46] The provincial auditor's report was released two months later, and it identified that total misspending was closer to $1.7 million, a number that grew to $2.3 million by mid-2001.[47] SIGA openly disagreed with its conclusions, although it was later revealed that despite having made $7.5 million more than the previous year, the Gaming Authority experienced a $3.3 million drop in profit.[48]

Additional research uncovered that several board members were hired as SIGA consultants and that Lerat was not interviewed for the CEO position, against an FSIN consultant's advice. Wendel's report indicated Lerat did not submit a resumé and that the SLGA did not conduct a background check, since the applicant was an FSIN vice chief.[49] Regarding board members hired as SIGA consultants, the key example cited was the $6,000/month contract given to former FSIN chief and board member Roland Crowe. Crowe was hired in 2000 on a seven-month contract; it was reported that upon that contract's expiration it would be renewed until July 2001, and then extended again for another three years. Crowe claimed the contract was to become permanent. Furthermore, the contract was for Crowe and his partner Mick Ryan to develop the Moose Jaw casino proposal and to negotiate management contracts with three Manitoba First Nations interested in operating casinos.[50] The negotiation of contracts with Manitoba First Nations would be beyond the scope of the 1995 Framework Agreement. Crowe insisted, however, that no conflict of interest existed due to widespread knowledge of the contract.

Wendel's subsequent two reports cited continuing discrepancies while suggesting that SIGA failed to implement the changes needed to secure the public's trust. In December 2001, SIGA's failures to develop a business plan and hire a chief financial officer were identified. Wendel also cited room for additional fraud at SIGA, including ease of access to blank cheques and automated systems lacking password protection that allowed "unauthorized persons [to] make changes to the systems to conceal frauds and errors."[51] The review unearthed additional fraud, including an employee who made improper payments worth $30,000 and a former employee who, with a partner, defrauded SIGA of $66,000 by falsifying account entries.[52] An update in December 2002 indicated that SIGA "continues to make payments beyond its authority and without due care. Saskatchewan Liquor and Gaming Authority (SLGA) is responsible for the supervision of SIGA. While (SLGA) has good practices in other areas, its supervision of SIGA remains deficient." In this regard, Wendel noted that the SLGA authorized SIGA to pay $400,000 to the FSIN for legal fees in connection with negotiating the new twenty-five-year gaming agreement and $150,000 to the SIGL without proper authority. As of December 2002, SIGA had implemented only seven of the original nineteen recommendations. It had ignored critical suggestions included establishing adequate policies to "ensure its books and records reflect its business operations" and "compliance with the casino operating agreement."[53]

In December 2003, a fourth consecutive report critical of SIGA's spending was published identifying a $446,000 unauthorized expenditure promoting the creation of a Saskatoon casino, well above the $100,000 approved payment. Most of the expense was recorded in other categories on the balance sheet.[54] In December 2004 Wendel again reported questionable spending practices. This time, SIGA had spent $480,000 on disputed marketing and promotional items.[55]

Challenging Provincial Jurisdiction over Reserve Casinos. In June 2000, renowned *Star-Phoenix* columnist Doug Cuthand promptly identified the FSIN's reliance on jurisdiction claims to deflect outside criticism: "The jurisdictional argument was a non-starter and clearly dealt with in the agreement. The FSIN wisely backed away from that argument and saved the issue of provincial jurisdiction in First Nations affairs for another day." He also astutely concluded, "This whole incident has the potential to haunt self-government if the First Nations leaders don't take decisive action and get SIGA under control and gain back its credibility."[56]

Cuthand was, however, somewhat optimistic in proclaiming the FSIN had backed away from this discourse. Rather, the FSIN continued to aggressively challenge provincial jurisdiction over reserve casinos. Despite several Supreme Court of Canada cases concluding that gaming jurisdiction rested with the province,[57] Bellegarde insisted provincial officials were "overreaching their bounds as far as we're concerned. Is it their jurisdiction to say, 'You can't do this?' No." He later added, "We've ultimately been working towards First Nations jurisdiction and control over management and operations of our gaming industry here in Saskatchewan. Unfortunately, the 1995 gaming agreement does give the power, authority and control to Saskatchewan Liquor and Gaming right now."[58] This argument was later altered in late 2000 to reflect on the nature of First Nations jurisdiction on reserves as opposed to gaming in general.[59] Bellegarde cited provincial jealousy as the motivating factor driving what he claimed many in the First Nations community would characterize as a witch-hunt: "Is it because they're [the SLGA are] upset with the success of our operations? That's something you've got to speculate about because [the government-owned] Casino Regina was going into Moose Jaw. One of our other tribal councils was going to go into Moose Jaw. So we had competing interests."[60] He added, "There's some other political agenda [government officials] aren't coming clean with."[61]

Former Assembly of First Nations (AFN) grand chief David Ahenakew in December 2000 answered the claims that the FSIN had given up jurisdiction by insisting Saskatchewan's First Nations were taking jurisdiction back or "we close all casinos. The ultimate bottom line is to close all casinos; not just the Indian casinos but all the casinos. There will be no gambling in this province." Willing to throw all provincial casino employees under the bus to regain jurisdiction, including an estimated 900 First Nations workers, Ahenakew demanded provincial officials "back off and allow us our money, our jurisdiction, get the hell out of there, then everything would be fine." He also implicitly suggested if the FSIN were not granted jurisdiction, SIGA's continued role as corporate sponsor would be compromised, as would its charitable work.[62]

This response was multifaceted. Take SIGA's two-pronged response to the auditor's nineteen recommendations, for example. Publicly Bellegarde admitted that they were logical responses to the situation and that they would be implemented. However, as of December 2002 Wendel highlighted SIGA's unwillingness to implement change: "SIGA has no clear plan to improve its spending practices."[63] For instance, it was some time before the positions of CEO and board chair were officially separated, and SIGA resisted recommendations to overhaul the board structure. The FSIN attempted to placate the print media and therefore the public by making aesthetic changes to the board structure. The new rules instituted for appointing trustees included stipulations that criminal background checks be conducted; all candidates be bondable; trustees be provided training in due diligence; and that the provincial government make the appointments.[64] Acknowledging this resistance, the SLGA unilaterally fired the board members and instituted its seven-member model in its place.

In another instance, the FSIN attempted on three separate occasions to re-hire Lerat, despite his being the subject of a very public RCMP investigation. Within two weeks of the mismanagement story breaking, in June 2000, the FSIN tried to secretly re-hire Lerat. The rational: Lerat was "still a First Nations citizen member, he will always be a Cowessess band member. So people thought he's got a lot of experience in gaming, there are financial obligations from the individual to SIGA."[65] The Saskatchewan Indian Institute of Technologies (SIIT) later provided Lerat with a six-month, $30,000 contract. SIGA also refused to furnish the SIGL (SIGA's regulatory authority) with financial statements, and the SIGL was blamed for doing a poor job of monitoring the gaming authority.[66] First Nations Trust Fund financials were withheld in 1997, defying a provincial auditor's request to review the records, as were board minutes.[67] This despite the FSIN's justice commission and economic development commission demanding their release.[68] SIGA begrudgingly relented and delivered the minutes to Ernst and Young—in effect bypassing Wendel on the basis of proprietary interest. The review reported that the board ran informally; multiple people attended and influenced the outcome of meetings; it was difficult to ascertain who was supposed to be in attendance or what the rules were leading to vital corporate decisions.[69]

It is interesting to note that as the inherent right to self-government and the corresponding right to regulate reserve casinos was being cited, FSIN leaders consistently referred to the SLGA's failure to monitor and regulate SIGA spending. Ahenakew opined, "All of us are to blame for allowing the province to do what it's doing to us."[70] Bellegarde claimed that the SLGA was partly responsible: "Every year they had the authority and responsibility. They vetted SIGA's operating expenses and budgets. They knew what was going on."[71] Interim chair of the board Gerry Merasty also questioned the province's competency: "They were made aware of the situation in 1998 and they approve all budgets and audits and they were aware—why did they choose to raise it [this issue] at the end of 2000?"[72] Bellegarde blamed neo-colonial attitudes for his and SIGA's difficulties: "Every year they [SLGA] had the authority and responsibility. They vetted SIGA's operating expenses and budgets. People don't talk about that."[73] Bellegarde's parting comments were provocative: "Every time First Nations people try to do something for their people in a good way, there's still oppression." He added, "There's that control. There's still that colonialism that exists."[74]

Bellegarde potentially undid any good will when he asserted that jurisdiction over reserve gaming was "the jewel in our crown ... and that if it is our sovereign territory, we should be able to do what we want, when we want, in our land."[75] Then, in June 2003, the FSIN vice chief responsible for economic development, Guy Lonechild, announced that Lerat had once again been hired, this time to expose the province's influence in the SIGA scandal. Attempting to deflect blame, Lonechild informed the print media, "The province was regulating SIGA and they approved all the expenses. The province regulated all the operations and they were licensing all the casinos and the people who managed them. So the province was responsible." He added, "We're going to expose those, like they did to us. From the First Nations' point of view, its time for us to tell the truth about the province. And that's what I'm going to do."[76] As a *Star-Phoenix* editorial later suggested, "It's as pathetic as it's galling to see Lonechild trying to play the victim card in suggesting that intelligent and competent Native persons responsible for the profitable casinos were powerless to act ethically."[77]

Citing the Province's Imposed Changes as a Missed Opportunity to Learn from Mistakes. SIGA responded slowly to the nineteen recommendations to improve government and accountability, although on 16 November 2000 the entire SIGA board of directors was fired. A seven-member board was established in its place with the following criteria: members must demonstrate proper educational qualifications and business experience, with three positions designated for government appointees. SIGA hired an internal auditor, limited credit card availability, and introduced new conflict-of-interest guidelines. Bellegarde's demeanour at times suggested a willingness to meet with government officials to resolve the situation, with him claiming, "We've got to sit down and work this out."[78] On other occasions, he claimed that the scandal was simply reflective of the growing pains associated with self-government.[79] In what was described by the Harvard Project as practical sovereignty, those communities and their leaders will benefit directly from good decisions while suffering the consequences of bad decisions: "Once decisions move into Indians' hands, then the decision-makers themselves have to face the consequences of their decisions." This, the authors argue, provides a learning curve resulting in "the quality of their decisions" improving.[80] It seems that the province agreed with this general assessment: in April 2002, a new twenty-five-year agreement was signed that permitted SIGA to install an additional 125 machines, bringing its total to 625. It then allowed for the installation of 250 more at the anticipated casino in Moose Jaw.[81]

Blaming the Print Media for Undermining the FSIN's Ability to Self-Regulate. The print media made convenient targets for an FSIN leadership frustrated with having its every action in the spotlight. Although this tactic played out minimally in the print media, it was, all the same, an aspect of an overall response whereby the FSIN blamed others for its inability to self-regulate. This unusual situation was arguably the result of many FSIN leaders' unfamiliarity with the internal workings of the print media and their minimal experience working with non-government agents seeking out corruption. Frustration boiled to the surface on 18 October 2000, following the publication of the FSIN's internal audit of SIGA, acquired by a *Star-Phoenix* reporter. The SIGL chief executive asked the reporter to refrain from publishing from the report, arguing that it was destined for internal [read "FSIN and affiliated agents"] consumption.[82] As *Star-Phoenix* columnist Murray Mandryk, who closely followed the scandal, wrote, "The FSIN chiefs and their overpaid spin doctors were busy playing the race card Wednesday, desperately trying to make this issue about something that it is not. The issue is the print media, they charged."[83] Doug Cuthand identified that during the FSIN chiefs' assembly the print media came under attack and were accused of muckraking and meddling. However, as he noted, "What they failed to mention is that the document was leaked to the media by someone within the First Nations community. The report came from within the offices of the Saskatchewan Indian Gaming Licensing Commission."[84]

FINAL THOUGHTS

The Dutch Lerat Affair had the potential to compromise the public's trust in SIGA, and to a lesser extent in the FSIN, resulting in diminished gambling revenues. First Nations officials responded immediately to a torrent of negative publicity, highlighting financial impropriety with two identifiable strategies: (1) establish a dialogue that would shape its official corporate response to perceived wrong-doing; and (2) cite the inherent right to self-government as a justification for First Nations mistakes made in pursuit of self-determination. These responses reflect the economic and political dimensions First Nations communities contend with daily, and how contradictory the responses can become when informed exclusively by political agendas. The failure to separate politics and economics in this case led to the misappropriation of funding, but more importantly it hindered the FSIN's public response. The Harvard Project's findings anticipated this result: SIGA's corporate structure means that it is a branch of the FSIN, informed by and answerable to politicians. Even if SIGA's gross revenues had not taken a significant hit, suggesting that the public's trust had not been compromised, the central issues identified in this case study resonate with the Harvard Project's long-standing contention that First Nations must separate politics and economics. As of 2010–11, SIGA is successfully operating six casinos and the Dutch Lerat Affair is largely forgotten—notwithstanding a poor corporate response to a troublesome episode that could have turned out unfortunately for all involved.

GAMBLING IN SASKATCHEWAN: A TIMELINE (1993–2002)

26 FEB. 1993 — The White Bear Indian Band opens a casino on reserve, in apparent contravention of the Criminal Code, which gives the provinces exclusive jurisdiction over gambling. The province threatens to shut down the operation.

22 MARCH 1993 — The RCMP raid a newly opened casino on the White Bear reserve, storming the building with an armed tactical squad.

30 NOV. 1993 — First video lottery terminals (VLTS) arrive in Saskatoon following government approval of machines as a means of helping rural hotels stay afloat.

14 DEC. 1993 — White Bear chief Bernie Shepherd and Alan King, the vendor of the slot machines sold to the reserve, begin their defence on charges of operating an illegal casino. The following day, the Crown stays the charges against Shepherd.

4 APRIL 1994 — Plans are unveiled for the Landing, a south downtown redevelopment including a casino, to the approval of a majority of city councillors.

20 MAY 1994 — NDP provincial government and the Federation of Saskatchewan Indian Nations sign a casino development policy that would put major casinos in both Regina and Saskatoon. The deal features a profit-sharing formula giving the province 50 percent, the Indian Nations 25 percent, and exhibition associations 25 percent.

1 JUNE 1994 — A group calling itself Citizens for a Quality South Downtown formally launches a petition drive to force a plebiscite on the south downtown casino.

3 AUG. 1994 — Anti-casino group tables petition at city council with 21,428 names, forcing a bylaw vote on whether Block 146 downtown could be used for a casino.

4 OCT. 1994 — Provincial court judge Wallace Goliath dismisses all gambling related charges in the White Bear case, saying the defendants had no criminal intent but were in the belief they had jurisdiction over casinos on reserve.

26 OCT. 1994 — Electors overwhelmingly reject a casino in Saskatoon's south downtown, by a margin of 50,938 to 13,182.

3 DEC. 1994 — Public opinion poll shows 82 percent of the Saskatoon public remains opposed to a major new casino in Saskatoon, an almost identical result to the plebiscite. Unlike the plebiscite, this question is not limited to a specific location.

9 FEB. 1995 — Province signs new gaming agreement with the FSIN raising the number of casinos it can develop to five, including one in Regina and four reserve casinos around the province. Saskatoon is specifically excluded from the deal. It suggests Saskatoon could be the site of an FSIN casino at some later date if it is approved by city council and proven to be economically viable.

12 APRIL 1995 — Premier Roy Romanow rejects calls for a province-wide referendum on maintaining VLTS in the province.

14 JULY 1995 — FSIN chooses four casino sites: North Battleford, Yorkton, Prince Albert, and the White Bear Reserve.

25 NOV. 1995 – The FSIN signs an agreement with government for four casinos, but Regina is left off the list.

18 DEC. 1995 — SIGA hires American Kelvin Lawrence, who established a number of casinos in South Dakota, as CEO.

25 JAN. 1996 — Casino Regina opens.

19 FEB. 1996 — Petition aimed at forcing a casino plebiscite in Prince Albert falls just short of collecting enough names to force a vote.

12 NOV. 1996 — Bear Claw Casino on the White Bear Reserve opens.

15 DEC. 1996 — Painted Hand Casino in Yorkton opens.

1 MARCH 1996 — North Battleford's Gold Eagle Casino opens.

7 MARCH 1997 — Province finally abandons the legal case against White Bear casino and agrees to help the FSIN lobby the federal government to give Natives jurisdiction over casinos.

1 NOV. 1997 — SIGA is given an ABEX (Achievement for Business Excellence) award for exceptional performance by a new company.

24 FEB. 1999 — Gaming minister Doreen Hamilton says the FSIN would have to show that public attitudes have changed before the government could consider another casino proposal and there would have to be a clear demonstration of public support before the province would approve a new casino for Saskatoon. It would not necessarily have to be a plebiscite, but "certainly it would have to be a democratic process that clearly demonstrates the majority will."

25 FEB. 1999 — Former Saskatoon mayor Henry Dayday calls for a plebiscite prior to construction of any new casino. "The people have spoken once with regards to a casino. And the people of Saskatoon said no they don't want one. I think it still stands that the public would have to speak to whether or not there would be one by way of a plebiscite."

DEC. 1999 — Canadian Auto Workers union wins right to represent employees at Northern Lights Casino.

7 JUNE 2000 — Dutch Lerat scandal breaks when the provincial auditor informs the SLGAOF irregularities in its annual audit of the Saskatchewan Indian Gaming Authority. Lerat is found to have spent more than $800,000 without proper authority.

9 JUNE 2000 — The SLGA cuts off Lerat's corporate debit and credit cards.

16 JUNE 1999 — The FSIN accepts Lerat's resignation as chair of SIGA, but endorses his decision to stay on as CEO. They also vote to approve retroactive salary increases totalling $360,000. FSIN chief Perry Bellegarde says the province can not fire Lerat.

19 JUNE 2000 — The province threatens to cut off VLT gambling at the four SIGA-run casinos unless Lerat steps down.

21 JUNE 2000 — The SIGA board fires Lerat as CEO and splits the chair and CEO positions. Lerat is ordered to repay $360,000 to SIGA.

27 AUG. 2001 — Government announces a new casino for Moose Jaw, just one day after lifting a moratorium on casino expansion imposed after the Dutch Lerat scandal.

10 NOV. 2001 — A *Star-Phoenix*/University of Saskatchewan poll shows that more than 85 percent of Saskatoon residents want a chance to vote on a casino before any decision is made about building a new one. More than 66 percent of respondents either disapproved or strongly disapproved of the idea of a new casino.

30 JAN. 2002 — City council puts off casino consultations, saying it would wait until there is a specific proposal to deal with.

15 OCT. 2002 — Saskatoon Tribal Council launches public consultation meetings on a new city casino.

22 OCT. 2002 — Robert Charles Head, former chief financial officer for the Saskatchewan Indian Gaming Authority, pleads guilty to fraud after embezzling $66,000 from the organization. He was sentenced to two years less a day, to be served in the community.

NOTES

* This article is reprinted with permission of the *Journal of Aboriginal Economic Development* 7, 1 (2010): 69–83. Thanks to Tammie Belanger, Chartered Accountant, Meyers Norris Penny, for her helpful suggestions.

1 For these data, see Yale D. Belanger, "First Nations Gaming as a Self-government Imperative? Ensuring the Health of First Nations Problem Gamblers." *International Journal of Canadian Studies* 41 (2010), p. 24.

2 Warren Skea, "Time to Deal: A Comparison of the Native Casino Gambling Policy in Alberta and Saskatchewan" (PhD diss., University of Calgary, 1997), 103.

3 Skea, "Time to Deal," 110.

4 Saskatchewan Government, "Casino Expansion Policy Paper," Feb. 1993 (photocopy in author's possession).

5 Skea, "Time to Deal," 14.

6 The information for this paragraph was gleaned from Cathy Nilson, "The FSIN-Province of Saskatchewan Gaming Partnership: 1995 to 2002" (master's thesis, University of Saskatchewan, 2004), 49–50.

7 See Lorna Wenger and Beth Mckechnie, *FastFacts on Gambling* (Manitoba: The Awareness and Information Unit of the Addictions Foundation of Manitoba, 1999), 22.

8 Jason Warick, "Casino Books Opened: FSIN Takes Audit Process One Step Further," *Saskatoon Star-Phoenix*, 31 May 2000, A1.

9 Murray Mandryk, "Nothing Learned in SIGA Affair," *Saskatoon Star-Phoenix*, 17 Nov. 2000, A14.

10 Ibid.

11 Ibid.

12 G.R. Dowling, "Developing Your Corporate Image into a Corporate Asset," *Long Range Planning* 26, 2 (1993): 102–109; and Cees Van Riel and John Balmer, "Corporate Identity: Its Concept, Its Measurement and Management," *European Journal of Marketing* 31, 5–6 (1997): 342–355.

13 Charles Fombrun and Cees Van Riel, "The Reputational Landscape," *Corporate Reputation Review* 1, 1–2 (1997): 5–13; Steven L. Wartick, "The Relationship between Intense Media Exposure and Change in Corporate Reputation," *Business and Society* 31 (1992): 33–49.

14 D.A. Gioia, M. Schultz, and K.G. Corley, "Organizational Identity, Image, and Adaptive Instability," *Academy of Mangement Review* 25, 1 (2000): 63–81

15 Allen Weiss, Erin Andreson, and Deborah J. Macinnis, "The Impact of Reputation on the Choice of Sales Organization," *Journal of Marketing* 63, 4 (1999): 75.

16 Claudia Simoes, Sally Dibb, and Raymond P. Fisk, "Managing Corporate Identity: An Internal Perspective," *Journal of the Academy of Marketing Sciences* 33, 2 (2005): 153.

17 Petya Pucheva, "The Role of Corporate Reputation in the Stakeholder Decision-Making Process," *Business and Society* 47, 3 (2008): 272.

18 Jeffrey R. Cohen and D.M. Hanno, "Auditor's Consideration of Corporate Governance and Management Control Philosophy in Preplanning and Planning Judgements," *Auditing: A Journal of Practice and Theory* 19, 2 (2000): 134.

19 C.T. Bathala and R.P. Rao, "The Determinants of Board Composition: An Agency Theory Perspective," *Managerial and Decision Economics* 16 (1995), 59–69; and Jeff Cohen, G. Krishnamoorthy, and A. Wright, "Corporate Governance and the Audit Process," *Contemporary Accounting Research* (2002): 579.

20 R.D. Kosnick, "Greenmail: A Study of Board Performance in Corporate Governance," *Administrative Science Quarterly* 32 (1987): 163–185.

21 Tracey Swift, "Trust, Reputation and Corporate Accountability to Stakeholders," *Business Ethics: A European Review* 10, 1 (2001): 18.

22 Yale D. Belanger, *Gambling with the Future: The Evolution of Aboriginal Gaming in Canada* (Saskatoon: Purich Publishing, 2006).

23 Jason Azmier, *Canadian Gambling Behaviour and Attitudes: Summary Report* (Calgary: Canada West Foundation, 2000), 8–9.

24 Stephen Cornell and Joseph P. Kalt, *Two Approaches to Economic Development on American Indian Reservations: One Works, the Other Doesn't* (Cambridge, MA: Harvard Project on American Indian Economic Development and the Native Nations Institute for Leadership, Management, and Policy, on behalf of the Arizona Board of Regents, 2006), 17.

25 Ibid. See also "Harvard Project Lessons on Self-Government: Improving Aboriginal Self-Government in Canada," *Frontier Centre for Public Policy: Backgrounder*, http://www.fcpp.org/main/publication_detail.php?PubID=517 (last accessed 16 Dec. 2008); and Stephen Cornell, Miriam Jorgensen, Joseph P. Kalt, and Katherine A. Spilde, *Seizing the Future: Why Some Native Nations Do and Others Don't* (Cambridge, MA: Harvard Project of American Indian Economic Development, 2005).

26 David B. Farber, "Restoring Trust after Fraud: Does Corporate Governance Matter?" *The Accounting Review* 80, 2 (2005), 540.

27 Ibid., 540.

28 J. Daly, A. Kellehear, and M. Gliksman, *The Public Health Researcher: A Methodological Approach* (Melbourne: Oxford University Press, 1997).

29 R. Boyatzis, *Transforming Qualitative Information: Thematic Analysis and Code Development* (Thousand Oaks, CA: Sage, 1998).

30 See Jennifer Fereday and Eimear Muir-Cochrane, "Demonstrating Rigor Using Thematic Analysis: A Hybrid Approach of Inductive and Deductive Coding and Theme Development," *International Journal of Qualitative Methods* 5, 1 (2006): 3.

31 Jason Warick, "Reins Tighten on SIGA Spending: Native Group Puts Strict Policy in Place for Executives Doling out Cash," *Saskatoon Star-Phoenix*, 16 June 2000, A1.

32 Colleen Silverthorn, "New Controls for SIGA," *Regina Leader-Post*, 16 Sept. 2000, A1.

33 Parker, "SIGA Fires its Chief," A1.

34 Randy Burton, "One of the Most Offensive Defences Imaginable," *Saskatoon Star-Phoenix*, 14 Dec. 2000, A2.

35 Dan Zakreski, "Purge SIGA Board," *Saskatoon Star-Phoenix*, 8 July 2000, A1.

36 James Parker, "FSIN Should Open SIGA Board: Election Hopeful: Native Casino Authority Should Recruit Indian Businesspeople," *Saskatoon Star-Phoenix*, 23 Sept. 2000, A10.

37 James Parker, "Tribal Council Member to Complete SIGA Term: Appointments to SIGA Board under Review after Management Crisis," *Saskatoon Star-Phoenix*, 21 Oct. 2000, A4.

38 *Gaming Framework Agreement* (2002), http://www.igr.ca/pub_docs/2002_Gaming_Framework_Agreement.pdf, 23.

39 Ibid., 17.

40 Ibid., 17.

41 Saskatchewan Indian Gaming Authority (SIGA), *Our Journey Forward: 2003–2004 Annual Report* (Saskatoon: SIGA, 2004), 12–13.

42 Jason Warick, "SIGA Won't Dump Lerat: FSIN Chief Says Provincial Dictates on CEO, Spending out of Bounds," *Saskatchewan Star-Phoenix*, 17 June 2000, A1.

43 Parker, "SIGA Fires its Chief," A1.

44 Silverthorn, "New Controls for SIGA," A1.

45 Parker, "FSIN Should Open SIGA Board," A10.

46 James Parker, "Province Fires SIGA Directors: Auditor's Report Shows Misspending Problems Went beyond CEO Lerat to Include Board," *Saskatoon Star-Phoenix*, 16 Nov. 2000, A3.

47 Colleen Silverthorn, "SIGA Misspending Tops $2.3 Million," *Regina Leader-Post*, 27 March 2002, A3.

48 James Parker, "New Faces on Board with SIGA: Seven-member Slate in Place to Begin Cleanup," *Saskatoon Star-Phoenix*, 14 Feb. 2001, A1.

49 Murray Mandryk, "Lerat Owes $800,000: Auditor: Many Expenses were for 'Personal' Services: Report," *Saskatoon Star-Phoenix*, 16 Nov. 2000, D7.

50 James Parker, "Ex-FSIN Chief Sues SIGA over Firing: Crowe Claims Breach of Contract after Audit Rules Consultant Role Posed Conflict of Interest," *Saskatoon Star-Phoenix*, 25 July 2001, A3.

51 Colleen Silverthorn, "Auditor Slams SIGA," *Regina Leader-Post*, 14 Dec. 2001, A1.

52 James Parker, "SIGA not Doing Enough to Clean House: Wendel's Update Shows Indian Gaming Authority Still has Problems to Tackle," *Saskatoon Star-Phoenix*, 14 Dec. 2001, A4.

53 Murray Mandryk, "Osika Must Crack down on SIGA," *Saskatoon Star-Phoenix*, 13 Dec. 2002, A18.

54 James Parker, "Auditor Blasts SIGA's Spending," *Saskatoon Star-Phoenix*, 12 Dec. 2003, A1.

55 Randy Burton, "SIGA Still Missing the Fairway," *Saskatoon Star-Phoenix*, 11 Dec. 2004, A2.

56 Doug Cuthand, "FSIN Faces Hard Work to Restore SIGA Credibility," *Saskatoon Star-Phoenix,* 23 June 2000, A13.

57 *R. v. Pamajewon,* [1996] 2 S.C.R. 821.

58 Warick, "SIGA Won't Dump Lerat," A1.

59 James Parker, "FSIN Ready for Casino Talks: Native Jurisdiction FSIN's First Priority as it Calls Gov't to Table," *Saskatoon Star-Phoenix,* 7 Dec. 2000, A3.

60 Dan Zakreski, "Scandals 'Growing Pains on Road to Governance,'" *Saskatoon Star-Phoenix,* 8 July 2000, A1.

61 Jason Warick, "Bellegarde Blasts Gov't Handling of SIGA," *Saskatoon Star-Phoenix,* 30 June 2000, A4.

62 "Ahenakew Urges Indians to Control Casinos, or Close Them," *Regina Leader-Post,* 6 Dec. 2000, A6.

63 Mandryk, "Osika Must Crack down on SIGA," A18.

64 Betty Ann Adam, "Chief Demands Integrity in Handling of Casino Profits," *Saskatoon Star-Phoenix,* 20 Oct. 2001, A4.

65 Dan Zakreski, "FSIN Wanted to Hire Lerat after Firing," *Saskatoon Star-Phoenix,* 8 July 2000, A10.

66 Dan Zakreski, "Report Raises Stakes in Battle to Control Gaming: Province Keeps Cards Close to Vest as Talks Proceed on New Deal," *Saskatoon Star-Phoenix,* 16 Nov. 2000, D7.

67 Ibid., D7.

68 James Parker, "Lerat Goes on Spending Spree: Probe *The Star-Phoenix*: Report Finds Former SIGA CEO Spent $500,000 in Last Fiscal Year," *Saskatoon Star-Phoenix,* 18 Oct. 2002, A1.

69 James Parker, "Gov't Tightens SIGA's Reins: Province Promises to Carry out all 16 of Auditor's Recommendations," *Saskatoon Star-Phoenix,* 16 Nov. 2000, A1.

70 Betty Ann Adam, "SIGA Told to Gain Control or Shut down Industry: Province Must 'Back-off': Former AFN Chief," *Saskatoon Star-Phoenix,* 6 Dec. 2000, A6.

71 Parker, "FSIN Ready for Casino Talks," A3.

72 Silverthorn, "New Controls for SIGA," A1.

73 Parker, "FSIN Ready for Casino Talks," A3.

74 Murray Mandryk, "SIGA Slow to Learn from Mistakes," *Saskatoon Star-Phoenix,* 23 June 2000, A1.

75 "Reveal Intent of SIGA Deal," *Saskatoon Star-Phoenix,* 4 May 2002, A12.

76 Parker, "FSIN Hires Lerat to 'Expose' Government," A1.

77 "Hiring Lerat Absurd Move," *Saskatoon Star-Phoenix,* 12 June 2003, A14.

78 Warick, "SIGA Won't Dump Lerat," A1.

79 Ibid., 14.

80 Cornell and Kalt, *Two Approaches to Economic Development on American Indian Reservations*, 14.

81 James Parker, "SIGA Hits Jackpot: Better Management, Cost Cutting Improve Financial Picture: CEO," *Saskatoon Star-Phoenix*, 28 Aug. 2002, A1.

82 Parker, "Lerat Goes on Spending Spree," A1.

83 Murray Mandryk, "FSIN Should Explain Spending," *Saskatoon Star-Phoenix*, 20 Oct. 2000, A11.

84 Doug Cuthand, "SIGA Mess Part of Broader Provincial Problem," *Saskatoon Star-Phoenix*, 27 Oct. 2000, A17.

CHAPTER 11

CASINO RAMA: FIRST NATIONS SELF-DETERMINATION, NEOLIBERAL SOLUTION, OR PARTIAL MIDDLE GROUND?

DARRELL MANITOWABI

INTRODUCTION

In the early 1990s, the province of Ontario and the province's First Nations agreed to establish a commercial casino sited in a reserve community.[1] The Rama-Mnjikaning First Nation (hereafter referred to as Rama[2]) near Orillia was selected as the host site for the venture, which was anticipated to benefit all provincial First Nations. In 1996, Casino Rama was opened to the public.[3] The casino is marketed as First Nations–owned and the largest single-site employer of First Nations people in Canada.[4] To date, the province's First Nations have benefitted from casino profits despite a prolonged disagreement between the province, First Nations, and Rama concerning profit distribution. Rama and the First Nations argue the casino is First Nations–owned and a symbol of First Nations self-determination. Ontario's officials counter that the casino is an extension of provincially regulated gaming and a revenue source for the provincial treasury.[5] Drawing on Richard White's "middle ground" concept,[6] this chapter proceeds to unpack the nature of the polarized belief that the casino must be either a form of First Nations self-determination or a strategic neoliberal solution to First Nations socio-economic difficulties. This is arguably not an "either/or" question, for elements of both options are evident. Further, this chapter argues that the First Nations' response was strategically designed to adhere to community-based needs that simultaneously enabled First Nations leaders to gain a partial middle ground on the road to self-determination.[7]

As a secondary line of investigation, this chapter also contributes to our knowledge of economic self-determination specific to First Nations–provincial relations, and, most importantly, it expands our understanding of how neoliberal reforms impact First Nations people in Canada.[8]

BACKGROUND

The following is based on two years of doctoral research undertaken between 2002 and 2004. This research included personal interviews, participant observation, and a literature review of documents related to Rama and Casino Rama. Officially I interviewed thirteen First Nations casino employees and thirty-seven Rama members. However, during my research I had countless discussions with various First Nations employees and Rama members. My perspectives are informed by these formal interviews, discussions with numerous individuals, and my day-to-day interactions in various social settings, ranging from the Orillia bars frequented by First Nations casino employees to the Orillia Native Woman's Group (a non-profit urban drop-in centre), and from the Rama administration office ("band office") to the casino and other social gatherings.

Prior to my arrival, Rama community member Karen Campbell produced a master's thesis concluding that as of 1999 the casino experience had increased employment, provided much-needed infrastructure, and enhanced social and administrative services. However, two specific problems had developed: (1) a significant increase in traffic volume through the heart of the community; and (2) a disruption of locals' peace and privacy. Campbell's fieldwork was accomplished roughly one year after the casino opened, and she limited her focus to community reactions to the physical changes.[9]

Building on the work of Campbell, my research at the time focused on the cultural negotiation of the emergence and impact of Casino Rama in the context of colonial history and neoliberal reforms in Ontario during the 1990s.[10] Insights presented in the following are based on this original research, though my focus differs here in that it emphasizes the political negotiations surrounding casino development and the discourse of First Nations self-determination within the context of neoliberalism in Ontario.

RAMA–MNJIKANING FIRST NATION

Rama is located on the eastern part of Lake Couchiching in south-central Ontario. Eight separate parcels of land amounting to 2350 acres compose the community's land base. In 2001, the on-reserve population was listed at 597, with the total (on- and off-reserve) membership of Rama as of 2003 reported to be approximately 1300.[11] One chief and six councillors govern the community on two-year terms.[12] Rama was once part of a larger reserve known as "the Coldwater and the Narrows Reserve." Coldwater was a colonial experiment designed to contain, remove, and isolate southern Ontario's First Nations on a narrow tract of land. The colonial government unilaterally terminated the experiment in 1836 after First Nations refused to settle.[13] Upon termination, the inhabitants of Coldwater dispersed under the leadership of hereditary chiefs Yellowhead, Assance, and Snake. Assance's group moved to Beausoleil Island in Georgian Bay and later to Christian Island (today known as the Beausoleil First Nation). Snake's moved to Snake Island and later to Georgina Island in Lake Simcoe (today known as Georgina Island First Nation). Yellowhead's group moved to the present location of Rama in 1837.[14] From 1837 to the mid-1950s, the First Nation engaged in a variety of economies that included hunting, fishing, and some on-reserve farming. A bartering economy also emerged, with members exchanging surplus fish or farm produce. Limited involvement in the market economy occurred, and men worked as hired hands in off-reserve agriculture and logging, and as fishing guides. Women acted as housekeepers and sold crafts.[15] By the 1980s, Rama was involved in tourism and had a wilderness park, marina, and small industrial mall in operation.

EMERGENCE OF CASINO RAMA

Since opening in 1996, Casino Rama has been marketed as a First Nations enterprise. This implies that it is representative of economic self-determination. With this in mind, and to meet the objective of this chapter, it is useful to examine the circumstances of the casino's development.

In 1989, the Chiefs of Ontario (COO), the political body representing Ontario First Nations, initiated discussions to develop and expand Ontario's gaming operations. The Union of Ontario Indians (UOI), a political body representing most Ojibwa/Anishinabek First Nations in Ontario, followed by developing a gaming work plan.[16] In April 1993, the provincial NDP government and the COO entered First Nations casino development discussions.[17] These deliberations focused on establishing regional catchment zones to avoid fostering unwanted competition between the various provincial casinos and the planned First Nations operation. Envisioning a casino operating on an Ontario reserve and benefitting all First Nations, the COO strategy was designed to counter the anticipated emergence of several Ontario First Nation casinos, which could lead to increased competition and ultimately diminished returns for all First Nations.[18]

In the early part of 1994, the province and Ontario First Nations established a site selection committee composed of forty-five representatives from various provincial First Nations groups responsible for selecting the proposed First Nations casino. The committee participated in a series of meetings with the province to establish criteria for the selection of a host community. Eventually it was agreed that a four-person independent selection panel be established to arrive at a final decision.[19] In April 1994, the provincial government informed the First Nations that the proposed casino would not be used as a source of government revenue.[20] It further stated that a First Nations entity would be established to administer casino profits to all Ontario First Nations.[21] The province also stipulated that 20 percent of gross profits would be put in a "First Nations Fund" to be controlled by a First Nations entity. The province introduced this condition to decrease the existing provincial contributions to economic and social development in First Nations communities.[22]

The COO invited all Ontario First Nations to submit a proposal to host the casino. In total, twenty-seven First Nations submitted fourteen proposals (several were joint proposals between multiple nations). By November 1994, the selection committee had narrowed the fourteen submissions to three finalists: Wahta (Mohawk community in central Ontario, northwest of Rama on the Gibson River); Munsee-Delaware (Delaware community near London on the Thames River); and Rama. On 5 December 1994, the selection committee announced that Rama had been chosen as the host community. The committee selected Rama based on its location, its experience with tourism, community support for the project, and, most importantly, the proposed revenue-sharing agreement, which was the most generous of all proposals.[23] In their proposal, Rama set out the following objectives:

♦ to ensure that the First Nations Casino ... provides increasingly progressive economic opportunities to the First Nations of Ontario both within and external to the operation

♦ to act as a catalyst for economic development for Rama and in the surrounding communities

♦ to provide revenue to all First Nations in Ontario

♦ to promote the tourism and hospitality industries

♦ to create jobs.[24]

In September 1995, Carnival Hotels and Casinos, based in Miami, Florida, was selected to manage the casino for the first ten years.[25] During this period, however, the Mike Harris–led Progressive Conservative Party was elected to power, which in turn led to an alteration in the casino agreement. The Harris government halted casino construction on 9 February 1996, claiming the previous agreement with the NDP government was verbal and not legal.[26] A compromise was proposed: casino construction would commence once the First Nations agreed to a 20 percent "win" tax (casino tax) on net revenues. The Rama chief echoed the feelings of community members: "This has to do with our self-esteem and our dignity and the future generations of our children. There's a lot at stake here."[27] A member of provincial parliament and a critic of the PC government stated, "And for what? So they can take an additional 20 per cent—intended for First Nations economic development—to pay for an irresponsible tax cut?"[28] At a news conference a few weeks later, a leading PC government member stated, "The previous government made an arrangement with the Rama organization. This is a different government."[29] In response, the Rama chief stated, "We were led to believe the government was working with us in good faith."[30] The chief further noted, "It is a repeat of history, but this time it's different."[31] These verbal exchanges provide useful insight. The provincial government interpreted an agreement in a way that benefitted its interest, whereas Rama viewed the agreement on a nation-to-nation scale, similar to a treaty.

Rama's United Church minister brilliantly articulated the parallels to the historical Coldwater experiment:

> When the white settlers from the south started moving in
> during the 1830s, they said "that land is too good for the
> Indians, we want it." The situation with the casino is very
> much the same as this. "This is too good a deal for those
> Indians, for 131 First Nations, to get a bit of income to be
> self-sufficient. That's too good." What happened then was a
> phenomenal sense of disillusionment. That sense of disillu-
> sion that the historians write about, I observe today. There
> is a phenomenal sense of betrayal at the lack of integrity of
> the government in power. Whether it was in 1830 or the
> Harris government of today.[32]

This cleric exposed the government's rhetoric and framed the situation as a continued extension of colonization with a non-First Nations government oppressing "Indians." One community member experienced in First Nations politics explained the problems arising from the government impositions: "One of the conditions the government placed on us was that the issue had to be reached before any construction was restarted. Our position here in Rama is that, that is not realistic or fair. You're talking about various components of the leadership, 131 personalities. You're trying to get them to agree and how long will that take?"[33] Evident in this statement are the unequal power relationships. The province dictated to Rama and the Ontario First Nations the criteria for the agreement rather than respecting the autonomy of First Nations people by allowing a cooperative decision to be made.

After weeks of halted construction, a deal was finally reached on 8 March 1996, leading to resumed casino building. The deal included the 20 percent win tax.[34] A Chiefs of Ontario leader summed up frustration with the situation: "From our point of view, we've never agreed with the 20 per cent the province is taking. It was a unilateral decision on their behalf."[35] In response, provincial officials claimed that their actions ensured "that [the] taxpayer's money is well spent."[36] Clearly an unequal manifestation of power determined the outcome; unwilling to remain silent, Rama and the Chiefs of Ontario echoed dissatisfaction. Meanwhile, the province's actions suggest their decisions were structured to serve dominant non-First Nations interests.

In anticipation of the casino's opening, excitement grew in the community. One member stated, "Everybody is running around like chickens with their heads cut off.... When the casino lights go on, it'll never be dark here again."[37] Such a perspective echoed the realization that the community would change forever. On 31 July 1996, Casino Rama opened to the public.

It should be noted that conflict over casino revenues extended beyond the provincial–First Nations interface. A decade-long dispute between Rama and the uoi in many ways eclipsed all other animosities emerging from the casino project. Initially, the casino documents proposed that casino revenues be distributed to Ontario First Nations to address social, cultural, educational, health, and economic needs.[38] The agreement stipulated that during the first five years of operations, Rama would take 35 percent of net revenues for casino enhancements, and the remaining 65 percent would be distributed to all other Ontario First Nations. At the end of five years, a provision called for a revised sharing formula to reflect changing circumstances.[39] In 2001, Ontario First Nations voted against renewing the 35 percent allocation to Rama, agreeing instead that Rama should receive the agreed-to First Nation percentage distribution. In October 2001, Rama filed a claim against the province of Ontario seeking to retain the 35 percent. When the initial revenue formula expired on

31 July 2001, Rama ceased receiving this 35 percent, pending the results of their legal case; meanwhile Ontario First Nations continued to receive funds until December 2006.[40] After an additional disagreement between the Ontario First Nations and Rama regarding a casino hotel loan, the province froze revenue dispersal to all Ontario First Nations in January 2007.[41] On 7 February 2008, the Chiefs of Ontario and the province struck a new agreement effective as of 2011. The deal includes an immediate $201 million payment to address socio-economic challenges and a 1.7 percent cut of provincial gaming revenues over twenty-five years, estimated to be worth $3 billion. The chiefs, in exchange, agreed to abandon the 20 percent win-tax lawsuit and other claims to Casino Rama revenues.[42] On 15 September 2008, the Ontario Superior Court of Justice dismissed Rama's claim to retain 35 percent of net casino revenues permanently. Rama is currently appealing this decision.[43]

NEOLIBERALISM IN ONTARIO

The concept of neoliberalism can be traced to the period before the 1980s when the relationship between the wealthy and poor was expressed by the terms "modernization" and "dependency." David Harvey suggests the period between 1978 and 1980 was a "revolutionary point" in the social and economic history of the world. Key events in China, Britain, and the United States helped to shape this revolution.[44] In particular, China opened itself up to the global economy in 1978; one year later the United States Federal Reserve attempted to curb inflation regardless of the consequences. That same year, Britain sought to minimize the power of unions and also deal with inflation. In 1980, Unites States president Ronald Reagan implemented various measures to control unions; deregulate industry, agriculture, and resource extraction; and liberate financial institutions domestically and globally.[45] Harvey contends that, combined, China's, Britain's and the Unites States' actions generated a "revolutionary impulse" felt internationally. The doctrine behind this impulse, which became known as "neoliberalism," is characterized as those political and economic practices designed to improve human well-being through state-sanctioned liberalization of market forces. In doing so, the state ensures military, police, and legal infrastructures are in place, thereby allowing the market to operate freely without state intervention.[46] Neoliberalism further posits that the liberalization of the market is necessary to resolve poverty.[47] According to Michael Peters, this collective articulation established a model for neoliberal governments that was based on the following mandate: "[The] economic liberalization or rationalization characterized by the abolition of subsidies and tariffs, floating the exchange rate, the freeing up of controls on foreign investment; the restructuring of the state sector, including corporatization and privatization of state trading departments and other assets, 'downsizing', 'contracting out', the attack on unions, and abolition of wage bargaining in favor of employment contracts; and, finally, the dismantling of the welfare state through commercialization, 'contracting out', 'targeting of services', and individual 'responsibilization' for health, welfare, and education."[48]

In theorizing neoliberalism, Pierre Bourdieu suggests it attaches a Western mathematical model of economics to human behaviour. Neoliberalism posits "that maximum growth, and therefore productivity and competitiveness, are the ultimate and sole goal of human actions; or that economic forces cannot be resisted."[49] Neoliberalism then becomes a political agenda: it imposes a "legitimate" vision of how the world should operate. Propelled by the "objective" discourse of academics, businesses leaders, and the media, this truth is eventually absorbed by the public and emerges as an unquestionable certainty.[50] In the process, "it has become incorporated into the common-sense way many of us interpret, live in, and understand the world."[51] Neoliberalism affects human social relations by applying economic solutions to them. It also challenges state sovereignty by empowering the market. At the local level, it affects divisions of labour through union-busting and through divestments of social welfare programs, affecting quality of life. The underlying problem is that it seeks to bring "human action into the domain of the market" under the guise of salvation.[52]

The topic of neoliberalism is certainly complex. For the purposes of this argument, my interest is limited to examining the link between neoliberalism, Casino Rama, and First Nations socio-economic disparities. Furthermore, I am interested in how neoliberalism affects social relations for First Nations employees of Casino Rama and members of Rama. To examine these links, I will focus on the socio-economic conditions that propelled the creation of, and eventual partial reliance on, casinos in Ontario.

Ontario emerged as Canada's leader in neoliberal reforms during an economic downturn in the 1980s. With the crash of the New York stock exchange in 1987 followed by that of the Toronto stock exchange, Ontario soon found itself in its worst recession since the 1930s.[53] This economic circumstance proved disastrous for the ruling David Peterson Liberal government during the late 1980s, and in 1990 Ontario's electorate responded by voting the Bob Rae–led New Democratic Party government into power.[54] The NDP platform was presented as an "Agenda for the People" that embraced a social charter (embedded social rights) and First Nations self-government and economic unification with

Canada.[55] Rae proclaimed his support for First Nations rights, specifically that his "government [was] committed to negotiating self-government agreements that will have real meaning, in this term in office."[56] Rae proposed a "Statement of Political Relationship" on 6 August 1991, while promising a "government-to-government" relationship with Ontario's First Nations.[57]

Unfortunately for Rae, the economic conditions in Ontario prevented him from fulfilling his agenda. During the period between 1990 and 1992, the province lost 437,000 jobs,[58] and the unemployment rate hit a high of 10 percent.[59] Desperate for economic stimulus, Rae seized upon gaming as a government revenue source. This represented a drastic ideological shift, for Rae had concluded in 1990, "The casino plays on greed. The sense of the ultimate chance, the hope against hope that the spin of the wheel or the shot of the dice will produce instant wealth, instant power, instant gratification. The work ethic 'steady as you go' appears alongside as fundamentally boring, goody two-shoes values."[60] A scant two years after Rae's statement, the NDP produced a policy paper on gaming. Then, with little public input, the government established a casino in Windsor in 1994.[61] During the planning process, the NDP decided against becoming operators, and instead demanded that the private sector build and operate the casinos, with the province collecting the profits.[62] At the same time that it began provincial casino planning, the government initiated negotiations with First Nations to explore casinos and gaming authorities.[63]

Rae, who supported First Nations' inherent right to self-government, envisioned First Nations controlling their government programs. Despite his public enthusiasm for First Nations self-government, however, and with the exception of the proposed casino and one land-claim negotiation, he accomplished little else that would feasibly lead to improved First Nations socio-economic conditions. Meanwhile, provincial economic conditions failed to improve, and the NDP struggled to reduce the growing deficit. Viewed through this lens, it appears Bob Rae accepted neoliberal reforms in Ontario. This is evident in the following statement he made on 5 April 1993: "Unless we reduce operating costs through restructuring and reforming government departments and programs and through agreements with public sector employers and employees, we will no longer be able to afford the level of public investment Ontario needs in jobs, training and capital to meet the economic challenges of the 1990s."[64] The growing importance of the market over social spending ultimately proved disastrous to the NDP government. The Mike Harris Progressive Conservative government exploited this diminished support and rose to power in 1996 on the wave of the "common sense" revolution. The hallmark of this "common sense" agenda was deficit control by slashing social programs and establishing greater reliance on the market. In the process, the neoliberal reforms initiated by the NDP were completed by the PCs.[65]

NEOLIBERAL SOLUTION OR FIRST NATIONS SELF-DETERMINATION?

Casino Rama's website reads as follows: Casino Rama is "Ontario's only First Nations commercial casino," and "the largest single site employer of Aboriginal people in Canada with over 700 Aboriginal employees."[66] Here it is implied that Casino Rama is First Nations–owned and operated. Is this, however, an accurate assertion? Based on fieldwork, I would argue this statement on employment is inaccurate. Although I was unable to acquire statistics examining this issue, based on my observations at the casino and discussions with First Nations employees, most on average are part-time, entry-level workers, usually assigned the graveyard shift (midnight to 8:00 a.m.) and working on a short-term contract (there is no union at the casino). This type of employment leads to high turnover (people were either fired or quit). In effect, the casino as a whole has a high turnover rate. I had two First Nations casino employees board with me; both lasted about a year. Landlords are also hesitant to rent to casino employees because the length of their employment is unpredictable. Only five of the twenty First Nations employees I knew remained upon my departure in 2004. I observed that with the exception of the few who do have sufficient work experience and education, the harsh reality is that most First Nations casino employees arrive with a sense of optimism but are forced to return to their communities.

In spite of the high turnover, there is a portion of casino employees that remains. Based on observations, I found that if an individual has significant education and work experience, desirable employment opportunities can be secured either at the casino or at Rama's administration. As well, a small number of First Nations with less education and/or work experience are able to persist at the casino and acquire more desirable employment. As regards the contention that the casino is exclusively "First Nations," the majority of employees are non-First Nations (78.6 percent in 2002); Penn National Gaming of Pennsylvania manages it; and the Ontario Lottery and Gaming Corporation defines the rules for casino operations.[67] The irony of Casino Rama's inaccurate marketing was perhaps best articulated by a First Nations casino employee: "It's weird living in the white world, even though I'm working on the rez."[68]

On the other hand, outside of Casino Rama, a greater sense exists concerning the casino's direct social and economic impact on both the Rama community and surrounding area. In the years prior to the casino opening, Rama's unemployment rate hovered around 80 percent. The year the casino opened (1996), that rate dropped to 10 percent and the regional number of jobs rose by 38 percent.[69] In 2006, the casino claimed a $122 million payroll for 3500 employees, and gross annual revenue of $500 million.[70] The resulting new infrastructure in Rama includes a gas station, an elementary school, a food services outlet, a small retail outlet, government offices, an elders' residence, a sports and recreational facility, a skateboard recreational park, a fire and police station, a daycare, a water treatment plant, improved roads, and numerous residential subdivisions. The majority of Rama's community members work within the band administration, which employs approximately 300 people. In 2007, the unemployment rate had dropped to about 5 percent, and according to the chief, "Anybody that is able to work is pretty well working."[71]

Unseen social and cultural impacts nevertheless exist beyond the financial and physical changes. For instance, as part of the agreement with the province, no other gaming may occur in Rama, which has affected fundraising efforts for hockey teams and other non-profit activities. The province justifies this proviso by citing the casino's generous compensation to the community. A problem with this is that community-based empowerment through fundraising is replaced with a provincially imposed agreement assigning narrowly delineated authority to a small group of political leaders. The provincially imposed agreement has in turn affected social relations. For instance, even though something may be funded, the corresponding sense of community ownership and empowerment normally associated with fundraising fails to materialize. An example of this was reported in the local community newspaper: "[An elder] and others set up a raffle to raise funds for the Fire Department and were told they could not continue or they would face legal action. Something about the raffle being in conflict with our agreement with the province. She was livid, and very afraid Rama had gained yet another oppressor."[72] Casino revenues paid for the new fire department—however, community members were ultimately excluded from direct participation in the process.

Steady employment provides a sense of well-being that did not previously exist; yet problems in the community still exist. One is an alteration of the family. Prior to the casino's introduction, it was common for one parent to remain home for child care, or for extended family to help with child care. With two parents now working, children must often attend daycare, which in turn has resulted in altered family dynamics. One member I interviewed stated:

People are feeling secure, psychologically, socially, there is now disposable income, people are happier on the surface than 10 years ago; there is a lot of two family incomes, on the downside though, the kids suffer, the core family is gone, kids are raising themselves. There's traffic, drugs and more drugs, cocaine and crack... There's gambling addiction, it is silent but here. I see it, when I did research, in the general public, I see the same people all the time, you get a broad perspective, people were working, they go home, go to work, became severe gamblers. On the positive side, it is a small portion, I estimate 75 percent don't use the casino, 25 percent use it, but there is [sic] teenagers now.

The previously quiet and secluded community disappeared with the flood of casino patrons. To make space for casino infrastructure such as administration buildings, government offices, and a gas station, the casino purchased property and houses near the site. Following its opening, many community members established homes away from the casino in an attempt to regain a sense of peace and seclusion. I recall driving down the main Rama road with an elder, and he told me where his house once stood: it has since been replaced by a gas station. He further detailed whose houses once stood where and metaphorically remarked to me, "the casino is buying all the houses." Regarding community dynamics, one member I interviewed stated,

Since the casino came almost everyone has a job, there's jobs, we have more resources such as our police and fire, we have an arena, better health services, paved roads, more housing, a higher standard of living, but I think also in that change the sense of community isn't what it once was, when we had a lot less. Community gatherings don't seem to be as prevalent as they once were.

When asked, "Is there any specific reason why you think a sense of community is changing?" this was the reply:

With the higher standard of living, people are much busier now, there's more services and options for people to have their kids in different sports, different activities. With everyone working their free time is often spent just relaxing at home, as opposed to when you had lots of free time it was a big deal such as a ball tournament when at the time you had something to look forward to, now people look forward to relaxing.

Investments in culture and identity are occurring, and a greater standard of living appears to support improved well-being. One member stated, "Our people are educating themselves, many are taking pride in their culture, there's more jobs, better lifestyle." There is hope for the future, that education can serve the needs of the community and the youth will advocate on its behalf. He added, "The government still wants control but it's not to be that way because we're gonna win there and we have to work together, I've always said that, I said to a judge you can only stand on people's back so long." And, "there's more lawyers, more and more First Nations, their kids are coming along becoming lawyers and become educated and this is really gonna hurt the government."

It appears neoliberalism has affected First Nations casino workers and Rama members. For First Nations casino employees, a non-union work environment comes complete with challenging working conditions. Entry-level, part-time work during the graveyard shift makes the transition to more desirable full-time employment difficult. The high turnover rate is a testament to the challenges of these working conditions. Those I spoke to who were familiar with casino employment highlighted how difficult the transition can be for First Nations people without employment experience. They added that a mechanism was needed to nurture successful employment transition.

Employment opportunities abound at the community level. As a consequence, a sense of community has been lost that is attributable to social adjustments to market integration. Furthermore, volunteerism has been compromised due to casino stipulations banning community-based capital fundraising events. These impacts are consistent with neoliberalism in that the government ensures the empowerment of a market enterprise (in this case, a casino) by proclaiming the nurturing of regional economic advancements—including the associated job creation and improvements to First Nations unemployment rates—as "common sense." Infrastructure such as new police and fire departments, a water treatment plant, and improved roads help make the casino a success. Unfortunately, the former power broker for the Rama First Nation was Indian and Northern Affairs Canada. Now, under neoliberalism, the casino represents an additional broker that has entered the power-relations dynamic on the nation.

From the perspective of Rama and the Chiefs of Ontario, Casino Rama is a First Nations casino. From the province's perspective, Casino Rama is an extension of provincially regulated gaming. A provincial crown agency, the Ontario Lottery and Gaming Corporation, regulates all gaming.[73] Furthermore, Penn National Gaming of Pennsylvania manages Casino Rama. The component of the casino defined as First Nations is limited to the Rama land the casino is built upon, and the revenue-sharing agreement, of which all Ontario First Nations are beneficiaries.[74]

Most of the public discourse surrounding Casino Rama revolves around the economic benefit and potential social problems. Newspapers and political leaders, both First Nations and non-First Nations, champion the socioeconomic benefits for Ontario First Nation communities, the central Ontario region, and the individual First Nation members who are employed at the casino (this is consistent with the neoliberal "common sense" rhetoric). Negative discussions focus on crime and addiction, and concerns that casinos on the U.S. border in Michigan and New York State may undermine Ontario's casino economy.[75] Absent from these discussions is the newly created influence the province has on Ontario First Nations communities.

In the broader historico-political context, United States Native American groups involved in gaming prompted the Ontario First Nations to explore gaming options of their own. Despite Rae's purported support for First Nations self-determination, it is suggested that potential First Nations casinos posed a dilemma for the province.[76] The potential proliferation of First Nations casinos would inevitably compete with provincial casinos, including the proposed large, provincially sponsored First Nations casino. The provincial two-pronged solution was to construct one casino as a means of exerting control over First Nations gaming, and to promote the creation of a revenue-sharing agreement needed to address Ontario First Nations socio-economic disparities. This allowed for an offloading of social welfare costs associated with Ontario First Nations, resulting in gaming revenue supporting First Nations socio-economic needs. As to the first part of this solution, critical discussions of economic self-determination are absent from the Casino Rama discourse. Before the casino, Ontario First Nations were deemed a federal responsibility, with First Nations striving for self-determination. In the process of negotiating the creation of Casino Rama with the province, the Ontario First Nations compromised effective economic self-determination, since ultimately the province exercises control over the casino.[77] As to the second part, this is the hidden element of the casino. It appears Casino Rama represents a case of First Nations economic salvation marked by modern symbols of development in the form of infrastructure and low unemployment.

The proposed First Nations casino was to generate a beneficial source of employment and revenue. The NDP provincial government supported this notion, especially since it would decrease provincial contributions to economic and social development in First Nations communities.[78] In the fine print of the original casino proposal, Rama promised to provide "progressive economic opportunities," to "act as a catalyst for economic development," to "provide revenue to all First Nations in Ontario," to "promote the tourism and hospitality industries," and to "create jobs."[79]

According to this scenario, we may conclude that neoliberal logic served as the basis of the proposed solution to the problem of poverty on Ontario First Nations and the associated social welfare costs. From the First Nations perspective, a casino was envisioned as a self-determining solution to unemployment. It is possible that neoliberal ideology drove the province to permit a First Nations casino. Furthermore, true to neoliberal logic, in order for the casino to be accepted, the government required an assurance of "economic sustainability" and a guarantee that Rama would share social welfare benefits, such as revenue, with all Ontario First Nations.

The logic of neoliberalism was also employed during the casino site-selection process. Location is important for economic reasons, since casinos require a large gaming clientele, which south-central Ontario (especially Toronto) provides. Those who formulated the casino proposal were keen to include such phrases as "economic catalyst," "creating jobs," and "providing revenue," which were needed to satisfy neoliberal logic. It appears the site of the Rama First Nation was chosen primarily because it adhered to the neoliberal creed, but also because of the perceived "community support." Therefore, it appears that Casino Rama is not *wholly* an example of First Nations economic self-determination, given the province's tactics to use it as a solution to First Nations socio-economic disparities while controlling and containing casino proliferation.

THE END, OR A PARTIAL MIDDLE GROUND?

In his influential book *The Middle Ground*, historian Richard White examined indigenous-settler relationships in the Great Lakes region during the period between 1650 and 1815.[80] White argued that indigenous history is much more complex than the dominant historical narrative of conquest and assimilation, especially when considering the multiple instances when indigenous and settler leaders willingly chose to accommodate one another. According to White,

The middle ground depended on the inability of both sides to gain their ends through force. The middle ground grew according to the need of people to find a means, other than force, to gain the cooperation or consent of foreigners. To succeed, those who operated on the middle ground had, of necessity, to attempt to understand the world and the reasoning of others and to assimilate enough of that reasoning to put it to their own purposes. Particularly in diplomatic councils, the middle ground was a realm of constant invention, which was just as constantly presented as convention. Under the new conventions, new purposes arose, and so the cycle continued.[81]

White's middle ground concept has been applied to modern economic contexts. For instance, Beth Conklin and Laura Graham examined Amazonian indigenous activist negotiations with the media, NGOs, and sympathetic Western intellectuals.[82] With the help of these allies, the indigenous activists were able to generate a "shifting middle ground" in opposition to dams, roads, and mining development in Brazil. Sabin suggests a middle-ground compromise led to the formation of the Mackenzie Valley Pipeline Inquiry, wherein Canadian indigenous political voices sought compromise in light of socio-economic dilemmas.[83] Sabin applies a similar argument to the indigenous experience with Ecuadorian oil extraction. In this case, market impositions were rejected, but not the idea of oil extraction. Indigenous Ecuadorians sought conditions in oil extraction, such as employment, market access, health care, and community development.[84] These case studies show that the middle ground concept, when employed as a conceptual scaffold, demonstrates that market interests are at stake. Or, as Conklin and Graham suggest, this "shifting middle ground" has moved beyond indigenous-settler relationships to indigenous-state-market relationships. This necessarily more complex matrix of relationships compels all parties to acknowledge the intersection of competing interests and the possibility of a middle ground compromise, in which neither side dominates the relationship.

The question that arises is: is Casino Rama an example of hegemonic market domination in neoliberal times, or is it an example of a modern middle ground? In order to answer this question, it is useful to reiterate, in summary form, the important events that led to the emergence of Casino Rama:

> 1) Ontario First Nations sought gaming as an economic option in light of the success of United States indigenous gaming.

2) Concurrently, the Bob Rae NDP provincial government came to power with a mandate sympathetic to First Nations self-determination.

3) Ontario experienced its worst recession since the 1930s and introduced casinos as a solution.

4) The NDP government agreed that one casino be established to benefit all First Nations socio-economic and self-determining needs.

5) The PC government defeated the NDP and imposed a casino win tax while sponsoring a "common sense" (neoliberal) revolution in Ontario.

6) A revenue-sharing agreement was struck that met First Nations health, economic, social, cultural, and community needs for five years (1996-2001), during which time Rama received 35 percent to deal with initial impacts of the casino.

7) In 2008, a revised revenue agreement was struck, resulting in a 1.7 percent cut of all provincial gaming revenues for Ontario First Nations for twenty-five years, effective 2011, and Rama lost a court case to retain 35 percent of Casino Rama profits permanently (under appeal at the time of writing).

8) Casino Rama became the "largest single-site employer of Aboriginals" and transformed the infrastructure and employment prospects in Rama. Community concerns include loss of privacy, loss of community, and drug and gambling problems.

According to this scenario, it is possible to envision the emergence of Casino Rama as a simultaneous force of state hegemony and indigenous counter-hegemony that is under "constant invention," to use White's phrase quoted earlier. Despite this interplay of countervailing forces, it appears this is not a case of a true middle ground as articulated by White. This is due to the overwhelming hegemonic influence of the province and the neoliberal context of casino development and containment, and the imposition of a revenue agreement.

However, Ontario First Nations and Rama are not absolute victims of provincial hegemony and neoliberal motivations. The distribution of casino revenue to all First Nations and the detailed structural changes evident at Rama bear evidence to this. Accordingly, I suggest that partial self-determination is at work. This is not a true middle ground, given the major concessions; rather, it is demonstrative of the difficulties associated with any cross-cultural economic development project such as a casino-resort. Simply by entertaining the idea and choosing to move forward, Ontario First Nations and Rama were forced to endure one another, the regulation of the province and, in Rama's case, bear the brunt of arbitrary changes to the original agreement. It is, however, possible to identify partial compromises, or what I define as a "partial middle ground." This partial middle ground is achieved through indigenous manipulation of competing interests. At the time of the casino discussions, Ontario was in a recession, the province was desperate for an economic stimulus, and casinos became an option. At the same time, First Nations observed the success of United States indigenous casinos, leading to their demands for like enterprises at a time when the province proclaimed its interest in promoting First Nations self-determination. First Nations utilization of available resources, combined with a shrewd read of the unfolding political environment, led to their influencing the emergence of a partial middle ground where they have increased political and economic influence. With the emergence of the casino, despite provincial hegemony and the influence of neoliberalism, all First Nations in Ontario have achieved a partial middle ground that provides capital used to address community-based needs.

CONCLUSION

Casino Rama emerged as the result of a deal between the province of Ontario and Ontario First Nations. Originally, the casino was envisioned as a First Nations casino designed to provide a solution to Ontario First Nations community, cultural, educational, economic, and health needs. On the surface, the casino appears successful: there is direct positive economic and infrastructural impact on Rama, and the casino is the largest single-site First Nations employer in Canada.[85] Since the casino is marketed as First Nations–owned, the impression is that it is evidence of First Nations economic self-determination in Canada. A closer look at the casino and its development in the context of First Nations–provincial relations suggests, however, that those casino administrators' claims are questionable. Here First Nations autonomy has been restricted and manipulated—one need refer only to the history of casino development and the botched revenue agreement to confirm this. It is evident the province embraced an active role in casino development and failed to respect First Nations autonomy in the process. Again, this is evidenced by a unilateral tax applied to the casino and the publicly proclaimed provincial belief that Casino Rama is an extension of the Ontario Lottery and Gaming Corporation.

During casino negotiations, Ontario was in the midst of a recession and confronting high unemployment and a growing deficit. In this situation, casinos made economic sense. This suggests that a First Nations casino was simply part of a larger provincial strategy designed to contain and control the proliferation of additional First Nations casinos provincially, while simultaneously offering a convenient neoliberal solution for First Nations socio-economic disparities. In sum, Casino Rama's construction was borne of economic necessity as opposed to state accommodation of First Nations' economic self-determination aspirations. Despite this rather negative pronouncement, Ontario First Nations have been able to manipulate elements of the competing interests of neoliberalism and of the province to control and contain First Nations casinos. This has ensured that, at a minimum, a partial middle ground has been reached to ensure community-based needs are met. Data collected during my fieldwork at Rama confirms this conclusion, as do the form of community-based investments, which include an elders' residence, a school, a daycare, and residential subdivisions. First Nations have secured a portion of casino profits to meet community-based needs and ensure an investment in the present and future. However, the cost of this investment has been independently guided, economic self-determination.

NOTES

1   This chapter is based on research undertaken for my PhD in anthropology at the University of Toronto. I greatly benefitted from the supervision of Krystyna Sieciechowicz. I especially thank Hilary Cunningham for suggesting a neoliberal connection to my casino research. I also thank members of the Rama-Mnjikaning First Nation for allowing me to conduct research within their community, and I am grateful for the funding provided by an Ontario Problem Gambling Research Centre Doctoral Fellowship (2002) and a University of Toronto Lorna Marshall Doctoral Fellowship in Social and Cultural Anthropology (2003). Versions of this paper have been presented at various conferences. For this chapter specifically, I have benefitted from discussions with Yale Belanger, Julie Pelletier, Heather Howard-Bobiwash, Susan Krouse, and Kevin Fitzmaurice, and from the comments of two anonymous reviewers. The perspectives contained in this chapter are, however, my own.

The Mississaugas of Scugog First Nation have a charity casino called the Great Blue Heron Charity Casino. The First Nation is west of Rama, near Port Perry, northeast of Toronto. As well, the Anishinabe of Wauzhushk Onigum First Nation run a charity casino named the Golden Eagle Casino in Kenora, Ontario. For a survey of First Nations casinos in Canada, see Yale Belanger, *Gambling with the Future: The Evolution of First Nations Gaming in Canada* (Saskatoon: Purich Publishing, 2006).

2   This change is reflective of the broader indigenous social movements in Canada towards challenging the colonial relationship with the Canadian state. A portion of the community sees the term *Rama* as a colonial imposition and prefers the Indigenous term *Mnjikaning*, which means "fish fence" (see note 3). Since the use of the term *Mnjikaning* is relatively recent, *Rama* is still common in community discourse. I heard *Mnjikaning* used when communication occurred outside the community, or in reference to the collective indigenous identity. At the community level, I heard *Rama* more than *Mnjikaning*. In Mnjikaning, I used the word *Rama* like everyone else. Some of the elders of the community are not comfortable with the term *Mnjikaning* and still use the word *Rama*. Further, since leaving the field, I have read media reports using the hybrid term *Rama-Mnjikaning First Nation* (as of 2006). I have sided with the elders and have chosen to use the term *Rama* in this document.

3   *Mnjikaning* is a Chippewa word meaning "fish fence" and refers to the remnants of fish weirs at the narrows between Lake Simcoe and Lake Couchiching that date back 4,500 years. See Richard Johnston and Ken Cassavoy, "The Fish Weirs at Atherley Narrows, Ontario," *American Antiquity* 43, 4 (1978): 697–709.

4   Casino Rama, About Casino Rama (2005), http://www.casinorama.com/aboutcr. aspx (accessed 13 January 2006).

5   The term *self-determination* is complex and open to a variety of meanings. For the purposes of my argument, I have chosen Ponting's definition of self-determination as the "degree of autonomy that enables individuals or collectivities to shape their own economic, social, cultural, and political destiny." See J. Rick Ponting, ed., *First Nations in Canada: Perspectives on Opportunity, Empowerment, and Self-Determination* (Toronto: McGraw-Hill Ryerson, 1997), 355. I am sensitized to the complexity of this issue as it relates to topics such as "self-government," "sovereignty," and "governance." Due to my objectives and space limitations, I have chosen to simplify this issue to "self-determination" as it relates to neoliberalism.

For comparative approaches see Gabrielle Slowey, *Navigating Neoliberalism: Self-Determination and the Mikisew Cree First Nation* (Vancouver: University of British Columbia Press, 2008).

6　Richard White, *The Middle Ground: Indians, Empires, and Republics in the Great Lakes Region, 1650–1815* (Cambridge: Cambridge University Press, 1991).

7　The province of Ontario administers many federal First Nations programs and recognizes a relationship with Ontario First Nations. See Ministry of First Nations Affairs (2008), http://www.First Nationsaffairs.gov.on.ca/english/onas.htm (accessed 2 June 2008), and W. Warry, "Ontario's First People: Native Children," in *Children, Families and Public Policy in the 90s*, ed. Laura Johnson and Dick Barnhost (Toronto: Thomson Educational Publishing, 1991).

8　For an exception see Slowey, *Navigating Neoliberalism*.

9　Karen Campbell, "Community Life and Governance: Early Experiences of Mnjikaning First Nation with Casino Rama" (master's thesis, University of Manitoba, 1999).

10　Darrell Manitowabi, "From Fish Weirs to Casino: Negotiating Neoliberalism at Mnjikaning" (PhD diss., University of Toronto, 2007).

11　J. Hall, "Casinos Roll Dice in Legal Game; Native Bands Fight Over Rama Profits. Province's 20% Take Also Disputed," *Toronto Star*, 23 August 2003, A1.

12　Canada, *Indian Act* (R.S. 1985, c. 1–5), Department of Justice Canada (2001), http://lois.justice.gc.ca/en/I-5/index.html (accessed 14 January 2006).

13　Peter Schmalz, *The Ojibwa of Southern Ontario* (Toronto: University of Toronto Press, 1991): 160–162.

14　Ibid., 160–162.

15　Indian and Northern Affairs Canada, Indian Affairs Annual Reports 1864–1990, (2004 [1997]), National Library of Canada and Indian and Northern Affairs Canada, http://www.nlc-bnc.ca/indianaffairs/index-e.html (accessed 14 January 2006).

16　"Maintain, Protect, Enhance: A Discussion Paper on Casino Rama," *Anishinabek News*, 11 February 2005, 3.

17　Ontario First Nations Limited Partnership. Copy of partnership agreement in author's possession.

18　Casino Rama Revenue Agreement (2000), http://www.ofnlp.org/revenue_agreement.html (accessed 15 January 2006).

19　D. Henton, "Muskoka Favoured for Next Casino," *Toronto Star*, 3 November 1994, A36.

20　Chiefs of Ontario, Past Community Profiles: Chippewas of Rama (2004), ontario.org/profiles/pr_chippewas_rama.html (accessed 28 June 2005).

21　"Maintain, Protect, Enhance," 3.

22　Campbell, "Community Life and Governance," 23.

23　Ontario Casino Corporation and Ontario Lottery Corporation, *Working and Winning: Annual Reports* (Toronto: Ontario Casino Corporation and Ontario Lottery Corporation, 2000), 18.

24 Campbell, "Community Life and Governance," 22.

25 Ibid., 22; Chiefs of Ontario.

26 *Toronto Star*, A3.

27 W. Walker, "Tories Broke Casino Deal, Indians Say," *Toronto Star,* 16 February 1996, A4.

28 Ibid.

29 D. Dutton, "700 Show Up at Rama Site to Hear Why Work Halted," *Toronto Star*, 23 February 1996, A11.

30 Ibid.

31 M. Welsh, "Indians Feel Betrayed Over Casino," *Toronto Star,* 25 February 1996, A10.

32 Ibid. At the time these statements were made, there were 131 First Nations recognized in Ontario; today there are 134.

33 Ibid.

34 W. Walker and B. DeMara, "Casino Construction Resumes, But Without Deal, Indians Say," *Toronto Star,* 9 March 1996, A17.

35 Ibid.

36 Ibid.

37 M. Welsh, "Rama Gambles Future on Casino: 'Nothing Will be the Same' with New Complex," *Toronto Star,* 27 July 1996, A1, A18.

38 Ontario First Nations Limited Partnership.

39 Ibid.

40 "Maintain, Protect, Enhance," 4.

41 N. Taylor, "Greed Behind Deadlocked Talks: Official," *Orillia Packet and Times,* 12 March 2007, electronic edition, http://www.orilliapacket.com (accessed 12 March 2007).

42 C. Puxley, "First Nations Get $3B from Gaming Revenue; Ontario Chiefs Sign 25-year Deal for Share of Casino, Lottery Money," *The Toronto Star,* 8 February 2008, electronic edition, http://thestar.com (accessed 2 November 2008).

43 *Chippewas of Mnjikaning First Nation v. Ontario*, 2008 CanLII 4633 (On S.C.), available electronically, http://www.canlii.org); "Rama Appeals Ruling," *Anishinabek News*, November 2008, 1.

44 David Harvey, *A Brief History of Neoliberalism* (Toronto: Oxford University Press, 2007).

45 Ibid., 1.

46 Ibid., 1.

47 Sarah Babb, "The Social Consequences of Structural Adjustment: Recent Evidence and Current Debates," *Annual Review of Sociology* 31 (2005), 199-222. See also Harvey, *A Brief History of Neoliberalism.*

48 Michael Peters, *Poststructuralism, Marxism and Neoliberalism: Between Theory and Politics* (New York: Rowman and Littlefield, 2001), 18–19.

49 Pierre Bourdieu, *Acts of Resistance: Against the Tyranny of the Market* (New York: The New Press, 1998), 31.

50 Ibid., 30.

51 Harvey, *A Brief History of Neoliberalism*, 3.

52 Ibid., 3.

53 Chuck Rachlis and David Wolfe, "An Insiders' View of the NDP Government of Ontario: The Politics of Permanent Opposition Meets the Economics of Permanent Recession," in *Government and Politics of Ontario*, 5th ed., ed. Graham White (Toronto: University of Toronto Press 1997), 335.

54 Rachlis and Wolfe, "An Insiders' View of the NDP Government of Ontario," 331.

55 Peter Graefe, "Striking a New Balance: Neoliberalism, the Provinces and Intergovernmental Relations in Canada, 1985–2002" (PhD diss., Université de Montreal, 2002), 130. See also Kendra Coulter, "Chameleons, Chimeras and Shapeshifters: The Production of Neoliberal Government in Ontario" (PhD diss., University of Toronto, 2007).

56 Thomas Walkom, *Rae Days* (Toronto: Key Porter Books, 1994), 224.

57 Bob Rae, *From Protest to Power: Personal Reflections on a Life in Politics* (Toronto: Viking, 1996), 167.

58 Rachlis and Wolfe, "An Insiders' View of the NDP Government of Ontario," 336.

59 Walkom, *Rae Days*, 99.

60 Ibid., 82.

61 Ibid., 82, 110–111.

62 Ibid., 112.

63 Ibid., 224.

64 Rachlis and Wolfe, "An Insiders' View of the NDP Government of Ontario," 353.

65 Graefe, "Striking a New Balance," 97–53. See also Kendra Coulter and Kirsten Kozolanka, *The Power of Persuasion: The Politics of the New Right in Ontario* (Montreal: Black Rose Books, 2007).

66 Casino Rama, *About Casino Rama*.

67 Initially, Carnival Resorts and Casinos, a division of Carnival Corporation of Miami, Florida, operated the casino. However, in 2001 Penn National purchased the resorts and casinos division from Carnival Corporation and thereafter inherited the management of Casino Rama.

68 Author's field notes, 2003.

69 Ontario Casino Corporation and Ontario Lottery Corporation, *Working and Winning: Annual Reports*, 19.

70 T. Moro, "Region's Economic Engine to Mark Milestone," *Orillia Packet and Times*, 24 July 2006, A1.

71 Moro, "Region's Economic Engine to Mark Milestone."

72 Brenda Ingersoll, "In Memory of Joan MacDonald Sandy, Simcoe," *Ojibway Times* (May 2003), 56.

73 Ontario Lottery and Gaming Corporation, *Annual Report 2004–2005* (Toronto: Ontario Lottery and Gaming Corporation, 2005), http://www.olgc.ca, 29.

74 Ibid.

75 Ibid., 47.

76 From the non-indigenous perspective, granting true sovereignty to indigenous groups is problematic because doing so would undermine state sovereignty. See Ronald Niezen, *The Origins of Indigenism: Human Rights and the Politics of Identity* (Berkeley: University of California Press, 2003).

77 Ontario Lottery and Gaming Corporation, *Annual Report 2004–2005.*

78 Campbell, "Community Life and Governance," 23.

79 Ibid., 22.

80 White, *The Middle Ground*; see also Sarah Carter, *First Nations People and Colonizers of Western Canada to 1900* (Toronto: University of Toronto Press, 1999) and Darcee McLaren, "Living the Middle Ground: Two Dakota Missionaries, 1887–1912," *Ethnohistory* 43 (1996): 277–305.

81 White, *Middle Ground*, 52.

82 Beth Conklin and Laura Graham, "The Shifting Middle Ground: Amazonian Indians and Eco-politics," *American Anthropologist* 97, 44 (1995): 695–710.

83 Paul Sabin, "Voices from the Hydrocarbon Frontier: Canada's Mackenzie Valley Pipeline Inquiry (1974–1977)," *Environmental History Review* 19 (1995): 17–48.

84 Paul Sabin, "Searching for Middle Ground: Native Communities and Oil Extraction in the Northern and Central Ecuadorian Amazon, 1967–1993," *Environmental History* 3, 2 (1998): 144–168.

85 Casino Rama, *About Casino Rama.*

CHAPTER 12

LABOUR UNIONS AND FIRST NATIONS CASINOS: AN UNEASY RELATIONSHIP

YALE D. BELANGER

INTRODUCTION

Native resistance to labour unions plays itself out in dynamic and often contradictory ways. There are several historic and social reasons that lead contemporary Native casino employees to oppose union membership, thereby hampering present-day attempts to organize. An additional site of resistance occurs at the political level, where organizations such as the Federation of Saskatchewan Indian Nations (FSIN), which controls the Saskatchewan Indian Gaming Authority (SIGA); the Rama-Mnjikaning First Nation, Casino Rama's home community; and the Mississaugas of Scugog Island First Nation, which operates the Great Blue Heron Charity Casino, have actively attempted to halt labour organizing. Political leaders consistently claim that the Aboriginal right to self-government and existing treaty rights combined shield reserve casinos from outside union dictates and provincial legislation. Others maintain that labour unions are not traditionally "native," and that their "un-indigenous" nature drives community resistance.[1] Casino Rama has resisted the Teamsters and five other unions, while SIGA has on two separate occasions broken organizing resolve even if union organizers have made some headway.[2] The Great Blue Heron Charity Casino, the third casino to oppose union organizing recently, failed as union busters.

Canadian dynamics parallel recent events in California, where American Indian leaders continue to fight the institution of unions. Strategies they use to intimidate works include using divide-and-conquer strategies, fostering distrust amongst workers, and threatening termination of all individuals discovered attending organizing meetings.[3] Responses such as this may suggest that First Nation governments (and American Indian tribes) are distinctly anti-worker. On the surface, First Nations leaders also appear to undermine provincial legislation designed to protect both Native and non-Native casino employees. The print media reinforce this image by portraying First Nations casino managers as union busters playing outside the Charter of Rights and Freedoms' legal framework. It would seem sensible to protect First Nations employees new to the casino's fast-paced work environment, where they face unique working conditions such as noise, violence, and patron harassment.[4] Answering why First Nations leaders/casino operators resist labour unions is a complex undertaking, and space limitations preclude an extended discussion. This chapter will posit several theories potentially explaining this resistance while reflecting on the historic, social, and political reasons driving First Nation's casino operators' resistance to union organizing.

HISTORIC AND SOCIAL FOUNDATIONS OF RESISTANCE

First Nations economic adaptability is a key theme in Native-newcomer relations. So is the impressive intercultural interface that characterized the extractive economy known as the fur trade. The resulting cross-cultural economic relationships remained strong until European settlers asserted self-government in the late eighteenth century, effectively altering inter-cultural trade, and established kinship ties. The new economies now embraced a unique order characterized by European-derived class structures[5] distinguishable "by their exact method of dispossession, which tended to focus on alienating Aboriginal land instead of appropriating Aboriginal labour."[6] First Nations adapted and by the mid-nineteenth century accepted wage labour working as guides and transporting goods and people, and functioned as commodities suppliers.[7] Pacific coast fisheries and canneries employed both First Nations women and men, the latter of whom also found work as loggers and in factories. Similarly, in eastern Canada First Nations worked in road construction, ship loading, cutting pit props for the coal mines, or producing arts and crafts. On the prairies many became farmers, ranchers, and, in certain cases, miners.[8] Federal officials nevertheless remained convinced that alternate strategies were needed to complete Indian integration into Canadian society, which necessitated abandoning the reserves for the cities. The Indian Act (established in 1876) was implemented to facilitate this process. Accordingly, the legislation contained limited economic development provisions, which continues to impact reserve economic development to this day.[9]

Many First Nations adopted farming and/or ranching as their leaders actively lobbied local Indian agents for permission to employ modern economic development processes. Reserve economic depression in the late nineteenth and early twentieth centuries suggests these requests were ignored.[10] Disturbingly, Indians were blamed for this malaise. Indian Act criteria made it nearly impossible for individuals to secure personal business loans. Simply put, federal reserve economic development policies were out of touch with the emergent industrial reality promoting large-scale farming, mining and mineral exploration, and manufacturing. Driving this point home was the residential school system, which advocated a curriculum emphasizing agriculture, rudimentary carpentry, animal husbandry, blacksmithing, shoemaking or boot making, and printing, for boys, while the girls were taught laundering and ironing, gardening, and basic household chores.[11]

A poor federal education program combined with the Indian Act and a minimal infusion of capital into reserve communities meant that First Nations were ill prepared for the economic reality confronting their people upon leaving the schools, and most reserve economies eventually collapsed. Determined federal attempts to compel land surrenders heightened First Nations' fears that to lease their agriculturally lucrative reserve lands would result in loss of traditional territories.[12] An infusion of financial capital would have improved the situation, as would proper education, although it is likely that the placement of reserves on agriculturally suspect land located sizeable distances from urban centres would have offset any potential gain.[13] Their location on the physical periphery of Canadian society made an integration of reserve economies into larger regional and provincial economies difficult. Indian officials were also convinced that members of communal societies that demonstrated constrained individualism possessed limited individual labour power. Personal productivity was seen as inhibited, and Indians, as a result, were depicted as lazy, shiftless workers.[14] Labour unions nationally internalized the emergent Canadian class structure, and many initially excluded Indians from the rank and file.[15] Once consigned to Canada's physical and social margins, First Nations found it increasingly difficult to bolster failing reserve economies.

In certain regions Native labour and union participation was pronounced. Rolf Knight's groundbreaking study of Native labour that identified a West Coast Native proletariat confirms this, even if his work is undermined by a lack of complementary research.[16] Perhaps the best known union is that of the Caughnawaga Skywalkers, which boasted a large Native membership as of the 1920s.[17] Guiding our understanding of Native labour advocacy is West Coast research highlighting Native people working in local sawmills and as lumber loaders and handlers as early as the 1860s. By 1893 it was estimated that at least one-third of the 2350 fishermen working on the Fraser River were Native, and many were coerced into strike activity by the Fraser River Fishermen's Benevolent and Protective Association. Native fishermen and female cannery workers brought production to a halt along the Skeena River and the Nass River valley the following year. This activism was followed by strikes in 1896 and 1897. The Industrial Workers of the World (iww) Local 526 was founded by William Nahanee, Dan Paull, and Joe Capilano.[18] Although smashed in 1923, the union produced several future labour and political organizers, including Andrew Paull, who in 1944 formed the North American Indian Brotherhood. This would morph into the National Indian Brotherhood (nib) in 1968 and eventually transform into the Assembly of First Nations (afn) in 1982.

Our understanding of Native union participation is largely confined to research examining labour militancy in the fishery and Native fishers' inclination to align with non-Native unions.[19] It is vital that we also acknowledge academic work linking labour militancy with Native political growth and the evolution of Native class structures.[20] There are a few instructive examples from which to draw. The Mohawk World War I veteran F.O. Loft, upon returning to Canada, formed the League of Indians of Canada in 1919. Loft's actions, specifically his use of trade union organizing principles, are worthy of careful examination, according to Native Studies scholar Peter Kulchyski. "Union is the outstanding impulse of men today," Loft proclaimed, "because it is the only way by which the individual and collective elements of society can wield a force and power to be heard and their demands recognized. Look at the force and power of all kinds of labour organizations, because of their unions."[21] Loft advocated a union model utilizing a collective bargaining framework that would foster a working relationship with Canadian officials.[22] His union template also promoted Native empowerment by reclaiming the social capacity needed to influence Canada's development.

Unions would eventually be utilized by First Nations as de facto political organizations after *Indian Act* amendments in 1927 made it illegal to use band funds to pursue land claims.[23] Since most political groups organized with this goal in mind, the resultant loss of funding negatively impacted the majority of operations.[24] In an attempt to safeguard operations from Indian agent scrutiny, the Native Brotherhood of British Columbia was established as a labour union in 1931.[25] The Métis Association of Alberta (maa) formed the following year and modelled its operations after the Worker's Unity League (wul), which "headed the struggle for industrial unions throughout this period."[26] Instrumental in the MAA's success were Métis leaders James Brady and Malcolm Norris, socialists who embraced organized labour movement's key ideologies. The MAA employed a WUL model that involved seeking out sympathizers and then critiquing poor worker conditions to government officials.[27] The organization published an elaborate constitution and fashioned a centralized decision-making structure that guided a network of "locals," or individual Métis communities. An executive was tasked with communicating with government officials.[28] By 1933, the MAA claimed 1200 members in forty-one locals.[29] Norris and Brady helped write the constitution for the Indian Association of Alberta (IAA) in 1939, which was adopted almost verbatim in 1946 by the fledgling Union of Saskatchewan Indians, the precursor to the FSIN (est. 1982). Following this period there are few studies examining Native union participation. This suggests either that academics found the phenomenon undeserving of their time, or that fewer Native people were actively employed and engaged in labour advocacy.[30]

Available evidence suggests that following an extended period of labour advocacy, Native people either voluntarily withdrew or were forcibly excluded from labour union membership. There are several reasons to suggest both conclusions. The lack of Native migration to the cities meant there was limited Native employment in manufacturing and service sector businesses, which were quickly becoming the nation's primary employers. Wage labour prospects declined during the Great Depression, which was a period of amplified societal questioning of Native peoples' ability to adapt to industrial wage labour.[31] Contemporary political discourse concerning Native issues confirms these attitudes. Future head anthropologist for the Department of Mines and Resources Diamond Jenness noted in 1932, for example, that the Native "world has fallen into ruins, and, helpless in the face of a catastrophe they cannot understand, they vainly seek refuge in its shattered foundation." Fifteen years later Professor Thomas McIlwraith echoed these values, concluding that "the White man's way is going to prevail, and I see no way on which we can, with the atomic age coming on, have a small group of our population going on as fishermen and hunters or as peasant farmers. It is a sad thought."[32] Federal Indian policy reflected these principles, seen specifically in the three Natural Resources Transfer agreements, implemented in the prairie provinces in the early 1930s, which transferred full administration and control of Crown lands to the provinces while limiting treaty rights to their exact wording (i.e., the right to hunt for food).[33]

By the 1940s, the majority of reserve economies were a mixture of agriculture and treaty-secured trapping and fishing, with a handful of communities accessing limited Indian Affairs Branch (IAB) funding to maintain reserve industries.[34] First Nations by this point were integrated into the federal welfare system. Racism was an issue. Limited urbanization and the distance from labour markets also hampered First Nations employment at a time when "the older paternalistic fur trade, a hybrid of European mercantilism and native reciprocal exchange traditions, was crumbling … and the groundwork for the modern welfare system so prevalent in the north today was laid."[35] Initially these issues did not concern those fortunate enough to live on reserves with good hunting, fishing, and fertile soil belts for farming.[36] In the late 1940s (1946–48) a special joint parliamentary committee investigating the *Indian Act* highlighted Native concerns about their economic future. Indian Affairs officials, anticipating the traditional Indian hunting economies' ruination, responded by establishing a socio-economic development program in the 1950s that failed to alleviate reserve impoverishment. Its demise was linked to the inability to integrate First Nations communities into the larger market economy, combined with increased federal and provincial demands for improved agricultural development and mineral exploration.[37] Further aggravating an inferior standard of living was the federal government's venerable policy orientation promoting First Nations' abandonment of the reserves for the cities.

The slow pace of Native urbanization led to fewer employment opportunities, thus restricting opportunities for Native people to become union members. This began to change in the 1960s as increasing numbers of Native people started to abandon reserves for the cities, in search of opportunities that often failed to materialize. Harry Hawthorn, commissioned by the federal government in 1963 to investigate Native socio-economic conditions nationally, highlighted a widening economic gap between Native and non-Native people in two separate reports published in 1966 and 1967. He concluded that not only did Native people make less than one-fifth the national per capita average income, but also more than one-third of Native households were welfare-dependent. The bulk of available employment was concentrated in primary, resource-based industries and occupations, including forestry, fishing, trapping, guiding, food gathering, and handicrafts. Only 14 percent of these jobs were considered skilled employment. The report provided no specifics concerning contemporary Native unemployment rates, but Hawthorn did forewarn of the inevitable rise in unemployed Indians due to technological change and increased urbanization.[38] If this wasn't dire enough, during the early 1970s the growth of urban Native populations corresponded with a decline in urban industrial growth. This resulted in additional "barriers of discrimination in employment, housing, and social life," suggesting "that a movement back to the reserves occurred, along with a diminution of the out-migration from reserves."[39] The earliest statistical data available to study these issues indicates that in 1974, 41 percent of the on-reserve population was receiving social assistance. During this period, the ratio of children and elderly people was expanding rapidly in relation to persons of labour-force age, and there was a scarcity of employment for those of working age.[40]

Things were not much better in reserve communities, where endemic economic crises tended to absorb much-needed social and economic capital. During this period, more than 70 percent of all bands were considered either remote or rural communities, and these bands represented 65 percent of the Native population.[41] By 1981, the failed promise of urban migration was apparent after it was reported that the Native unemployment rate was roughly 2.2 times higher than that of the non-Native population, rising to 2.5 times higher by 1991. Native individuals over fifteen years of age had limited employment opportunities: this cohort's unemployment rate was 15.8 percent in 1981, compared with 7.2 percent for the mainstream population. An estimated 38 percent of registered Indians aged fifteen and over were employed, compared with 60 percent of the general population. Those living on rural reserves or settlements faced an income disparity of nearly 1.75 percent compared with the general population.

Indicative of their dissatisfaction with their living conditions and labour's failed promise was the percentage (54 percent) of Native people who refused to participate in the labour force, compared to 35 percent of the general population.[42] Academics warned government officials of rampant un- and underemployment and growing welfare dependency.[43] Those with steady work witnessed their income levels drop behind their non-Native brethren: income levels in Canadian society increased by nearly 4.3 percent during the 1980s, while Native income levels dropped by 5 percent. Native people's average income plummeted 9 percent during the same period, as their populations grew.[44] An estimated 12 percent of First Nations men and women living on-reserve worked full time in 1990, compared with 28 and 20 percent, respectively, for off-reserve men and women. Accordingly, "in addition to carrying a penalty in terms of access to jobs, living on a reserve appears to carry a wage penalty with it as well: those few on-reserve Aboriginals who did work full-time, full-year earned 20 to 25 percent less than single-origin, off-reserve Aboriginals. Neither the reserve-employment, nor the reserve-wage gap can be entirely accounted for by differences in the observed characteristics of individuals living on and off reserves."[45]

As this brief survey has shown, a general lack of union and labour consciousness was borne of several independent and intersecting forces. Federal Indian policies of the late twentieth century encouraging Indian urban assimilation were coupled with Native people being taught agrarian skills in an increasingly industrialized society. These skills were applicable to the very reserve environment people were, ironically, being encouraged to abandon. When Native people did obtain union membership, they often found these agents embraced class structures that reflected societal trends promoting Native peoples' physical and societal marginalization. Eventually, those same trends led to the inculcation of attitudes equating Native people with poor workers. This barrier to gainful employment also hindered the generational transfer of a labour consciousness. The failure of reserve economies in the 1940s resulted in increased Native migration rates to the cities in the 1950s; however, labour exclusion in an already limited job market remained a noteworthy trend, as did noticeable income disparities. The dearth of literature allows us to only speculate about the role Native people see themselves playing in unions and where the non-Native rank and file situates prospective Native union members within existing hierarchies and operational models. That Native people see little value in seeking skilled, permanent employment or aggressively pressing for re-inclusion in unions that until recently failed to provide them sanctuary should come as no surprise.

CONTEMPORARY POLITICAL RESISTANCE

Despite this history of poor treatment and questionable benefits, Native people working in casinos continue to investigate union participation. In response, a range of labour unions, including the Teamsters, the Canadian Auto Workers (CAW), and the Canadian Union for Public Employees (CUPE) have attempted to organize the combined national Native and non-Native reserve casino workforce of approximately 7500 employees. In response, First Nations leaders have developed successful anti-union strategies that include offering workers competitive wages and benefits packages. Non-unionized employees realize, however, that they lack the collective bargaining strength needed to ensure the protection afforded union members. First Nations leaders have uniformly contested labour union certification, claiming that reserve casinos located on Crown lands fall under federal jurisdiction and, as such, are exempt from provincial labour standards. They also contend that the band councils have an inherent right to determine the substance of reserve economic development and its attendant policies; and that band council-established bylaws related to economic development and labour issues are immune from outside challenges launched by provincial officials seeking to affirm or extend their jurisdiction to reserves. In Saskatchewan, operators went so far in an attempt to undermine pro-union factions as to insist that since casinos were not a traditional aspect of indigenous societies, unions would negatively affect Native culture.

First Nations have challenged the Canadian courts on several occasions to determine the extent of their Aboriginal and treaty rights as they relate to reserve casinos. Most notable was the Shawanaga First Nation's contention that provincial (in this case, Ontario) authority for gaming did not extend to a reserve gaming house. Shawanaga leaders argued that Section 81 of the *Indian Act* provided for band "control and prohibition of public games" and "other amusements."[46] They insisted the provincial and federal governments accept the First Nations' right "to control public games," which included high-stakes bingos. Shawanaga's leaders proposed that reserve businesses, including the gaming house, were exempt from federal and provincial laws. Ontario's Eagle Lake First Nation followed this lead by contesting provincial authority over their bingo operation. Both communities believed their inherent self-governing authority and assertions of sovereignty were adequate to undermine provincial oversight on reserve, an argument the Court rejected. On appeal, the Ontario Supreme Court determined in 1994 that "the appellants had not demonstrated … that they were acting in 'obedience' to the Shawanaga First Nation's lottery law (it did not require them to act as they did) or that the band council had de facto sovereignty."[47] Gaming was not considered to be an Aboriginal right. As such, reserve gaming facilities were not exempt from provincial legislation according to Section 35(1) of the *Constitution Act*, 1982. Provincial jurisdiction for gambling thus remained intact.[48] Two additional cases confirmed, first, that a provincial legislature has jurisdiction to enact laws in the gaming area[49] and, second, that the *Indian Act* did not supersede "the application of the criminal code to gambling on a reserve."[50]

None of these cases dealt with a First Nation's ability to restrict labour organizing in a reserve setting generally, or in reserve casinos specifically. The FSIN seized upon this ambiguity to promote the organization's self-governing authority to manage labour relations. In 1999 the organization's leadership announced its intent to establish a labour code in response to the CAW's certification at the Northern Lights Casino in Prince Albert. That the FSIN challenged the encroachment of unions into reserve communities should come as no surprise, considering the organization's historic commitment to self-determination.[51] The FSIN argued that its four reserve casinos were distinct First Nations businesses that fell under federal legislation and were shielded from provincial regulation. Behind the scenes, FSIN leaders and provincial chiefs were concerned that CAW headway would inevitably lead to the unionization of bands, tribal councils, and other Native-run organizations.[52] Accordingly, the proposed labour code asserted the FSIN's authority over not only reserve casinos but also all individuals represented by the province's seventy-two member bands. The FSIN's intent was to immunize member bands from federal and provincial labour laws while simultaneously empowering the Chief's Assembly to certify unions. The chiefs spoke openly of unionization's potentially compromising effect upon First Nations' jurisdiction over reserve activities and their collective financial stability.[53]

At the centre of the controversy was the certification of CAW, the largest private-sector union in Canada, at Prince Albert's Northern Lights Casino. In a blatant attempt at union busting, SIGA's lawyers maintained that the four casinos fell under federal jurisdiction and, as such, were exempt from provincial labour standards. Before the Saskatchewan Court of Appeal, they argued that their employees should not be permitted to form a union. The court disagreed, ruling that the province has jurisdiction over the unionized employees at SIGA casinos. An independent mediator was appointed to produce a report as the basis of a collective bargaining agreement. The final pact was expected to raise employees' wages between three and four dollars per hour while providing a one-time, $650 payment in lieu of retroactive pay. Prior to the ratification a new vote took place that led to the CAW's decertification that December. By 2002, union advocacy was again in motion as Painted Hand organizers sought union certification from the Public Service Alliance of Canada (PSAC) in Yorkton. The PSAC applied for a certification order on 29 November 2002, albeit without majority support. A secret ballot was held 10 January 2003, and a majority of Painted Hand employees voted against the union. The PSAC's application was dismissed.

SIGA managers bought the time required to discourage employee union participation by petitioning the courts, according to several workers, who also cited employee intimidation as a discouraging strategy. During the union drive of 2002, for example, an organizer who received numerous official warnings was suspended several times from work and eventually fired in January 2003. In 2001 Saskatchewan Retail, Wholesale and Department Store Union (RWDSU) organizer Gord Schmidt was temporarily banned from the Painted Hand Casino premises. He also discovered that the majority of Painted Hand workers resisted becoming involved for fear of losing their jobs. The RWDSU eventually concluded that achieving the majority support needed for certification was not possible due to workers' fears of management retribution.

In April 2003, CUPE opened a Yorkton office to organize Painted Hand Casino employees. The ubiquitous threat of dismissals and suspensions came to fruition with the May 2 layoff of Trevor Lyons, who had signed a CUPE support card. Interest was soon rekindled once CUPE officials learned of the previous RWDSU drive and CUPE offered its support. In a deposition before the Saskatchewan Labour Relations Board, CUPE organizer Linda Pelletier stated that the union drive would likely be unsuccessful unless the two men were reinstated, although both reinstatement applications were denied.[54] Organizers in Saskatchewan continue their advocacy in the hopes of establishing labour unions in the six provincial First Nations casinos.

These decisions represented a clear blow to the First Nations self-determination movement. Since the release of two reports in 1977 and 1979, the FSIN has consistently demanded federal acknowledgement of traditional First Nations sovereignty, based upon the most fundamental right a sovereign nation holds: the right to govern its people and territory under its own laws and customs. Expanding on these ideas, the FSIN considers the right to self-government as "inherited ... from the people," and something that has never been extinguished voluntarily or by means of military defeat. This sovereignty, FSIN officials argue, has been eroded and suppressed by the legislative and administrative actions of Canada. First Nations leaders acknowledge that Section 91(24) gives the federal government the authority to regulate relations with First Nations, a power that does not permit federal or provincial regulation of internal band affairs. The courts disagreed with this analysis, concluding instead that the FSIN could not enact its own labour code. It is interesting to note that the courts were sought out by a political organization representing self-professed, self-determining nations to determine the pith and substance of Aboriginal self-government. Such an approach arguably undermines the certainty that treaties reserve a complete set of rights, including self-governing rights, and the right to control First Nations lands and resources without federal interference; and that First Nations have inalienable rights, including the "inherent sovereignty of Indian Nations, the right to self-government, jurisdiction over their lands and citizens and the power to enforce the terms of the Treaties."[55]

Three researchers observing events as they unfolded concluded that union opposition had more to do with "First Nations leaders not wishing to have the authority of Chief and Council challenged."[56] University of Winnipeg professor

Brock Pitawanakwat is equally frank: "In other words, organizing to protect workers' rights is 'un-indigenous'[57]." Pitawanakwat took particular aim at an FSIN strategy that spread the rumour that labour unions would negatively affect First Nations culture. He was especially critical of how the FSIN chiefs utilized a "false front of nationalism," described as a "red herring [employed] to maintain their power over labour relations in indigenous institutions."[58] Reflecting on increasing class divisions and fluid notions of citizenship, Pitawanakwat concluded, "The emerging capitalist class in indigenous communities has exploited ongoing and deep-seated fears of assimilation amongst our peoples. Indigenous organizations have used a nationalist and xenophobic propaganda campaign to oppose labour unions."[59] His concern here is the FSIN's internalization and replication of traditional colonial "divide and conquer" techniques, which seek to accomplish the collective political empowerment of the FSIN and band councils at the expense of Native workers.[60] Indigenous political theorist Taiaiake Alfred has argued that this could be considered a natural by-product of an Indian Act system Native leaders remain submissive to, unable to utilize historic societal and governing values.[61]

Similar events in Ontario sparked litigation after the operator of the Great Blue Heron Charity Casino, the Mississaugas of Scugog Island First Nation, established a labour code in its attempts to halt the CAW certification by casinos workers. Initially certified as bargaining agent for a unit of employees on 23 January 2003, CAW notified the First Nation of its intent to bargain. Without responding to CAW, the band's chief, Tracy Gauthier, and two councillors approved a Labour Relations Code at an informal band council meeting held 6 June. There are no meeting minutes to draw from, and none of the involved parties or government officials were informed of the band council's intentions. Generally speaking, the code would govern labour relations both on- and off-reserve as they related to activities involving First Nations commercial entities. Structured along the same line of the Canada Labour Code (CLC), the band council's code set out a number of questionable provisions that do not appear in the CLC, including denying workers the right to strike or lock out; demanding unions pay a $3,000 fee to speak with workers; and subjecting workers to a $12,000 fee to file an unfair labour practices complaint to be heard before a tribunal called the Dbaaknigeniwin, based on a traditional society. The code also prohibited First Nation officials from negotiating with unions not properly certified according to its regulations.

Responding to a CAW complaint of unfair practices to the Ontario Labour Relations Board (OLRB), the Mississaugas of Scugog Island First Nation refused to accept the OLRB's jurisdiction, countering that its inherent self-governing authority and actions were shielded from outside scrutiny. Furthermore, as leaders of a self-governing nation, the Mississaugas of Scugog Island leadership argued that they retained jurisdiction over, and a corresponding authority to develop, community bylaws related to labour relations, and that right superseded provincial legislation. The OLRB considered the arguments, but found the claims to be baseless, particularly those suggesting that the management of labour was an ancestral practice, custom, or tradition.[62] It was further determined that the CLC applied on-reserve, effectively overriding the newly enacted labour code. Following the ruling, approximately 850 CAW casino workers voted 92 percent in favour of a strike to support their demands for a collective agreement.[63] The bargaining issues included wages and benefits, shift schedules, contracting out, seniority provisions, and contract language. On 17 July 2004, the two sides agreed to a three-year contract that provided the 700 casino workers with wage increases ranging from two dollars per hour for those at the maximum wage rate to between 15 and 30 percent for those earning below the maximum rate.[64]

The Mississaugas of Scugog Island First Nation relied on three points to defend their Aboriginal right to excise labour unions from reserve casino operations: (1) the passage of the code was an exercise of the inherent right to self-government in relation to internal affairs and access to activities in the community's territories; (2) the passage of the code was an exercise of an inherent right to regulate work-related activities in the community's territories; and (3) the Covenant Chain treaty relationship dating back to the mid-seventeenth century both confirmed and sustained the community's rights to self-determination and self-government, which were unextinguished rights.[65] Reflecting the FSIN's position on the matter, community and organization leaders in each case asserted that passage of the labour code was an aspect or expression of Aboriginal self-government in relation to control over land, resources, and community labour management. The OLRB, however, refused to accept that the Mississaugas of Scugog Island First Nation's self-governing authority extended to it being used as a check against labour organizing on reserve lands. In response, the chief and council petitioned the Ontario Divisional Court for a judicial review seeking determination of one question: did the Mississaugas of Scugog Island First Nation have the legal right to "enact its own labour code to govern collective bargaining in relation to a commercial undertaking that operates on reserve lands"?[66] The petition failed and they were not granted a judicial review.

The court further noted labour relations were the subject of the band council's code, and not the regulation of work activities or control of access to reserve lands. In the court's opinion, it would "be a gross distortion to characterize the code as regulating access to reserve lands on the basis of a single provision that regulates access to reserve lands only where the party entering the land does so to solicit union members."[67] The integrity of arguments for territorial sovereignty also suffered. As for the question concerning the Aboriginal right to control labour relations, the court determined that no evidence of a similar pre-existing practice, custom, or tradition existed. The band council's code was deemed to exhibit no meaningful relationship or connection with pre-contact communal, non-hierarchical decision-making practices characteristic of the Mississaugas of Scugog Island First Nation's historic governance process. The court concluded the Aboriginal rights claims in this instance were "cast at a level of such generality that it amounts to an assertion that First Nations should be accorded a virtually unconstrained right of self-government in relation to any activity that takes place on aboriginal land."[68] First Nations leaders may rejoin that such is the definition of self-government; however, the courts reaffirmed the dissonance between the Native perspectives of self-government as right of self-determination and the Canadian belief in self-government as a delegated right.

The Mississaugas of Scugog Island First Nation also decided to test the nature of their treaty rights, specifically the characterization that they remained autonomous sovereigns in their territory. Citing the Silver Covenant Chain as confirmed by the Treaty of Niagara of 1764 as proof of the British Crown's acceptance of the community's continued right to economic development, Mississauga leaders argued that they had the right to establish and control reserve casino operations. Dating to a 1618 Dutch-Mohawk treaty, the Silver Covenant Chain was originally symbolized by a rope, which became an iron chain in 1643 when New Netherlands fashioned a pact with the Mohawks. After the English accepted the responsibility in the chain previously exercised by the Dutch in 1664, two supplementary peace treaties were negotiated in 1677, resulting in the chain becoming silver and a multilateral alliance being fashioned.[69] The Silver Covenant Chain "joined the Iroquois and English worlds and organized their discourse, but did not merge them, instead leaving each of them discreet."[70]

The Mississaugas of Scugog Island First Nation, however, did not become members of the Silver Covenant Chain until 1764, the same year the Treaty of Niagara was formalized.[71] After King George III issued his famous Proclamation of 1763, declaring all lands west of the Appalachian mountain chain to be British sovereign territory reserved for the Native peoples' use and benefit, indigenous leaders who had been reluctant to permit colonial officials to arbitrarily ratify legislation affecting their political autonomy demanded a meeting with Crown officials. Conceding to these demands, the Crown invited Native leaders of the Great Lakes and the upper Ohio Valley to attend a conference at Niagara in 1764. There they expected to discuss principles for governing Native-Crown relations. It was hoped this would also help establish "the framework by which the parties would relate to one another."[72] An estimated 2000 chiefs representing two dozen indigenous nations from throughout North America met at Niagara Falls in June and July to clarify the proclamation's provisions and to renew political relationships. A leading historian has suggested that even though existing evidence tends to downplay the aforesaid interpretation, existing archival materials tend to confirm that British agents explained the proclamation's territorial guarantees to the Iroquois, suggesting further that they were discussed with and explained to other regional First Nations.[73] The Mississaugas of Scugog Island First Nation consider their membership in the Silver Covenant Chain, which stressed First Nations' autonomy rather than the union of tribal nations and British, Dutch, and/or French political representatives into a single political unit, as proof of their autonomy.[74]

The court concluded there is no evidence "arising from the records and conversations that comprise the Covenant Chain and the Treaty of Niagara of any specific term or promise" that would suggest that First Nations were considered imbued with a self-determination right when they acknowledged Crown sovereignty over their territories.[75] Affirming the OLRB's interpretation, the court further emphasized that the "rights which might have been continued from this 'treaty' have nothing to do with and do not speak in any way to the regulation of activity as between employers and employees."[76] Suggesting that the Covenant Chain and the Treaty of Niagara "reflect the general nature of the relationship between the Crown and First Nations at the time and confirm the basic common law doctrine of inherent Aboriginal rights,"[77] the court expressed its concern that "to accept the treaty argument would be to accept an aboriginal right of self-government on reserve lands of virtually unlimited breadth and amplitude and exceed anything seen to date in the jurisprudence of aboriginal treaty rights."[78] The Ontario Superior Court of Justice denied the Mississaugas of Scugog Island First Nation request for a judicial review of the decision. It further suggested it did not have a constitutional right to enact it own labour codes. This decision was upheld on appeal.

CONCLUSION

First Nations casino operators' resistance to labour unions is multifaceted and dynamic. As demonstrated, resistance that began in the late 1990s in Saskatchewan took root in Ontario and is likely to flower presently at Alberta's First Nations casinos. First Nations individuals challenging labour advocacy's legitimacy often portray unions as a colonial manifestation that fails to represent their needs. First Nations' lack of labour consciousness is attributable to the labour movement's historic unwillingness to consider Native members and to the lack of job opportunities afforded First Nations people in urban centres, where they would have likely been introduced to labour advocacy. Note well that First Nations would have also been aware of wage disparities at a time when unions were claiming to improve worker egalitarianism. The literature examining these trends is limited, but it informs our understanding of why First Nations individuals tend to avoid union membership. This does not suggest an absence of Native labour advocates; the heterogeneous nature of First Nations communities and the unique nature of politics and economic development at the national, provincial, regional, and community levels denies this possibility. Additional research into First Nations casinos and individual perceptions of unions would benefit the larger discussion of Native people and labour advocacy.

At the political level, First Nations leaders who oppose unions in casinos follow a different tack: they cite their inherent right to self-government and treaties as evidence of their internal ability to regulate labour relations as a component of self-government. Labour relations are framed primarily as a sovereignty issue and as part of an inherent right to self-govern traditional lands. The resulting overlap in jurisdiction, which in this instance enables provincial discretionary authority on reserve land, is considered an assault on First Nations sovereignty. With this in mind, First Nations leaders likely view labour unions as yet another group of non-Native individuals infiltrating the reserve and telling them how to self-govern. Court petitions to resolve the issue have failed, and the courts have responded that the right to control labour was not demonstrated to be an historical Aboriginal right. Contemporary First Nations, as a result, lack the Aboriginal right to control reserve labour.

Resistance to labour unions in the name of nationalism has resulted in two developments. First, a rather unflattering portrait has emerged that portrays First Nations as anti-labour and willing to sacrifice their employees' workplace satisfaction and security in the name of vague Aboriginal and treaty rights. Not all employees are Native, however. The Great Blue Heron Casino employs approximately 1150, for example, of which 85 are employees from the Mississaugas of Scugog Island First Nation (pop. 173). SIGA currently employs 1700 people, of which approximately 1241 are Aboriginal, whereas 461 are non-Native.[79] During the CAW's attempts to organize Casino Rama workers in the early 2000s, Mnjikaning First Nation leaders focussed exclusively on the impact of the union on Native employees without mentioning non-Native workers. In this instance, only 700 (19 percent) of the 3700 casino employees were Native. This is a dangerous strategy, for non-Native employees will always be needed to maintain operations, and workforce harmony is the key to corporate stability. The second development is that the substantial cost of First Nations litigation has been paid from existing casino profits originally intended to aid in community socio-economic development. Depleted financial resources and limited social capital have led to minimal advancement of Aboriginal and treaty rights claims, suggesting alternate strategies need to be developed.

The nature of labour advocacy has shifted in recent years. In its attempts to remain relevant, the labour movement has responded to contemporary trends by embracing fresh ideas among an increasingly multicultural membership.[80] The recent CAW–Assembly of First Nations alliance points to a new relationship between the labour movement and First Nations that is difficult for First Nations employers to dismiss or distance themselves from.[81] There is a movement afoot in Saskatchewan to create a First Nations union, similar to British Columbia's Bow and Arrows of the 1920s.[82] And in Nova Scotia an Aboriginal union was formed in 2004 intent on organizing all Eskasoni band workers.[83] In all, the labour environment and First Nations casinos appear to be locked in a tortuous relationship that has failed to achieve equilibrium. Only time will tell whether this will lead to a mutually acceptable union (if I may) or if the relationship will remain contentious and divisive.

NOTES

1 Brock Pitawanakwat, "Indigenous Labour Organizing in Saskatchewan: Red Baiting and Red Herrings," *New Socialist* 58 (Sept.–Oct. 2006): 32–33.

2 "Union Still Gambling on Casino," *Barrie Examiner*, 31 July 2004, A3; and Yale D. Belanger, *Gambling with the Future: The Evolution of Aboriginal Gambling in Canada* (Saskatoon: Purich Publishing, 2006), 159–162.

3 See, for example, Bryan H. Wildenthal, "Federal Labor Law, Indian Sovereignty, and the Canons of Construction," *Oregon Law Review* 86, 2 (2007): 413–530; and Wenona T. Singel, "Labor Relations and Tribal Self-Governance," *North Dakota Law Review* 80 (2004), 691–730.

4 Alison Dubois, Wanda Wuttunee, and John Loxley, "Gambling on Casinos," *Journal of Aboriginal Economic Development* 2, 2 (2002): 58.

5 Frank Tough, *As Their Natural Resources Fail: Native Peoples and the Economic History of Northern Manitoba, 1870–1930* (Vancouver: University of British Columbia Press, 1996).

6 Adele Perry, "'The State of Empire: Reproducing Colonialism in British Columbia, 1849–1871," *Journal of Colonialism and Colonial History* 2, 2 (2001), http://muse.jhu.edu/login?uri=/journals/journal_of_colonialism_and_colonial_history/v002/2.2perry.html.

7 For an excellent collection of essays dealing with this and like issues, see Martha C. Knack and Alice Littlefield, "Native American Labor: Retrieving History, Rethinking Theory," in *Native Americans and Wage Labor: Ethnohistorical Perspectives*, ed. Alice Littlefield and Martha C. Knack (Norman: University of Oklahoma Press, 1996), 3–44; also, see Arthur J. Ray, "Periodic Shortages, Native Welfare, and the Hudson's Bay Company, 1670–1930," in *The Subarctic Fur Trade: Native Social and Economic Adaptations*, ed. Shepard Krech, (Vancouver: University of British Columbia Press, 1984), 1–20.

8 Rolf Knight, *Indians at Work: An Informal History of Native Indian Labour in British Columbia, 1858–1930* (Vancouver: New Star Books, 1978); Sarah Carter, *Lost Harvests: Prairie Indian Reserve Farmers and Government Policy* (Kingston and Montreal: McGill-Queen's University Press, 1990); Harald E.L. Prins, "Tribal Networks and Migrant Labour: Mi'kmaw Indians as Seasonal Workers in Aroostook's Potato Fields, 1870–1980," in *Native Americans and Wage Labour: Ethnohistorical Perspectives*, ed. Alice Littlefield and Martha C. Knack (Norman: University of Oklahoma Press, 1996), 45–65.

9 The *Indian Act* contained fewer economic development provisions than rules to punish First Nations leaders for failing to cooperate with government demands for access to reserve lands for mineral exploration, rights-of-way for highways and railways, and the leasing of land to local farmers and ranchers. See Treaty 7 Elders and Tribal Council with Walter Hildebrant, Sarah Carter, and Dorothy First Rider, *The True Spirit and Intent of Treaty 7* (Kingston and Montreal: McGill-Queen's University Press, 1996), 217.

10 Robert N. Wilson, *Our Betrayed Wards: A Story of "Chicanery, Infidelity, and the Prostitution of Trust"* (Montreal: Osiris, 1973).

11 See John S. Milloy, *A National Crime: The Canadian Government and the Residential School System, 1879–1986* (Winnipeg: University of Manitoba Press, 1999).

12 See, for example, Peggy Martin-McGuire, *First Nations Land Surrenders on the Prairies, 1896–1911* (Ottawa: Indian Claims Commission, 1998).

13 Mark S. Dockstator, "Toward an Understanding of Aboriginal Self-Government: A Proposed Theoretical Model and Illustrative Factual Analysis" (PhD diss., York University, 1993); and Anne-Marie H. Mawhiney, *Towards Aboriginal Self-Government* (New York: Garland Publishing, 1994).

14 There are several studies demonstrating how socially constructed images hampered indigenous economic, social, and political development in North America. See, for example, Daniel Francis, *The Imaginary Indian: The Image of the Indian in Canadian Culture* (Vancouver: Arsenal Pulp Press, 1992); and Robert Berkhofer, *The White Man's Indian: Images of the American Indian from Columbus to the Present* (New York: Vintage Books, 1979).

15 Brian D. Palmer, "Nineteenth-Century Canada and Australia: The Paradoxes of Class Formation," *Labour/Le Travail* 38 (Fall 1996): 28.

16 Rolf Knight, *Indians at Work: An Informal History of Indian Labour in British Columbia, 1858–1930* (Vancouver: University of British Columbia Press, 1978).

17 Edmund Wilson, *Apologies to the Iroquois* (Syracuse, NY: Syracuse University Press, 1992), 278.

18 Andrew Parnaby, "'The Best Men that Ever Worked the Lumber': Aboriginal Longshoremen on Burrard Inlet, B.C., 1863–1939" *Canadian Historical Review* 87, 1 (2006): 53–78.

19 See Miriam Wright, "'Building the Great Lucrative Fishing Industry': Aboriginal Gillnet Fishers and Protests over Salmon Fishery Regulations for the Nass and Skeena Rivers, 1950's–1960's," *Labour/Le Travail* 61 (Spring 2008): 103; also Percy Gladstone, "Native Indians and the Fishing Industry of British Columbia," *Canadian Journal of Economics and Political Science* 19, 1 (1953), 20-34; Stuart Jamieson and Percy Gladstone, "Unionism in the Fishing Industry of British Columbia, Part I," *Canadian Journal of Economics and Political Science* 16, 1 (Feb. 1950), 1-11; and "Unionism in the Fishing Industry of British Columbia, Part II," *Canadian Journal of Economics and Political Science* 16, 2 (May 1950); Phillip Drucker, *The Native Brotherhoods: Modern Intertribal Organizations on the Northwest Coast*, Smithsonian Institute Bureau of Ethnology Bulletin, No. 168 (Washington, DC: Smithsonian Institution, 1958).

20 Parnaby, "'The Best Men that Ever Worked the Lumber'"; also Yale D. Belanger, "Seeking a Seat at the Table: A Brief History of Indian Political Organizing in Canada, 1870–1951" (PhD diss., Trent University, 2005).

21 Quoted in Peter Kulchyski, "'A Considerable Unrest': F.O. Loft and the League of Indians," *Native Studies Review* 4, 1–2 (1988): 101.

22 Ibid., 101.

23 The amendment resulted in Section 141 of the *Indian Act*. One of the anticipated benefits of the legislation was that outside consultants assisting Indian organizations or Indian leaders wishing to pursue land claims against the federal government would forever be silenced.

24 See Belanger, "Seeking a Seat at the Table."

25 See generally Paul Tennant, *Aboriginal Peoples and Politics: The Native Land Question in British Columbia, 1849–1989* (Vancouver: University of British Columbia Press, 1990); and Drucker, *The Native Brotherhoods*.

26 Murray Dobbin, *The One-and-a-Half Men: The Story of Jim Brady and Malcolm Norris* (Vancouver: New Star Books, 1981): 110.

27 See Desmond Morton, *Working People: An Illustrated History of the Canadian Labour Movement*, 4th ed. (Montreal and Kingston: McGill-Queen's University Press, 1998), 142–143.

28 The information for this paragraph was gleaned from Murray Dobbin, "Métis Struggles of the Twentieth Century," *New Breed* (Aug.–Nov. 1978) and his *The One-and-a-Half Men*.

29 Dobbin, *The One-and-a-Half Men*, 77.

30 As an example of this literature, see Janet Mary Nicol, "'Unions Aren't Native': The Muckamuck Restaurant Labour Dispute, Vancouver, B.C," *Labour/Le Travail* 40 (Fall 1997): 235–251; and Julie Guard, "Authenticity on the Line: Women Workers, Native 'Scabs,' and the Multi-Ethnic Politics of Identity in a Left-led Strike in Cold War Canada," *Journal of Women's History* 15, 4 (2004): 117–140.

31 See generally Robin Jarvis Brownlie, "'Living the Same as the White People': Mohawk and Anishinabe Women's Labour in Southern Ontario, 1920–1940." *Labour/Le Travail* 61 (Spring 2008): 41–68.

32 Canada, Parliament, *Special Joint Parliamentary Committee of the Senate and the House of Commons appointed to examine and consider the Indian Act*, Minutes of Proceedings and Evidence, No. 9 (3 June 1947): 1529.

33 See Frank Tough, "The Forgotten Constitution: The *Natural Resources Transfer Agreements* and Indian Livelihood Rights, CA. 1925–1933," *Alberta Law Review* 41, 4 (2004): 999–1048; and Brian L. Calliou, "Losing the Game: Wildlife Conservation and the Regulation of First Nations Hunting in Alberta, 1880–1930" (LL.M. thesis, University of Alberta, 2000).

34 Responsibility for Indian Affairs at Confederation was vested with Secretary of the State Responsible for Indian Affairs. In 1873, responsibility for Indian Affairs was transferred to the Department of the Interior. The Department of Indian Affairs, a branch office of the Department of the Interior, was created in 1880. It operated until 1935, when it was dissolved as a cost-cutting measure. Responsibility for Indian Affairs transferred to the Department of Mines and Resources, and a sub-department was established: The Indian Affairs Branch (IAB). Responsibility for Indian Affairs was reassigned to the Department of Immigration and Citizenship in 1950, where it remained until an independent Department of Indian Affairs and Northern Development was established in 1966.

35 Arthur J. Ray, *The Canadian Fur Trade in the Industrial Age* (Toronto: University of Toronto Press, 1990): 221.

36 See Cam Mackie, "Some Reflections on Indian Economic Development," in *Arduous Journey: Canadian Indians and Decolonization*, ed. J. Rick Ponting (Toronto: McClelland and Stewart, 1986); and T.R.L. MacInnes, "History of Indian Administration in Canada," *Canadian Journal of Economics and Political Science* 12, 3 (1946): 393.

37 For this detailed history see Canada, *For Seven Generations: An Information Legacy of the Royal Commission on Aboriginal Peoples*, CD-ROM (Ottawa: Canada Communications Group, 1996).

38 Harry Hawthorn, *Survey of the Contemporary Indians of Canada*, vols. 1 and 2 (Ottawa: Department of Indian Affairs and Northern Development, Indian Affairs Branch, 1966–1967).

39 J. Rick Ponting and Roger Gibbins, *Out of Irrelevance* (Toronto: Butterworths, 1980), 34.

40 J. Rick Ponting, "Historical Overview and Background, Part II: 1970–96," in *First Nations in Canada: Perspectives on Opportunity, Empowerment, and Self-Determination*, ed. J. Rick Ponting (Toronto: McGraw-Hill Ryerson, 1997), 61.

41 Ponting and Gibbins, *Out of Irrelevance*, 46.

42 Andrew J. Siggner, "The Socio-Demographic Conditions of Registered Indians," in *Arduous Journey: Canadian Indians and Decolonization*, ed. J. Rick Ponting (Toronto: McClelland and Stewart, 1986), 72.

43 Ponting and Gibbins, *Out of Irrelevance*, 43.

44 Royal Commission on Aboriginal Peoples (RCAP), *For Seven Generations: An Information Legacy of the Royal Commission on Aboriginal Peoples*. CD. Ottawa: Libraxus, 1997.

45 RCAP research reports record number 48002.

46 Hal Pruden, "An Overview of the Gambling Provisions in Canadian Criminal Law and First Nations Gambling," *Journal of Aboriginal Economic Development* 2, 2 (2002): 40.

47 *R. v. Pamajewon*, [1996] 2 S.C.R., 821.

48 Thomas Isaac, *Aboriginal Law: Cases, Materials and Commentary* (Saskatoon: Purich Publishing, 1999), 526.

49 *R. v. Furtney*, [1991] 3 S.C.R., 91.

50 *E. v. Gladue and Kirby*, [1986] 30 CCC (3d) (Alta. Prov. Ct.), 308

51 See Belanger, "Seeking a Seat at the Table," and his "Federation of Saskatchewan Indian Nations (FSIN)," in *The Encyclopedia of Saskatchewan: A Living Legacy* (Regina: Canadian Plains Research Center, 2005), 324–325.

52 James Parker, "Top Court Slams Door on SIGA Appeal of Casino Union: Rights of P.A. Workers to Unionize Upheld; Sides Eye First Collective Agreement," *Saskatoon Star-Phoenix*, 31 August 2001, A6.

53 "Sask. Aboriginal Chiefs Try Union-busting," *CBC News*, 4 June 1999, http://www.cbc.ca/canada/story/1999/06/04/sk_native_union990604.html.

54 *The Labour Relations Board, Saskatchewan, Saskatchewan Joint Board, Retail, Wholesale and Department Store Union v. Saskatchewan Indian Gaming Authority Inc. carrying on business as the Painted Hand Casino*. LRB File Nos. 067-03, 068-03 and 069-03 (29 Aug. 2003), http://www.sasklabourrelationsboard.com/recent-board-decisions/2003/067-03.pdf (accessed 31 Jan. 2006).

55 Federation of Saskatchewan Indians (FSI), *Indian Government* (Saskatoon: 1977).

56 Dubois, Wuttunee, and Loxley, "Gambling on Casinos."

57 Brock Pitawanakwat, "Indogenous Labour Organizing in Saskatchewan: Red Baiting and Red Herrings," *New Socialist* 58 (Sept-Oct. 2006), 32.

58 Ibid., 32-33.

59 Ibid., 33

60 Ibid., 33.

61 Taiaiake Alfred, *Peace, Power, Righteousness: An Indigenous Manifesto* (Toronto: Oxford University Press, 2008); see also Howard Adams, *A Tortured People: The Politics of Colonization* (Penticton, BC: Theytus Press, 1995).

62 *Ontario Labour Relations Board,* 12 December 2003.

63 Chris Hall, "Contract Talks to Begin between Great Blue Heron Casino, Union," *This Week,* 14 Aug. 2007, 1.

64 UNI Global Union, "Casino Workers Ratify First Contract and Great Blue Heron," http://www.union-network.org/ UNICasinos.nsf/0/ 4077ec5be6caa599c1256ee500 24d66d?OpenDocument (last accessed 1 June 2005, site no longer active).

65 "National Automobile, Aerospace, Transportation and General Workers Union of Canada (CAW-Canada) and its Local 444, Applicant v. Great Blue Heron Gaming Company, Responding Party v. The Attorney General of Ontario and the Attorney General of Canada, Intervenors." *Ontario Labour Relations Board* (30 November 2004).

66 *Mississaugas of Scugog Island First Nation v. National Automobile, Aerospace, Transportation and General Workers Union of Canada,* [2007] ONCA 814, 2.

67 Ibid., 2, 7.

68 Ibid.

69 Gilles Havard, *The Great Peace of Montreal of 1701: French–Native Diplomacy in the Seventeenth Century* (Kingston and Montreal: McGill-Queen's University Press, 2001), 38.

70 Matthew Dennis, *Cultivating a Landscape of Peace: Iroquois-European Encounters in Seventeenth-Century America* (Ithaca, NY: Cornell University Press, 1993), 69.

71 See David T. McNab, *Circles of Time: Aboriginal Land Rights and Resistance in Ontario* (Waterloo: Wilfrid Laurier Press, 1999), 49.

72 John Borrows, *Recovering Canada: The Resurgence of Indigenous Law* (Toronto: University of Toronto Press, 2002), 125.

73 Jim R. Miller, "Compact, Contract, Covenant: The Evolution of Indian Treaty Making," in *New Histories for Old: Changing Perspectives on Canada's Native Pasts*, ed. Ted Binnema and Susan Neylan (Vancouver: University of British Columbia Press, 2007), 78.

74 See Francis Jennings, *The Ambiguous Iroquois Empire: The Covenant Chain Confederation of Indian Tribes with English Colonies from Its Beginnings to the Lancaster Treaty of 1744* (New York: Norton, 1984).

75 *Mississaugas of Scugog Island First Nation v. National Automobile, Aerospace, Transportation and General Workers Union of Canada*, 14.

76 Ibid.

77 Ibid.

78 Ibid.

79 Saskatchewan Indian Gaming Authority (SIGA), *Celebrating 10 Years: Annual Report, 2006–07*, http://www.siga.sk.ca/06SIGA1008_AR_lo.pdf (accessed 26 February 2008).

80 See generally Craig Heron, *The Canadian Labour Movement: A Short History*, 2nd ed. (Toronto: James Lorimer and Company, 1996); Bryan D. Palmer, *Working-Class Experience: Rethinking the History of Canadian Labour, 1800–1991* (Toronto: Butterworths, 1992); also Morton, *Working People*.

81 Joanna Smith, "CAW Union and Natives Team up to Fix Centre," *Toronto Star*, 26 Oct. 2007, A10; "CAW Tradespeople Donate Skills to Help First Nations," *Kamloops Daily News*, 26 Oct. 2007, A11; John Bonnar, "Canadian Auto Workers and Assembly of First Nations Work Together to Fight Poverty in First Nations Communities," *Toronto Social Justice Magazine*, 26 Oct. 2007.

82 Anne Kyle, "Aboriginal Union Sought," *Regina Leader-Post*, 20 May 2006, B4. For information on the Bow and Arrows, see E. Palmer Patterson, "Andrew Paull and the Canadian Indian Resurgence" (PhD diss., University of Washington, 1962); and Parnaby, "'The Best Men that Ever Worked the Lumber.'"

83 T.J. Colello, "Aboriginal Union Has its First Executive: All Band Corkers on Group's Agenda," *Cape Breton Post*, 23 March 2004, A3.

SELECTED BIBLIOGRAPHY

Ackerman, William V. "Indian Gaming in South Dakota: Conflict in Public Policy." *American Indian Quarterly* 33, 2 (2009): 253-279.

Belanger, Yale D. *Gambling with the Future: The Evolution of Aboriginal Gaming in Canada*. Saskatoon: Purich Publishing, 2006.

———. "First Nations Gaming as a Self-government Imperative? Ensuring the Health of First Nations Problem Gamblers." *International Journal of Canadian Studies* 41 (2010): 1-24.

Binde, Per. "Gambling across Cultures: Mapping Worldwide Occurrence and Learning from Ethnographic Comparison." *International Gambling Studies* 5, 1 (2005): 1–27.

———. "Gambling, Exchange Systems, and Moralities." *Journal of Gambling Studies* 21, 4 (2005): 445–479.

Burnett, Jody L. "Coming Full Circle: Aboriginal Family Members' Experiences of Problem Gambling." Master's thesis, University of Regina, 2007.

Campbell, Karen. "Community Life and Governance: Early Experiences of Mnjikaning First Nation with Casino Rama." Master's thesis, University of Manitoba, 1999.

Cattelino, Jessica. *High Stakes: Florida Seminole Gaming and Sovereignty*. Duke University Press, 2008.

Cheska, Alyce T. "Native American Games as Strategies of Societal Maintenance." In *Forms of Play of Native North Americans: 1977 Proceedings of the American Ethnological Association*, edited by Edward Norbeck and Claire R. Farrer, 227–248. St. Paul, MN: West Publishing Company, 1979.

Cornell, Stephen. "The Political Economy of American Indian Gaming." *Annual Review of Law and Social Science* 4 (2008): 63-82.

Cozzetto, Don A., and Brent W. Larocque. "Compulsive Gambling in the Indian Community: A North Dakota Case Study." *American Indian Culture and Research Journal* 20, 1 (1996): 73–86.

Culin, Stewart. *Games of the North American Indians*. New York: Dover Publications, 1975 (1907).

DeBoer, W. "Of Dice and Women: Gambling and Exchange in Native North America." *Journal of Archaeological Method and Theory* 8, 3 (2004): 215–268.

Deiter-Buffalo, Constance. *The Handgame Project*. Hobbema, AB: Indian Association of Alberta, 1996.

Desbrisay, Dave. "The Gaming Industry in Aboriginal Communities." In *For Seven Generations: An Information Legacy of the Royal Commission on Aboriginal Peoples*. CD-ROM. Ottawa: Libraxus, 1996.

Desmond, Gerald. *Gambling Among the Yakima*. Catholic University of America Anthropological Series 14. Washington, DC: Catholic University of America Press, 1952.

Dubois, Alison, Wanda Wuttunee, and John Loxley. "Gambling on Casinos." *Journal of Aboriginal Economic Development* 2, 2 (2002), 56-67.

Elia, Christopher, and Durand F. Jacobs. "The Incidence of Pathological Gambling among Native Americans Treated for Alcohol Dependence." *The International Journal of the Addictions* 28, 7 (1993): 659–666.

Frits, Paul K. "Aboriginal Gaming—Law and Policy." In *Aboriginal Issues Today: A Legal and Business Guide*, edited by Stephen B. Smart and Michael Coyle. Vancouver: Self-Counsel, 1997.

Gabriel, Kathryn. *Gambler Way: Indian Gaming in Mythology, History, and Archaeology in North America*. Boulder: Johnson Books, 1996.

Grant Thornton, LLP. *Review of First Nations Gaming Commissions: Sources and Uses of Funds Analysis*. Nova Scotia: Office of Aboriginal Affairs, Sept. 2000.

Guth, Francis R. *Western Values Comparison in Gambling: With a Comparison to North American Aboriginal Views*. Sault Ste. Marie, ON: Algoma, 1994.

Heine, M.K. "The Symbolic Capital of Honour: Gambling Games and the Social Construction of Gender in Tlingit Indian Culture." *Play and Culture* 4 (1991): 346–358.

Hewitt, David. *Spirit of Bingoland: A Study of Problem Gambling Among Alberta Native People*. Edmonton: Nechi Training and Research and Health Promotions Institute/AADAC, 1994.

Hewitt, David, and Dale Auger. *Firewatch on First Nations Adolescent Gambling*. Edmonton: Nechi Training, Research and Health Promotions Institute, 1995.

Kainaakiiski Secretariat, *Gaming Research Report: Final Report Prepared for the University of Lethbridge*. Lethbridge, AB: Rob Williams, 2005.

Kelley, Robin. *First Nations Gambling Policy in Canada*. Gambling in Canada Research Report 12. Calgary: Canada West Foundation, 2001.

Kiedrowski, John. *Native Gaming and Gambling in Canada*. Ottawa: Indian and Northern Affairs, 2001.

Lange, Phil. "A First Nations Hand Game: Gambling from Supernatural Power." *Journal of Gambling Issues* 11 (2004). [online] http://jgi.camh.net/doi/full/10.4309/jgi.2004.11.10

Lazarus, Morden C., and Brian Hall. "The Need for the Creation of a Framework for Aboriginal Gaming to Legally Exist in Canada: The Compelling Case of the Mohawks of Kahnawa:ke." *Gaming Law Review and Economics* 14, 2 (2010): 95-99.

Lazarus, Morden C., Edwin D. Monzon, and Richard B. Wodnicki. "The Mohawks of Kahnawá:ke and the Case for an Aboriginal Right to Gaming under the Canada Constitution Act, 1982." *Gaming Law Review* 19, 4 (2006): 369-378.

Little, Margo. "The Moral Dilemma of High Stakes Gambling in Native Communities." Master's thesis, Laurentian University, 1997.

Luna-Firebaugh, Eileen M. & Mary Jo Tippeconnic Fox. "The Sharing Tradition: Indian Gaming in Stories and Modern Life." *Wicazo Sa Review* 25, 1 (2010): 75-86.

Manitowabi, Darrel. "From Fish Weirs to Casino: Negotiating Neoliberalism at Mnjikaning (Ontario)." PhD diss., University of Toronto, 2007.

Maranda, Lynn. *Coast Salish Gambling Games, Canadian Ethnology Service Paper No. 93*. Ottawa: National Museums of Canada, 1984.

Mason, W. Dale. Indian Gaming: Tribal Sovereignty & American Politics. Norman: University of Oklahoma Press, 2000.

McGowan, Virginia, and Gary Nixon. "Blackfoot Traditional Knowledge in Resolution of Problem Gambling: Getting Gambled and Seeking Wholeness." *Canadian Journal of Native Studies* 24, 1 (2004): 7-35.

McGowan, Virginia, Lois Frank, Gary Nixon, and Misty Grimshaw. "Sacred and Secular Play among Blackfoot Peoples of Southwest Alberta." In *Culture and the Gambling Phenomenon*, edited by Alex Blasczynski, 241-255. Sydney: National Association for Gambling Studies, 2002.

Nilson, Cathy. "The FSIN-Province of Saskatchewan Gaming Partnership: 1995 to 2002" Master's thesis, University of Saskatchewan, 2004.

Oakes, Jill. *Gambling and Problem Gambling in First Nations Communities*. Winnipeg: Native Studies Press, 2005.

Oakes, Jill, Cheryl Currie, and David Courtney. *Gambling and Problem Gambling in First Nations Communities: OPGRC Final Report*. Winnipeg, MB and Guelph, ON: University of Manitoba Press and Ontario Problem Gambling Research Centre, 2004.

Peacock, Robert B., Priscilla. A. Day, and Thomas D. Peacock. "Adolescent Gambling on a Great Lakes Indian Reservation." *Journal of Human Behavior in the Social Environment* 2, 1/2 (1999): 5-17.

Peroff, Nicholas. "Indian Gaming, Tribal Sovereignty, and American Indian Tribes as Complex Adaptive Systems." *American Indian Culture and Research Journal* 25, 3 (2001): 143-159.

Pitawanakwat, Brock. "Indigenous Labour Organizing in Saskatchewan: Red Baiting and Red Herrings." *New Socialist* 58 (Sept.–Oct. 2006): 32-33.

Pruden, Hal. "An Overview of the Gambling Provisions in Canadian Criminal Law and First Nations Gambling." *Journal of Aboriginal Economic Development* 2, 2 (2002): 37-40.

Research and Health Promotions Institute, *Firewatch on Aboriginal Adolescent Gambling*. Edmonton, 1995.

Salter, Michael A. "An Analysis of the Role of Games in the Fertility Rituals of the Native North American." *Anthropos* 69 (1974): 494-504.

———. "The Effect of Acculturation on the Game of Lacrosse and its Role as an Agent of Indian Survival." *Canadian Journal of History and Sport and Physical Education* 3 (1972): 28-43.

————. "Play in Ritual: An Ethnohistorical Overview of Native North America." In *Play and Culture: 1978 Proceedings of the Association for the Anthropological Study of Play*, edited by Helen B. Schwartzman, 70–82. West Point, NY: Leisure Press, 1980.

Schaap, James I. "The Growth of the Native American Gaming Industry: What Has the Past Provided, and What Does the Future Hold?" *American Indian Quarterly* 34, 3 (2010): 365-289.

Shanley, Kathryn. "Lady Luck or Mother Earth? Gaming as a Trope in Plains Indian Cultural Tradition." *Wicazo Sa Review* 15, 2 (2000): 93–101.

Skea, Warren. "Time to Deal: A Comparison of the Native Casino Gambling Policy in Alberta and Saskatchewan." PhD diss, University of Calgary, 1997.

Smith, Karen Lynn. "The Role of Games, Sport, and Dance in Iroquois Life." Master's thesis, University of Oregon, 1975.

Sommerfelt, Daniel M. "Comparison of Blackfoot and Hopi Games and their Contemporary Application: A Review of the Literature." Master's thesis, University of Lethbridge, 2005.

Steane, P.D., J. McMillen, and S. Togni. "Researching Gambling with Aboriginal People." *Australian Journal of Social Issues* 33, 3 (1998): 303–315.

Volberg, Rachel A., and Max W. Abbott, "Gambling and Problem Gambling among Indigenous Peoples." *Substance Use and Misuse* 32, 11 (1997): 1525–1538.

Volberg, Rachel A., and Precision Marketing, Inc. *Gambling and Problem Gambling among Native Americans in North Dakota*. Fargo: North Dakota Department of Human Services Division of Mental Health, 1993.

Wardman, Dennis, Nady el-Guebaly, and David Hodgins, "Problem and Pathological Gambling in North American Aboriginal Populations: A Review of the Empirical Literature." *Journal of Gambling Studies* 17, 2 (2001): 81–100.

Zitzow, Darryl. "Comparative Study of Problematic Gambling Behaviours between American Indian and Non-Indian Adolescents in a Northern Plains Reservation." *American Indian and Alaska Native Mental Health Research* 7, 2 (1996): 14–26.

————. "Comparative Study of Problematic Gambling Behaviors between American Indian and Non-Indian Adults in a Northern Plains Reservation." *American Indian and Alaska Native Mental Health Research* 7, 2 (1996): 27–41.

CONTRIBUTORS

JAMES BATTLE is a registered psychologist who has worked as a university professor, therapist in forensic psychiatry, teacher, vocational rehabilitation counsellor, school psychologist, consultant, and professional football player in the CFL and NFL. He has conducted more that 50 research studies, produced thirty books, twelve poems, two audiocassette tapes, a thirty-six-minute video and a large variety of assessment instruments including the popular Culture Free Self-Esteem Inventories. He is president of James Battle and Associates, founder and president of the Self-Esteem Institute of Canada.

YALE D. BELANGER, PhD, is an associate professor of Native American Studies (NAS) at the University of Lethbridge, Alberta. In 2006 he published *Gambling with the Future: The Evolution of Aboriginal Gaming in Canada,* the first book-length treatment tracing the emergence of casino gaming among Canada's First Nations seeking improved economic development opportunities.

CHERYL CURRIE is a PhD candidate in the School of Public Health at the University of Alberta. Her work is oriented toward the social, economic, and cultural forces that shape public health, with a particular emphasis on Indigenous health and well-being.

DAVID GREGORY, RN, PhD, is Professor and Coordinator, Graduate Program and Research, Faculty of Health Sciences, University of Lethbridge.

MORDEN C. LAZARUS is a Partner and head of the Gaming Law department at Lazarus Charbonneau, a Montreal law firm. He is past president of the International Association of Gaming Attorneys (IAGA) based in Las Vegas, and has recently served as the chairman of the Gaming Law Committee of the American Bar Association.

BONNIE LEE, PhD, is an Assistant Professor in the Faculty of Health Sciences, University of Lethbridge and a couple and family therapist. Her research has focussed on relational and ecological conceptualizations and approaches to healing in addictions. Her articles on Congruence Couple Therapy (CCT), CCT training evaluation, CCT's effectiveness, Chinese immigrants, and pathological gambling have appeared in international peer-reviewed journals.

DARREL MANITOWABI is assistant professor of Native Studies at University of Sudbury College, Laurentian University. He is a member of the Wikwemikong Unceded First Nation, Three Fires Anishinaabek Confederacy on Manitoulin Island, Ontario. Manitowabi's research interests include indigenous well-being, economic and political development, ethnohistory, and indigenous anthropology.

EDWIN D. MONZON is a lawyer who handles a wide range of matters in litigation and gaming at Lazarus Charbonneau, a Montreal law firm. Mr. Monzon holds a BA from Concordia and a law degree from the University of Montréal.

GARY NIXON is a psychologist, associate professor and director of the Addictions Counselling program at the University of Lethbridge. His clinical, teaching and research work focuses on the quest for wholeness both in long-term recovery from addictions as well as in transpersonal and non-dual psychology which integrates Eastern and Western contemplative pathways with conventional psychology.

GARRY SMITH is a University of Alberta Professor Emeritus and currently works as a gambling research specialist with the Alberta Gaming Research Institute. His research interests include public policy issues related to gambling, gambling and crime, and sports gambling.

RHYS M.B. STEVENS is the librarian and information specialist for the Alberta Gaming Research Institute and is based at the University of Lethbridge Library in Lethbridge, Alberta. His primary focus is to support the Institute's research activities by working with Institute-funded researchers and the general public who are interested in issues related to gaming and gambling. He obtained his Master of Library and Information Science degree from the University of Western Ontario in 1997.

ROBERT J. WILLIAMS is a professor in the Faculty of Health Sciences, University of Lethbridge, in Lethbridge, Alberta, and also the Lethbridge Coordinator for the Alberta Gaming Research Institute. Dr. Williams is a co-editor of International Gambling Studies, one of the two leading journals in this field; and an internationally recognized expert in gambling and a leading authority in the areas of: prevention of problem gambling; Internet gambling; the socio-economic impacts of gambling, the proportion of gambling revenue deriving from problem gamblers; and the etiology of problem gambling.

RICHARD B. WODNICKI is a member of the law firm Lazarus Charbonneau in Montreal, Quebec.

HAROLD J. WYNNE is a renowned Canadian researcher, teacher and administrator with three decades of experience as a community development practitioner, adult educator, and social scientist who has planned and implemented hundreds of social service, adult education, and research programs. Over the past twenty years, Dr. Wynne has conducted many seminal problem gambling studies and he is co-developer of the widely used Canadian Problem Gambling Index and the new Canadian Adolescent Gambling Inventory.

SHARON YANICKI is coordinator of the public health degree program (undergraduate) and a lecturer with the Faculty of Health Sciences, University of Lethbridge. Sharon is a registered nurse, and a doctoral student (Faculty of Nursing, University of Alberta). Sharon completed a BSN (University of Saskatchewan), and a MSc in health promotion (University of Alberta). Sharon has many years of experience as a public health nurse, a manager, a public health consultant, and an evaluator of health promotion programs.